SCOTTISH HISTORY SOCIETY

SIXTH SERIES

VOLUME 6

—

The McCulloch *Examinations* of the Cambuslang Revival (1742)

Volume II

The McCulloch *Examinations* of the Cambuslang Revival (1742)

A Critical Edition

Conversion Narratives from the Scottish Evangelical Awakening

Volume II

Edited by
Keith Edward Beebe

COLLIGITE FRAGMENTA NE PEREANT

SCOTTISH HISTORY SOCIETY
2011

THE BOYDELL PRESS

First published 2013

A Scottish History Society publication
in association with The Boydell Press
an imprint of Boydell & Brewer Ltd
PO Box 9, Woodbridge, Suffolk IP12 3DF, UK

and of Boydell & Brewer Inc.
668 Mt Hope Avenue, Rochester, NY 14620-2731, USA

website: www.boydellandbrewer.com

ISBN 978-0-906245-33-0

A CIP catalogue record for this book is available
from the British Library

The publisher has no responsibility for the continued existence or accuracy of URLs for external
or third-party internet websites referred to in this book, and does not guarantee that any content
on such websites is, or will remain, accurate or appropriate.

Papers used by Boydell & Brewer Ltd are natural, recyclable products
made from wood grown in sustainable forests

MIX
Paper from
responsible sources
FSC® C013604

Typeset by Word and Page, Chester, UK

Printed and bound in Great Britain by
CPI Group (UK) Ltd, Croydon, CR0 4YY

CONTENTS

ILLUSTRATIONS

INTRODUCTION

The Reverend William McCulloch's *Examinations of Persons under Spiritual Concern* (1742) and its background are described in detail in the Introduction to Volume I.

In Volume II, the documents include:

1. the collective *Examinations of Persons under Spiritual Concern* (324 leaves including the acquired title page, recto and verso);
2. a misplaced index of 48 respondents in Volume I (one leaf, recto);
3. an 'index to the corrected copy' (one leaf, recto and verso); and
4. an index of 88 'ministers and others' (1 leaf, recto).

Besides the five duplicate accounts shared with Volume I, one narrative in this volume (A. B. Janet Berry) contains duplicate fragments of text within the same account (which is indicated with notes in square brackets within the body of the text). This volume also contains a misplaced extraneous page of text that, according to McCulloch, 'belongs to another composure'; however, because the textual fragment relates directly to the revival activities at Cambuslang, it has been retained in its original location in the manuscripts (see p. II:42). Of the original narrative accounts and three indices in Volume II, only two are not handwritten by McCulloch, but were submitted by Mary Scot (II:107–9) and an anonymous individual (II:286–97), presumably in their own handwriting. Volume II was not circulated to the clerical redactors, and thus contains only McCulloch's editorial markings and no extraneous marginal annotations. While most of the accounts in this volume have only one set of pagination located at the top center of each page, five accounts contain two sets of pagination.

EDITORIAL PROCEDURES

This volume of the critical edition reproduces the text of the *Examinations* as recorded, arranged and revised by William McCulloch. All spelling variations, grammatical and factual errors, as well as edited text and marginal annotations found in the original handwritten text, have been preserved. However, catchwords have been eliminated, pagination errors have been noted in footnotes, and folios arranged out of sequence or indices bound with the wrong volumes have been rearranged. A glossary of terms that may be unfamiliar to modern readers may be found at the end of each volume of the narrative accounts.

Volume II of the McCulloch manuscripts differs from Volume I in three respects. First, Volume I contains editorial annotations by four of McCulloch's ministerial colleagues, but Volume II does not. Second, all accounts in Volume I are written in McCulloch's hand (and subsequently marked in the hands of the clerical redactors), whereas Volume II contains two testimonies written in the hands of two persons other than McCulloch. Third, nearly all the accounts within Volume I—but only a handful in Volume II—are marked with two sets of pagination, both of which are indicated by square brackets within the text. The first numeral indicates McCulloch's ultimate pagination, with the second numeral indicating penultimate pagination (from previous casebook assemblages). Where there are omissions of pagination that might normally have been implemented by McCulloch (usually located at the top center and top fore-edge corners of the page), such lacunae are indicated here by an en-dash (–).

Text in some locations has been partially obscured or rendered illegible owing to multiple factors, including unclear script, crowded text, ink stains or smears, closely cut or badly worn page edges, tight bindings, or textual strikethroughs. Every effort has been made to supply the actual text if possible, and in the case of duplicate accounts, a comparison of identical texts has been made to supply the correct text, if possible. Words deemed illegible are indicated by a horizontal ellipsis within square brackets '[. . .]' if it belongs to the main body of text, and by a horizontal ellipsis in angle brackets '<. . .>' if it belongs to a marginal annotation.

Biographical information on narrative respondents and persons mentioned in the text is drawn from both internal and external sources. The internal sources include the various indices accompanying the accounts that were produced by William McCulloch. Most of the biographical information on clergy mentioned in the text has been derived from Hew Scott, *Fasti Ecclesiae Scoticanae*, and whenever other external sources have also been utilized, they are specifically identified in the footnotes.[1]

Marginal annotations found in the original manuscripts are comprised of two general types: revisions (corrections, deletions, and insertions) and commentary, which are readily distinguished in the explanatory footnotes. In Volume I, the following editorial protocols have been implemented: routine editorial markings made by McCulloch consist of deletions with strikethroughs (i.e. 'I ~~said~~ to my self'). Insertions made by McCulloch through the use of carets or superimposition of text are indicated by empty brackets '[ ]' followed by a footnote that provides the inserted text (i.e. '[thought]'). Where text has been marked out for deletion, but the text remains legible, the text is retained using a strikethrough (i.e. '~~said to myself~~'). Where such text is replaced with a substitution, it is indicated by a footnote (i.e. 'then I ~~said to myself~~ [ ]'[2]) When referring to textual additions or insertions made within the manuscripts, such changes are here indicated by a pair of empty brackets ('[ ]') at the point at which the insertion is to be made, followed by a footnote with respective text to be inserted contained within brackets (e.g. ['and I took stronger hold of Christ's covenant toward me']). Various symbols used by McCulloch (e.g. 'Ø') to indicate the location and insertion of larger portions of text (e.g. paragraphs) are indicated and utilized in the critical edition whenever possible. Wherever the exact placement or location of a textual insertion is unspecified by such symbols or indicators, reconstruction of the textual placement has been accomplished either according to the obvious context, or by comparison with a duplicate narrative account, where it may exist.

---

[1] Hew Scott, *Fasti Ecclesiae Scoticanae: The Succession of Ministers in the Church of Scotland from the Reformation* (Edinburgh: Oliver and Boyd, 1915).

[2] ['thought to myself'].

Examinations

of persons

Under Spiritual Concern

at Cambuslang, During

The Revival, in 17-41–42;

By

The Revd William Macculloch

Minister of Cambuslang,

With

Marginal Notes by Dr. Webster

And Other Ministers.

Vol. II.

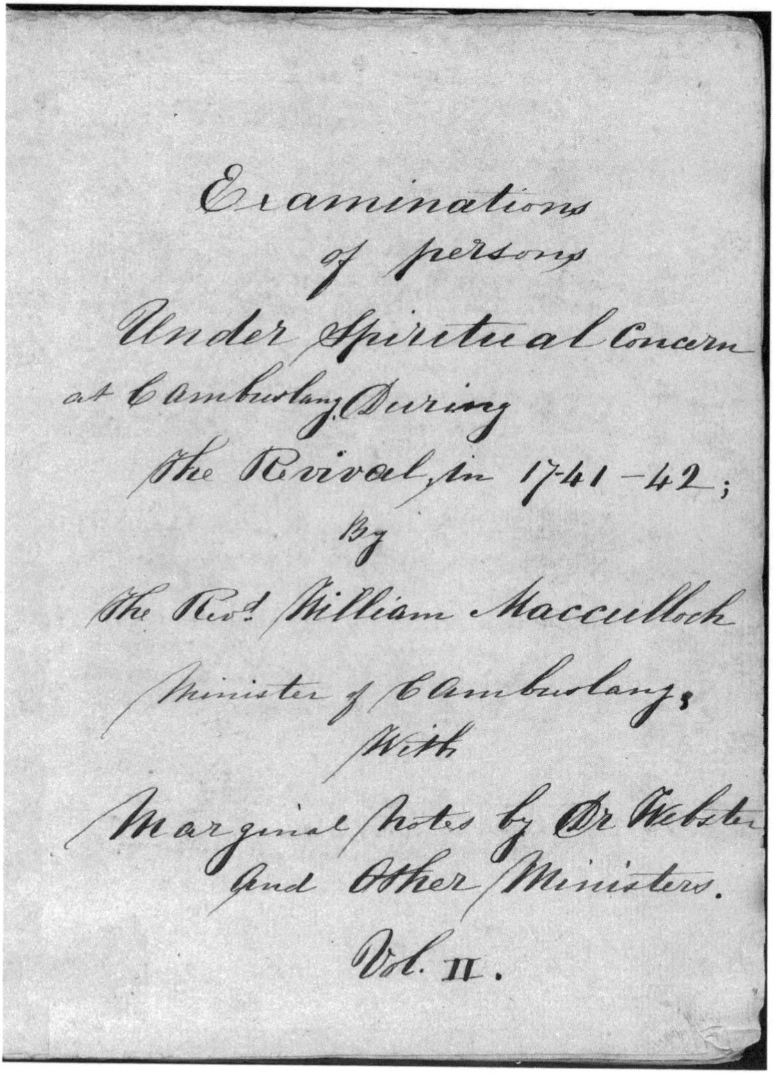

Figure 1. William McCulloch *Examinations*, title page (Volume II)
Courtesy of New College Library, University of Edinburgh

[1/–] b.n. A young Woman of 19 years[1]

I was thro' mercy, kept from any gross Outbreakings before the world all along hitherto; and had some form of Secret Devotion, which I ordinarily kept up once a day, & sometimes but rarely twice a day, but it went all against the grain with me, till within these two years past. I very seldom read the Bible by my Self in the former part of my life, because I had then no delight in it. For the fashions sake however, I went to the Kirk on Sabbath days, but had no concern whether I heard the Sermon or no, & brought none of it along with me: & never found any word I read or heard come with any Power to me. I never thought seriously what would become of me after death, or whither I would go: only sometimes when I fell sick, I thought if I recover'd I would be more taken up about Soul-Concerns; but when I came to health, I was just what I us'd to be.

And thus matters continu'd with me, till One Sabbath sometime in the Spring 1742, Hearing a minister (26)[2] preach on the Brae [2/–] at Cambuslang on a Text which I do not now remember, these words he had in his Sermon, "When a Room is full of darkness, the ~~noisom things~~ []³ that may be in it are not seen : But if a beam of light be let in by any small hole, these ~~noisome things~~ []⁴ come to be discovered, and the air in the Room is seen to be full of them: So, said he, it is with the heart: it is a room full of darkness by nature, & you that are unrenewed see nothing much amiss there: but if it would please God to cause a beam of his Light to Shine into that dark heart of thine, thou would see it multitudes of abominations swarming in it [].⁵ At that Instant, I felt the words spoken powerfully get home on my heart & Conscience, and a Ray of Light came along that discovered to me the many corruptions of my heart, & was made to see what an ugly loathsome & polluted creature I was in the sight of God by these multitudes of corruptions of my heart & all the sins of my Life : I was made to loathe my self for all my iniquities & abominations & to wonder that I had lived so long in the world & under the Gospel, & had never seen any [3/–] thing at all my Vileness by Sin. I was now made to grieve & mourn for the offences & dishonours I had done to God by Sin, & thought that I was now quite lost & undone, and that I was just at

---

¹ Jean Anderson – the shorthand text in McCulloch's 'Index of persons' names who gave the foregoing accounts to Mr. McC' states: daughter of James Anderson, tenant in Shawfield. Taught to read the Bible, got the Shorter Catechism when young, and retained it.
² William McCulloch (1691–1771) – minister, Cambuslang.
³ Insertion ['little moles']: McCulloch.
⁴ Insertion ['little moles']: McCulloch.
⁵ Insertion ['or words to that purpose']: McCulloch.

that time sinking down into Hell, & with that thought I could not forbear crying out among the People on the Brae, Oh lost & undone! What Shall I do?

For about a month after this, I continued in great Distress of Soul on the account of my Sins actual & Original, Sins of heart & life. I was much bowed down & asham'd of my Self before God on the account of my ugliness in his Sight by Sin. Fears of Hell & Sense of Sin whereby I had dishonoured God were mixt together oftimes in my Exercise: sometimes fears of being thrust down to Hell for my Sin pressd me down with the greatest Weight: sometimes again these fears would have vanished for a time; & then that which was most grievous & afflicting to my Spirit, was that I had so greatly offended & dishonoured a gracious God by my Sin. And my Distress of Spirit under these sorts of Exercise was so great, that for about a months time after [4/−] my awakening, I could not apply my Self to work tho' I often essayd it, nor could I eat drink or sleep, any at all, or but very little, but inclined to be almost always at Secret Prayer reading my Bible, or hearing Sermon [ ]⁶ at Cambuslang. I had all along a deep Sense of my need of Christ to Save me from Sin & wrath, & an earnest thirsting after him, & restlessness without him.

But I got no Sensible Outgate or Relief, till one day when I was at Camb. being an ordinary week day : & that day the number of People not being great a minister (26) preachd in the Hall in the Manse, and before Sermon, a part of the 51ˢᵗ Psalm being appointed to be sung, while the 18ᵗʰ verse was a singing

[Of Gladness & of joyfulness
make me to hear the voice,
That so these very bones which thou
hast broken may rejoice,]⁷

especially at the singing of these two last lines, my heart so filled with joy ~~that~~ at the thoughts of what God had done for me, in giving me a Sense of my Sins, & Shedding abroad his Love in my heart as he now did, that I could not forbear crying out aloud for joy, & thought I could never [5/−] praise him enough for his mercy to me. But after Sermon, coming from the Hall into the Ministers Closet to give him an account of what God had then done for me, [ ]⁸ I fell under a strong Apprehension, that Hell was just before me, & that I was just ready to fall down into it, & durst not go one step further, but [ ]⁹ cry'd out aloud for fear. This Dread of Hell I took to be from Satan, to put me into a Confusion when I was going to tell what God had done for

---

⁶   Insertion ['every day']: McCulloch.
⁷   Ps 51:8, Scottish Psalter (metrical); bracketed by McCulloch.
⁸   Insertion ['as I was at the stairhead betwixt the two doors']: McCulloch.
⁹   Insertion ['fell down and']: McCulloch .

my Soul. A minister (38)[10] coming & Speaking to me. I turn'd some calmer & more composd.

Next Sabbath I fell under great darkness & fears about my own condition: but on Munday morning when I was at Secret Prayer, these words in Isai.41.16. came into my heart with great Power & Sweetness, Thou Shalt rejoice in the Lord, and Shalt glory in the Holy One of Israel, and made indeed greatly to rejoice in God in Christ & to glory & triumph in him, but with fear & reverence. And I was then made to accept of the Lord Jesus Christ, as my Redeemer & Saviour & to ~~accept of~~ [ ][11] him in all his Offices of Grace as my Prophet Priest & King & to give up my Self to him to be Saved by him in His own way.

[6/– through 8/– blank]

---

[10] John Scott (d. 1759) – minister, Stonehouse.
[11] Insertion ['close with']: McCulloch.

[9/–] a.k. A woman of 30 years.[1]

When I was a child at Schools I had a great delight in praying often by my Self, and in reading my Bible: but after that I turn'd more & more careless of any thing of that kind: tho' frequently urg'd to read and pray by my Parents, I lost all relish for these things so far, that for 12 years after I had done with the Schools I scarce ever bowd my knee to my Maker by my self: yet I went Sometimes to the Kirk for fashions sake, but had no pleasure in doing so, or in hearing any thing there. But about ten years ago, I thought I had livd a very careless graceless life, & thought I must change my way of life, & so fell to praying again : but yet I had no sense of my lost condition by nature, or of the evil of Sin on my Spirit. I continued however to keep Stated times dailie for prayer, & reading a chapter of my Bible morning and Evening: but all was still but a dead form. About a year after I had begun this course, Satan troubled me much with his Temptations, particularly in urging me to take away my own life, and he press'd me so hard to it, that when there was any Instrument ~~about~~ [ ][2] me, to do it with, I was forc'd to put it away out [10/–] my sight, the better to get rid of the temptation: and by continuing in Prayer, & running to God for power against the Temptation, I was enabled to get the better of it. And sometimes I got great comfort in that and other duties.

When the awakening brake out at Camb. in Feb. 1742, I came over & heard Sermons, & was much affected in seeing the people there in such distress : and I thought that unless I got out of the State I was in I would never be Saved. One day I was much affected in hearing a Minr (26)[3] preach on that Text, And when he is come, he will convince the world of Sin.[4] Another day hearing a Minr (26) preach on these words, He that believeth not hath made God a liar,[5] & shewing the hainous nature of the Sin of Unbelief, when he said among other things, That Unbelief was a greater Sin than murder, than even the murdering of father or mother, for that was but murdering a creature, but unbelief was a murdering of the Son of God, or an approving of his murder by the Jews: I found these words brought home with great power to my heart, was made sensible that I was an unbeliever, & that by my unbelief, I had murderd Christ, kill'd the Prince of life and crucified the Lord of glory or caused him to be kill'd & crucified. [11/–] Upon this I

---

[1] Janet Tennant – the shorthand text in McCulloch's 'Index of persons' names who gave the foregoing accounts to Mr. McC' states: daughter of David Tenant, weaver in Old Monkland. Taught to read the Bible and got a good part of the Catechism by heart.

[2] Insertion ['near']: McCulloch.

[3] William McCulloch (1691–1771) – minister, Cambuslang.

[4] Jn 16:8.

[5] 1 Jn 4:20.

was brought into great distress of soul, & was just at the point of crying out among the people, but got it refrain'd. But at that time I did not get a sense of any of my Sins but my Unbelief: which was very distressing to me for a considerable time.

While I was in this Soul-trouble, that Tempter one day suggested to me, That Christ never came into the World to Save Sinners, and he urg'd this upon my mind for about half a day: but God let me see That this was but a Temptation of Satan to think so; & gave me faith to believe the contrary Truth revealed in the Word, & so the Temptation went off. Sometime after this the Devil tempted me to give my Self away Soul and body to him, for that there was no mercy for me: I was indeed under great fears that there was no mercy for me, but I abhorr'd the vile suggestion of the Evil One of giving my Self away to him: and the Lord was pleased to give me some hair of hope, that he would yet shew me mercy: but it was but a very small glimmering of hope I got ; till one night in my bed, wishing the Lord might have mercy on me, but fearing he would not, that word came into my mind, Return unto me and I will turn unto you, saith the Lord of hosts [12/–] This gave me some little comfort to think that the Lord was calling me to turn to him, & that the door of mercy was yet open to me, & I got some more liberty in praying after this.

About the 17ᵗʰ of June 1742 having come over to Camb. to hear Sermons, before Sermon began, a Glasgow-man sitting on the Brae beside me was telling how the Seceding ministers & their followers, were calling all this Work at Camb. a Delusion, and particularly how ~~Mr~~⁶ Seceding Minr at Stirling, at the late Sacrament they had there, had been exclaiming [ ]⁷ bitterly against it, and had pitch'd upon these words in Jude for his Text at his Action Sermon, Raging waves of the sea, foaming out their own Shame, wandring Stars to whom is reserv'd the blackness of darkness for ever.⁸ This put me into so great Confusion, that I could give little heed to what was said in the Sermons, & I went home that night in great perplexity, & continu'd so ~~that~~ after I was got home. But next morning, while I was at ~~Secret Prayer~~, begging the Lord might remove that temptation, I was under, as to the Work at Camb. being a Delusion, and might shew me from his Word if it was right, within two minutes after I had begun to pray thus, those words came into my heart

> For God of Zion hath made choice,
> There he desires to dwell
> This is is my Rest here Still I'll Stay,
> For I do like it well.⁹

---

⁶   Textual overwrite from 'Mr' to 'a'.
⁷   Insertion ['for that purpose']: McCulloch.
⁸   Jude 1:13.
⁹   Ps 132:13–14, Scottish Psalter (metrical).

[17/–]¹ b.y. A widow woman aged about 34 years.²

I had not the advantage of a Religious Education in my younger years; & so began only when I was about twelve years of age to pray some in Secret and continued to do so for about two years: after which I turn'd quite careless of all that was good, & laid aside praying by my Self altogether till of late. I us'd to go to Kirk on Sabbath days, but did not mind what was said in earnest. I thought if I could read the Bible & go to the Kirk & lead a moral life; & not wrong my ~~Self~~ neighbours, that all was well enough. After I have been sometimes recovered from danger at childbearing, I have had some kind of impressions on my Spirit to return God thanks; but I Soon forgot all again, & return'd to my former careless unconcern'd way of life, and seldom ever thought at all of an after state, or what would become of me after death.

    And thus matters continued with me till the year 1742, When I resolvd to go to Cambuslang about the first of May and on Sabbath Morning, before I went out that thought came into my mind, now I am going to Seek the Blessing & I know not where. When I came there, I heard a Minister (26)³ preach on that Text, When the strong man armed keeps the house [18/–] all his goods are in peace; but when a stronger than he cometh, he will bind the strong man and Spoil his goods & cast him out.⁴ While he shewed that the strong man armed was the devil, the house or palace, the heart; his goods the lusts & corruptions of the Soul, and the methods he took to keep the Sinners heart with all his corruptions in it, in peace & quiet but that Christ who was infinitely stronger than the Devil, would come & bind the devil and cast him out of the ~~Sinners~~ hearts of his Elect, & the way he us'd to take to do so: While I heard these things discours'd at large, I found a secret & mighty power, applying them to my soul, giving me such a sight & sense of my lost and wretched condition, and such a sense of my Sins as dishonouring to God as well as exposing me to Eternal Misery, that my inward agony made me fall into such a sweat, that one might have wrung my Gown from my Shoulder to my Belt as if it had been drawn thro' the water; and yet at the same time I was made to tremble as if I would have shaken to pieces: [ ]⁵ and this was joind with a sweet melting of heart for sin, & Secret praising and blessing of God in my heart, that he had not cast me into Hell but Spared me so [19/–]

¹ Primary pagination numbers 13–16 omitted by McCulloch.
² Margaret Boyle – the shorthand text in McCulloch's 'Index of persons' names who gave the foregoing accounts to Mr. McC' states: relative to James Scot, shoemaker. Taught to read, got the Catechism, and retained it mostly.
³ William McCulloch (1691–1771) – minister, Cambuslang.
⁴ Lk 11:21–2.
⁵ Insertion ['but cry'd not out, tho I refraind with difficulty']: McCulloch.

long & was now giving me such a Sight and Sense of things as I now had. And all this was accompanied with such a Love To Christ, that I could have been content, if it had been his will, [.....] never to have seen my husband or nearest Relations or any body in the world, but to have been just swallowed up of that Love to Christ, I then felt poured into my soul. And after that Sermon was closd, while that Portion of the 68th Psalm was a singing

> (Thou hast O Lord most glorious
> Ascended up on high
> And in triumph Victorious led
> Captive captivity
> Thou hast received gifts for men
> For Such as did I rebel
> Yea even for them that God the Lord
> In midst of them might dwell)[6]

I was made to rejoice with joy unspeakable, that Christ, had bound Satan & cast him out of my heart, or in hopes that he would do so, & would rid my heart of the Devils goods, the hellish trash of lusts & corruptions in my heart, that he would captivate Me to himself, who had been so long a captive to the Devil, that he would receive such a Rebel as I had been into favour, & come and dwell in my heart.

[20/–] But after this frame had lasted about ten or twelve days, in a good measure, it wore off & I fell under great distress of Soul, at the thoughts of my Sins, & danger of Eternal misery, & [][7] that all I had met with was but delusion I had met with, tho at times it was otherwise, & I durst not deny what the Lord had done for me: but I got no Sensible Comfort for about a Quarter of a year after this, tho, blessd be God I was still kept close to the way of duty & diligent in the use of all the Means of grace, I could get access to, as hearing of the word & reading it, Meditation Christian Converse & Prayer, especially Secret Prayer: I slept very little for that Quarter of a Year, but sate up often till twelve o'clock at night, and got up again about two in the morning for Secret Prayer & other duties: Some about me seeing me so much taken up that way, Said I was turn'd light in the head & would certainly go to distracted, and would pray my Self to Hell. At length one night very late, while I was first at meditation then at Secret Prayer, 'ere I was aware my Soul was made as the chariots of Amminadab,[8] while I was musing the fire burnd meditation was turnd to Prayer, and Prayer [21/–] into praise: and praises proceeded from love & joy in God thro' Jesus Christ by whom I thought I had received the Atonement. My heart was led out to close with

---

6   Ps 68:18, Scottish Psalter (metrical).
7   Insertion ['often thinking']: McCulloch.
8   SS 6:12.

Christ in all his Redeeming Offices, as Prophet to teach Priest to save & King to Rule me. I could not forbear crying out Bless the Lord O my Soul & forget not all benefits &c: as in the 103ᵈ Psalm.⁹ ~~My heart was~~ I had then an ardent desire, if it had been possible to have had 1000s of congregations employed in praising him, & that Heaven & Earth Should sing with his praises.

But about five or six days after this [ ]¹⁰ I was tempted to think all I had met with was but Delusion, upon which I was brought under great distress, and thought I was a Cast-away, & that the Lord would never have mercy on me, or forgive such heinous sins as I had been guilty of; Shortly after, while I was under much perplexity with such apprehensions, that word came into my heart, I say I even I am he that blotteth out thy transgressions & will not remember thy sins, for my own names sake:¹¹ this word came with such power, as eas'd me of the burden that had been on my Spirit, and caused me to rejoice at the hopes of Gods pardoning & pitying me & sending such a word to relieve me & to ly low before him for my unbelief & distress.

[22/– through 24/– blank]

---

⁹   Ps 103:2.
¹⁰ Insertion ['when this frame went off']: McCulloch.
¹¹ Isa 43:25.

[25/–] b.l. A young woman of 19[1]

My parents being Religious Persons, by any thing I could formerly, or can yet judge, brought me [][2] in a Religious way: and I conformed to their Instructions and Example, in an outward way, & was restrained in mercy from things vicious before men, usd to go to Kirk on Sabbaths & to pray twice or once at least Every day from [][3] Childhood. I usd however sometimes in converse, when I would have the person that spoke to me, & seem'd to doubt of what I told, have said, In Truth it is so, or Faith, Haith it is so: I saw no evil in that way of speaking then, but I often since have been made to see much evil in my speaking so, & to mourn in secret for it. And because I kept up a form of Religious Duties, I made no doubt but this would take me to Heaven.

    And thus things continued with me, without any thing like an awakening, or sense of sin or my natural lost state, till in October 1740, when the Sacrament Occasion at Glasglow drawing near, my mistress said to me, Are you not thinking to partake of the Sacrament at this time? I said No, I was not, for I was not prepar'd: She answered, I'll warrant there will many as unprepared there []:[4] I then began to think with my Self, Surely I [26/–] must be a great Hypocrite when my Mistress has such thoughts of me. And tho' I saw I was not fit to go to the Lords Table, yet I thought it would be fit for me before such an occasion to read the History of Christ' Sufferings in the Gospel: but as I turn'd over my Bible, I saw a mark (or corner of my Bible-Leaf folded down) & knowing that I did not use to put a mark, but in places where I had formerly observd something remarkable, I asked a Blessing on what I was going to read, as I always usd to do when I was going to read in the Bible, [][5] give me the sanctifyd use of it; and resolvd, I would read what was there before I went any further: & as I read there [][6] and came to the 41st verse, And Jesus moved with compassion, put forth his hand and touched him (the Leper) and said, I will, Be thou clean:[7] upon which I was made to believe that Christ was willing to heal & cleanse my Soul from the leprosy of Sin; But I was wofully averse to come to be healed & cleansed by him: at the thoughts of this, I fell into great uneasiness & distress of mind. I asked my

---

1   Mary Shaw – the shorthand text in McCulloch's 'Index of persons' names who gave the foregoing accounts to Mr. McC' states: daughter of Duncan Shaw, ship-carpenter in Greenock. Taught to read the Bible when a child, got the Shorter Catechism by heart, and retained it.
2   Insertion ['up']: McCulloch.
3   Insertion ['my']: McCulloch.
4   Insertion ['as you']: McCulloch.
5   Insertion ['that the Lord would']: McCulloch.
6   Insertion ['Mark. 1. at the beginning']: McCulloch.
7   Mk 1: 41.

Mistress, if she would allow me to go to that Sacrament Occasion, no she said, but she would allow me to go to the next after that. All the Winter & Spring following (in 1741) I continued under more concern about my Soul than before, and was much grievd to find my heart so hard, and my mind wandering in time of duty, & thro disquiet of [27/–] my heart, when there was none within by my self, I have been made to roar, & I would then have found my heart very sore, and lest any body should have overheard me, that I might conceal my inward distress that was the spring of all, I would have cry'd, my Head, my Head!

At the Barony-Sacrament that year, hearing a Minister ( ) on that Text, Choose ye this day whom you will serve,[8] I thought I will for my part choose the Lord to serve him only: But I was sensible, that I had so often already broke so many promises, resolutions, & vows to serve God, that I was afraid that I would do so still. And when he said, There are many that drew near to God, rushing into his presence, as the horse into the Battel, without considering whom they approach; that they did not consider what a Holy & just God, they had to do with: I thought that this had indeed been my way too much & too long already; but I thought I would try for a week or two, If I could once refrain from Sin and after that I would be more fit to come before him in prayer. I accordingly essayed to do so, for two weeks, & after that essaying to pray, I [ ][9] I was more unfit & out of order in that duty than before: & sitting down & reflecting how things were with me since I had refraind prayer for two weeks: I found things had turn'd still worse & worse. Upon which I resolv'd to return to my former course of prayer daylie. And that word coming into my mind, encouraged [28/–] me much to that duty, And Isaac said, Here is the Wood and the fire, but where is the Lamb for a burnt offering: And Abraham answered, My Son the Lord will provide himself a Lamb for a burnt offering.[10] So Is was made to hold on at the duty & to go about it, when I was sensible of my unpreparedness for it, hoping the Lord would give what he required of me. And sometimes when I went out into the fields alone, for the more secrecy & liberty at this duty, I would have fainted & swarfd & been seized with great tremblings of body at the apprehension of the Greatness & majesty of God, & because I thought he would pour down his infinite wrath upon me, because I so richly deserved it. And under such apprehensions I would sometimes be made to cry out in the fields, and sometimes in the House too, & when I could not otherwise get crying refraind, I would, to prevent it, have sometimes stopt my mouth with my Napkin, or if I was near a Bed, would have wrapt my Head in the Bed, close with the Bed-Cloaths. And all this was in the Summer 1741.

---

[8]   Jos 24:15.
[9]   Insertion ['found']: McCulloch.
[10]   Gen 22:7–8.

And in this condition I continued oftimes till a Stranger Minister ( ) came to Glasglow in Septr thereafter (1741.) & hearing him preach in the High-Church-yeard concerning Sauls conversion, when he said, Some of you will not pray for a week or more, hoping you'll grow better, & then you'll pray: I thought he was just speaking to [29/–] me and was going to name me out, for a hypocrite: upon which I was put to great confusion, and was like to cry out. When he further said, If one should ask many of you, How long since you lov'd Christ, you would answer, Ever since I was born, or ever since I can remember. And some of you would say, I thought I lov'd Christ once, but I do not love him now: I thought here he was just describing me, & the thoughts of my heart, & was in such distress, that I was afraid I would cry out, and rather than do that, I choosd to withdraw from among the people, & did so, & heard him no more.

Next Sabbath I was afraid I would be made to cry out in the Kirk, & therefore I thought I would rather go to hear some of the Seceding Ministers at Corshill; for I had observd, that in hearing them sometimes before, I was never so nearly touchd with what they said, as in hearing some Ministers in the Kirks; and so I thought I would not be in such hazard of crying out among them as in the Kirks. Accordingly I did go to Corshill, & heard a Seceding Preacher ( ) there, who among other things said, You may remember, my Friends, that I prayed that we might be sanctifyd, tho ye are all sanctifyd by the word that I have spoken—and a little after that he said again, Ye are sanctified. He also said, when our First Parents sinned; the Sun & Moon & Stars and all things frowned upon them, & yet by the bye Christ died for us, and within a little, [30/–] he repeated these words over again, by the bye Christ died for us. I rose up & looked about me, & thought, it's a strange thing if all this multitude be sanctify'd, & I unsanctify'd: And Christs dying by the bye, lookt to me, as if he had said, He dyd by chance or by accident: & if he dyd in that manner, I thought his death could never avail me to Salvation, or any other. I had before, thought that Christ dyd according to God's purpose and his agreement with the Father from all Eternity: and so did not at all die by the bye. Finding my self put into great confusion by these things, I had not patience to sit out the rest of the Sermon, but came away home: & because I could scarce trust my own Ears, that I had heard such shocking Expressions, tho they had been repeated over & over, I asked two other persons (&) if they had noticd any such Expressions, & they both said they did; one of them, saying he had heard many Sermons, but he had never heard such things before: The Effect however on me was sad, for I was tempted to think for several days after, that it might be that Preacher was in the right in saying That Christ dyd by the bye; but that seemed so unreasonable-like, that rather than think so, I thought it would be better to believe that he did not die at all: and accordingly I did at length conclude that it was so: but was some time after mercifully recovered from that horrid piece of unbelief, by reading

Mr. Dan. Campbells little Book on the Sacrament,[11] whereby I came to be confirmed in the belief of the reality of Christs death, as had been designed & agreed upon from Eternity.

[31/–] Next Sabbath, hearing a Minister ( ) on that Text Rom. 8.10. But ye are not in the flesh but in the Spirit: Now if any man have not &c:[12] when he said, It was strange that people heard the Gospel every day with so much quietness, & heard him often Gods wrath was denouncd against Sinners, & were not moved: if some Sinners who have only an ~~sense~~ apprehension of Gods wrath, & some little drops of it let into their souls at a time, are in such agonies, what would it be for sinners to have their whole souls filled with that wrath to all Eternity, & their own Consciences made to owne that it was all just & due: I felt some such drops of wrath let into my soul, & my conscience was made to owne that this wrath to the uttermost was what was justly due to me: & was scarce able to refrain crying out in the Kirk, but got out immediatly to the Church-yeard and cryd out there: and went home, but durst not go back in the afternoon.

Next Sabbath hearing a Preacher ( ) when he said, These that break one of Gods commandments broke all: I found my Self in great disorder, & got out of the Kirk, & cryd in the Kirk-yeard, because I thought I had broken all Gods commandments, slighted his Providences & abused his mercies, And I thought I heard every one of these [ ][13] saying, Broken me! and Broken me! A woman nearby hearing me, & thinking I was crying to some dead Relation in the grave, or so, said, you need not cry so, your cry will not be heard. I was afraid that it would be so, that a Righteous God would refuse to hear my cry: & went home in great anguish. [32/–] I then went to a Minister ( ) who asked me what was the matter with me, I told him that as I had never closed with Christ, I was afraid I was under the curse of a broken law. He asked me if there was any other sins I was touchd with the sense of? I told him that I usd sometimes to say Faith and Truth. He said far be it from him to desire me to confess my secret sins to him, that these were to be confessed to God only. I told him that mercy had restrained me from any gross Outbreakings beside these, but that I was under much hardness of heart. I also told him that I had cut down a man who hang'd up himself in a rope to dispatch himself, & that that man was often angry & in a heat of rage afterward at me for doing so, upon which I had been often tempted to think that I had done wrong in cutting him down, & preventing his death. The Minister said, you are not in

[11]   Daniel Campbell, *Sacramental Meditations on the Sufferings and Death of Christ. In which the humiliation and sufferings of Christ, in his birth, in his life, before, at, and after his death, with the end of his sufferings, and the sacramental promise is consider'd. By Mr. Daniel Campbell, minister of the Gospel in Kilmichael of Glasrie, within the presbytery and synod of Arglye* (Boston, Printed by D. Fowle, for S. Kneeland and T. Green, in Queen-Street near the prison, 1740).

[12]   Ro 8:9.

[13]   Insertion ['commandments as it were']: McCulloch.

the right way. I continued uneasy about my cutting down the man; till one Sabbath night as my Minister was asking the Questions in the Catechism[14] at me & the rest in the Family, it fell to my share to answer that Question, What is required in the 6th Commandment, and in repeating the Answer, The 6th Commandment requires all lawful Endeavours to preserve our own life & the life of others: I was made to see I had been only doing my duty in that matter.

But after this, thinking I was not in a right way, I laid by my Bible, & refraind prayer, thinking that my reading & praying when I was not right, would but aggravate my Condemnation: & continued to do so for four days: But at the end of the 4th day, that word came into my mind with great life & power 'Return O Shulamite, return,[15] & after that, it was added, For I am God & there is none else beside me:[16] which engagd me to return to reading the Bible & Prayer, which I never ommitted one day since.

---

[14] *Larger Catechism of the Westminster Assembly. The humble advice of the assembly of divines, now by the authority of Parliament sitting at Westminster, concerning a confession of faith: With the quotations and texts of the scripture annexed. Presented by them lately to both Houses of Parliament.* Printed at London; And reprinted at Edinburgh by Evan Tyler, printer to the King's most Excellent Majesty, 1647. (London; Edinburgh: Evan Tyler, 1647).

[15] SS 6:13.

[16] Various forms found in Isaiah 45–7.

[33/–] b.w. A Man of 50 years[1]

I was train'd up by my Parents to a custom of praying in Secret, when I was
a Child, but when I advanced to youth and manhood, I in a great measure
laid it aside; and when at any times I went about it, it was always cross the
grain. I went however usually to Church on the Sabbath days, but it was in
a great measure only out of custom. I usd in my former life to be too much
addicted to several evil ways, particularly keeping idle company, playing at
cards & drinking to excess. And thus it continued with me, till about till about
two years ago. And some more, when going to Cambuslang about the end of
February 1742, and hearing a Minister (26)[2] preach [34/–] from a Text which
I do not now distinctly remember, concerning the exceeding evil & sinfulness
of Sin, as dishonoring to God & piercing to the blessed Redeemer, as well as
exposing the Sinner to Eternal misery [],[3] I found a strange stirring in my
heart, & got such a sight & deep sense of the evil of my sins both of heart &
life that I could have found in my heart to have torn my self all to inches, for
my sins whereby I had offended such a gracious & glorious God, & wounded
such a merciful & compassionate Saviour: and it was with great difficulty that
I could get my Self refrained from crying out among the people. And this
distress of soul continued with me near to a month thereafter.

[35/–] During that Month, I was often reduc'd to so great confusion, that
I thought sometimes I should have gone distracted. I went every Lord's day
to Cambuslang, & often also on week days, to hear Sermon there, and got
always further and clearer Convictions of my sin and the lost condition I
was in. I was also led to be very much in Secret Prayer, at least essaying it:
for sometimes I could pray none at all, when I essay'd it. Sometimes when I
would have gone about that duty, I have continued kneeling for about half an
hour before I could get one word uttered. And Satan laboured hard to drive
me from that duty, & all others, telling me, That now it was too late & to no
purpose. Yet there was still a hankering in my heart to go to Cambuslang,
to hear Sermon, & to pray by my self, and some ~~small~~ glimmering hope of
mercy, tho but very small, & scarce discernible.

[36/–] About a month after this first awakening, hearing a Minister (who
it was I do not now remember) at Camb. cite some passage of Scripture in
his Sermon, I turn'd over the leaves of my Bible to find it; and while I was
seeking for it, another Text which he did not cite, cast up to me, & my eyes

---

[1]   Ballie Weir – the shorthand text in McCulloch's 'Index of persons' names who gave the
      foregoing accounts to Mr. McC' states: from Hamilton; taught to read and write, and later
      got the Catechism to heart and retained it.
[2]   William McCulloch (1691–1771) – minister, Cambuslang.
[3]   Insertion ['that there was no remedy but the application of the blood of Christ']: McCulloch.

were kept staid on it, Isaiy. Look unto me all ye Ends of the Earth & be ye saved,[4] and Oh! What a greedy grasp did my poor Soul give at Christ at the reading of it, and I thereupon found my mind much composed, & framed to attend to the Sermon. About an hour after this, that word came into my mind, The blood of Jesus Christ cleanses from all Sin,[5] which gave a vast deal of ease to my mind and conscience; and Satans temptations to think that my Salvation was impossible, were not so strong & powerful on me, & I thought that precious blood of Christ might yet cleanse me from all my sins, how many & hainous so ever. I came [37/–] straight home to prayer, & hastned to retire by my self, & found more freedom in that duty [ ][6] than ever I did all my life before. And ere I rose from my knees, I got such a persuasion of the All sufficiency of the merit of Christs blood, that I saw it was perfectly able to wash away all my Sins. And at the same time I got such a Sight by faith of the infinite amiableness of Christs person, that I was, so to speak, o're head & ears & all in love to him. And ever since that time, hearing Christ preached, praying and praising God in my Family, & by my Self alone, is just become a perfect pleasure and a delight to me. And every time I hear his Gospel and partake of the Holy Sacrament of the Supper, I see more & more of his Beauty and desirableness; & more and more of Fullness and fittedness in him to answer all my wants and neccessities. My soul is more & more [38/–] led out to a hearty well-pleasedness with the method of Gods Saving Sinners by Jesus Christ; & despair of all other ways of Salvation but that & that only. My soul now trembles at the thought of sin, and particularly, the remembrance of my former evil ways is terrible and bitter to me. I have a daylie fight and struggle with a body of Sin and death within me, which draws many a weary groan from me, and reconciles me to the thoughts of death, & makes it in some measure sweet to me, in hopes that then I shall be delivered from the very being of [. . .]. I have no delight in conversing with one living soul, but such as I think have the grace of God in them. I have no ambition to be rich in the world. I would not give a fig for all the Riches of the Indies; if I might be rich in faith, food and raiment is all I want of worldly kind, and I trust God will not deny me that. Carnal & worldly pleasures are now turn'd insipid & tasteless to me, and my only the great pleasure [ ][7] now is to be found in Christ, & to enjoy communion with him here & for ever hereafter. To his name be Glory. Amen.

[39/–] I find Satan very often assaulting me, by his suggestions, tho he never appeard to me in any visible shape. One time lately this same Summer (1744) when attending at the Sacrament Occasion at Kilsyth, and being out in the

---

4 Isa 45:22.
5 1 Jn 1:7.
6 Insertion ['of Secret Prayer']: McCulloch.
7 Insertion ['I now aim at']: McCulloch.

fields by my Self, and having sung two or three verses by [. . .] [. . .] and read
a Chapter of my Bible, in prayer while I was very earnest for the pardon of
Sin, and peace & reconciliation by Jesus Christ; Satan suggested to me that
all this was needless; that these things were but meer Chimera's and fanesis,
& that my own vile & wicked heart was but deceiving me with notions about
these things all this while. I was then much dejected & put to confusion, &
did not know what to say. After Prayer, I resolvd that I would walk about a
little & meditate, and while I was going to do so, the passage Rom. 10. 9, 10.
came into my mind, If thou shalt confess with thy mouth the Lord Jesus, &
shalt believe in thine heart that God raisd him from the dead, thou shalt be
saved, for with the heart man believeth unto righteousness, & with the mouth
[40/–] confession is made unto salvation: upon which I was made to say, O
Lord I confess before thee the heart-searcher, that Jesus Christ, the merit of
his obedience & sufferings is the only ground of all my hope & trust & I can
appeal to Thee who knoweth all things, that I believe with all my heart &
soul that thou raised him up from the dead, & that he is now at thy right hand
in heaven; upon this I found the power of Satan's Temptation broken, & my
spirit was relieved from that dejection under which I was sinking.

[41/–] a.a.[1]

My Life, thro' mercy has not been stain'd with gross vices before the world: only I have sometimes been drawn away by commorades to drinking more than was convenient. I had early desires after what what is good, & a great inclination after knowledge and reading of Books. I was put to pray by my Self by my mother when very young, but I did not much mind it out of choice then but when I came to more years I usd to go pretty oft about it. I usd all along for ordinary to go to the Kirk on Lords days, and to read the Bible & other good Books now & then when alone. And found the Word sometimes sweet to me, and would have long'd for the Sabbath before it came: and had much pleasure in the Work of it when it came. But when I came to more years, I was drawn away for sometime by bad company to break the Sabbath day, & sometimes to drink to excess: but came afterwards to see something of the evil of these ways & to refrain them. I went sometimes to hear the Seceding Ministers, & thought sometimes I was under much concern in hearing them, particularly in hearing one of them ( ) on that Text, whom say men that I am—but [42/–] whom say ye that I am, and he answered Thou art Christ the Son of the living God,[2] where I was made to see that I had not yet received Christ in the offers of the Gospel, nor yielded my self to him: And found some desires then to do it. After this one day; walking out by my self, I began to think, That within a little while & these heavens over my head would be folded together like a Scroll & the Earth with the works therein would be burnt up, and if I did not get an Interest in Christ, I would certainly be miserable for ever. And the Sacrament Occasion in the place I liv'd in drawing near, I went by my Self, and essay'd to give my self away in Covenant to God, engaging to fear & serve him & to walk in his ways, if he would give me grace. When first admitted to that holy Ordinance, I made some preparation for it, but cannot say, That I met with anything sensibly to my soul.

[43/– through 48/– blank]

---

[1]   James Lang – the shorthand text in McCulloch's 'Index of persons' names who gave the foregoing accounts to Mr. McC' states: weaver in Kilmarnock, son of John Lang, also a weaver in Kilmarnock. Taught to read the Bible and write, got the *Larger Catechism* by heart, and retained a good part of it.

[2]   Mt 16:15–16; Mk 8:29–30; Lk 9:20–1.

[49/–] c.h. A man of 40 years.[1]

I was put to school when a child, but would not apply my self to learn to read, only I learnd the Letters & to read the Catechism[2] some way; & was entred in the Psalm Book when I left the school; but when I came to be about twelve years of age, I took a fancy to learn to read, thinking I would not be like another man when I came to be of age if I could not read: and these with whom I liv'd being me incline to learn to read, both gave me liberty to learn & put me to it and so I proceeded till I could read the Bible tolerably. But for Prayer in secret I never usd so much as a form of any thing of that kind, till I came to be a man, if it had not been that I would sometimes, tho but seldom, have gone to my Knees, and said Lord keep me: and that was all my Prayer. After I came to man's age, I would sometimes have gone to my knees & prayed for some space of time, at once: but it was only at some rare times when I took it in my head, like a freak, when any thing provokd or vexed me. ~~But after I was~~

[50/–] But after I was married, I began to thrive very fast in the world; and then I thought it was a very odd thing that God in his Providence should make me to thrive so fast in the world, & that I should never acknowledge him for it: upon that I fell to pray both in my Family & by my self, and went on in a custom of doing so for some time, till one night that I was in the stable giving my horse his supper, and after I had done so [ ][3] when I had fall'n down on my knees there, to pray; ~~and just as I was going to do so,~~ I thought I saw like a long black man before me, and heard him as it were whisper to me, What art thou going to do? Is there such a thing as a God? At which I fell into a great Fright, but continued for some little space on my knees, thinking I would not not rise till I got praying, but the apparition and the terror continuing, I could get nothing out but, God keep me. And with that I got up, & away to my house in a great hurry & confusion. But after that, for about six years (viz. till the year 1742) I left off all praying both by my self & in my Family, tho' frequently urged to it by my Wife. both because of the Fright I had got when last at it, & because I turnd very near an Atheist in Opinion, so that a very little arguing by a man, speaking in favours of Atheism

[1]   Thomas Foster – the shorthand text in McCulloch's 'Index of persons' names who gave the foregoing accounts to Mr. McC' states: from Ridley-Wood.

[2]   *Shorter Catechism. The humble advice of the assembly of divines, now by the authority of Parliament sitting at Westminster, concerning a confession of faith: With the quotations and texts of the scripture annexed. Presented by them lately to both Houses of Parliament.* Printed at London; And reprinted at Edinburgh by Evan Tyler, printer to the King's most Excellent Majesty, 1647. (London; Edinburgh: Evan Tyler, 1647)..

[3]   Insertion ['tho the place was dark']: McCulloch.

would have, I think, persuaded me altogether, That there was no God. [51/–]
And indeed I had been a kind of Atheist in practice almost all along before:
I livd without God in the world: my life had been a continued Tract of Sin
& Folly. I had not the Temptations & Opportunities to sin that many have,
else, I think, there was scarce any sin but I would have committed it. I car'd
not what mischief I did, so be I could get it hid from the eyes of the world.
Yet the many of the Evils I was guilty of I was drawn into by others, thro'
a natural easiness of temper. I usd to be just & honest in my dealings: In my
younger years, till I was about fourteen years of age I could drink no ale or
other liquor, but would have trembled when any would have put a cup of
ale into my hand: At length, when about that age, two men offered me each
a penny, if I would drink one cup full of ale: I took the two pence & drank
it off, and after that I learn'd to drink better from time to time, at length I
could not want it, and came just to make a Trade of it, and often abus'd my
self with it & drank to Excess.[†]⁴ I sometimes usd to let an oath fly, when in
passion or in drinks; but I could not endure to hear others swear; and if any
of the company drinking with me fell a swearing, I would have immediatly
run to the door and away. And if I was bad before, I turnd much worse and
wickeder, during that six years that I quite left off all Prayer.

[52/–] In the year 1742 hearing a minister ( ) at the Brae of Cambuslang,
on that Text, Is there no balm in Gilead, is there no physician there,⁵ I fell
under a great terror of the wrath of God, so that I thought I felt the ground
where I was sitting all shaking: and thought oh how shall I be able to endure
the punishment due to my sins! [ ]⁶ I was seizd with much horror for fear of
the punishment of sin, but I had no sense of the evil of sin as dishonouring
to God; I fell however again to pray both by my self & in my family; and
continued to do so, but, I continued still my drinking Trade: [ ]⁷ That Summer
I heard another minister (12)⁸ preach at Camb. I fell again under great Terror
and thought I would certainly perish for ever: and while I was hearing in this
condition, with my hand over my Eyes, Hell was represented to my mind, as
a Pit at the foot of a Hill, and a great drove of people marching into it, & I

---

⁴ Insertion ['† Sometimes I have workd all day & drunk all night after, & then followed my
 work the next day again. And once, I remember, I wrought each lawful day of the week &
 drank every night of that week out & out without sleeping any at all till Saturdays night']:
 McCulloch.
⁵ Jer 8:22.
⁶ Insertion ['I then thought I was caught up between the sky and the ground, & there I thought
 I shrank altogether when up in the air but fear'd I would fall down again & be crushd all to
 pieces.']: McCulloch.
⁷ Insertion ['I went often to Alehouses and drank long there and still after my great fit of
 drinking, I could scarce sleep above an hour when I came home; being startled with uneasy
 thoughts & fears of judgment ready to overtake me for it, & yet when inward I would seek
 to it yet again.']: McCulloch.
⁸ George Whitefield (1714–70) – evangelist.

along with them, & when I was got very near it, I thought I looked over my shoulder & saw a very beautiful man, who smild on me and made a motion to me with his hand to come back, at which I was very glad. And for some time after that Sermon; I refrain'd my course of drinking much, at least I did not drink so oft to excess as I usd to do, and heard sermons with more pleasure. But []⁹ I returned gradually to my former Drunken way again, my concern wore gradually off, I turnd more & more loose and careless of prayer & sermons & all that was good: & for about a month before I fell under a fresh awakening & abiding concern about Religion in Summer 1744, I had left off praying altogether both in Secret and in my Family.

[53/–] One day in July, 1744, after I had been drinking hard two days ~~together~~ & one night and part of the third day altogether without intermission, on the third of these days, in the afternoon, []¹⁰ coming by the Manse of Cambuslang, as I passd thro' the Church yeard there, I slept a little & look't on a Grave-stone lying above one I had been acquainted with, & thought it would not be long till I would be lying in the grave too: upon which I said within my self, It is a strange thing that I am so enslaved to drink, that I cannot get free of it: I'll go away in to the Minister there, and see if he will say any thing to me that will rouse me & put me from it. I accordingly went in to the Manse, & calld for him: he was then at dinner with several persons & some strangers with him: he came to the door & spake a word or two to me, and then bade me come forward into the room where he was dinning, & desir'd his wife to give me a drink, & sate down to meal again. When I got the drink into my hand, []¹¹ I had been full of drink the day before: What say ye, said the Ministers wife, are you going to speak that way to the Minister: Yes, said I, I was as full as I could hold both of ale & brandy; The minister said nothing, but look'd me broad in the face, & then I turning to the Company at Table, said, I take you all witnesses to this [54/–] confession. Upon hearing that I was immediatly struck with terror & confusion at the thought that I should have spoke so to a Minister & offended his people present with him, and ran to the door, and as I lookd back over my shoulder, going out of the door, that word struck in suddenly in my mind, He that toucheth you toucheth the apple of my eye, which greatly increasd my confusion & uneasiness at the thoughts of my behaving so unsuitably there: I ran off in a hurry however to a Change-house near by the Manse, & fell to drinking there, hoping by that means to drink away my trouble of mind: I would gladly have been merry & jolly, but when I essayd to be so at my Cups, my mirth would have died quickly away; and my sadness & uneasiness (which I would fain have conceald

---

⁹   Insertion ['after some months']: McCulloch.
¹⁰ Insertion ['being refreshd by some sleep the night before, & having the exercise of my sense & Reason pretty well, after what I had drunk on that day']: McCulloch.
¹¹ Insertion ['I said I had little need of drink for']: McCulloch.

from the company) returnd. And so finding no ease by drinking there, I went from that Ale-house to another, & drank a little, & from that to another, & so till I had gone thro' about half a dozen of them & drank a while in each: but my trouble of mind did not abate but increase by all that cursed pains I look to extinguish it. In passing from one of these Ale-houses to another, while I lookt to the grass on the ground where I was going, I thought not only these in the Manse, would bear witness, but that every pile of grass would I saw would witness against me. And as I was on the road from the last of them coming home, I fell under so great Terror of the wrath [55/–] of God as just ready to crush me, that I could not walk further, but sate down [ ][12] for some time full of dread & horror. After a while, I got up, & essayd to go home, and as I walkd along, I began to get a more distinct and amazing sight of my sins, particularly my Drinking to which had been the In-let to so many other sins, the ten Commandments were brought into my mind, & I was made to see that I had broken them all, & that I had been doing nothing but dishonouring God & rebelling against him all my life. The thoughts of this was now very distressing to my conscience: I essayd to wrestle out the way home, but was not able; but after going forward a little, I turnd back with a design to go into an Elders House ( ) near by the Road; but being very averse that any should know the Case I was in, I came went homeward again: but my trouble increasing, after going by the house & returning toward it again, I at length went to the door & knock'd (& by this time it was about midnight.

[56/– blank]

---

[12] Insertion ['on the ground']: McCulloch.

[57/-] c.c. A Single woman about 26 years[1]

I was brought up religiously by my Parents, who kept up the worship of God twice a day in their Family, and set me upon a Custom of praying twice a day by my Self, when I was a Child, and being under their Inspection when I came to years, I continued all along to keep up that Custom; and usd to go the Kirk for ordinary on the Lord's days; only in the year 1741, I turnd very careless and indifferent about it, & sometimes stayd at home. I was also outwardly civil & moral all along. And I thought no more was needful but these things, going to the Kirk, keeping up a form of Prayer and giving no body offence: But I never met with any Communion with God in these duties, nor did I know what it meant, and I had little or no concern about my heart or state.

[58/-] About the beginning of March 1742 I came to Camb. & heard a Minister (26)[2] on that Text, What shall it profit a man if he gain the whole world & lose his own Soul, or what shall a man give in exchange for his Soul,[3] at hearing of which I began to turn thoughtful and concernd, about my Soul & my Eternal Salvation, and thought that I had all along before that, liv'd without any thought or concern about it: And for a long time after, when I was at home, that word What shall a man give in Exchange for his Soul, came every now & then into my mind, & made me look on all worldly concerns as nothing compard to Soul-Concerns. I came frequently to Camb. but nothing I heard there further touchd me, till toward the End of April 1742, when hearing a Minister ( ) on a Thursday preach on that text, They shall look on him whom they pierced & mourn,[4] at which I was made to see that I had been along my life piercing and wounding Christ by my sins, and was made to weep and mourn and melt on that account.

[59/-] That same day in hearing another minister (26) on that Text, Awake thou that sleepest arise from the dead & Christ shall give thee light,[5] I was made to see that I had been all along my former life been dead and sleeping in my sins, and was made to long for the light of life from Christ; But then, I thought, How could it be that ever he would shew himself in mercy to me, who had so wounded & pierced him. And when he said, If one of you had murderd a man or woman, & the judge should come & ~~ask~~ enquire after the

---

[1]   Helen Finlay – the shorthand text in McCulloch's 'Index of persons' names who gave the foregoing accounts to Mr. McC' states: daughter of John Finlay, farmer in Calder. Taught to read the Bible, got the Catechism by heart, and retained it.

[2]   William McCulloch (1691–1771) – minister, Cambuslang.

[3]   Mt 16:26.

[4]   Zec 12:10.

[5]   Eph 5:14.

murderer, every one of you would be ready, to say, It was not I, & it was not I, & so would the guilty person too with his lips; but his Concsience would fly in his face & give him the lie, & say, Thou art the man. You have all of you, said he, been guilty of Sins that murdered the Saviour, & yet ye are all ready to deny it, & where is the person that takes with the guilt, & says Thou art the man or women. I found my conscience then charging me with that horrid guilt, & thought I had been doing [ ]⁶ all my life, but embruing my hands in the blood of the Son of God by my Sin. And this for a long time [60/–] stuck close to my Conscience. At hearing a Minister (26) after this, on that Text, He that believeth hath the witness in himself, & he that believeth not hath made God a liar; because he hath not believed the record God gave of his Son;⁷ I was made to see the hainous nature of unbelief as it was a Giving God the lie: I then thought I could believe nothing God had reveald, & had never believd on his Testimony: I had all along my life come to the Kirk only out of custom & form, but had never believed what I heard: that there were none that belongd to God like me: they had the witness within themselves that they did believe, but I had a warm witness within me that I did not believe; & that my unbelief would ruin & undo me for ever. I never however cryd out in publick; but thought they were happy that ~~did so~~ [ ];⁸ for that they certainly had other sort of Sights & Sense of Sin than I that forcd them to cry out. Only once at hearing a minister (⁓) preach on that Text, concerning these that were invited to come to the marriage, feast & would not, but all began to make Excuses,⁹ [61/–] when he said, These that had been often invited to come to Christ & would not were worse than the Jews ~~that~~ or Pilate that crucified him & set a crown of thorns upon his head, I could not forbear crying out in anguish of heart, thinking my self to be indeed worse than any of them.

At the Sacrament-Occasion in the place where I live, when I was at the Lords Table (to which I was with much difficulty persuaded to go) when the minister then Exhorting (12)¹⁰ Repeated these words of Job, I have heard of thee by the hearing of the Ear, but now mine eyes have seen thee, wherefore I abhor my self in dust & ashes;¹¹ I was at that instant made to see a Fulness and Sufficiency in Christ to save to the uttermost, & was persuaded that he would save me, and had my heart drawn out to accept of him and to close with him on the terms on which he offered himself in the Gospel; my heart was melted & drawn out in love to him, but was grieved I could not love him more.

---

⁶   Insertion ['nothing']: McCulloch.
⁷   1 Jn 5:10.
⁸   Insertion ['could do']: McCulloch.
⁹   Mt 22:2–14; Lk 14:16–24.
¹⁰ George Whitefield (1714–70) – evangelist.
¹¹ Job 42:5–6.

For about a month after this, I fell into a very dead lifeless condition, and was afraid all my concern would wear off. [62/–] I then thought I was a great hypocrite, that I had been crying out in the congregation, & making a great profession, but now all was come to nothing. I heard a minister (12) at Cumbernald on these word, Thou hast a name to live and art dead, which I thought was just my case, & this rousd and startled me much again. But when he preachd again on that text, And yet there is room, I could not be brought to think that that concern'd me, or that there could be any room in Gods mercy for me, who had been such a sinner, & such a hypocrite: but in hearing another minister ( ) on that text, As many as received him to them gave he power to become the sons of God,[12] I was made to see that if I could come weary & heavy laden to him, he would receive me however great a sinner I had been: and was helped to aim to do so, and for a considerable time after that found much love in my heart to Christ, but was grieved it was so little.

[63/– and 64/– blank]

---

[12] Jn 1:12.

[65/–] c.f. a Young Woman of 23 years[1]

I had scarce any form of Prayer in Secret when I was Child, or even after I came to Womans age: it was so much against the grain with me, that I rarely at all minded it, if it was not when I was put to it by some Friends about me. I scarce at all thought of what would become of me after death. But still the Lord kept from many gross Out-breakings, only I got a wicked custom of taking his holy name in vain, & I spent much precious time in vanity and idly company. I went however for ordinary on Sabbaths to church, but it was more to see & be seen than for any thing else.

In May 1742, I came to Camb. of heard Sermons on the Brae; but without any Effect: but hearing these word in Ps. 96.6. read & sung in the Kirk at night,

> O come & let us worship him
> let us bow down withal
> And on our knees before the Lord
> Our Maker let us fall[2]

[66/–] I could not forbear bursting out in tears, feeling some warm motions on my heart and hearing a woman there cry out, O Christ come, her words affected me much, for I thought I had as much need to cry that as she. This however wore off in a short time. I came back to Camb. next Lord's day, but got nothing sensibly. Next Sabbath after that, I came back to Camb. & ~~heard~~ while I heard a minister (26)[3] preach on that Text Ps. 68 Thou hast ascended up on high, thou hast led captivity captive, thou hast receivd gifts for men, even for the rebellious also &c.[4] I found all my sins that I had committed since my Infancy brought as fresh to my remembrance, as at the time I committed them, & set in order before me: and I made thereupon greatly to mourn & grieve for all my sins, as they were dishonouring to God & rebellious against him, and as thereby I sin my self liable to hell & damnation: and for two [67/–] days after, I thought I would certainly perish, & that there was not mercy for me: these despairing thoughts went off, but I continued in Soul-distress for about a quarter of year after. Hearing a Minister (26) preach at Camb. on that Text, Thou hast a name that thou livest and art dead,[5] I thought I was one of these & nothing but a hypocrite: and this exercised me much for

---

[1] Janat Alston – the shorthand text in McCulloch's 'Index of persons' names who gave the foregoing accounts to Mr. McC' states: daughter of Gavin Alston in Dalserf. Resides in Milton, taught to read the Bible when young, got Catechism by heart, retained it mostly.

[2] Ps 95:6, Scottish Psalter (metrical).

[3] William McCulloch (1691–1771) – minister, Cambuslang.

[4] Ps 68:18.

[5] Rv 3:1.

some time. I heard him also preach on that Text, O Jerusalem wash thine heart from wickedness &c.[6] I then got a deep conviction of heart Evils and pollutions of nature, which continued to grieve me much.

I went to attend the Sacrament-Occasion at Paisley about Lambas 1742 and, had a great deal of comfort & satisfaction, in hearing two ministers (&) preach in the forenoon of the Fast-day: But the afternoon I turnd very dull & dead[7]

[68/– through 72/– blank]

---

[6]   Jer 4:14.
[7]   Account ends abruptly.

[73/–] a.t.   A Young Woman of 22 Years.[1]

I was brought up by my Parents under the Influence of good Instruction and Example. I was set [ ][2] to pray in Secret when I was a Child, and continued in that custom of praying by my self twice a day all along my Life from my Childhood: and usd to attend publick Ordinances to see if I might get any good to my Soul: and was in mercy restrain'd from any thing grossly vicious before the world. But alas! all my Religion formerly was but a dead Form. I never felt the word of God when I read or heard it make any Impression on me: nor had I any Communion with God in Prayer [ ].[3] I little thought what would have become of me if I had died in that Condition.

Coming over to Camb. In March 1742, on a Sabbath, I got nothing by ordinary on that day; but coming back there again the Munday thereafter; I heard a Minister (26)[4] preach in the Kirk, on a Text that I cannot now recollect: but hearing him frequently speak of the State of Condemnation that all unregenerate, <u>unbelieving</u> Persons are in; that Word Condemnation, struck me to the Heart, & made me cry out under a Sense of my being in a lost condemn'd State, and that there was no Relief for me. My Convictions of Sin then [74/–] began and went on with me. I was then grieved that I had heard so many Sermons in such a careless way, and dishonoured God by many other sins: but ~~that~~ I was most of all, at this time, griev'd for my coming to the Lords Table so unpreparedly, & joining at that Solemn Ordinance in such an unconcerned manner, as I had done when I communicated formerly.[5]

---

[1]   Rebecca Reid – the shorthand text in McCulloch's 'Index of persons' names who gave the foregoing accounts to Mr. McC' states: daughter of James Reid, tenant in Barony. Taught to read the Bible, got and retained the Catechism to heart.
[2]   Insertion ['by them']: McCulloch.
[3]   Insertion ['or other duties']: McCulloch.
[4]   William McCulloch (1691–1771) – minister, Cambuslang.
[5]   Account ends abruptly.

[75/–] b.c. A Man of 29 years of Age.[1]

When I was put to School, I inclind so much to reading that I would oftimes have stayd ~~withal~~ of my own accord, with the Master that taught me reading, after the School was dismissd, & rest of the Scholars were gone away. But I had no delight in Prayer, nor did I ever once essay it all my life, till I was about twelve years of age, when one night over-hearing a Lad in the House where I livd, praying by himself in the Stable, I resolv'd that I would essay it also, and did so now and then in the fields; but finding it burdensome I laid it aside again. Some years after, when I came to serve my Apprentiship, my Master being a Religious man, oblig'd me morning & evening every day to retire for Secret Prayer: but having no heart to it, I oftimes stood still a while in the Closet where I retir'd without ever bowing a knee to God. At that time, tho' I learn'd my Trade, & apply'd my self to it, yet I had no pleasure at all in it, nor in any thing under the Sun, nor in any Company I happened to fall into: I had no Sense of Sin nor fear of Hell; only, I do not know how, life became a Burden & every thing was [76/–] irksome: and hearing of a Young man in the place being found dead, who was thought by some to have cut his own Throat, Satan urgd me often strongly to do the like, and the suggestion haunted me wherever I went night and day, and was pressd on me with great violence, tho' it was very contrary to my inclination, & I would fain have escapd it, if possible. The Tempter told me that it was better do so than live as a poor Slave as I did, and that the longer I livd I would still be the worse: but all the time of this Temptations continuing, I never had one thought that I would go to Hell; by doing it, or that it was dishonouring to God. After I had been toss'd almost continually with these Suggestions for about a Quarter of a year, One [ ][2] night when I retir'd to Secret Prayer, I got great liberty in that Duty & continu'd long at it, & was made to rejoice & bless God that he had not suffered me to give way to that horrid Temptation; & resolvd by his Grace, I would never do so. And after this; tho the Temptation sometimes return'd, yet I was made more to abhor it, & got several Psalms by heart, & oftimes repeated them in my mind, in order to keep such wicked thoughts out of my heart, & found this way useful for that end. [77/–] After this also, I needed not be put to my Secret Prayers by my Master, but took much delight in that duty for some time, till falling into a fever, & relapsing again & again into it, & apprehending that I was in great danger of death;

---

[1]   Robert Hamilton – the shorthand text in McCulloch's 'Index of persons' names who gave the foregoing accounts to Mr. McC' states: weaver in Anderston; taught to read and write, and had the Catechism to heart.

[2]   Insertion ['Sabbaths']: McCulloch.

I made many vows & promises that if God would spare me & recover me
to health, I would live another sort of life & be another sort of man than
I had been. But I was no sooner recovered, than I forgot & broke all these
Promises, & turnd drunken & looser than ever I had been, and fell into [ ][3]
uncleanness with a woman who at length bore a child to me, whereby this
sin I had secretly livd in coming to light, I was much grievd for what I had
done, & subjected my self to Church Discipline for the Scandal. But coming
to be much harrassd by that Woman, for money, I resolvd to have gone away
out of the Country, but was hindred by a Relation from that design: then
I listed my self to be a Soldier, but was bought oft again. A little after that I
married, & set up Family Worship, and continued to keep it up daylie for a
considerable time, but in the meantime neglected Secret Prayer: Afterward,
I got into a course of Secret Prayer also: & continued for some time in the
practice of both: at length I was wearied of both & laid them both aside, &
neglected my Trade, & turnd more loose than ever. But after I had taken full
Swing in my Dole [78/–] and loose way of living thus for a good while, my
wife telling me that I would ruin my self & her both by this way of doing,
& chiding me often for it, I again altered this course of Life, [ ][4] & return'd
to my Work, & to Family worship and Secret Prayer; and was admitted to
partake of the Sacrament: And now I thought all was well with me; and I
did not see wherein I came short of any of my Neighbours, & thought I was
as fair in the way to Heaven as any of them.

And thus it continued with me till I came to Cambuslang about the
beginning of March 1742, and was much delighted to hear to hear some
very young persons pray there in Companys by themselves: and somewhat
affected to see so many persons in time of Sermon in the Church-yeard
crying out & falling down, but was not moved by any thing I heard that
day in the Sermon, or afterwards when I came out there: till one Sabbath
hearing a minister ( ) on that Text, If ye continue in my word then shall
ye be my disciples indeed,[5] where he shewed how far persons might go,
& yet after all be but hypocrites, and he instanced, among other things in
the Young man in the Gospel whom Jesus is said to have loved, & in these
hypocrites Isai. 58.2. that sought God daylie delighted to know his ways
as [79/–] a nation that did righteousness & forsook not the Ordinance
of their God, they askd of him the Ordinances of justice & took delight
in approaching to God. I was not moved with these things while I heard
them, but after I came home taking my Bible & reading these Passages,
I was then convinc'd that I was not only a hypocrite, but that I had not
come the length that some hypocrites had done: & therefore that I was

[3]   Insertion ['a course of']: McCulloch.
[4]   Insertion ['turnd sober,']: McCulloch.
[5]   Jn 8:31.

yet in the gall of bitterness & bonds of iniquity; that all my Prayers had
been but a mocking of God, & that by approaching to the Lords Holy
Table while I was in this case, I had prophan'd that Ordinance, & had eat
& drank damnation to myself. And the thoughts of my Hypocrisy filled
me with great anguish & bitterness of Soul, so that I could sleep none that
night. My distress continued for about eight days before I got any ~~hopes~~
relief; I came out to Camb. on Thursday & heard Sermon & went home
in great Bitterness. I often essayd Secret Prayer, but no liberty in it. On
Friday I was almost like one distracted, apprehending that there was no
mercy for me & that I would surely go to hell for my great & many sins.
I went & spoke to ministers but found no relief. One ( ) said, other things
were expected of me, I told him, I had been but deceiving him & others
all my life. Another (26)[6] [80/–] mentioned that word Ps. 66.18. If I regard
iniquity in my heart the Lord will not hear me, and bade me take that
home with me, & think on that. I thought much on these words on the
way going home, & apprehended that that minister had seen hypocrisy in
my face, or some way or other discernd that I was certainly an hypocrite,
& therefore had given me that passage of Scripture to think on. And after
I came home thinking much on it, I was then made to see that it was no
wonder that the Lord did not hear my prayers, when I indulg'd so many
lusts & corruptions in my heart. And whereas all my grief & sorrows since
last Sabbath proceeded only from fears of Hell, & from reflecting on the
gross Evils of my outward life & practice; now I was made to see the Secret
lusts & corruptions of my heart to be more in number than the hairs of
my head: and was made to mourn bitterly for my regarding and indulging
iniquity in my heart, & for my natural corruption that was the Spring of
all.

Next Lords day hearing a Minister ( ) on that Text, Be sober be vigilant for
your adversary the Devil goes about always as a roaring Lyon seeking whom he
may devour,[7] I was much refreshd by many things in that Sermon, particularly
in the Directions he gave him to resist the Evil One, as by habituating [81/–]
our selves to good & holy thoughts & meditations and resolvd in the strength
of grace to do so, & that I would not yield to his temptations as I had done.
And after this I found my self sometimes raised above my self, & thought I
got my eyes singly fixt on the Glory of God in what I did, so that I could
have been content to lay down my life for Christ, if it might any ways tend
to advance his Glory. I got also great liberty & joy & enlargement of heart in
Prayer: and one time in particular at the Close of Prayer [ ],[8] I was made to say

[6]   William McCulloch (1691–1771) – minister, Cambuslang.
[7]   I Pt 5:8.
[8]   Insertion ['when at Cambuslang']: McCulloch.

with David, If I regard iniquity in my heart the Lord will not hear me,[9] and then the words that follow, came with a strong impression my heart, & I was made to pronounce them with a full assurance, Surely the Lord hath heard me.

I heard that Minister ( ) at that time, on these words, He that covereth his sins shall not prosper, but he that confesses & forsaketh shall find mercy:[10] & was made humbly to confess all my sins before the Lord & to hope for mercy not for my Confessions or any thing of mine, but for the sake of the merit of the blood of Christ. After Sermons I came in to the Manse & heard a minister (26) exhort in the Hall & could have been glad that if it had been possible, the whole world might have heard these Exhortations, & been brought in to Christ by means of them. On Mundays night [82/–] I went home filled with joy & peace in believing & could have been content to have got leave to die & go to Christ, as what was best of all, yet had my will resign'd & subjected to the will of God, to dispose of me as was most for his Glory.

After this, tho I essayd to apply to my work, yet for some time it did go well on with me, my mind running still after spiritual things: and I had not been able to work for a good while before this while I was in distress of Soul; & my Family had no other visible way to be maintaind but by my work: I therefore earnestly pleaded that the Lord would either enable me to apply to my work, or that he would provide for my Family in some other way. Next day my Landlord sent enquiring if we wanted any meal? I was glad of the offer, but told him I could not pay for it at the time, but hopd to pay it before it was eaten. And accordingly, e're it was done, tho' I could not pay it by what I made of my work, yet money owing to my Wife came to hand, in good Providence, in an unexpected way, by which it was cleared.

After this, I applyd to my work: But Satan attacked me fiercely with atheistical & unbelieving Suggestions, making me to doubt If there was a God, & If Jesus Christ was the Son of God & the promised Messias: But good Providence brought a little Book called Bishop Beveridges Thoughts[11] to my hand at that time, which was made greatly useful to me in establishing me in the Truth, in opposition to these horrid Suggestions.

---

[9]   Ps 66:18.
[10]   Pr 28:13.
[11]   William Beveridge, *Private Thoughts upon a Christian Life; or, Necessary directions for its beginning and progress upon earth, in order to its final perfection in the beatifick vision* (London: Printed for R. Smith, 1712).

[83/–] D. E. A Married Woman aged 38 years.[1]

It was observ'd of me, by some serious ~~people~~ [ ][2] about me, that I gave many signs of what they took to be, Early Piety, or at least of some good inclinations of that kind. This some of them have said, they notic'd when I was but about 4 years of age. But my own Memory serves me only to go back to some things that looked that way, when I was about 7 years: about which time I felt Love to Christ, his Ordinances & People, working in my heart. From 7 to 9, I usd to pray daylie, Morning and Evening, & to retire from my play-fellows to pray by my Self, & tho I could but say little when I went to my Knees, yet I was usually much in a praying frame. About 9 years of age, ~~the Devil attack'd me with blasphemous thoughts~~ and from that to 11, I fell under much slavish fear. In the Morning Satan would have hurried me away to my worldly Work, telling me, it would lay behind if I would go to pray: & at night, threatning to devour me & carry me away with him to Hell, if I offered to go to pray in any place by my Self. So that under these Slavish fears and cares of the world I refrained from Secret Prayer for these two years [ ].[3] After that time, I got more Love to Christ, & my Slavish fears wore off, and, I fell to pray in Secret again.

[84/–] When I was about 13, about Whitsunday betwixt my leaving the Service I had been at in one family & going to another, I one day in the fields, turnd exceeding hungry, & knew not what to do for relief: but I took up a handful of Earth & lookt to it, & was going to eat it, at which instant that word came into my mind, ~~man should~~ The Lord is able of these Stones to raise up children to Abraham, upon which I was made to believe that er'e I was suffered to perish for hunger, God was able to turn that handful of Earth into Bread to me [ ];[4] and at that thought [ ][5] the Hunger went off me; And ever after that time to this (Apr. 25.1745) I have had it to remark, That I was never hungry but I knew ~~not~~ where to get food, or I was not so hungry, but I could wait patiently & easily till I got it. From this time for about 2 years & a half, that is, till I was about 15 years & a half, I had a Sweet & pleasant time of the Love of God shed abroad in my heart, one Promise of the Covenant still coming in with great Sweetness into my Soul after another.

After this for about 4 years & a half, that is, till I came to be about 21 years of Age, I fell under great Temptations, and was haunted almost continually

---

[1]   Partial account with no record of respondent's name.
[2]   Insertion ['friends']: McCulloch.
[3]   Insertion ['tho still at my work I was every now & then putting up Petitions to God']: McCulloch.
[4]   Insertion ['or provide for me some other way.']: McCulloch.
[5]   Insertion ['I laid down the handful of Earth']: McCulloch.

with horrid blasphemous thoughts, & ~~hellish~~ wicked Suggestions of the Devil. This made [85/–] my life bitter & burdensome to me, and when I was sore vexed, and in great bitterness of Spirit with these Suggestions, the Evil One would have ply'd me hard with Temptations to Dispatch, or Make away my self, one way or other: At length one day as I was at my Secret Prayer in the Stable, & happening to lift up my Eyes to the Roof of the House, my Eye fixt on one of the Sticks there, & Satan suggested, that there was now a Stick, about which I might very conveniently fasten a Rope, & hang my self. At that instant, that Word came into my mind, "I have with-held thee from sinning against me". This came with so much Power & Life to my Soul [ ][6] & fill'd me with much Love & Thankfulness to God and admiration of his Goodness, in keeping me back from yielding to that dreadful Temptation to destroy my self with my own hands; & that had kept my will from consenting to these wicked & blasphemous thoughts with which my mind had been so long pester'd. But after this, I was no longer troubled with these temptations & suggestions, as I had been.

For about 3 years after this, that is, till I was about 24 years of age, I was kept on in a course of rejoicing in God, & in Endeavours to mortify sin, & specially my Beloved Lusts & Corruptions. Some-time in these 3 years, I communicated for the first time at [86/–] Biddernock. Before I went to the Table of the Lord, & [ ][7] [θ In the time of the Action-Sermon, Satan disturbd me much with his Temptations, to keep me back from the Table; but when the Minister ( ) came to show who might communicate & who not, I felt my heart fill'd with hatred of these sins, for which persons were debarrd, & could humbly apply the Marks on these Invited to come there: And God was pleasd to rebuke the Tempter, & to restrain him from giving me any trouble. And I was helped to apply the promises with much comfort.][8] On Munday morning, my master with whom I servd, refusd to allow me to go to hear ~~that~~ Sermons, at which I was much vex'd, ~~and,~~ but as I was out in the fields, going quick [ ][9] I fell o're a Dyke & had almost broke my neck, but that word coming at that Instant, into my mind, grieve not the Holy Spirit by which ye are sealed unto the day of Redemption:[10] after this going in to my Masters House, he spake to me in a very kind way, & bade me put on my Cloaths & go to the Ordinances, at which change I was surpris'd & overjoy'd.

---

6   Insertion ['that I fell back from my knees on the ground with joy & wonder']: McCulloch.
7   Insertion ['before I went to it my right to come was made clear from that text of the Action Sermon I <...><...><...> & at the Table Christ was made very precious to my Soul']: McCulloch.
8   Marked for removal and placement moved to [θ]: McCulloch.
9   Insertion ['& resolving I would not go there']: McCulloch.
10   Eph 4:30.

At Rutherglen-Sacrament a little about 3 years after this, when he [θ].[11]
After I had been at the Table, going out by my self to Secret Prayer, I fell
under great deadness, I came back to the Tent & heard a Minr ( ) describe my
Condition very particularly what it was & had been for many years back: yet
my deadness continued & while I was in great perpexity at it; it was suggestd
to me were it not better for thee to be out of the world than to be in that
Case: my heart replyd, I do not know but it might be so: & I secretly wishd
I might drown as I went thro' the [87/–] water I had to cross going home,
but I did not wish or design to do any thing willingly to drown my self: but
as I came thro' the water, I was seiz'd with fear of drowning, and had almost
drown'd my self in a hurry of confusion seeking to escape drowning. When I
went home I was thinking not to return next day to Sermons in Rutherglen;
but that word next morning coming into my heart, If any man thirst, let him
come to me & drink:[12] & with that word, such a power of the Holy Ghost
came along as made me thirst after Christ & the water of life, & made me
earnestly Desirous to come & receive & accordingly I came to Rutherglen
that day and was, I think, made there to drink of the water of life.

[88/– through 90/– blank]

---

[11]   Insert text here: [θ].
[12]   Jn 7:37.

[91/1] A. B. a married woman about 30 years of age.[1]

I was kept thro the mercy of God all my Life hitherto, from any gross Vices and Outbreakings before the World. I had some kind of form of Secret Prayer when young; but when I came to years, I ofter neglected it than I minded it. I went for ordinary to the Kirk on Sabbath days, but it was more to see and to be seen than for any other thing. But I never felt the Word at all come home to my heart with Power, when I read or heard it preach'd, till I came to Camb. about the beginning of March 1742 on a Thursday; where hearing sermons (14 & 26)[2] I was greatly affected, ~~I was greatly affected~~ and made to weep under my concern about my Souls condition: but it wore off again. But at the singing of the Psalms in the Family next night, I fell under great concern again: so that I was made to burst out in Tears: and my concern increased in time of Prayer: & immediatly after it, my distress was such that I was made to roar out twice in the hideous and terrible manner: the sound was not like that of a humane voice, but it came up my throat to my mouth like Thunder, bursting up suddenly, and coming out with a loud frightful, indistinct sound as that doth. It was not in my power to help it, for I apprehended that I was just going to sink into Hell that moment. My Husband was afraid to come near me, & ran out and got some neighbours to hold me. I was all like to [92/2] shake to pieces with trembling: but a man sate behind me, and a woman at each knee and held me fast. For a while I was not able to speak any, but made a sign to some about me to get me a drink, being scorched with thirst. I had nothing then upon my spirit but a dread of Hell, and a sense of the wrath of God, which was so great that I [ ][3] had no sense at all of sin, or dishonour done to God by my sin. Only I thought that in time of Family Prayer, when my bodily Eyes were shut, that I got a sight of my sins set all before me in general: there appear'd to my mind as it had been a Sclate House, and my sins were represented to me as the sclates on the House, set in ranks, & one rank rising higher than another. But this was but as a passing on wast disappearing from my mind again in less than a minutes time: But this dread and terror of Hell I was under, lasted only that night, after which I was no more under it. And for about four months after that my distress was all about sin, and the dishonour I had done thereby to God

---

[1]   Janat Berry – the shorthand text in McCulloch's 'Index of persons' names who gave the foregoing accounts to Mr. McC' states: spouse to John Sheddon, carter in Rutherglen. This account contains two duplicate fragments.The 'second' fragment (indicated later in the text) was an earlier version that was subsequently transcribed.

[2]   John McLaurin (1693–1754) – minister, Glasgow/Ramshorn, and William McCulloch (1691–1771) – minister, Cambuslang.

[3]   Insertion ['thought there was no mercy for me but']: McCulloch.

Next day after this, I was much grievd for my sin, and for the hardness of my heart and because I could get no Love to God. Some Neighbours coming in to see me, some of them said, what need you be so vexed: I have known you so long, & never saw any ill in you. I answered, I thought I was in a right way before this; but now I saw all was wrong with me. And so went on bewailing my own sad case, and that I could not get a [93/3] a heart to seek God. While I was in this condition, I went almost every day to Camb. and heard sermon, but got nothing for my Relief. But while I was in great grief for my sins, there were three words that came into my heart with power on different nights, when I was in my bed. The first of these was, Thou shalt be whiter than the snow,[4] which tho it did not lift me up with joy, yet much refreshed me. And tho I was shy to admit of it as from God; yet it came still back on me; and I was made to repeat it six times over in my own mind: but within a day and a half, I was as much in the dark as formerly. The second word was, I will give thee a new heart;[5] I will take away the stone heart, and I will give thee a heart of flesh: and this filled me with much joy and comfort, which lasted for two or three days. And while this continued, the Bible when I read it seem'd to be just new to me. The third was, My stripes are sufficient for thee: but this last came not with such power as the first two.

For a long time my grief & distress for sin was such, that I could scarce work any at all; nor could I eat but against my inclination: but my great Thirst made one drink water much and oft. I was frequently seizd with great Trembling, so that I could not keep my legs & arms from shaking like a Leaf before the wind. I durst not look my self in a Glass, I thought I was so loathsome and

[Recension 1][6]

[Recension 2]

[94/4] vile even in my bodily shape, that I greatly abhorr'd my self, and could not endure that my Husband should come near me I was ugly & vile. I was in a Terror when coming by a Looking-Glass, lest I should see my self, thinking that the Devil was just looking out at my face. I felt sometimes a most loathsome Smell about me, like the stinking smell of hair when it is burning, which I took to be the smell of the bottomless pit. One day hearing

[100/–] near I was so vile; I was in a terror when I coming by a Looking Glass, lest I should see my self, thinking the devil was just looking out at my face: and I felt some times a most loathsome smell about me, like the stinking smell of hair when is burning, which I took to be the

---

[4]   Ps 51:7.
[5]   Multiple variations: Ez 11:19, Ez 18:31, Ez 36:26.
[6]   Duplicate fragments of corresponding text within the same account.

a Min. (12)[1] he said, Ye wonder what makes these people cry so: but if the Lord would be pleased to open your Eyes, as he has done theirs, ye would see your hearts all crawling with Toads of Corruptions, and surrounded with Legions of Devils. This did not much affect me at the time, yet when I came home I took a strong apprehension that it was so, and imagin'd that I felt them within me, crawling up my Throat to my mouth, and turn'd away my eyes that I might not see them coming out of my mouth. And together with this I had a most affecting sense of the vileness & filthiness of my heart by sin: and often thought, if I be so vile in my own sight and in the sight of men, how much more vile must I be in the sight of a Holy God. And yet even in these days, when I read or heard of the name of Christ my heart would have taken a beating or leaping out of Love to Christ: and I aimed to trust in him, being never left to despair, but having always some Hope; but fearing he would never accept of me I was so vile, yet believing that his Blood [95/5] was able to cleanse from all sin & pollution.

I was much concern'd to know whether I had any Faith or no; but could not get to any satisfaction about it, till one day I was hearing a Min (79)[2] preach at Camb. & telling, That if a person could pray as heartily and sincerely for others & their Salvation as for themselves, that this was a sign

smell of the bottomless pit. And one day hearing a minr (Mr Wh—d)[1] he said, Ye wonder what makes those people cry so, but if the Lord would be pleasd to open your eyes as he has done theirs, ye would see your heart all crawling with toads of corruptions, & [ ][2] legions of devils and tho this did not much affect me much at the time, yet when I came home, I took a strong apprehension that it was so, & imagin'd that I felt them within me crawling up my throat to my mouth, & turnd away my face, that I might not see them coming out of my mouth. And together with this, I had a most affecting sense of the vileness & filthiness of heart by sin; & often thought if I be so vile in my own sight & in the sight men, how much more vile must I be in the sight of a holy God. And yet even in these days, when I read or heard of the name of Christ, my heart would have taken a beating and leaping out of love to Christ, and aimed to trust in him, being never left to despair but having always some hope, but fearing that he would accept of me I was so vile, yet believing that his blood was able to cleanse from all sin & pollution. I was much concernd to know whether I had any faith or no; but could not get any satisfaction about it, till one day, I was hearing a Minr (Mr John H—n in Barony)[3] preach at Camb. & telling that if a person could pray as heartily & sincerely for others &

[1] George Whitefield (1714–70) – evangelist.
[2] John Hamilton (d. 1780) '(19)' – minister, Glasgow/Barony.

[1] George Whitefield (1714–70) – evangelist.
[2] Insertion ['surrounded with devils']: McCulloch.
[3] John Hamilton (d. 1780) – minister, Barony/Glasgow; translated to St Mungo's in 1749.

the Person had some Faith: At which I was made to conclude, That if that were a sign of true Faith, I had some Faith. For tho formerly I thought it was enough to pray for my self & my Relations, I now could and did pray for others, even my Enemies, and heartily desir'd their Salvation, & wish'd well to all: I could not so much as come by a poor Beggar-Child in the way, without wishing and saying in my heart, O that it might please God to make thee one of his Children. And some time after that, while I was among the People that day, I felt my Heart fill'd with great Love to Christ & joy in him: and this frame continued with me in some measure during the time of Sermon, and when I was going home.

And frequently after that, this Love & joy would arise in my Soul at times, and I would find my heart as it were all smiling within me, & a softness & sweetness of heart that I cannot express: and always when I heard of the name of Christ, my heart would take a beating, & make even my Body to leap. And this continues to be the case oftimes still; and especially in the morning when I awake

[96/– through 98/– blank]

their salvation, as for themselves that this was a sign they had some faith. At which I was made to conclude that if that were a true sign of faith, I had some faith, for tho formerly I thought it was enough to pray for my self & my Relations, I could now & did pray for others, even my enemies & heartily wish for their salvation & wishd well to all & I could not come by a poor beggar child in the way [. . .] [. . .] [. . .] [. . .] [. . .]⁴

[99/–] my heart, O that it might please God to make thee one of Gods children: And some time after that while I was among the people that day I felt my heart filled with great love to Christ and great joy in him: & this frame continued with me in some measure during the time of sermon & when I was going home. And at times frequently after, this love & joy would arise in my heart, & I found my heart as it were all smiling within me & a softness & sweetness of heart which I cannot express and always when I heard the name of Christ, my heart would taking a beating & make even my Body to leap, and this continues to be the case oftimes still, & especially in the morning when I awake with thoughts of Christ, that motion of heart after him will be so vehement, that I cannot forbear making all the bed under me to shake: and a little after I come from Secret prayer, I will find all within me, & even my whole Body in a motion: being made to think that I see Christ

---

⁴   Illegible text due to worn fore-edge. The text continues in the side margin, which reads: ['I find my heart now running always after spiritual things, & even when I am sitting talking about < . . . >'].

smiling upon me, & not being able to refrain from smiling my self.

Hearing a minr (Mr. McC)[5] preaching of the man in whom there is no guile: & was made to see several marks of such a Person in my self, particularly ~~which he said~~ that, That such a one is as careful to watch & guard against sin when he is in secret, & no eyes but Gods sees him, as if the whole world were looking on. This my conscience bare me witness was my care and Endeavour.

Another day hearing a Minr (Mr McC) preach on that Text, That which is born of the Spirit is spirit,[6] I was then enabled to apply all the Marks that were then given (of which that Sermon was full) to my self, & found the disposition of my heart answer to them, & was so filled with love & joy that I thought I was in Heaven already; & could not refrain crying out among the People for joy.

*I have frequently had as much of the Love of Christ & of the joys of heaven let into my soul at certain times as I could well contain, particularly at the first Sacrament at Camb. & another time at home. [ ][7] but at other times I feel my heart dead, as it were, but it pleases the Lord again to quicken & enlarge [. . .] my heart: He has now given me a [. . .] [. . .] [. . .] [. . .][8]

---

5   William McCulloch (1691–1771) – minister, Cambuslang.

6   Jn 3:6.

7   Insertion ['† when I thought I saw not w*t* the eyes of my body but of my mind & spiritually Christ, in heaven, as it were, standing as w* a fine wig on him, & his face shining brighter than the Sun And all the saints before him sitting as < . . .>']: McCulloch.

8   Illegible text due to worn tail edge.

[101/–]¹

[Note - This Page should not come in here at all, but belongs to another composure.]²

or with the greatest part of them, or with such as had done so which I suppose this author will not pretend to have done. And if they did so, what was amiss in it.

16. What the nature of it was I have not learnd; but was a sermon on that text, This is the name whereby he shall be calld, even the Lord our Righteousness:³ the nature & scope of it was to shew the necessity of every way an perfect Righteousness in which to appear before God: our own utter inability to furnish out such a Righteousness of our own, & liableness to Eternal Sufferings for the want of it, & that betaking our selves by faith to Christ the Lord our Righteousness in order to escape those sufferings.

17. The issue of the Sermon was That 40 or 50 persons were affected in the same manner as the first convert had been the Lords day before. As this author represents it, the girl whom this author in way of derision, calls the first convert, had the Lords day before, been affected first in agony of Despair, & then raisd to the greatest Transports of the most triumphant assurance & declard her conversion to others. Now it is false there were 40 or 50 thus affected on the Thursday. About 40 or 50 as some present have reckond them, fell that day under convictions or alarming apprehensions about the state of their souls; but there only about 19 who that night got any Outgate or relief from their soul distress.

18. They were brought into the house fainting & screaming in a very astonishing mannor They were not brought but all of them came without help of their own accord: these were none of them screaming nor [. . .] [. . .] [. . .] []⁴

[102/– through 108/–blank]

---

¹ Page [101/–], which was bound with the narrative accounts, is a misplaced fragment of another document written by McCulloch.
² A note by McCulloch inserted on top margin. The page has been scored with three diagonal lines.
³ Jer 23:6.
⁴ Insertion ['& they could not come in a <. . .>']: McCulloch.

[109/–] a.o. A Woman about 23 years of age.[1]

I was put to a course of praying in Secret when very young, and continued in it for some Years: but when I grew older, I turn'd careless of it in a great measure, and neglected it very much, tho' I did not lay it altogether aside. But I never from my Infancy felt my heart engag'd to draw near to God, [ ][2] nor did I know what the presence of God in that or any other Duty meant: but reckon'd all was well when I spent a little time in the external part of that Duty. I do not know what I would have been or how I would have behav'd if I had been in other Circumstances: but as it was, my Lot having been ordered to be a great part of my Life in Ministers Houses; I did for the forms sake, attend on Publick Ordinances on the Lords day, & at other Occasions. In my outward conversation and behaviour before the world, I was all my life kept from any gross Out-breakings, except one; that Instance of Fornication, which thro' the permission of God & Temptation of Satan, I fell into, about five years ago, with a Servant-Lad who was in a ministers house with me at the same time.

[110/–] After that gross Out-breaking I was several times made to see, That I was in a natural state; and that if I died in that condition, I would certainly be miserable for ever: and I was often afraid, that death would overtake me before I got out of it: and I would fain have turn'd, but yet I was unwilling to turn from all my Sins to God. I was made to see and feel in part, that Sin was the cause of all miseries, and brought many Calamities on Sinners in this life, & had done so upon me; and made to fear that it would bring Eternal Misery upon me hereafter. A young Sister of my own, coming to my house and dying beside me, after her death, I would have often thought, Oh had I died when she died, where had I been!

And as I was often wishing to be turn'd, so when a Stranger Minr (12)[3] came to Glasgow in Septr 1741, & preach'd there five days; I long'd much to hear him preach, having heard that he spake much of Conversion, and had been the mean of converting many, & I thought that was just what I wanted, & I would go & hear him: but having a Child on my breast, and being in low & straitning Circumstances, I could never get the Opportunity to hear him all the five days he was at Glasgow; at which I was much griev'd. But when the great Awakening began in Camb. in Feb. 1742, I was very glad to hear of it, &

---

[1]   Agnes More – the shorthand text in McCulloch's 'Index of persons' names who gave the foregoing accounts to Mr. McC' states: daughter of John More, tenant in Carmunnock. Put to school when a child, taught to read the Bible, got the Catechism to heart, and retained it mostly.
[2]   Insertion ['till of late']: McCulloch.
[3]   George Whitefield (1714–70) – evangelist.

began to say with my self, O will I be disappointed there, as I was when that Stranger Minr came, will there be nothing for me! I resolv'd I would come & see what I might with [ ]⁴ The week before I came, that word,

> Let God arise and scattered
> Let all his Enemies be⁵

[111/–] one morning when I was rising came into my mind, and, as it were, sounded loud, I was not at that time usd to such secret ways of Gods communicating his mind, and was much amaz'd what it might mean: however, I found my heart disposd to say Amen, Let him arise, and let all his Enemies in my heart and in the hearts of others be scattered. Next morning that word came into my mind in a powerful way, as the other had done the day before

> And under thy Subjection
> The people down do bring.⁶

At which I fell a wondring what that and the former word might mean. But afterward, (about two days after my Convictions began at Camb.) when I was by my self, both these words were brought to my mind, tho not with the power they came at first, and then I was made to understand them better, namely, That the Lord was about to arise, and bring the people under his Subjection.

I came to Camb. on a Munday, about two weeks after the Awakening brake out there, and heard a Minr (26)⁷ preach that day on Luk. 23.27,28, And there followed him a great Company of people & of women, which also bewailed & lamented him: but Jesus turning to them, said, Daughters of Jerusalem weep not for me, but for your selves, and for your children. At hearing of that Sermon, I was first made my heart was first moved with Compassion toward Christ, that he should have been so cruelly used, and should be going in that manner to his Cross: and I was very much affected with that Condescending Love he manifested, [112/–] that in these Circumstances he should turn and speak with such kindness to the women that followed him. But a little while after that, I was made to weep for my self, and my Concern came to be for my self and my own sins: and I then first found, as it were, a great darkness rising in my understanding, with which I was much affected, at the sense I got of my ignorance of God and spiritual things. And then I got an amazing and humbling sight of all my Sins, as in one Heap or Pile; [ ]⁸ And I was

---

⁴   Marked for textual insertion; sentence ends abruptly.
⁵   Ps 68:1, Scottish Psalter (metrical).
⁶   Ps 45:5, Scottish Psalter (metrical).
⁷   William McCulloch (1691–1771) – minister, Cambuslang.
⁸   Insertion ['But in that great Heap of my Sins, one, as it were rose up & overlopd all the rest, and that was my uncleanness, which appeard to me as the greatest of all my Sins at that time, and was then most of all wounding & affecting to my Spirit']: McCulloch.

made to mourn & weep & cry out bitterly, under the Sight and Sense of all my Sins, as committed against God and dishonouring to him, and as by them, I had wounded that Glorious Saviour, who suffered for poor perishing Sinners; and that spoke so kindly to these women, that were following him to his Cross. I would have refrain'd from crying, if I had been able; but it was not in my power, I got such a Sight of my Sins, as was amazing to me; and I apprehended that God with whom I had to do, was infinitely greater than ten thousands of worlds of creatures: and so my regard to what these about me might think or say of me, for my crying out, quite vanished: and I thought that God was about to be aveng'd on me for all my Sins & Rebellions against him; and did not know but that every moment I might drop down into the Pit of eternal destruction. And I was thorowly convinc'd that God would have been just if he had sent me to Hell, and wondered [113/–] that he had spared me 'till that time.

But this Sight and Sense of my Sins continu'd with me but for a little time; for it went off before the Sermon was done. But then it return'd upon me again as I went home: and sometimes it turn'd so strong, that several times by the way, I was neither able to go forward nor stand still; but dropt just down under the terrible Apprehensions I had of Gods wrath against me. And one time I fell down, I thought I saw the Lord Jesus coming thro' the Clouds with his holy Angels, appearing with awful Majesty, & in the terrors of his Justice, ready to take vengeance on me: and thereupon I thought I was just ready to sink into Hell; & cry'd out bitterly for mercy: and oftimes as I went forward, I thought that at every step I was about to perish. I often & almost continually as I went along, was essaying to pray: but I thought that my Prayer was still, as it were, driven back again into my face. And many a time I was concluding or just ready to conclude, that the Lord would never hear me or shew me mercy. As I went along, that word Is. came with great Power to my Conscience, They speak peace when there is no peace, there is no peace saith my God to the wicked.[9] And these words went and came several times, but [114/–] with lesser Power afterwards than at first, and greatly increasd my Agony; for I was made to see that I was among the wicked, and that I had been speaking peace to my self when there was none. I got home that night with much difficulty and the terror & anguish I was under, continued after I was at home, & sometimes increas'd: but before Supper-time the strength of that terror in some measure abated; and I became, as it were, dull & stupid.

I had no more of these distressing terrors, for about eight days; yet still I was a great deal more restless and uneasy than I usd to be, and always filled with one fear after another; such as, That my convictions would not return, and that God would cease striving with me, and leave me just where I was. About eight days after, intending to go to Camb., before I went I took my

---

[9]   Isa 57:22.

Bible, and before I opened it, desired of the Lord, That he would direct me to somewhat that might be useful to me, & shew me what course I ought to take; and then opening it, the first word that cast up to my Eye, was that in Jer. Call unto me & I will answer thee, and I will shew thee great and mighty things which thou knowest not.[10] this came with much power to me in the reading of it, and I was to wonder to see that verse appearing in such a distinguishing way from all the rest beside it, printed as it had been in large letters. In obedience to this command of God to call on him, I set my self to Secret Prayer: but found my self exceedingly straitned, so that I could scarce utter a word. I essay'd the Duty however three times, & at the third time, that word came with [115/–] exceeding great power to my heart, ye will not come to me that ye might have life,[11] which words were repeated three times on end; whereby I was made to see that Christ was calling me in his Word to come to him, but that I was unwilling to come. And when I came to Camb. a Minister (26) no sooner began to preach, but the same words, Ye will not come &c: (tho not uttered by him) came to my heart with very great power, whereby I was made to see, that it was my unwillingness to come to Christ, that was the great obstacle that kept me back from him, & from getting life in him & by him: And after that, the threatning things that were said thro' the whole Sermon, of which there were many, were set powerfully home on my heart, as if they had been all spoken to me in particular; but I could get no hold of any thing that was spoken of a comfortable nature. And my Soul-Agony and distress was so great, at hearing of these Threatnings, and being made to see that they really belong'd to me, that I was made to cry out very much and often, in time of that Sermon, tho I endeavoured all I could to refrain.

That week I heard several people talking of the Work at Camb. and calling it all a Delusion, and saying that it was mostly so reckoned. I then began to think & say with my self, It may be it is all a Delusion: but when I reflected, I thought that could scarce be a Delusion that made me cry out so, and that I thought I did not cry but when I could not help it. I then resolvd that I would go again to Camb. And [116/–] would set my self with all my might against crying, and would by no means cry if I could possibly help it. But when I came there, the minister (26) no sooner began to preach, but I was forcd to cry out, notwithstanding all my Endeavours to the contrary. And now I could no longer look upon the work as a Delusion; but was fully persuaded in my own heart, that it was indeed the work of Gods Spirit, by feeling his power on my own soul. I was so ashamed before God for my sin, that I could not lift up my face as others did, & it was what I strongly inclin'd to, to hold down my face to the ground; & by doing so, & striving against crying, all I could,

---

[10] Jer 33:3.
[11] Jn 5:40.

my crying differed much from the crying of many, being neither so loud nor constant, but now & then a kind of half-smothered cry.

The Effect that my Soul-distress, at this and other times, had upon my Body, was very great pains afterward. In the time of my Soul-Agonies, I never felt any pain at all in body, but only, as it had been a racking of my bowels, besides which I felt no bodily pains, nor had I any leisure to think on what concern'd the body. Some trembled in the time of their inward soul-distress, but I never did so; but when my convictions were very strong, I fell into a great sweat, and when the distress was over, I turnd colder and fell a shivering, I felt my bowels & breast as it had been crushed, and all my body as it had been beat & bruised in great uneasiness & soreness, like one that had been in a great hot Bath. And I believe these bodily pains were much occasion'd by my strongly endeavouring to refrain crying; [117/–] for I found my self like a Bottle ready to burst, and when I gave vent to the griefs wherewith my heart was overcharg'd by crying, I found my breast much eased. And these bodily pains after my distress were always alike, except in so far as the degree of the soul distress made the difference in the degree of these pains of the body.

Some time after this, after I had been seeing a young woman who had got an Outgate from her distress, and having also heard of many Instances of that kind; I thought with my self, The Lord is giving Outgates from Soul-trouble to many, but it seems he is to give none to me: I did not however repine & fret against this Dispensation of God; but only the greatness of my soul trouble made me think the time very long, and I was afraid he would not give me a gracious Outgate as he did to others. I thought however, that if God would save my Soul at last, I could be continued under trouble never so long. Full of these fears and being under a very deep sense of my sins, and apprehending they were so great & hainous, that tho they were not such but that God could pardon them; yet that God was provok'd by them that he would not pardon them; I went to Prayer by my Self, & while praying, that word came into my mind with power, Tho your Sins be as crimson & Scarlet I will make them white as wool Isai. 1.18 upon which I was made to believe, that however heinous my Sins were; yet God could & would [118/–] wash from them all in the blood of Christ, and my heart was made to relent & break and melt, at the thoughts of the great dishonour done to God by my great sins, & of the Sufferings of Christ for sin, and the riches of Gods mercy in pardoning them; and was filld with great peace and comfort in the hopes I was made to conceive of the pardon of them: and I was made to wonder and admire at the mercy & Love of God so much the more, that he sent me such intimations of peace & pardon, at a time when I was so far from expecting any such thing. Tho I knew that these words were in the Bible, yet I did not know in what place to find them, 'till I ask'd at a woman who shewed me the place; and upon seeing the words, they appear'd to me to be exceeding beautiful, bright & shining; & I was made to burst out again, wondring &

adoring at the pardoning mercy of God in Christ, and being – made to hope that he had pardoned or would pardon my many and great sins.

However this sweet frame did not continue with me long, but I lost it mostly that same night and my former fears returnd again. One—morning I awaked in great terror, & I found my understanding, as it were in an instant, filled with great darkness, and afraid that God would give me up to Satan to be devoured, as a just reward of my Sins. And while I was tossing in great Agony of Soul under these fears, & apprehending my self just ready to sink, [119/–] that word was suddenly darted into my mind, Behold the Lion of the tribe of Judah![12] But alas I wanted faith, and could not behold him, tho I knew it was Christ was signified by that name: the thoughts of Christ however reviv'd my spirit, & it gave me some comfort that he was calling me to behold him, tho I could not do it. And I was made to wonder at his Long-Suffering toward me, and to say, O why am I not shut up in Hell among Devils & damned Spirits! And every hours respite & preservation from the pit of perdition seem'd precious to me: and I thought, Oh if I might if it were but for one hour see his face. I had an earnest desire to praise God for his forbearing mercy toward me, but finding my self incapable to do it, I earnestly wish'd that I had all these beside me, who had tasted how gracious he is, that they might do it.

I came to Camb. and heard a Minister (26) preach on these words, There are some of you that believe not:[13] but felt nothing at that time by ordinary. Next morning, when I was in prayer, pleading that God might accept of my unrighteous person and imperfect services and save me, these words came with power to my mind, Go to the gods whom you have served, and let them deliver you:[14] upon which I was made to cry out bitterly, and to break off Prayer: and while I was crying out and bewailing my sad state under a deep sense of my sins, an [120/–] Elder came in and asked, What was the matter? And when I told him, he said I should not seek after such Scriptures, saying, They did not belong to us but to the Idolatrous Israelites of old that worshiped Idols & stocks & stones; and that I had not been doing so. I told him I was not seeking out such places, but I got them by way of Refusal, when I was petioning for mercy & acceptance, and I took them as sent from Heaven to me: and that tho I had not been worshipping stocks & stones, yet I had been serving the world & the flesh, in gratifying my lusts: and therefore God might justly reject me & my services. Many other threatning words were also [ ][15] set home on my Conference with power, particularly the Text I had been hearing preachd on the day before at Camb. There are some

---

[12]   Rv 5:5.
[13]   Jn 6:64.
[14]   Jdg 10:14.
[15]   Insertion ['that day']: McCulloch.

of you that believe not; whereby I was made to see my self an unbeliever or much under the power of unbelief; and that word, What hast thou to do to take my Covenant in thy lips;[16] Ephraim is joined to his idols let him alone:[17] and several others beside these, And when I opened the Bible, or other good Book to look into it, I met with nothing but Threatnings there that I could apply to my self; and every word of comfort, as it were, hid it self from me: and I began to lament that ever I had taken any comfort at all. But while I was bitterly lamenting my sad case, and I could do little else all that day but do so, and was beginning to think my Case was quite desperate and past remedy; that word came into my mind with some power, It may be there may be hope: this revivd me a little, and made me conceive some hope, whereas immediatly before I had none: and in the afternoon the same day, that passage Ezek. [121/–] 16.62, 63. And I will establish my Covenant with thee &c: came with great power, as if it had been spoken loud, which tho' it did not give me present sensible comfort, confirm'd me in the belief that comfort would come, & that there might be hope.

One Sabbath day being in Carmunnock Kirk about the beginning of Publick Worship, turning over my Bible to seet out the Psalm appointed to be sung, these words in Hos. 5.14, 15. cast up lo to me, & my eyes were fixt upon them, I even I will tear &c: and at reading them I found them come home to me with power, especially the former part of these words, and I thought the Lord was just pointing at me in particular; & therefore I fell into great distress and confusion of Soul: but looking about, and seeing several persons who usd to mock at the Work at Camb. and the crying out there; I begg'd of the Lord, that if it were his holy will, I might be kept from crying out in the Congregation, and becoming an Object of derision to them or others: upon which the distress I was under somewhat abated: but in time of Sermon these words returnd upon me with greater power than before, and reduc'd me to greater distress than formerly: and I was made to cry out before them all: and such an awful apprehension of God, and of the terrors of his Majesty & justice fell upon me, that I had no regard to those about me, if there had been millions more of them, or what they might think or say of me for my crying. The Speaker ( ) either because the strain of this Discourse led him, or [122/–] out of compassion to me, hearing me in such distress, cited a great many comfortable places of Scripture, which I would gladly have taken hold of, but could not: and indeed I was not willing to take comfort till God gave it, and I was waiting till the same blessed hand that had wounded should heal. But hearing him cite many comfortable Places as particularly that text, When thou passes thro' the fire and water I will be with thee;[18] I

---

16   Ps 50:16.
17   Hos 4:17.
18   Isa 43:2.

thought I would turn over my Bible, & seek the places he cited, & I did not know what I might meet with: and while I was looking for one passage he cited, another passage he cited not cast up to me, and my eye was kept upon it, because it appeard with a peculiar brightness & clear splendor, to my outward eye, as well as to the eye of my mind [ ][19] in reading it, Is. 41.10, Fear not for I am with thee, be not dismayed, I am thy God, I will strengthen thee, yea I will help thee & uphold thee with the right hand of my righteousness: upon reading of which, my fears were immediatly banishd, and I was made to believe that he was my God, and that he would indeed be with me, & that he would help uphold & strengthen me; & I felt him doing so at the time. And thereupon I was made greatly to rejoice, even as much as I had griev'd & sorrowed before, & felt my heart drawn out toward God & Christ, & was made to lament over my former Rebellion; especially when turning over to Is. 48.18, I read that verse, & felt a Divine Power accompanying it to my heart, O that thou hadst hearkened to my Commandments, then had thy peace been as a [123/–] river & thy righteousness as the waves of the Sea: in which words Jesus Christ seem'd to me, as if he had been lamenting over my former obstinacy & disobedience, which greatly affected and melted my heart.

About the middle of April 1742, hearing a Minister (26) preach at Camb. on a Sabbath on these words, To day if ye will hear his voice,[20] while he said, It is not to morrow or the day after that ye are called to hear Christs voice, & to believe on him, but to day, now while ye are hearing his Call, I found my heart much affected: & immediatly that word that had come to me often before, (tho not uttered by the Speaker) came into my mind with power, Ye will not come to me that ye may have life:[21] this word that came to me so frequently for a while at first had no more added to it; but afterwards, it came with these words after it, and that ye might have it more abundantly;[22] but whether these last words were added at this time or not I do not remember: however I was now made to see more & more of my backwardness and unwillingness to believe & to come to Christ. But a while after, during the time of that Sermon, while I was much cast down, these words (tho not spoken by the Minister) were sent into my heart, I will be as the dew to Israel, which was a sweet softning oil to my hard heart & made me to relent before God:[23] and I was made partly to believe it, but at the same time I was filled with many doubts & fears as to my self saying, Oh can it be that Gods grace will be as the dew to my unbelieving heart. Betwixt Sermons when at Secret Prayer, I fell under a terrible [124/–] apprehension that Satan was coming to devour me: and tho my face was toward the ground, & I saw nothing with

---

[19]   Insertion ['and it was']: McCulloch.
[20]   Heb 3:7,15; 4:7.
[21]   Jn 5:40.
[22]   Jn 10:10.
[23]   Hos 14:5.

my bodily eyes, yet I strongly fancy'd that I saw him behind me, like a swine, coming to destroy me. I pray'd that God might rebuke and restrain him, and I thought God answered me, for the terror immediatly left me, and I got to more freedom in Prayer, & brokenness and relenting of heart for sin.

In the afternoon of the same day, I was much affected with the Minister's first Prayer: and in the beginning of his Sermon, going to speak of particular Cases, he said, It may be ye want a renewed will: at which I was much affected, feeling the backwardness of my own will; and immediatly came these words I had so often met with before (tho not uttered by the Minister) Ye will not come unto me that ye may have life: upon which I was cast into my former distress, and fell under Convictions of my unbelief & several other sins I had not been convinc'd & humbled for before, and was made to cry out in my agony under these Convictions: & continued in this distress till toward the end of the Sermon, when these words, Be of good cheer thy sins are forgiven thee,[24] came in with some power into my mind; but I did not receive them or believe that they were from God, but thought that Satan had suggested them to me to deceive me. But immediatly that word Fear not for I am thy Shield and thy exceeding great reward,[25] came into my mind with great power, and attended with a Spiritual Light shining as it were before & behind the word the word of comfort, as it came into my heart, [125/–] tho no light appeard to my outward eyes, but it was a spiritual light discernd by my mind and felt by my heart (and such a Light often usd to accompany words of sensible comfort sent to my Soul at other times also:) And the Power & Light wherewith this Word was accompanied, immediatly scattered my fears, and made me to believe and receive the other comfortable word that had come immediatly before it, Be of good cheer thy sins are forgiven thee, as from God, as well as this Word it self, and made me admire the riches of his grace, in sending me such a Word of comfort, when I had been rejecting & disbelieving the word he sent me before, and I was made to receive this Word, fearing I should grieve Gods Holy Spirit, if I should put it away from me. My mind then was quieted & comforted, and I believed that it would be to me even according to this Word, That he would be my Shield & exceeding great reward:[26] yet still some unbelieving doubts & fears now & then return'd upon me.

After Sermon I came into the Manse, to speak to a Minister (26) to see if I might further grounds of comfort from what he might say. But after I had told him what I had met with, all he said to me was, Then shall ye know if ye follow on to know the Lord, and that sometimes people when they had got deliverance & comfort that was really from Heaven, might be like Peter when he was brought out of Prison by an Angel, he wist not that it was true

24 Mt 9:2.
25 Gen 15:1.
26 Ge 15:1.

that was done of the Angel; but that afterwards [126/–] they might come, as Peter did, to see & know certainly, that all was true & real they before doubted of. I came off much cast down at my disappointment; for I was expecting that he would have spoken a great deal to comfort and encourage me. As I was on the way home, I fell under great terror that Satan was about to start up in some shape or other & devour me, and this terror increasd as I went on in company with another woman; but a little after I had told her my condition, the terror went off, & we went on pleasantly together, talking of the Scripture & Spiritual things. But after I came to my house, the fire being out, & it being dark, I fell under my former terror, that Satan would appear & destroy me: but there being another family separate only by a wall from the end of my house, when I was under these frights, it was suggested to me to cry to them, and it would be some comfort to me to know that they were awake, and to hear them speak: but I was made to see that this would be to trust in man & make flesh my arm, & so forbare speaking to them. I then resolvd to pray before I went to bed, but was greatly afraid that Satan would appear & disturb me. But then I thought with my self again, If I neglect my duty for fear of the Enemy of Souls, it may justly provoke the Lord to let him loose upon me to destroy me after I am got to bed. I was also afraid, as I have been at several other times when I have been going to pray, that the Spirit of Prayer would be deny'd me, and I would get nothing to say, or [127/–] be able to say nothing aright; but then that word in such cases, usd to encourage me to the duty, To him by whom I live I'll pray. After I was on my knees that night going to pray, I thought Satan was going to pull me backward off my knees: but going on in that duty, that word came into my mind with great power, The Angel of the Lord encamps round about them that fear him, upon which all the Terror of Satan I was under, immediately went off. I was then, I think, made to fear God with a fear of holy awe & reverence, and to believe that he would send his angel and deliver me from Satan,[27]

[128/– through 132/– blank]

---

[27] Account ends abruptly.

[133/–] a.v. A Woman of 23 year. Of Age.[1]

As to my former manner of life, it was before the world all along blameless. I had the advantage of a Religious Education & Example from my Parents, who train'd me in the way I should go when I was a Child, tho' alas I have in many Instances too much departed from it: I usd to keep up a form of Secret Prayer for daylie, tho sometimes I neglected it. Sometimes when I was very young, when I was in Secret Prayer, the Lord would have brought in some Convictions upon me, ~~but they~~ and I would have taken much delight in that duty, but after some time, these would worn off & I would have turn'd more careless again. I also heard many Sermons in my younger years, with which I have been much affected, particularly, by a minister (81)[2] on that Text Is.55.3. Incline your ear, hear & come unto to me, & I will make with you an everlasting covenant, & I will give you the Sure mercies of David. Many a time in my younger years, when I have been pleading the Lord might give me a discovery of my own Condition, he has given me a Sight and Sense of my lost & undone State by nature, that I was guilty of Adams first Sin, & that my nature was universally corrupted & polluted, that all my righteousness were as filthy rags, & that there were as much Sin in my best duties as might justly damn me for ever.

[134/–] When I was about 17 or 18 years, my Convictions and distress under them arose sometimes to as great a height, I have often thought since, as any I saw at Camb. at the time of the Awakening there in 1742: []³ and however outwardly blameless before the World, I verily thought I had the wickedest heart of any in the Earth []⁴ And under these Convictions of Sin, I was in mercy led to flee to Jesus Christ & to close with him as my alone Saviour; And that very quickly, one time when I was at Secret Prayer, and I was in very great Agonies of Soul in the Sense of my Sin Actual & Original, & my lost state by it, and was made to See the Sword of Divine justice drawn against me, or in other words, that I was made deeply sensible that, I was exposd to the Stroke of Gods just vengeance by my Sin, & had his wrath abiding on me, & that it would have been perfectly just with God to have crushd me under the insupportable weight of his wrath in hell for ever: while I was in

---

[1]   Sarah Gilchrist – the shorthand text in McCulloch's 'Index of persons' names who gave the foregoing accounts to Mr. McC' states: daughter of James Gilchrist, schoolmaster in Cardross. Taught when young to read and write, got the Shorter Catechism to heart, and retained it.

[2]   Elizabeth Jackson – lay person, Cambuslang.

[3]   Insertion ['tho' not so observable to others']: McCulloch.

[4]   Insertion ['And my rejecting of Jesus Christ in his kind Invitations & Calls in the Gospel to come to him, was of all other things, most grievous and affecting to me.]: McCulloch.

this condition, the Lord enabled me to cast my Self at the feet of his mercy, and to put my Self under the Covert of the Redeemers blood & to trust in him for mercy & pardon [ ]⁵ But I was, some time after this, on the first of June 1740, on Saturday before the Sacrament at Cathcart, in hearing a minister (26)⁶ preach on that Text, Wherefore he is able to save to the uttermost all them that come to God by him,⁷ under a sense of my lost condition, more distinctly made to close with Christ Jesus in all his Offices, as an All-Sufficient [136/–]⁸ Saviour, being then persuaded not only of his being able but willing to save to the uttermost, upon my coming to God by him, which I was then in some measure enabled to do.

After this, I was much in pleading that the Lord might make me more watchful against Sin, & break the power of my heart corruptions more & more: but I found them often prevail against me, which was very grieving to me.

In hearing a Minister (12)⁹ preach in the High-Church-yeard in Septr 1741, & insisting much on making sure an Interest in Christ: While he said, never call your selves Christians, unless ye can say, God has made you sensible of your lost and undone state by nature, & drawn out your heart to close with Christ on his own terms; I could appeal to God that this was what [ ]¹⁰ wrought in me & for me: but I was still under doubts, whether this was a saving & thorow work, & if God had accepted of me. And I was thereupon made to plead more earnestly than ever, that he would clear up to me my Interest in Christ; & he was pleasd to give me clear & satisfying views of the Covenant of Redemption, wherein a certain Select number were given to Christ to be redeemed and Saved by him, & that I was among that number. And after this I continu'd closs at my duty, with some composure, till the Awakening broke out at Camb, when I fell into new plunges again.

[137/–] About ten or twelve days after that Awakening began, I came out to Camb. on a Tuesday, & heard a minister (26) preach on that Text, A bruised reed will he not break &c:¹¹ and was made to hope, that he had put some spark of grace in my heart, & would blow it up into a flame, & that tho I was but as a bruised reed, he would not break but heal & strengthen me: and that he was now about to return in mercy to this poor Land & his Church in it. After Sermon [ ]¹² I went into the Manse, & while the Minister one was praying in a standing posture I kneeld down: but hearing the people

---

⁵ Insertion ['and I was made to hope he would shew mercy and pardon: & found my heart easd of the sinking load I was under, but no sensible joy came in']: McCulloch.

⁶ William McCulloch (1691–1771) – minister, Cambuslang.

⁷ Heb 7:25.

⁸ Primary pagination number 135 omitted by McCulloch.

⁹ George Whitefield (1714–70) – evangelist.

¹⁰ Insertion ['he had']: McCulloch.

¹¹ Isa 42:3, Mt 12:20.

¹² Insertion ['Before Sermon']: McCulloch.

in time of Prayer, cry out much, I got up again off my knees in great fear &
astonishment, remembering what I had heard some adversaries of the Work
say, That a Quaker-Spirit was got in among them, and for some little time I
thought that it was indeed so. But within a short space I altered my thoughts
of them, seing them make so much use of their Bibles, & looking out for
places there, by which they had got relief: and bewailing their Slighting of
the Gospel, & the offers of Christ and Salvation that had often been made to
them in it: And while I beheld them in their Agonies I was putting up many
Petitions to God for them: but at the same time was afraid matters were not
right with my self, because as I then thought, my distress had not, in some
respects, resembled theirs, which was [ ]¹³

[138/–] grieving to me to think, & made me suspect my Self more than I
had done them a little before. But in hearing some of the Prayers there, I felt a
sweet melting on my heart which greatly refreshed me: and went home ~~rejoic~~
perfectly confirm'd that it was the Lords work, & the rejoicing at the hopes
that the Lord was about to do some good & great thing in that place & about
it: And when at home was much enlarged in praying for these in distress at
Camb., that the Lord might give them a Sight of Christ in his All-Sufficiency
to save them, & hearts to embrace him; & that the Lord carry on his work
where it was begun, & spread it into other Places. And for several days I had
them so much upon my heart, that I was not pleasd with my Self when any
worldly affair fell in & took off my thoughts from them, & interrupted my
concern & pleadings for them, tho but for a very little time.

I came out very oft to Camb. from time to time, usually twice a week, and
when I came would sometimes have stayed two days together; and in time
of the Exhortations prayers & singing of Psalms in the Hall of the Manse,
have often ~~enjoyd~~ had much of heart-meltings & great sweetness in my own
Soul: & would every now and then have been putting up Petitions secretly
in my heart to God, for the People that were there in distress.

[139/–] I heard the Sermons there with great satisfaction. But when I saw
& heard many persons there crying & fainting & swooning in their agonies
of soul, I have made to wonder at my own stupidity, that what I heard did
not affect me as it did them. I knew by what I had formerly sometimes felt,
that it must proceed from the quick sense they had of the wrath of an angry
God let in upon their Consciences: but I sometimes thought they had a
more affecting sense of the Evil of Sin than I had ever got, when it had such
outward Effects on them, that I had never been acquaint with. And this often
occasion'd much Self-jealousy. But the awful terrors of the Law against them
that transgressd it, & the terrible things pronouncd in the Gospel against them
that believe not which were then often preach'd, & that had such affecting
impressions on others, had very little effect on me: but what then affected me

¹³ Insertion ['some of them crying out']: McCulloch.

most was the sweet & gracious offers of Christ & the Promises of the Gospel, which sometimes were made sweetly to draw and melt and warm my heart.

When I heard & was well informd [ ][14] of the many sweet Outgates & ravishing joys that many were getting, after they had in their Distress been made to close with Jesus Christ on his own terms; I was frequently [140/–] taken up in earnest pleadings with the Lord in Prayer that he might give me also some clear & satisfying discoveries of my Interest in Christ, and that he had graciously accepted of me, & was reconciled to me in this Son ~~Jesus Christ~~ of his Love.

At the first Sacrament at Camb. in July 1742, I got nothing sensibly, but only was much in these sorts of Pleadings: but while I was thus imployed on Saturdays night, Satan was very active in endeavouring to keep me back from communicating, and to make me to throw up my Hopes of Blessings from God, & often urg'd that word upon me, When Esau would have inherited the Blessing,[15] he was rejected, & found no place for Repentance, tho he sought it carefully with tears: and by this he much discomposd and discourag'd me: Yet I was helped still to go on praying, that the Lord might in his own good time send me some clear and satisfying token of his love & favour, and that if it might make for his Glory, that he might give me the joy of his Salvation, and in the mean time, keep me waiting till his good time should come. And while I was thus pleading, that word come into my heart The Vision is yet for an appointed time, tho it tarry wait for it, it will surely come & not tarry:[16] ~~and that, I will remember my holy Covenant with Abraham with Isaac and with Jacob:~~ this gave me some comfort, & made me hope, that refreshing times from the presence of the Lord would come, & were drawing near.

[141/–] When I heard of another Sacrament Occasion to be shortly after that at Camb. I was exceeding glad of it, & essayd thro' grace to prepare for it, tho yet my preparation work went but heavily on. On Friday Evening before it having heard Sermon there, I went apart by my Self in the Fields, and aim'd at the duty of Personal Covenanting with God, & renewed my former pleadings for a Manifestation of the Love and Favour of God to my Soul. On Saturday, I was much affected in hearing the Sermons, particularly one (12) on that Text Except I wash thee thou hast no part in me.[17] That might after taking some Refreshment in my Quarters in Camb. I went out to the Fields by my Self for Prayer, & there falling down, while I was earnestly pleading, That the Lord might give me a clearer Sight & more affecting Sense of the Evil of my Sins as dishonouring to him, and as the procuring Cause of Christs Sufferings, than ever I had yet got: the Lord was pleased accordingly to give

---

[14]   Insertion ['from time to time']: McCulloch.
[15]   Gen 27.
[16]   Hab 2:3.
[17]   Jn 13:8.

me the desire of my heart in that matter, & more than I ask'd or could think of. For I then got a most humbling Sight & Sense of the exceeding Sinfulness & hatefulness of Sin; and I was made to see my Sins especially my Unbelief as the nails [ ][18] that pierced his hands feet & side, & was made Spiritually & in the most evident manner by faith to look as it were thro' his pierced side into his heart, & see it filled with Love to me, & his Love engaging him to undergo all these his bitter sufferings for me.

[142/–] And that yet after all the Evils I had done he was willing to forgive and had forgiven me all my Sins, that tho my Iniquities should be sought for they should not be found. Many passages in the 53d Chapter of Isaiah were then brought to my mind with greater power than any thing ever I had met with, particularly these, He was wounded for our transgressions and bruised for our iniquities, the Chastisement of our peace was upon him and by his stripes we are healed:[19] he shall see the travel of his Soul & shall be satisfied[20] —And I was these were brought home to my heart, with a particular application to my Self; & I was really persuaded that Christ was thus wounded and bruised for me & my Sins, & for purchasing Eternal life & Salvation to me, & that he would see the fruit of his soul travel in conferring that Salvation upon me that he had purchased for me by his death & sufferings. And under all these views & discoveries that were made to me, I found a heat of Indignation raisd in my Soul against Sin, melt a sweet kindly melting of heart under the sense of it, as that which crucified the Lord of Glory, and killd the Prince of Life. And while Christ was pleasd to Speak in to my heart, saying, Open to me my Sister my Spouse my head is wet with dew & my locks with the drops of the night,[21] I was made to grieve [143/–] that I had kept him so long knocking at the door of my heart for access, & that I had never so fully opened to him, as I ought to have done: & now he was pleasd himself to open these everlasting doors, & to enable me by faith to close with him in all his Redeeming Offices & to devout & dedicate my self to be wholly & for ever his; and to draw out my Affections in the most ardent manner toward him: And all this was followed with a beam of heavenly light (I know not how else to express it) shining into my heart or mind, for a little, giving me the most ravishing discoveries of the transcendent Glory & Excellency & amiableness [ ][22] in his Person as God-man Mediator, & in all his Offices of Grace & his perfect suitableness to all my wants & desires [ ].[23] And this was followed by that word quickly but sweetly darted into my mind, I have heard of thee by the hearing of the Ear, but now mine eyes have seen thee, therefore I abhor my self in dust and

---

18 Insertion ['& spear']: McCulloch.
19 Isa 53:5.
20 Isa 53:11.
21 SS 5:2.
22 Insertion ['of Christ']: McCulloch.
23 Insertion ['& made me long to be with him in heaven']: McCulloch.

ashes:[24] and along with this word, I got the most humbling & self abasing Sense of my own vileness by sin, & was made indeed to loathe & abhor my self in dust & ashes by reason of it, & to wonder that ever he should have shewd me mercy & set his love on such a vile unworthy & polluted sinner as I; & to praise him for the Soveraignty of his mercy & the wonders of his Love & free grace.

[144/–] For some ~~time after this, that night~~ [ ],[25] I scarce knew where I was or how I was, my mind was so [ ][26] taken up with these glorious views & ravishing Enjoyments I was favoured with. But after some time, I began to reflect on the former treachery & deceitfulness of my heart, and how frequently I had broke my Vows and Resolutions to live wholly to God: & therefore I now earnestly begg'd of the Lord, That if it might make for the Glory of his own name, he might take me immediatly to himself in Heaven, & not suffer me to return to the World ever to offend him any more as I had done: But if it was more for his Glory that I should continue for some time in the Body, ~~that he would~~ I was willing by his Grace to serve my Generation according to his will, only I begg'd he might undertake for me, & keep my feet from falling & enable me to walk before him in the Land of the Living. I was then forecasting & laying my Account with great Tryals, & could then have been content if if every hair of my head had been a life to have laid them all down for Christ; yet I was afraid, that I might be left to my self when I met with the Tryals. While I was thus pleading for strength and support those promises came with great sweetness into my heart, When thou passest thro' the Waters I will be with thee, & thro' the rivers they shall not overflow thee: the [145/–] mountains shall depart & the hills be removed, yet shall not my loving kindness depart from thee nor the Covenant of my peace be removed, saith the Lord that hath mercy on thee.[27]

Next day the Lord was pleasd to give me much of his Presence & much Communion with himself in the Time the Tables were a serving, & in Secret Prayer: and so also on Munday in hearing the Sermons. And much of this sweet frame continued with me for some weeks after that Sacrament-Occasion. And very often since that time, I have been allowed much nearness to God in duty.

And now to close: as to the habitual temper of my heart & spirit: I find a Principle within me opposing & striving against corruption & Sin of all sorts: when I fall into sin there's nothing so bitter to me as to think I have been sinning against so much Love and manifestations of the Love of God to me. I look upon all things as Enemies, that would separate between Christ & me, or interrupt & marr the communications of his Love to me. Ordinances

---

[24] Job 42:5–6.
[25] Insertion ['while this manifestation lasted']: McCulloch.
[26] Insertion ['Entirely']: McCulloch.
[27] Isa 54:10.

are dear to me: yet I am restless & unsatisfied in attending them, unless I
meet with Christs presence in them. I long often to be with him in Heaven,
yet am satisfied to wait his pleasure. The advancement of Christs Kingdom
in the World is my chief desire. If I forget thee, O Jerusalem, let my tongue
cleave to the roof of my mouth.[28] Come Lord Jesus, come quickly in the
manifestation of thy Glory & the Advancement of thy Kingdom Amen.

[28] Ps 137:5–6.

[146/–] Margt Shaw Daughter to Wm Shaw Tenant in Rutherglen age abt 20

I was put to School when young & taught to read & also to write some. I got my Shorter Cat. By heart and retain it still. I was put by my Parents when a child to pray by my Self, and continued to keep up a form of praying in Secret twice a day []¹ all along. However that was all but a meer form with me till about 4 years ago when hearing Minr (Mr Alexr Maxwell)² preach on that text, We must all appear &c:³ at which time I fell under great Concern, being made to think, what way shall I appear before his judgment-seat, who have been so great a sinner, and after that I took more delight in reading & hearing of the word and in Secret Prayer. I had thro mercy been kept from gross outbreakings before the world but many gross corruptions prevaild in my heart, tho I did not notice them till then. And after this Sermon, I began to be more affected with them, & was roused from my carnal Security and yet was excited to more diligence in duty, and some longing desires after Christ & an Interest in him & communion with him. but never got a deep and humbling sight of the Evil of Sin, and discoveries of the Glory & Excellency of Christ, or any Sensible communion with him, nor any Satisfaction as to my Interest in him, till I came to Cambuslang, on the first Sabbath in Febry 1742 after the Awakening began there: and at hearing a minr preach that day on that Text []⁴ You who were sometime alienated &c:⁵ I fell under much concern & was made to shed a great deal of tears at the thoughts of my being alienated from God by nature, & an Enemy to him by wicked works; but that concern wore off, I came next day & heard Sermon, & fell under Concern again; but it wore off again after I went home; & thus I continued coming out to Camb. & being affected while I was hearing, but the Concern wearing off again afterward; till I heard a mnr (Mr Bane of Killairn)⁶ []⁷ preach on that Text at Camb—And to Jesus the mediator of the new Covt⁸—at which time, I fell under strong Convictions [147/–] of the evil of Sin & of my great Sinfulness, of my heart & life, & of the original corruption I brought into the world with me, & was even weighted & pressed down under the Sense

---

¹ Insertion ['& all my other duties']: McCulloch.
² Alexander Maxwell (c.1687–1741) – minister, Rutherglen and Polmadie; brother of William, minister, Rutherglen.
³ 2 Co 5:10.
⁴ Insertion ['Mr McC.']: McCulloch.
⁵ Col 1:21.
⁶ James Baine Jr (1676–1755) – minister, Killearn.
⁷ Insertion ['in May']: McCulloch.
⁸ Heb 12:24.

of all those, & particularly of the Sin of unbelief & pride of my heart; and my slighting of Christs calls & offers in the Gospel. And for 7 weeks after this, I continued in great distress under a sense of these things [ ][9] One day after I had been hearing a minr[10] on that Text, Pardon mine iniquity, for it is very great,[11] being at my Secret Prayers, I thought I was just hanging over the mouth of Hell, & ready to drop down into it. One night when I was in my bed, these words were darted in upon me, Because I have called—ye set at naught all my counsel & would—I will laugh—[12] those words were set home upon my Conscience with such power that I was struck with great terror, & was like to go beside my Self, not knowing what to do. In these 7 weeks I could neither eat nor sleep nor work, except some very little, thro' the agonies of heart I was under. The first thing that ever gave me any Relief, was in hearing a Minr (Mr McC)[13] preach one day, that word (tho not utterd by him) darted into my heart, I love thee with loving kindness:[14] on which I was made to admire the Love of Christ, that had sent such a word to me who had been so great a Sinner; but yet I could scarce believe that it was from him, but though I was but taking it to my Self. Some days after, while I was sitting on the Bed-side, these words came and darted in upon me, Seek ye the Lord while he may be &c:,[15] on which I was made to wonder at the love & patience of God toward me, that he should yet be near & willing to be found of me, after I had so long neglected & provoked him, & felt some love in my heart kindled toward him, & was soberfully inclined to seek him with greater earnestness than ever I had done, & a little after that went to Secret Prayer & got liberty to pour out my heart before him. [148/–] and hearing a Minr (Mr McC) that day preach my distress of Spirit under a Sense of my lost condition increased in the time of his Sermon: I came back on Saturday & got more of my Sins discovered to me [ ],[16] but no comfort at all that day. I came back on the Sabbath, & heard Sermon & was in great distress in the time of it, & betwixt the forenoon & afternoon Sermons I fell into a Swarf twice, thro' the great fears & terrors of that fell upon me, but in the time of the afternoon Sermon, I got some Comfort for a little (tho' I do not remember what were the words that were the mean of it) only I mind these words in the Psalm that was sung [ ][17] These that are broken in their hearts & grieved in their minds, he healeth, & their painful wounds he tenderly

---

9   Insertion ['without getting any relief comfort']: McCulloch.
10   Insertion ['Mr McC.']: McCulloch.
11   Ps 25:11.
12   Pr 1:24–6.
13   William McCulloch (1691–1771) – minister, Cambuslang.
14   Jer 31:3.
15   Isa 55:6.
16   Insertion ['hring sermons']: McCulloch.
17   Insertion ['were sweet to me']: McCulloch.

upbinds.[18] On Munday I came back, & my distress still continued, but I was not under so great Terrors as before: on Tuesday I was going to stay at home, but while I was thinking to do so, I fell into great distress, & was made to cry out, what should I do here, there is no comfort for me here: & so I came to Camb, & had more composure to hear the Sermon; And that night when I was in bed, these words came into my heart with power, O thou of little faith why didst thou doubt,[19] & I was thereupon fill'd with comfort & love to God and all that was good, & I got some faith to believe & rely on Christ alone for Salvation. During that ten first days of my distress, I slept some but little & was grieved at my self for it when I did sleep, for I thought it was a dreadful thing for me to sleep, when I did not know but I might waken in Hell: & I also thought I was such a great Sinner, that I ought not to take any meal, & took very little but as my friends about me compell'd [ ][20] me to it. I also wrought little at all, in that time, my heart not lying to it, but being always carried away ~~after~~ in thoughts about my Souls condition & I thought what signifies the world to me if I perish at last. In these days, especially my distress was great I thought a great darkness was all about me, & one night [148/–][21] at home, I thought I saw a flash of fire on the Brae which I look to be hell-fire, that came very near me, but did not touch me: and I had a strong apprehension at that time that I felt the Smell of brimstone, which ~~I too~~ which was very choaking to me, & I thought it would have taken away my breath, & took it to be the Smell of the lake of fire & brimstone in the bottomless pit but I was never left altogether to despair of mercy, but was helped to wait with patience till his time w'd come.

On Thursday hearing a Minr (Mr Connel)[22] preach on these words, Hath the Lord forgotten to be gracious &c:[23] I was hereby comforted & encouraged to a patient waiting on the Lord in his own way. After this for some time I was more settled in my mind & heard the word with pleasure, & particularly one Sabbath when I heard a Minr (Mr McC) preach on that Text, What is a man profited &c:[24] I got much composure & comfort But hearing a Minr (Mr McC) some time after, preach on that Text, Joh. 3.all. He that believeth not on the Son shall not see life &c:[25] I fell under great distress in hearing of which I got a great sense of my Sin of unbelief, and thought the wrath of God was abiding on me for my unbelief: I was very distressd all that night, &

---

[18]   Ps 147:3, Scottish Psalter (metrical).
[19]   Mt 14:31.
[20]   Insertion ['oblig'd']: McCulloch.
[21]   Primary pagination repetition.
[22]   David Connell (1706–90) – minister, E. Kilbride. Son and ministerial successor of Matthew Connell (d. 1743) – minister, E. Kilbride.
[23]   Isa 49:14.
[24]   Mt 16:26.
[25]   Jn 3:36.

next day came & heard Sermon at Camb. & after it was over, I came & spoke
to a Mnr (Mr McC) who among things advis'd me to read the 4th Ps. looking
up to God for his Blessing every might when I was going to bed, which I did,
& found much benefit by it and I was never so distressd after that, except at
some particular times for a short while [ ][26] & then the word would come
into my heart with power [ ][27] Fear not for I am with thee, be not dismaid for
I am thy God,[28] which would immediately banish my fears & compose me.

One day coming out of Glasgow, & finding unbelieving thoughts arise &
prevail much in my heart That word came into my heart with power Look
unto all ye ends of the Earth & be ye Saved &c:,[29] on which I got strength
to trust & rely on Christ, being made Sensible that I could nothing of my
Self without him, & gave me some love to him.

[149/–] One day retiring to Secret Prayer in the fields, I got great liberty
and enlargement of heart in that duty, and I was coming homewards from
that duty, these words came into my heart with very great power, Thou art
an heir in Christ, thy Sins are forgiven thee. These words came with such
a mighty Sweet & heart overcoming power, that I felt, as it were the Holy
Spirit come rushing as with a strong Stream of Divine Influences into my
heart, & I was thereupon like to fall into a swoon; & was made to believe that
it was even as it was told me by these words, and a flame of Love to Christ
was kindled in my Soul, & I was filled with joy in God thro' Jesus Christ.
And coming into the house I took up the Bible to read, and the first thing
that cast up was the 51st Psalm w[c] I intended before I opened the Book to
read, & all along as I was reading the whole Psalm, I felt every verse of it
come, as it were rushing with a Divine Power into my heart, and my heart
was made to express all the words of it, as if they had been my own words,
and expressions of my own case. And thus it continued with me for about a
month after this: & every morning almost when I awaked, these words came
with great sweetness into my heart Thou art an heir in Christ, thy sins are
forgiven thee: and these words accompanied me almost wherever I went.
And in that in that time I slept very little at all, but rose often at Midnight
& at other hours to praise him; for I never wearied of that Exercise, & never
thought I could praise him enough. And all that time I could never doubt of
my Interest in Christ in the least: my mountain stood strong by Gods favour,
& I thought I should never be moved.

One [ ][30] day[ ][31] coming to Camb. & hearing a Mnr (Mr Arrat) preach
in the Kirk on a Munday, wn he said wn relief comes to a person in distress

[26]   Insertion ['& at several other times when in great distress']: McCulloch.
[27]   Insertion ['& <. . .> by it']: McCulloch.
[28]   Isa 41:10.
[29]   Isa 45:22.
[30]   Insertion ['of these']: McCulloch.
[31]   Insertion ['s']: McCulloch.

of Soul, ~~it cures~~ and Body both, it cures them of both at once: these words ~~came with power to me~~ were applied with Power to me, for tho' I had been brought very low in my body & thought long always that I was in a dying condition & would Die soon this Relief I had lately got restor'd me to health of Soul and [...] [...] [...].[32] [150/–] Being in Glasgow on the Street & seing a man coming out of a Closs, ~~when~~ I imdtly tk him to be a minister come from England, (Mr Whitefield) whom I had never seen or heard before []][33] but having heard much of him, I was exceeding earnest to hear him preach; but being obligd to wait on some worldly business I had just then on my hand, I burst out into tears, that I could not get across to go and hear him. But my idolizing an Instrument cost me dear, for I immediately lost that flame Sweet frame I had enjoyd so long, & going home I lost Sight of all together that had been so delightful to me. Next day I came to Camb. to hear him there, and did so that day & the following, but I heard with a very bad frame, & all the dreadful threatenings I heard, I thought always belongd to me & applied them all to my Self. The day after that, I went to hear him at Calder Sacrament & heard him there, but got nothing. On ~~Sabbath~~ Saturday while I was hearing another minister (Mr Burnside)[34] preach there, my heart was exceeding hard, & my mind was busy wandering after sinful & vain objects, when all on a sudden, I thought I heard a great number of Bells ringing & Drums beating just at hand and such a terrible noise that I thought the day of Judgment was come, and the wrath of God coming down upon all the people present, & just ready to consume them & my self among them: this put me into the greatest confusion & consternation that could be imagined. And I had such a strong Imagination & Persuasion of the Reality of all this, that I could not forbear crying out, ~~Do ye~~ to the people, Do ye not hear the Bells & Drums: a little while after that, the noise I thought I had been hearing ceased: The Sermon being ended I went away by my Self to Secret Prayer, thinking that if the Day of Judgment came on while I was so unprepared, I would be ruin'd forever: and getting some liberty in Secret Prayer, I came to some more composure & ~~returned~~ joined with some that were singing the Psalms & praying all that night. [152/–][35] And there about midnight, while one (James Knox in Ruglen[36]) was giving out the 40th ps. From the beginning for himself & the Company to sing, I got a ravishing discovery of the lovliness & glory of Christ & my heart so filled with his love, that I thought all that was within me was praising and adoring him: and my heart closed with him in all his Offices, & I devoted my self entirely to him to be

---

[32] Illegible text due to worn tail edge.
[33] Insertion ['but once when I could scarce get hearing him']: McCulloch.
[34] James Burnside (d. 1743) – minister, Kirkintilloch.
[35] Primary pagination number 151 omitted by McCulloch.
[36] Rutherglen.

saved by him on his own terms: & [†][37] that word came with fresh power to my soul again, Thou art an heir in Christ, thy sins are forgiven thee, & the joys of heaven came so rushing in upon me that I scarce knew where I was whether in heaven or Earth [T many other promises also came to me that I do not now remember.] And all that day both in hearing Sermons and at other times I was filled with the Love of Christ. I came in to Glasgow that night to hear that Stranger Minr (Mr Wh—d) that I was so fond of to an excess next morning there: but in hearing him I got nothing but disappointment again, my sweet frame wore off, & by the time I got home, I was looking upon all I had met with as delusion; I hrd him however at Camb. prch several times, but got nothing, but was in great terror, & under fears of wrath, & got a great affecting sense of unbelief, & going home I was so afraid that the Devil was coming to take me away, that I durst not go to the door: I heard him next day, but continued still in great distress, & remained in a very confused dead & unbelieving frame for about 14 days after that & could get no freedom in prayer: A little before the first Sacrament at Cambuslang, that former word came into my heart with power which revivd me much. And I had a great desire to be a Communicant there. Accordingly I did partake there but thought my heart was but very dead at the Table, but at joining in the Psalms at the close of all that Evening, I got my heart filled with love to Christ: & after that my love incrsd every day [153/–] Hearing a Mnr (Mr Wh—d) prch at Auchinloch in Calder, where he spoke of the danger of a Persons pleasing themselves with what they call'd the faith of Adherence, without (seeking after) the faith of Assurance: upon hearing of this I was reduc'd to a great plunge of distress again: going forward to Campsy Sacrament, I that night aim'd at what that Minr had recommended, Go & tell him, that ye will not leave him till ye get the seal of his Holy Spirit: but [][38] I did not obtain it at that time: In hearing the Action Sermon, I felt my heart very hard and dead, but in time of the Psalms after that sermon when that line Ps. 25[39] Whose hands are clean whose heart is pure,[40] a power came along that fill'd me with love & joy. And wn I saw the Elders brought forward the Elements, my heart was melted down with love to Christ, & was made to see my own vileness by sin, & yet made to believe that Christ shed his blood to cleanse me from my sins. When a Mnr (Mr Robe)[41] was serving a Table, he was saying, a believer if he were to be torn in pieces for Christ, he was willing: if he were to be burnt to death for Christ, he was willing: & looking about he seemd to

---

[37] Insertion ['† I thot I saw the golden scepter of free grace stretched out to me, & I took fast hold of it, & at <...><...><...><...><...> it was added <...> is thy <.....> T']: McCulloch.

[38] Insertion ['my faith faild and']: McCulloch.

[39] Should read Psalm 24:4.

[40] Ps 24:4.

[41] James Robe (1688–1753) – minister, Kilsyth.

point with his finger to me; but I found my heart very ~~hard~~ very unwilling, which was a great grief to me, that Christ should have laid down his life for me, & died & suffered so much for me, & that I should be unwilling to part with my poor worthless life for him! While I was thinking, these words came into my heart with power & immediatly made me willing to part with life & all things for Christ, When thou passest thro' the waters &c:[42] and I was then & all that day filled with love to him: hearing of threatnings I always find my heart turn harder: but in hearing of the Love of Christ & his own death & sufferings my heart was melted down: & it was so remarkably that day, when I heard the Tables served: ~~especially when~~ [154/–] and while I was weeping much for my sins, whereby I had pierced Christ, that word ws spoke in secretly to my heart, fear not, Christ is become thy salvation, my fears & griefs were removed & I got my heart just fill'd with love to Christ all that day, and so also all the next day; & I got still a further sense of my own vileness, and of Christs Excellencies: and when I heard many of the people crying out that day, it was a further addition to my joy: And I thought if I could have got all that there was there brought to Christ & to taste of the sweetness of his Love, It would have been the greatest joy to me. Coming away from that Occasion, I essayed by the way to plead as before [],[43] for the faith of Assurance & the Seal of the Spirit, & the answer at length came with a powerful impression on my heart with these words Thou art sealed by the Holy Spirit to the day of Redemption.[44] At which I was made to believe that it was so, was filled with more love to Christ, and had a full assurance of my Interest in him, & of Eternal Salvation by him. And thus it continued with me for 10 days thereafter when some doubts & fears & deadness return'd upon me: but it lasted but a little tillit was removed. And from that ten days to this day (Janry 21. 1743.) I have never been left under deadness or doubts or fears, except for some little time as for a day or two or so: but have always had a sense of the love of Christ on my soul, & sight of my Interest in him.

At the 2d Sacramt at Camb. Aug. 15, wn it was drawing near, I was much perplexed between desires of going to the Lords Table there, & fears of a rash approach: And looking on these words in my Bible, Let a man examine himself to which seemed to me to be very awful words; but these words being pressed on my heart, Go and shew forth the Lords death till he come[45] I was thereupon made very desirous to come & my former scruples were removed: accordingly I did come & communicate [155/–] there, & was helped to much of the exercise of faith in Christ and love to him: & this continued with me for a good while after.

---

[42]   Isa 43:2.

[43]   Insertion ['in secret petitions as I had been pleading all along at that occasion']: McCulloch.

[44]   Eph 4:30.

[45]   1 Co 11:26–8.

When I attended at Kilsyth 2nd Sacrament, I got my heart melted down in some measure with a sense of the love of Christ in his death & sufferings & my sins that procured them, and some love to Christ, but not so much as I would have wishd, but after I came from the Table my former dead frame returned again [].⁴⁶ On the Evening of that day, my former Sweet frame returnd: & on Mund: hr— a Mnr (Mr McC) preach on these words Blessed be the God & Father &c:,⁴⁷ at hearing of which I felt a Divine power come along with the text & all that was said, & my heart went along with every sentence and at singing the last Ps. at the conclusion of the work after that Sermon (O Let thy priests &c)⁴⁸ my heart was greatly lifted up & enlarged in love to Christ & rejoiced in him as God my Saviour. especially when in singing it, these words were pressd on my heart, I am thy Lord thy God & thy Savior. And going down from the Kirk to the meeting without at the Brae, & there hearing a Minr (Mr Robe) discourse a little at the close on the 118 Psalm, Save now I pray me &c:⁴⁹ he said, The Believer may go home rejoicing all the way calling him, my Lord & my God [---], which words were applied with power to my soul & I did accordingly go home in that manner.

Sabth after that, I hrd a minister (Mr McC) preach []⁵⁰ the same Sermon he had had at Kilsyth on Munday, at Camb. & found it again accompanied with the like power to my heart, or greater being just melted down

I heard a Sermon at Camb. a Sabbath after that []⁵¹ on that Text, That which is born of the Spirit is Spirit,⁵² where many works of regenerate persons were given, among others, he asked For what end is it that ye came to the ordinances of the Gospel: can ye say, it is not for customs sake or curiosity or other selfish end. but to enjoy communion with God here, & to be filled for communion with him for ever hereafter [156/–] this is a good sign: I found my heart go along in this mark, & all the rest then given, as expressing just the disposition of it.

Another Sabbath hearing a Minr (Mr. McC.) preach at Camb. on these words, We had the sentence of death in our selves that we might not trust &c:⁵³ which I found attended with power to my Soul, particularly when he said, If you run just to your friend, when you are in distress and danger, you just trust in the arm of flesh: if you then bear up your hearts with the thoughts of your money & wealth it shows that that is your idol god that

---

⁴⁶ Insertion ['that had been very dead and hard just before'] ['but those words he hath sealed you &c: again quickned me']: McCulloch.
⁴⁷ Eph 1:3.
⁴⁸ Ps 132:9, Scottish Psalter (metrical).
⁴⁹ Ps 118:25.
⁵⁰ Insertion ['over again']: McCulloch.
⁵¹ Insertion ['by a Mnr (Mr McC.)']: McCulloch.
⁵² Jn 3:6.
⁵³ 2 Co 1:9.

you worship and trust in: but when thou falls into extremities, dost thou run first of all and above all run to God for relief, this is the disposition of a true believer. And this I found to be an account of what by grace is my way.

Hearing a Minr anothr Sbth preach in Glasgow (Mr Stirling)⁵⁴ on that text, all things work together &c:⁵⁵ after reading the Text, he said, he was sure there are some here that can set to their seal to this Truth, That all they meet with from time to time works for their good: [ ]⁵⁶ I for my part could set my seal to it, since ever God put anything of his love into my heart, I see from day to day, the truth of it in my experience, If a person speak but a work to me by the bye I find it as over-ruld for my good & soul advantage.

It was among the first things whereby I discernd any change of my heart after I began to be affected at Camb. That I felt a love in my heart, not only to my friends, but to these I liked ill before, so that I could take them all in my bosom, & whereas I shund speaking with them before, I now wishd & longd for an opportunity to talk & converse friendly with them. And this continues still to be my disposition.

The greatest vexation I have now in the world, is evil & vain thoughts, particularly in the time of holy duties, as in prayer & reading & hearing of the word: but it was some relief to me to hear the Mnr (Mr Wh—d) say that such thoughts are hated strivn against & mourned over, God will not lay them to that persons [. . .] [. . .] [. . .] [. . .] [. . .] [. . .] [. . .]⁵⁷ [157/–] Hearing a minister (Mr Wh—d) preach on that text, The leaves of the tree are for the healing of the nations⁵⁸ And when he said Methinks, I hear some soul here saying I felt the Influences of the Holy Spirit flowing in upon my heart abundantly & greatly strenthning refreshing & rejoicing my soul.

I bless God, I have for ordinary ~~some~~ hope of heaven & sometimes also a full assurance of it: as ~~late~~, lately about the beginning of this new year (1743) when at Secret Prayer, I was allowed great liberty to ask blessings of God [ ]⁵⁹ these words were spoke in powerfully to my heart, Thy name is written in the Lambs book of life, which was attended with love to Christ the Lamb of God, & wrought in me a full Assurance of Eternal Life, & I was made to rejoice that my name was written in his book of life.⁶⁰

I desire to lean & rely on Christs righteousness every day; and to build all my hopes of all blessings in time and Eternity on what he has done & suffered for poor Sinners; and when God gives me assurance of Heaven I think it leans to the same foundation, the testimony of his word, & the witness of his Holy Spirit.

---

⁵⁴ James Stirling (d. 1773) – minister, Glasgow/Outer High Kirk.
⁵⁵ Ro 8:28.
⁵⁶ Insertion ['this was apply to me wt pwr &']: McCulloch.
⁵⁷ Illegible text at worn tail edge.
⁵⁸ Rev 22:2.
⁵⁹ Insertion ['& particularly that he would give me Assurance']: McCulloch.
⁶⁰ Rev 21:27.

[158/–] a.i. A Young unmarried man of 21 years.[1]

When I was about 12 year old, I was put to School, & was taught to read ~~both~~ the Bible in English & the Psalm Book in the Irish or the High-land Language, being taught first from my Infancy to speak Irish, and afterwards, by hearing some people about me speak English, I came also to learn that language: but I could have read most of the English Bible, before I knew anything of the sense or literal meaning of what I was reading. In my former life I was given to many Vices. I scarce ever usd to aim at Praying any at all, till about five years ago, that I had my Lot for some time in a Family, where there was much Religion, and observing all in the Family, retiring by themselves daylie for Secret Prayer, I thought it was a strange thing that I should be singular in neglecting it: and that I might not be so, I let about it too: and went on in it, twice a day ~~for ordinary~~ after that for ordinary, tho' yet it seems to have been but a form. I read the Bible however with some delight, & read it often, because I knew my Father would have been angry at me, when I came home to see him, if I had neglected my reading after I [159/–] had been taught to read. I also all along usd to attend publick worship on the Lord's day: But cannot say, That any thing I heard came with any power to me, or made any impression on me except that I would sometimes gone away resolving to mind some things that were wrong in my life, But I soon forgot them & broke them all.

At length hearing of the Awakening at Camb. in Febry 1742, I wish'd when I heard it, that I were there, thinking I might perhaps get something there too. I came frequently and heard Sermon there, & had some concern on me, & was very desirous to get more of a concern, wishing I might be in as great distress as any among all that were: But my concern did not come to any great height, till, one day hearing a Minr (11)[2] on that Text, The God of the Hebrews hath met with us:[3] at hearing the very words of the Text, I was much affected, because I thought he would never meet with me in a way of mercy. Hearing another Minr (26)[4] preach on that text,—'He that believeth not hath made God a liar, ~~because he believeth not~~ &c:[5] where he shewed the hainous nature of the Sin of unbelief, that it was a giving

1   Daniel McClartie – the shorthand text in McCulloch's 'Index of persons' names who gave the foregoing accounts to Mr. McC' states: raised in Naptal Parish, Kirkmichael, Argyleshire. Son of Angus McLartie, weaver in Naptal Parish or Kirkmichael. Servant in Argyleshire, also served in Paisley. Got Catechism by heart, and retained it.
2   William Hamilton (1689–1769) – minister, Douglas.
3   Ex 3:18, Ex 5:3.
4   William McCulloch (1691–1771) – minister, Cambuslang.
5   1 Jn 5:10.

God the lie, that in some respects, it was worse than the Sin of murder, or the gross wickedness of the heathens []⁶ or than Adams first Sin whereby he murderd a world; & in some sense worse than the Sin of Devils: and that it was a Sin that he was sure chargeable on all the people before him on the Brae, in [160/–] lesser or greater degrees: that all unregenerate persons were entirely under the guilt & dominion of that Sin, however blamless they might be before the world: & that believers themselves, had still much of remaining unbelief in them. I was much affected and astonished to hear this: but I could not admit that I was guilty of such a horrid thing as that: I thought indeed that I was an unbeliever, but I could not think, that by my unbelief I was guilty of as great wickedness as the Jews that murder'd Christ, or Adam that murderd a world. And I took up such a Dislike at the Speaker, for saying so, that I resolv'd I would never hear him again. And accordingly I did not come back next Lords day. I chang'd my mind however, and came back again to Camb. & heard that Minr ~~& others~~ often, on the same & other Subjects, & was made to believe that all he had said of unbelief was very true, & that I had been & was still deeply guilty of that hainous sin of unbelief: and was often in under great uneasiness of mind under the sense of this and my other sins. Yet it did not rise to such a height as I would have had it: and I thought it was nothing compard with what it ought to have been, & what I saw others under [].⁷ for I ~~still~~ never at any time cry'd out, & I continued still to eat & sleep & followed my work, tho' yet while I was at it, I never almost got Soul Concerns out of my thoughts, & came often to Camb. to hear Sermons. I was also often in Prayer, [161/–] not only on my knees but in ejaculatory Prayer at my work & walking out the way. Sometimes when I was on my knees at Secret Prayer, I got much freedom in pouring out my heart before God, but alas! I had no sooner done sometimes after I had got these Enlargements in Prayer, but a thought would have come into my mind, suddenly & violently, Surely God will hear thee now, there is no fear of answer to thy prayers after thou hast been praying so earnestly. This made me to cry out to the Lord, That he would keep me from Self: and there was nothing I was more afraid of than a Selfish Spirit, and hypocrisy. I had sometimes a fear of hell upon me, but I think the chief cause of my uneasiness was Sense of Sin as dishonouring to God.

At []⁸ Kilbride []⁹ hearing a Minr (12)¹⁰ preaching on that Text, Dost thou believe on the name of the Son of God,¹¹ As he gave some marks of believers and such as had a right to come to the Lords Table, I got freedom to

---

⁶   Insertion ['or the Sin of the Jews in crucifying Christ']: McCulloch.
⁷   Insertion ['tho I usually trembled & shook when I heard Sermon on the Brae']: McCulloch.
⁸   Insertion ['the fast before']: McCulloch.
⁹   Insertion ['Sacrament at']: McCulloch.
¹⁰ George Whitefield (1714–70) – evangelist.
¹¹ Jn 9:35.

apply these marks to my Self, and thought I might come to the Lords Table at the first Sacrament at Camb. July 1742, which then drew near, & where I intended to attend. But some time after this I was very afraid to think of coming to the Lord's Table, at the thoughts of my being so unprepared: And after I had one day in prayer been begging the Lord might direct me to some place of Scripture to clear my way to his Holy Table, [162/–] as I walk'd out the way, taking my Bible out of my Pocket, & going to read, the very first thing that cast up to my eyes, was that, But to do good & to communicate forget not, for with such sacrifices God is well pleased:[12] which gave me much satisfaction at the time: But my fears of an unsuitable approach afterwards return'd. After I had got a Token from a Minr (26) on Friday before the Sacrament, I spent most of that night in Secret Prayer on ~~Glasgow~~ [ ][13]–Green, & got some manifestations of the love of Christ, that warm'd my heart & made it glow, & filld me with joy. And this joy continued with me on Saturday hearing the Sermons at Camb, & in the Action Sermon: but when I came to the Table, the joy vanished, & I was seiz'd with great tremblings so that my body was like to shake in pieces. I had for a long time used to tremble in hearing Sermons at Camb. & could not refrain it, tho' I endeavour'd to my utmost: but this Trembling now at the Table, exceeded any thing of that kind I had been under before or since; and yet to this Day I cannot say what was the cause of it. Only I had been under great fears to come there, & fears of unworthy communicating when there: & I found my mind very confus'd & got nothing sensibly. On the Sabbath Evening hearing a Minr (12) on that [163/–] text, Thy Maker is thy husband,[14] I felt love to Christ in my Soul, & so much joy that the sweet offers of Christ as a husband to my Soul, That ~~my~~ the joy of my heart had almost made me to cry out among the people, That I was ready to strike hands on the Bargain. And after Sermon meeting with a Lad of my Acquaintance, who I knew had been under Exercise, I just flew with my arms about him, & said, such a Minr (12) has married my Soul to Christ. And I lay down on the Brae, & was so fill'd with the Love of Christ and contempt of the World, that I even wishd, if it were the Lord's will, that I might die on the Spot, & never more return to the world again; Yet rain coming on, I thought it was not my duty to ly still there, but went to a House for Quarters. And ever since this night, I bless God, these glowings & burnings of heart, & warm breathings on my Soul ~~with~~ [ ][15] love to Christ, and joy in him, have been continued with me. I never one day hear a Sermon or go to prayer, or read my Bible, or ask a Blessing to meal or return Thanks, or meditate on Spiritual things, which is now become ordinary to me, but

---

[12] Heb 13:16.
[13] Insertion ['Rutherglen']: McCulloch.
[14] Isa 54:5.
[15] Insertion ['working']: McCulloch.

I always feel this sweet warmth in my heart. And it is now [ ][16] very near twelve months since, it began to be so much with me.

[^][17] I never knew what it was to meet with any particular work of Promise, that came with power to my heart, till one night in Winter [164/–] last that I was much vex'd that both my master who was an Elder & a Preacher who lodg'd with him, put off Family Worship that night with Prayer only: & going out into the Yeard for Secret Prayer, I was pleading that the Lord might not forsake me; upon which that word of Promise, I will never leave thee nor forsake thee,[18] was instantly darted into my mind with great power & sweetness. At Glasglow Sacrament in April 1243. having come to one Kirk & communicated, & gone to another to hear the Evening Sermon, & one telling me that the words of the Text in the Evening Sermon in the Kirk where I had communicated were these, I will never leave thee nor forsake thee, & that the Minister discoursing on them, said, That from the original they might be read, 'I will not not not leave thee not forsake thee, or I will not leave thee nor forsake thee, three times repeated; which gave they continued running in my mind [ ][19] a long time after. And one day reading in my Bible, & meeting with these words 'ere I was aware, my heart was instantly so filld with joy, that for a while I could do nothing but ly down and weep for joy.

When I read my Bible & meet with the Threatnings there, I am not at all moved by them: but when I meet with the Promises, I find my heart melted with love and joy.

[165/–] In hearing Sermons, I have oft been made to think say with the two disciples going to Emmaus, Did not my heart burn within me while Christ opened to me the Scriptures, and talked to me. Particularly in hearing a Minr (26) about Candlemass 1743, lecture on Hos. 2. My love to Christ & joy in him was so great [ ][20] that my body was made to shake for joy, & was scarce able to stand, but was ready to fall down on the ground. Another time in hearing a Minr (15)[21] on that Text, In whom after ye believed, ye were sealed with the Holy Spirit of promise:[22] when he explain'd that Sealing, I was so filled with joy, that I had almost cry'd out for joy that the Lord had sealed me by his Holy Spirit. And at the first Sacrament at Camb. May 1743, while a Minr (13)[23] in the Evening Sermon, on the Lords day, discoursd on that Text concerning the disciples grief, That Christ would [ ][24] not take them to

---

[16] Insertion ['June 27. 1743']: McCulloch.
[17] [^] indicates bracketed [ ] material from p. 73 to be inserted in this place.
[18] Heb 13:5.
[19] Insertion ['with pleasure'].
[20] Insertion ['Especially when he repeated these words three times, I will betroth thee unto me, I will betroth thee unto me for ever saith the Lord'].
[21] James Stirling (d. 1773) – minister, Glasgow/Outer High Kirk.
[22] Eph 1:13.
[23] John Willison (1680–1750) – minister, South Church, Dundee.
[24] Insertion ['not stay with them'].

heaven with him, but yet promising to see them again & make them rejoice, I felt my heart glowing hot with love to Christ, and earnestly longing to be with him in Heaven, and joyful in the sense of his Love, & in the views of being for ever with him in glory.

I have oft been much troubled with base and wicked thoughts, many of them, its like, proceeding from the Devil & my corruption together, [166/–] some of them cast into my mind with violence, or urgd upon me again and again, without any shadow of reason, & contrary to my duty and inclination, which, its like, were more immediately from Satan!: I have by as one day when I was sharping my knife, urging me to cut my own throat with it &c: In such cases I have been in great bitterness and perplexity: And then I use to turn my thoughts to think on some part of Scripture, I have been reading or hearing of: Such as that, Ps. 16.1.

> Lord keep me for I trust in thee,
> To God thus was my speech[25]

And that, in Zech. The Lord rebuke thee, O Satan, even the Lord that hath chosen Jerusalem rebuke thee:[26] And I have sometimes thereupon been freed from these wicked thoughts. I have been oft troubled with them also, when I have singing Psalms with the Congregation, but I have use in that Case to sing so much louder, resolving by grace that I would go on & praise God Christ yet in spite of all the Devils in Hell: & then it has pleasd him sometimes to give me more courage & strength & joy, in his praises, & to rebuke the Adversary, so that he has departed from me for a Season.

[167/–] [One night a little after I had fall'n asleep, I thought I saw about a dozen of men from Greenock, that came to me & desir'd me to go along with them to Camb: at which I thought I heard the singing of Musick Bells, with which I awaked, & jogging another young man then asleep before me, & awaking him, O man what can that be? He said to me, What? I also & first heard as the sweet sound of Musick Bells; and then after that, a most sweet and melodious sort of Musick, somewhat like that of Viols & Harps together but vastly more delightful, that almost ravish'd my heart. When it ceasd, which was within a little after I awakened, that word came into my mind, & agreed well with my judgment at that time & what I then had enjoy'd, Surely the Lord is in this place & I knew it not.][27]

To conclude: I now for ordinary find my heart running out after Scriptural things, & have far more pleasure in Scriptural meditations than in carnal pleasures diversions: I find that to be Spiritually minded is life and peace: I have oft thought of what Christ says, concerning Spiritual drink & the water

[25] Ps 16:1, Scottish Psalter (metrical).
[26] Zec 3:2.
[27] Text in brackets marked for insertion after [^] on p. 72.

of life, Joh. If thou knowest the gift of God[28] —and Joh. If any man thirst let him come[29] —and Rev.n. The Spirit and the Bride say come—[30] & I bless the Lord, he has given me to know the meaning of these Scriptures in my own Experience, & I scarce ever come to publick Ordinances, but I get some more of these living waters; & I long & hope to be brought to that fulness of joy in Gods presence in heaven, & to drink of these Rivers of pleasures that are at his Right hand for evermore. To him be glory now & ever. Amen.

[28] Jn 4:10.
[29] Jn 7:37.
[30] Rev 22:17.

[168/–] b.z. A Widow Woman about 37.[1]

Tho' I had the privilege of many good religious Instructions & example, from my Father in my younger years; yet I slighted and neglected all. I seldom ever aim'd at praying any at all. I usd to go to Church in Sabbath, but I think it was only to see & be seen, for what I heard made no impression on me. I livd in a very careless life, & without the fear of God, & was given to some gross vices, not needful to be named. Sometimes when I fell under affliction, I would have resolvd to repent & ammend, but when I recovered, I turn'd back to any former evil ways. After I was married I fell under some concern to be religious, & prayed some, and left off some gross Evils I had been addicted to: I put up a Petition to God [ ][2] to be merciful to me; but never all the time of my married life, did I get a sight & sense of my lost state & the need I had of a Saviour, till toward that time of my husbands death in April 1742; I had had some concern upon my Spirit for my salvation for some time before that, but when I thought my Husband was drawing near to his latter end, my Concern [169/–] increasd, and I was much taken up in praying both for his Salvation & my own. After his death I continud under some concern still. At the first Sacrament in Camb. in July 1742, I was struck with a terror in hearing a Stranger Minister (12)[3] there & after I came home, & the terror increasd to that degree, that I durst not allow my self to sleep, for I thought I might awaken in Hell before the next morning; but fell a praying in my bed, being afraid to vise, & was overtaken with sleep, and when morning came, was awaked with that word, Rejoice and be exceeding glad, but could take no comfort from it. Another morning I was awaked with that word, How beautiful is thy feet with shoes, Song :[4] but I did not feel any Effect it had upon me, but still I went mourning, not only under fears of Hell, but because I had by my sins dishonoured a holy God.

And in this Case I continued till about Candlemass 1743, when after having talk'd a long time with a woman from Glasgow, who came to see me, & was much delighted in hearing her tell what God had done for her Soul, and calling Christ her Redeemer & saying, She could say it to the glory of free grace, That she knew whom she had believed; [170/–] hearing of these last expressions, I was so filld with grief that I could not join with her in saying so of my self, that I fell a weeping & trembling, & at length into a kind of

---

1   Jean Morton – the shorthand text in McCulloch's 'Index of persons' names who gave the foregoing accounts to Mr. McC' states: relative of William Edmiston, weaver. Taught to read, got Catechism by heart, and retained it.
2   Insertion ['now & then']: McCulloch.
3   George Whitefield (1714–70) – evangelist.
4   SS 7:1.

insensibility, at least I cannot now remember what condition I was in; but these about me, said afterward, that I imployed in blessing & praising God. After I came to my self, I found some Love to Christ in my heart. Some time after this, that word came into my mind, Jesus stood and cryed, & said, If any man thirst, let him come to me & drink:[5] I look'd my Bible & found it there, but got little comfort by means of it: but turning over my Bible another word cast up to my eye, And yet there is room,[6] which gave me comfort to think that there was yet room for me in the blood of Christ. And for about 2 weeks after this, I went on in the way of duty rejoicing in God, & praising him for giving his Eternal Son for a lost world of Elect Sinners & for some of the greatest of sinners such as I was; & glorifying Christ for his love in giving himself to death for his people, & I hoped for me among others & interceeding with God for them: and I had committed my cause to him, I was hopeful he would plead it.

[170/–][7] Another night I was meditating on the word, & felt more warmness of heart toward Christ than I had felt for some time before, and within a little I was made greatly to rejoice in God thro a Mediator, Christ Jesus & to cry out, How precious in thy grace.

I have several times, I think, closd with Christ in all his Redeeming offices; or have been made heartily willing to do so. I find for a considerable time past, my heart going out above all things after Christ, that I may know him with a heart-purifying knowledge. What I would desire above all things, is to have Saving Interest in Christ secured. I would not for a 1000 worlds return to my former sinful ways. And I hope thro' the grace & strength of Christ to be always kept on my guard against every known sins. I can never allow my self now to forget or ommit praying twice a day, & would incline to go about it oftener if I could have a closs. It is my grief that I cannot get that heart-brokenness I would have to melt and mourn for sin. I have no sinful way or lust that I would rather keep than part with. I desire that Christ may sit King & Lord over all in my heart. To him be glory. Amen.

[171/– through 174/– blank]

---

[5]   Jn 7:37.
[6]   Lk 14:22.
[7]   Primary pagination repetition .

[175/–] b.o. A Young Woman of 19 years.[1]

In the former part of my life till the year 1742, I had some little form of praying in Secret now & then. While at home in my Fathers house I got not leave to neglect it: but afterward when I went to Service I minded it but very seldom. In[2] was kept all along my life in merciful Providence from open gross sins before the world, except that for about a year and an half that I got into a wicked habit of Swearing, thro' the influence of bad Company that indulgd themselves in that practice, among whom I livd for a time, & from whom I too readily learnd it: but after a year and a half returning from among them to my Parents house, I refraind it, not from any hatred of it or sorrow for it, but because I durst not use such wicked ways of talking before my parents. I went however, in compliance with custom & the way I had been traind up to the Kirk on Sabbath for ordinary, but without noticing or regarding what I heard, & [176/–] never found the word touch my heart or Conscience: only sometimes I would have been a little uneasy, & would have gone away saying, I'm sure I shall not do as I have done: but it was still in my own strength I put on these Resolutions, & so came of them: all came to nothing.

And thus matters went on with me, till about two weeks after the Awakening brake out at Cambuslang in the Spring 1742, coming out there on a Saturday Afternoon, and having heard a Sermon in the Kirk, but without any Sensible Effect, I came in to the Manse, & went up to a Garret where I as had been told [ ][3] a Boy (82)[4] was praying, and several Persons about him hearing & joining him: Among other Expressions he had in that Prayer, he said Jesus Christ was knocking at the door of our hearts, & we will not open; these words I found piercd into my heart like a knife: when I thought Is Christ knocking at the door of my heart, & I refusing to open! & I was made to see that he had been knocking [177/–] at the door of my heart by a preached Gospel, but that I had not opened: I did not however fall into great distress at the time, but it came on more gradually, as I got more & more discoveries of my Sins & more & more of my lost state by nature without Christ, which the Lord was pleased to give me by several means from time to time after this. Next day, hearing a Minister (26.)[5]

---

1   Janat Turnbull (or Turnball) – the shorthand text in McCulloch's 'Index of persons' names who gave the foregoing accounts to Mr. McC' states: daughter of William Turnbull (Turnball), tailor in Rutherglen. Taught to read the Bible when a child, got Catechism to heart, and retained it.
2   Insertion ['I']: McCulloch.
3   Marking for insertion.
4   (82) is the code for female parishioner Jean Robertson; the more likely code is (62). referring to James Miller – weaver, Cambuslang..
5   William McCulloch (1691–1771) – minister, Cambuslang.

preach on that Text, A bruised Reed will he not break &c:[6] where I got more of a sight of being in a lost perishing Condition, & found my self cut off from all Interest in Christ. Some days after this, meeting with a Seceder, he made use of a great many arguments to persuade me, that I was under a Delusion, & that my Exercise & trouble & all of that kind with others at Cambuslang, was but meer Delusion: I was much vex'd at that thought, but knew not how to answer him.

Some time after this, being at Camb. on a Thursday, & hearing a Minister (26) on that Text, I know you that ye [178/–] have not the love of God in you:[7] I was made to see by the account he gave of the Love of God, and the marks & signs of it, he mentioned, that I had not the Love of God in me: but was made to resolve thro' Gods strength that I would take no rest till I found that love of God put into my heart, & a gracious Change wrought on my Soul, & that I would endeavour to aim, by grace, at complying with the Directions then given.

I applyd my self on week days to work some, but my heart was still running out after an Interest in Christ, & if I had had all the Earth, & could have freely parted with it all, if I might have an Interest in him. As I was at my ordinary work, the sins of my heart & life, would every now & then stard me in the face & made me very uneasy. I came frequently to Cambuslang on Lords days & other days, & got more & more of Awakenings & Convictions there. But I got no sensible Outgate, till one Night [179/–] that I was reading on Vincents Catechism[8] that the Minister of the Parish (19)[9] had given me, all the rest of the Family being in bed; as I read it meeting with that Citation Joh. 14.14. If ye ask any thing in my name I will do it, which came with such power & sweetness to my heart as I read it, that I could not forbear starting up from my seat to my feet, and crying out Praise him Praise him: I then thought I could never praise him enough for such a gracious word set home on my heart: for that him self knew that it was pardon of Sin & Salvation I was wanting, & that I desird to have it no other way but thro' Jesus Christ & his merits; & I had been often asking these & other blessings in the name of Christ. And O how delightful was it to my Soul, that Christ himself had said, That if I asked any thing in his name he would do it. And within a little after this, turning over the Leaf, that Citation cast up to my Eye, Heb. Wherefore he is [180/–] able to save to the uttermost &c:[10] which also was applied to my heart with

---

[6]   Isa 42:3, Mt 12:20.

[7]   Jn 5:42.

[8]   Thomas Vincent, *An Explicatory Catechism: Or An explanation of the Assembly's Shorter Catechism. Wherein all the answers in the Assembly's Catechism are taken abroad. under Questions and Answers; the truths explained, and proved by reason and Scriptures; Several cases of conscience resolved; Some chief controversies in religion stated, with arguments against diverse errors: Useful to be read in private families after examination of the Catechism itself, for the more clear and thorough understanding of what is therein learned* (Glasgow: Robert Sanders for James Brown, 1674)..

[9]   John Hamilton (d. 1780) – minister, Barony/Glasgow; translated to St Mungo's in 1749.

[10] Heb 7:25.

power: And I was made to see that if I was willing to come to Christ & to
God by him, Christ was willing to receive me: & I was now made willing
to come & accept of the Lord Jesus in all his offices; as my Prophet Priest &
King, & was made as heartily willing to be ruled & govern'd as to be taught
& saved by him. & I was made then actually to close with him & entirely to
give up my self to him.

[181/– and 182/– blank]

[183/–] b.e. A Woman of 25 years of age.[1]

In the former part of my life, tho I did not, for what I know, give any great
offence to man, by gross misbehaviours, and had a form of praying in secret,
& attended publick Ordinances, from my Childhood, and for some time usd
to hear the Seceding ministers often; yet I was always but a poor Stupid thing,
and knew nothing of inward heart Religion, till I came to Camb. in March
1742; And the first day I came there, I heard a Minister (26)[2] preach on that
Text There are some of you that believe not:[3] but felt nothing by ordinary
in hearing of it, but Satan was still busy in tempting me to take home an ill
report of the Work there, for that there was no difference between hearing
Preaching there from other places; & I too far complyd with his Temptations,
for I was all day resolving That if I saw any Person there any way misbehaving,
I should be sure to mind that, & to tell that when I went home. After Sermons
I endeavoured in to the Manse to see the People in Distress there, but could
not get in there, but went to the Kirk, where I heard a Preacher ( ) [184/–]
speaking on some text of the Song which I do not now remember; but just
as I entred, he was saying That for his own part, he would not want what
he had met with since he came to this Place for 10,000 worlds, upon which
I felt a power come down upon my heart, that [ ][4] made me quite to alter
my mind as to the work there, & resolve that I would not take home a bad
report of it, and made me grieved and ashamed that I had been thinking
thro' the day to do so: for I was then much affected & saw many about me so
likewise. After I went home, I was much taken up thro' that week in thinking
on the Work at Camb: & longing to return to it again & sometimes retiring
to Secret Prayer, where I had sometimes more sometimes less Liberty: and
besides these things I did not find any alteration on my heart from what usd
to be. Next Sabbath after this I returnd to Camb. and heard a Minister (26) on
that Text Joh. 3. last verse; He that believeth not the Son shall not see life,[5]
but the wrath of God abideth on him, and found the word preachd brought
home to my heart with Power, and made deeply sensible of that great sin of
Unbelief, that had never in all my life troubled me before, and was made to
think [185/–] that I would certainly go to Hell, for I had never believed in
Christ, & could not now believe. And after Sermon coming in to the Manse,

---

[1]   Agnes Buchanan – the shorthand text in McCulloch's 'Index of persons' names who gave the
       foregoing accounts to Mr. McC' states: daughter of James Buchanan, merchant in Shotts.
       Taught when a child to read the Bible, got the Catechism to heart, and retained it.

[2]   William McCulloch (1691–1771) – minister, Cambuslang.

[3]   Jn 6:64.

[4]   Insertion ['some way melted it &']: McCulloch.

[5]   Jn 3:36.

& seeing others in such distress, I thought mine was nothing equal to theirs; and I went away homewards, reckoning it was no matter what way I went, or what came of me, for I would never get to Heaven: but as I went on the way, I found my heart turn somewhat better, & began to check my self for such desponding thoughts & to hope that the Lord would yet help me to do what I could not do of my self. I continued in distress for my Unbelief, but sometimes having some little hopes that the Lord would help me against the power of my unbelief, thro' all the next week. Next Lords day I returnd to Camb. & heard a Minister (26) on that Text, While the Strong man armed keeps the house all his goods are in peace.[6] & in hearing that Sermon, got a humbling & affecting sense of multitudes of other sins besides unbelief, so that I thought the whole Sermon was directed as particularly to me as if there had not been another on the Brae to hear: I had some hopes however that the Lord might pardon these other sins, but still my unbelief appeard [186/–] so great and hainous a sin, that I could not get a sight of pardoning mercy for it. The same day I heard another Minister ( ) on that Text, The God of the Hebrews hath met with us,[7] and was earnestly to wish & long that he might meet with me, and could appeal to him that it was for that end, to get a gracious meeting with him in Christ that I came there that day. After that I also heard another Minister ( ) on that Text, Sir We would see Jesus,[8] and found my Errand & Exercise describd in that Sermon, and was full of longing desires to see Jesus in his beauty & glory.

I continued for some months in this condition: often under great fears of Hell; but more grieved for dishonouring God by my sin; & grieved that I could not be grieved enough for sin, or so much as others I thought were: my unbelief especially pressed me down, & my other heart Evils were a daylie burden to my Soul. I essayd all along to work as before, but still found my mind running after the work at Cambuslang and spiritual things meal was unsavoury & Sleep often almost quite departed from me, & I did not incline to allow my self in it till matters were better with me.

[187/–] A Little before I returnd to Camb. in July 1742, when I was one day coming out the way by my self, I sate down on a stone by the way side to rest my self; and found my heart very easy & quiet: but all on a sudden, tho I saw or heard nothing outwardly, a terror & trembling came on me, & a darkness, confusion & stupidity seiz'd on my mind and heart, and I thought a thought rose within me, Thou'lt be lost, & this was immediatly followed by that horrid Expression, Lord damn my Soul. I got up in great terror, & went homeward, and while I was by the way that horrid word was often repeated & urg'd upon my mind; and while I was endeavouring to reject it

[6] Lk 11:21.
[7] Ex 3:18, Ex 5:3.
[8] Jn 12:21.

with abhorrence, & begging the Lord might free me of it, & afraid that my heart had consented or might yield to it; that word came into my mind, Tho thou slay me yet will I trust in thee:[9] after which that Hellish word never troubled me again, and my heart was much easd & quieted.

Next Lords day after this, being the Sabbath before the first Sacrament at Camb. in July 1742, I came to that place [188/–] and heard a Minister preach on that Text, But let a man examine himself & so let him eat of that bread & drink of that Cup.[10] I found it to be a very sweet & agreeable Sermon to me & longd much to partake of that Holy Ordinance of the Lords Supper: And after I came home I essayd to examine my self by the marks I had been hearing in that Sermon, but could not find that clearness to apply them to my self I would have had, and was afraid I was not in a condition to partake there

I heard much concerning a Stranger Minister (12)[11] & came & heard him preach several times at Camb. but found my heart always more dead & stupid when I was hearing him than when I heard other ministers at that place: but hearing him at Kilbride Fast before the Sacrament there in June 1742, on Peters denying his master & repenting, I found my heart a little more softned than it had been before that, & continuing so for some time.

On the Fast before the first Sacrament at Cambuslang I heard a Minister ( ) on that Text, Abraham staggered not at the promises thro' unbelief,[12] where he spoke much of persons wavering between the motions of lust & the offers of God in the Gospel, & sometimes listning to the one & sometimes to the other, and that persons [189/–] might go on that way till they died & never come to a good issue, unless they closed with Christ in the Promise by faith. This I thought touchd me nearly, and my unbelief was yet so strong that I could not get resting on the Promise of God by faith. I heard also another minister ( ) on that Text, O Lord, I beseech thee, pardon mine iniquity for it is great,[13] & found it suited to my condition, for I had then a deep sense of the greatness of my Iniquity & need of a pardoning mercy of God.

On Saturday I found much sweetness in hearing some Sermons, tho I do not now remember the Texts or the Ministers that preachd on them. In the afternoon of that day hearing a Minister (12) preaching on Christs Sufferings, from Mat. 26 I think, & speaking of Christs going a little further from the disciples & praying again & again, saying O my Father if it be possible let this cup pass from me,[14] he said Christ had [ ][15] all the Elect then on his heart, & all the weight of all their sins on his back, so that the load of them made

---

9 Job 13:15.
10 1 Co 11:28.
11 George Whitefield (1714–70) – evangelist.
12 Ro 4:20.
13 Ps 24:11.
14 Mt 26:39.
15 Insertion ['those persons']: McCulloch.

him fall on his face, & had almost pressd him thro' the Earth. While he was speaking to this purpose, I felt much heart melting for my sins whereby I had thus pressed & pierced the Lord of Glory, and thought I would rather choose to die that minute, than to return to my former sinful ways.

[190/–] A Minister (26) at the Close told us that so much had been said, that he needed not to say any thing further; only he exhorted us to go aside & pour out our hearts before God, telling us tho' we might be ashamed to let men know what Evils in heart & life we were guilty of, yet we might freely open up all to God. I inclind much to do so: but found such a mass of sin in my heart that I knew not how to fall about the duty. Withdrawing up the brae, these words came into my mind, Hear and your soul shall live:[16] and after they had come once & again into my heart, I took out my Bible to see if I could find them there; but while I lookt for them, that Place cast up to me & was the very first I cast my eye on, Phil. 4. at the beginning, which I read on to the end, & found it all exceeding sweet to my soul; it seem'd as if it had been an Answer to what had been my thoughts all that day, or as if I had set down my thoughts and difficulties, about my Souls Condition & one had sent me what is writen in that Chapter by way of Answer [ ][17] But there were some passages there that were particularly applied to me with great light & power, such as these, Stand fast in the Lord,[18] [191/–] —whose names are written in the book of life[19] at reading of which, I felt a power come along with the Word, that persuaded me as fully that my name was writen in the Book of life, as if I had seen it there with my bodily eyes, And because the Lord had made it thus known to me that my name was in the Book of life, I thought this was ground for me, to do as the apostle enjoins in the very next word Rejoice in the Lord always & again I say rejoice,[20] & I was made accordingly to do so: the gift of 10,000 worlds would not have made me to rejoice so much as the light of Gods Countenance & assurance of his love did that night. And the passages that follow I thought were just ~~Exhortations~~ Directions to me how to walk after this, as particularly that Let your moderation be known to all men the, Lord is at hand,[21] —These things that ye have heard & seen in me do, and the God of peace shall be with you.[22] After I had read over the Chapter again and again, I found all my difficulties vanish, my heart was filled with the love of God, tho not so much as I desired, my soul was enlarged

---

[16] Isa 55:3.
[17] Insertion ['And tho' I saw or heard nothing, yet such was the Divine Power & Light that came along with the Word while I read it, that three several times I thought there fell from my Eyes as it had been Scales.']: McCulloch.
[18] Php 4:1.
[19] Php 4:3.
[20] Php 4:4.
[21] Php 4:5.
[22] Php 4:9.

and mouth opened to praise him with joyful lips in the place to which I had retird by my self. [192/–] My great concern now was to get this sweet frame continued, & what I would do if it should be removed; for I did not see how I could live, if the Lord should withdraw the light of his countenance. And whereas formerly when I came away home from Ordinances, I thought there was always something I had to do my self in way of duty, I now saw that I could do just nothing [ ],[23] of my self, but saw a Sufficiency of power and grace in Christ to help me in every weakness & in every difficulty, to which I desired to look & lean, & to submit my will to his to be disposed of by him in all things as might be most for his glory.

I spent all that night in prayer and praises. Next day wherever I turnd and read my Bible, I saw every passage I read concern'd my self. And whereas formerly the things I read there seem'd as if they had not been true, thro' the power of my unbelief, now I saw every thing I read to be true and real. And in hearing the Action Sermon, the Exhortations at the Tables, and the Evening Sermon, and all that was said that day in Publick Ordinances, came in to my heart, as if it had been so many words spoken to me immediatly from Heaven. I continued in a sweet [193/–] and heavenly frame all imployed in prayers and praises all that night also. On Munday hearing a Minister (12) on that Text, Let the same mind be in you which was in Christ Jesus,[24] my spirit was greatly weighted, how I should get a conformity to Christs Example in spirit and practice. But in hearing another Minister ( ) on that Text My God shall supply all your wants;[25] my heart was much lightned and easd in the hopes & belief that God would graciously supply all my wants from time to time: [ ][26] & was made to hope that I should be enabled to do all things thro' Christ that strengthening me.

I went home rejoicing. And now, I began to think with my self, This blessed Bible that I carry with me; where every thing I now see there is so plain & sweet, will tell me all things I need know: & therefore I need not care tho' I never come back to Cambuslang again, or go to publick Ordinances elsewhere: So foolish was I & ignorant; and the Lord soon made me sensible of my folly to my [. . . . .] but blessed be his name; he did so in a mild & gracious [194/–] way by giving me a humble & teachable disposition, and giving me to understand better the necessity of attending all the Ordinances whereby Christ communicates to us the benefits of his Redemption. And accordingly I took up my Shorter Catechism[27] when I went home, & began at the first Question in it, resolving to read it thro' & consider it, as I got leisure, as if I

---

[23] Insertion ['at all']: McCulloch.
[24] Php 2:5.
[25] Php 4:19.
[26] Insertion ['I was made now, & at other times, to close with the Lord Jesus Christ in all his Redeeming Offices']: McCulloch.
[27] *Shorter Catechism of the Westminster Assembly* (1647).

had never read it before: for tho I had very often read it & got much of it by heart, I reckoned I had formerly understood nothing in it at all to purpose.

This sweet frame the Lord gave me at the Sacrament in Cambuslang, was continued with me for about a Quarter of a year thereafter in some measure. Sometimes indeed [ ][28] that Love to Christ and joy & Spirituality would have abated: but upon retiring to Secret Prayer, or reading my Bible, or in hearing the Word, these would have returnd in a good measure again. Sometimes also I have been much quickened and enlargd in heart just when I have been following my lawful worldly affairs by some words of Scripture cast into my mind with much life and sweetness: as [195/–] particularly one day after I had been working hard and was ready to faint, that word came into my mind with a powerful Influence

> My heart and flesh doth faint & fail
> But God doth fail me never[29]

Immediatly after which I was as much refreshed & strengthned [ ],[30] as if I had never been wearied at all. Another time while I was beside one who digging up the Earth with a spade, a worm cast up to my sight, and at first sight of it these words came into my mind, with much sweetness, Tho after my skin worms consume this body, yet in my flesh shall I see God:[31] And I was hereupon made to rejoice in Christ, & in the hopes of seeing him in his Glory at the Resurrection.

To come to a Close: I can safely say in the sight of the Heart-Searcher that I have no malice enmity or ill-will at any person on Earth. I want & heartily desire that all that are strangers to Christ belonging to the Election of Grace may be brought in to him, and his Kingdom may be advanc'd all the world over.

[196/–] On the Monday after the Sacrament at Cambuslang my heart was so filld with love to Christ & the Souls of others, that I could have been content if it had been possible, to have taken all the multitude on the Brae in my arms & to have carried them all up to Heaven. Oftimes I find my self straitned when I would pray for blessings to my self: but when I begin to pray for others, & for the advancing of the Kingdom of Christ, I get much liberty & enlargement of heart; and after that I come to get much freedom in asking mercies for my self. I see a necessity of joining all duties of first & second Table together, and would fain study by grace to keep a Conscience void of offence both toward God & man, tho yet I'm daylie coming short of my Duty to both. I am not without fears sometimes of falling away: but I desire to rest on his word of promise on which he hath made me to hope &

---

28 Insertion ['now & then']: McCulloch.
29 Ps 73:26, Scottish Psalter (metrical).
30 Insertion ['in body as well as mind']: McCulloch.
31 Job 19:26.

to commit my all for Time and Eternity to Jesus Christ, to whom be Glory for ever Amen.

[197/– and 198/– blank]

[199/–] b.d. A Woman about 36 years of Age.[1]

I was traind up in my Childhood in a Religious way by my Parents, & usd all along to go to Publick Ordinances on the Lords day, and to pray for ordinary twice a day in Secret, and often read the Bible by my Self with some delight. When I was about thirteen years of age I fell under some concern about Salvation a little before the Sacrament was to be dispensed in the Place where I livd, and had a great Inclination to have come to the Lords Table to take my Baptismal Engagements upon my Self: and accordingly went there, and tho' I cannot Say I met with anything Sensibly there, yet I found from that time a great desire after that and all other Gospel Ordinances, and was careful to attend them when I had Opportunity. I am much indebted to the mercy of God for Restraining Grace, in keeping me all along my Life free of anything vicious & shameful before the World. But when I went to Service, that delight I had in Ordinances & duties of Gods worship, much abated, & I turn'd more ~~carnal~~ earthly in my disposition, & indulgd my Self in much vanity [200/–] my Conversation, & in carnal mirth and jollity [ ][2] tho' not directly sinful, yet blunted my desires after Spiritual things. But while I was going on in this way, ~~my Re~~ some of my near Relations dying, I was much affected with their death, and began to turn more thoughtful again about Soul-Concerns. And for a long time after that, I attended on Publick Ordinances with much Concern, and found my Case often described in the Ministers ( ) Sermons whom I usd then to hear, and the Word coming close home to my Conscience, and for about ten years time after this I always thought myself to be a hypocrite; yet I durst not then keep away from the Lords Table, for I thought that would be Rebellion, & I could not think of being guilty of that: And every week I usd to think long for the Return of the Sabbath, and still to be counting how many days were yet to it: & on Saturday's-Evenings, I would have begun to reckon the time to the Sabbath in hours, that now there were but so many & so many hours remaining till the Lords day would begin, & the thought of its being so near at hand, was matter of joy to me.

For about three years time before the [201/–] Awakening brake out at Camb. I was in a great strait betwixt the two, whether I should continue to hear my Parish Minister (. .) or if I should break off altogether & join the Seceders. I went as often on Week-days as I could have access to hear the Seceding ministers, even to the injuring my bodily health & weakening my

---

[1] Isobel Provan – the shorthand text in McCulloch's 'Index of persons' names who gave the foregoing accounts to Mr. McC' states: daughter of Robert Provan, tenant in Calder. Taught to read the Bible when a child, got the Catechism to heart, and retained it.

[2] Insertion ['which']: McCulloch.

strength in going to far distant Places to hear them; yet when I went to Pray & Seek Direction, I could never get freedom to go hear them on Sabbath days, but found my Self still as it had been constrain'd to go & attend Ordinances at home, and often found my Self obligd to be thankful that I had a Gospel minister at hand, who preachd so close to my Condition. And I did not find the Seceders way of Praying agreeable, because they seemd to me to be very narrow in their Prayers, and not to extend them to the whole Israel of God, but to confine them in a great measure to themselves.

When the Awakening brake out in Camb. In the Spring 1742, it was so surprizing to me to hear of it, and I was in such Confusion at the thoughts of it, that for about ten days after I first heard of it, I could scarce eat or drink or sleep any: the Seceders kept a Fast in oppositon to it, [202/–] which encreasd my uneasiness about it, & put me I know not what to think of it. After many struggles with my Self about it, I resolvd to go there & hear & see: & I was still in doubt, falling down by the way to pray, these words came into my mind, can any good thing come out of Nazareth, come & see: which determin'd me to go forward. When I came there, I heard two ministers (&), preach two Gospel Sermons, but felt nothing beyond ordinary: After I went home I was often thinking of the Lords way of dealing with his people by alluring their hearts, by the still calm voice of the Gospel, and could not get my heart brought to a liking of the work at Camb: Yet I had some thoughts now & then of returning to it some day or other; & one Sabbath morning, after lying & sleeping much longer in my bed than ordinary, for which I was much displeasd with my Self, I intended to have come to the Sacrament Occasion at Cathcart about the first of May 1742, and was in such a hurry that, I did not stay so much as allow my Self time to retire, & say God help me: but by the way when I fell down to prayer, that word came to my mind, Thou knowest the way that I take, when thou hast tried me I shall come forth as gold; I did not well understand the meaning of that passage as applied to my Self, [203/–] but found a heart melting impression made by it upon me, & a great Inclination to come to Camb: and I accordingly turn'd my course & did so: And went straight down to the Brae, never stopping till I got into the midst of the people before the Tent; and immediatly after I had down so, a minister (26)[3] came down & gave out the 126 Psalm to be sung, and he no sooner read the first line of it but I fell a trembling with concern, yet I sung the Psalm with great delight: and in time of the Prayer, I got more composure and attention of mind to go along with the minister than ever I had had in that duty before. When he read out his Text, While the strong man armed keeps the house all his goods are in peace,[4] the words came so home to me that I thought I was just the Person pointed at the words as directly as if I

[3]   William McCulloch (1691–1771) – minister, Cambuslang.
[4]   Lk 11:21.

had been mentioned name & Sirname. And it was the same way with me all along the Sermon. Every sentence was so powerfully & closly brought home & applied to me in particular, as if there had been no other to hear, & my Agony of Soul under the Sense of my Sin & thraldom to Satan was so great, that I was just ready [204/–] to cry out for Anguish at every sentence, yet with I got refraining but with much difficulty. In hearing another minister ( ) on that Text, The God of the Hebrews hath met with us,[5] I continued in great distress, at the thoughts that God had never met with me in a way of mercy, & fears that he never would: & when he said, That this Work was the Answer of the Prayers of those that had gone to heaven before us; & for some years past, some of us might as well preach to stocks & stones as to the people that sate before us: I thought that that had been just my case, & was so affected with grief at the thoughts of it, that I was just ready to cry out, & to prevent crying took so fast hold of my throat with my hand, that I had almost strangled my Self. Betwixt Sermons I read the 119th Psalm with some pleasure. In the afternoon hearing a minister ( ) on that Text, Sir we would See Jesus,[6] I thought it was my desire to see Jesus, but that I had been but hypocritically pretending to be seeking to see him before, & thought I was not as yet seeking him sincerely.

[205/–] After Sermon, several that were along with me proposd to go in to the Manse, I was very averse to do so, but would go away home, but a woman with me, saying Be as it would, she would go into the Manse, & doing so, I followed after, and standing still on one of the steps of the stair that led up to the Hall, I heard these Lines of the 6th Psalm a giving out to be sung, In thy great Indignation O Lord rebuke me not,[7] at hearing of which I fell a trembling so that I thought I should have shaken in pieces: recovering a little I went up to the stair-head, where a woman in the Hall gave a great Cry, saying, O What shall I do: A minister said to her, Believe on the name of the Son of God,[8] & thou shalt be saved. At hearing that, I could no longer contain at the thoughts that I had not yet believed, but cryed out too: And got forward into the Hall, & stayed there for some time: And while I was there, that word came in with power into my heart, Stand still & see the Salvation of God,[9] which encouraged me to hope I should yet see the Salvation of God: before this word [206/–] came my unbelief was very strong, & despairing thoughts prevaild, now I got some hope: before I was so feeble I could not stand but was obligd to sit down, now I could get up & go thro' the Room: and went home that night, tho I had several miles to go. After I was got home, for three days I could neither work sleep eat

[5]   Ex 3:18, Ex 5:3.
[6]   Jn 12:21.
[7]   Ps 6:1, Scottish Psalter (metrical).
[8]   1 Jn 5:13.
[9]   Ex 14:13.

or drink, except only that I drank water: & with great pressing of some, I took little bit of bread on Tuesday, but for several days I found that but still as it were sticking in my breast. All these 3 days I was in the greatest distress that one could be in under a Sense of unbelief & heart-corruptions, & the evil & hatefulness of them; and I thought they were so strong and powerful, that they would be my utter undoing. As for fears of Hell, I never had any either of that or any other time. A minister ( ) coming to see me, when he came in [ ]¹⁰ & saw me in distress, smil'd & said, What's is this that ails thee O'er thee now: thou never murderd any body, I believe. I replied, I might be was guilty enough of other sins, tho I was free [207/–] of that. He told me Manasses was guilty of as great sins as, I and yet obtaind mercy. And then began to ask me several questions how this distress had befallen me. When I told him I never had any fears of Hell, he said, Thou has war'd me then, for I have been fear'd for Hell many a time. One thing in my condition I believe, was very singular & very afflicting to me, that in all that time, I could not pray one word. I could not get into a frame for prayer, or any one word uttered to God either on my knees, when I went to them as I often did, nor could I put up one Petition to God at other times, when I was not on my knees, in an ejaculatory way. Only I got liberty to say often, with tongue and heart, That I was content to be Eternally oblig'd to Christ for the Work of Redemption, and immediatly after I had said so, those words were impressd with great power & vigour on my Spirit, The Seal of Heaven: and as oft as I repeated the former words in the time of these three days, the [208/–] latter words came always in at the back of them. I did not will and these words at the time, but came to understand them better to my Comfort afterward. I went and talkd with a minister ( ) and askd him, If he thought I should go back to Cambuslang again: he said, What should you do but go back? I think you have good reason to go back: So I resolvd to return there on Thursday. But before I did so, while I was at home essaying to pray, the first word I got uttered in prayer after three days time, was, Yet that of Jonah, which came in with power, & gave me liberty to pray, Yet will I look toward thy holy Temple:¹¹ and this was immediately followed by that of Job, Tho thou slay me, yet will I trust in thee.¹² On Thursday returning to Cambuslang I got liberty to hear two Sermons on the Brae with some composure, but cannot say there was much Concern on me. But after these two Sermons were over, hearing there was to be a Sermon in the Kirk, I went & heard a Sermon by a minister (26) on that Text Is. He feedeth on [209/–] ashes, a deceived heart hath led him astray so that he cannot deliver his soul, nor say, Is there not a

¹⁰ Insertion ['as soon as I saw him I just flew to him, for gladness & cry'd out']: McCulloch.
¹¹ Jnh 2:4.
¹² Job 13:15.

lie in my right hand.[13] Which he explain'd as chiefly pointing at the Spiritual
Idolater: I found the various ways & instances whereby persons commit
Spiritual Idolatry set home so particularly & powerfully on my Conscience
& heart, that I thought I was just the person describd & levelled at, & was so
filled with anguish on that account, that even my bodily strength was quite
overcome, & I fell down as dead, and after was carried out in time of Sermon
as one dead, & laid me in the Kirk-yeard where I lay for some time like one
really dead. Some about me applied their Spirit-glasses to my nose, and when
that had no affect to awake me, they poured in Spirits into my nose (as I was
informed afterward) but all that had no Effect on me, & I believe tho' they
had poured in these Spirits all the way up to my Brain, I would [ ][14] not once
have felt the Smell of them in the least. At length after a while [210/–] lying
in that Case, I was raisd out of that Swarf, tho not by the force of any thing
they applied; and after I had recovered a little out of it, they began to hold
their Spirit-Bottles again to my nose, to help me to recover better, as they
thought: but I bade them, Hold away their oyls & Spirits from me, it was not
that that I was wanting; what I wanted was the Oyl of the Spirit of Christ.
After I got a drink of water, I could then walk, & got up, & went in company
with another home: but after I got home I turnd stil more distress'd under a
sense of sin, especially my Spiritual Idolatry, and earnest longings after Christ.
I went to a Ministers ( ) house, & at his desire stay'd all night there; & he gave
me many good advices & Instructions, & good Books to read: yet my trouble
continued, & I could attain to no relief or comfort, till next when I was on
the way coming home, These words came into my mind, The Lord thy God
is mighty, he is in the midst of thee, he will save, [211/–] he will rejoice over
thee with joy, he will rest in his love, he will rejoice over thee with singing.
Zeph. 3.17. I had fallen down by the way to pray, when these words came,
& they were attended with such a melting & brokenness of heart, that I got
my heart pour'd out before the Lord. I got but a very wavering hold of them,
and unbelief so prevail'd, & I was filld with such a sense of my own sin and
unworthiness, that I could not get it believd that such precious words could
belong to such a sinner as I. And I could not think or remember that ever
I had read these words in the Bible. Nor did I ever know it, till about five
months after this, that I heard a minister at Cumbernauld Sacrament, cite
these words & the place they were to be found, saying they were worthy to
be written in Letters of gold, at hearing which joy filld & swelld my breast
that I was almost ready to burst, that it was with great difficulty that I was
able to refrain crying. But, tho' I can't say I had much joy by means of these
words at the time [212/–] they first came, but was rather filld with unbelieving

[13] Isa 44:20.
[14] Insertion ['threw water on my face and']: McCulloch.

wonder, yet these [ ][15] came often back with a new impression on my heart, when I was any way troubled, and for about a months time after this, I always lay down and waked with them.

[213/– and 214/– blank]

[15]   Insertion ['words rest in his Love']: McCulloch.

[215/–] Jean Hay Daughter to Hugh Hay Writer in Edr
her mother Widow Hay now living in Lismahago age 26.[1]

I was put to School when I was a Child & taught to read the Bible & got the
Shorter Cat. by heart, but had much neglected & forgot it till of late that I
have been learning it again. I have all along been kept from things outwardly
gross & vicious before the world: but tho' I had a profession of Religion, I
had nothing but a name to live: I had no form of praying in Secret till about
the time I was 12 years of age, when I was in a family where there was some
religion, & to please them more than any thing else, I put into some form of
religion too: but I laid aside any outward fashion of it again some time after
when I came into another family where it was not fashionable: till when I
was about 15 years of age, a young man making faith to me, & my Father
refusing to let me marry him, I left my Fathers house in resentment, & being
filld with much grief on this account, I fell to praying again to see if I might
be relieved out of that grief, but in a little time I left it off again, thinking I
was too young to serve God, and that it would be soon enough when the
next year was come. But next year, having many persons in the place where
I was, were to go to the Lords Table, I though I would go there too, that I
might get a name of religion, & without some kind of form of praying in
Secret I knew I would not get there. the time coming, Near, I went to the
Minr of the place & he askd me what is the Lords Supper, which I answered
& he [ ][2] admitted me. When I was at the Table, I sate next the Minr, like the
Pharisees seeking the uppermost seat & getting the cup out of the Minrs hand
I thought I was well enough. But I was dead & stupid all the time: Afterward
I went to a place by my self to pray, & there I thought I heard like the great
rushing of many waters, & I thought at the time it was the Devil was making
that noise, & that he & all his angels were triumphing that I had eat & drunk
damnation. I kept up the form of praying in secret once a day or once in two
days: but I waxed worse & worse from time to time; & fell into a custom of
swearing & profaning the Lords name almost at every sentence but went on
in a formal way, & it was two years after that before I came to the Sacrament
again: & went there again to get more of a name of religion. But going out
to hear at the Tent after I had been at the Table [216/–] & hearing a Minr (Mr
Linnen)[3] preach on those words, What think ye of Christ,[4] the Lord gave me

---

[1] This partial duplicate account is an earlier version of the version found in Volume
    I:154–69.
[2] Insertion ['without any more questions']: McCulloch.
[3] Thomas Linning (also Lining or Linen) (1657–1733) – minister, Lesmahagow.
[4] Mt 22:42.

a shake, [ ]⁵ & I was made to see that I had been a despiser of Christ, & thought that the whole heaven was above my head were hanging full of judgments for my sin: and from that time I fell about seeking God more earnestly than what I did formerly: and thus I continued for four years: But can not say that I forsook the evils of my life, nor was I much taken up about my heart either: at length being one day at prayer in a field of pease, the devil fright'd me from it, by throwing as it were stones among the pease near where I was, and sometime after that he appeard one morning before break of day when the fire in the room was giving some light, he appeard at my bed side like a brown cow with a white face, & lookd in at me in the bed where I was lying waking, which frighted me terribly, & after that I laid aside all praying at Secret, thinking it was better laid it aside than to be frighted with the devil: & slighted all the offers of Christ, & when the Minr spoke of the danger of hell and damnation I thought he was speaking what was not true, and thus I continued for about a year without ever bowing a knee to God in Secret, & when it was gone about in the family, I weary'd much of it & could not endure it. After that I went to a good Christian family, where I was allowed two hours every day for Secret duty, but I spent it very badly & imploy'd little of it that way. The Sacrament in the place drawing nigh, that I might not fall under my masters displeasure, I fell to praying again, that I might get access to the Table & communicated, but with no suitable frame at all. After that I sometimes kept a form of prayer; but ofter neglected it, pretending I could not get a part for prayer, but alas it was because I had not a heart for prayer: I went sometimes to the Lords Table after this with no better disposition, & particularly at Douglass, where a Minr (Mr Lawson)⁶ preaching on Munday, said, There's a great multitude of you here present, we will never all meet again on Earth: & many of you will never meet till ye meet in hell: at hearing of which my heart rose up against him for saying so, & I reckond that was what he could not know, & should not have said it. After that I had my lot in a family, where there was very little but sometimes a dead form of religion, & much carnality, & that pleas'd me well, &, yet such was my pretense to strictness, that I would not go to hear the Minr of that parish where I was because he had read Porteous Act.⁷ [ ]⁸ [217/–] Falling under affliction I came home to a near Relations house with whom I could well enough agree ther,

---

⁵   Insertion ['& saw that I had been a great sinner, & before all that I had not believed Gods Word']: McCulloch.

⁶   McCulloch's records makes identification difficult, but (46) is likely John Lawson (d. 1757) – minister, Closeburn & Dalgarno.

⁷   A 1736 act of Parliament which required all ministers to read to their congregation a statement condemning the mob lynching of Captain John Porteous. Any minister who refused to read the act faced the threat of deposition, yet public opinion largely supported the captain's informal execution, and the laity often resented those ministers who read the act.

⁸   Insertion ['but went & heard another']: McCulloch.

because we agreed much in the same careless temper and way about serious Religion tho' I bless God I cannot now so well agree with her as to that point. I continued in much outward affliction but all that time, I was so wofully stupid & hardned [ ][9] that I never so much as essayed to seek God in the time of my affliction. And when I recovered I returnd to my former Evil ways. About half a year after this affliction I fell into two fevers after one another & was in very great bodily distress, & thought I would have died, but alas! I had no thought how I would appear before God: When I recovered from this last fever, I resolvd that I would enquire what was the Achan in my heart that provokd the Lord to send so many troubles upon me:[10] but I found my heart so hard, that it would not yield to God or ply to duty at all: & so I enquird no more after that matter. I then learnd so obdur'd & unbelieving that I did not believe that God would punish sinners in the other world. I had all along from my Childhood kept the Kirk on Sabbath days when I could get to it; but now I turnd so hardened in sin, that I would not go to the Kirk nor pray nor read the Bible, and my practice was very coarse, and my heart filld with Enmity against God & all his people. And thus I continued for about a Quarter of a year viz. from Candlemass to May 1742, & then perceiving that no body liked me as I apprehended, & hearing that a great deal of people were become praying people that were not formerly so, I fell to praying again in Secret. I also went again to the Kirk, but nothing I heard made any impression on me; —And hearing of noise at Cambuslang, I thought I would pray more fervently, to see if I could win to be like the people that were crying out of their sins & their lost state there. But in my essays this way, I thought to break my own heart my self, & did not look to the power & grace of God to break it, & so came of it. My master feeling sick & seemed like to die, & having no serious impressions on his Spirit, by what appeared, I essayed to pray for him but yet could neither pray for him nor my self. I went to Dalserf Sacrament, & on the Sabbath day I fell, into a great flooding of tears, but could not tell for what, for I felt nothing working upon me. In hearing a Minr (Mr Wisharts)[11] there on that text, if ye love me, keep my commandments,[12] I fell under a great terror of the day of judgments, because I thought I had neither lovd Christ nor kept his commandments. [218/–] I came away with that terror of the day of judgment but knew nothing of the love of Christ, but this terror wore off in a few days: after which I returned to my old formal careless way. About 20 days after that at Lesmahago Sacrament hearing a Minr (Mr Wilson of Castairs)[13] on the Text, They that

[9]   Insertion ['in carnal security']: McCulloch.
[10] Jos 7.
[11] George Wishart (1703–85) – minister, Edinburgh/Tron.
[12] Jn 14:15.
[13] John Wilson (1683–1746) – minister, Carstairs.

are whole need not the physician, but they that are sick,[14] but I did not find my self sick & so thought I would not seek after the Physician. Hearing a Minr (Mr Wm Ham. D-ss)[15] on these words, This is the cup & the N. T. &c:[16] ~~I haved almost no~~ when he was exhorting several sorts of sinners to come to Christ, I found a great stir in me & after Sermon, tho' I had no thoughts before of communicating, I went & got a Token to communicate, but by as dead and stupid as a stone again, both at the Table & after it: But what I heard that Minr say concerning Camb. & the work there, That there were some that call it a delusion but for his own part, he durst not call it so for his life, no nor for his soul, which was more than life, or for 10,000 worlds: for he has been there & had seen with his eyes & heard with his ears & been acquaint with the work there & was persuaded that it was of God. This raisd in me a great desire in my mind to come, & I found an impression on my Spirit that I might go there. Telling it to one that I designd to do so, he said God pity thee, for if thou go there, thou'll be put stark mad, But I told him That to Camb. I would go, tho I should be both to bind & to hold. Before I came off next Sabb. [ ][17] to Camb. I prayd the Lord might carry me not go off the way nor fall into bad company, & ~~was kept~~ when going to could get no body coming to it to bear me company. Coming there & seing a Minr (Mr McC)[18] coming down the Path going to the Tent to preach, when ever I look'd to him my heart took a beating, tho' I did not know for what. I joind in singing the Ps. he appointed to be sung at the Entry with more than ordinary sweetness : & heard the prayer with a great deal of satisfaction. Hearing him preach on that Text, If ye live after the flesh ye shall die, but if ye thro' the Spirit mortify the deeds of the flesh ye shall live.[19] I found a stir in my heart at hearing the Text read, but felt not much more, till he said If ye will not take a look of the death & sufferings of the Lord Jesus Christ & will ye take a [219/–] look of your own death & then take a look of his. These words I found come home with great power on my heart & cryd out in my heart What shall I do to be saved: but I did not cry out among the people: I would have set my mind to think of my own death, but I got but a small glance of a thought of it, till I fell immediatly into great distress of soul for my sins on the account of the dishonour done to God by them, which I then saw to be so great that I thought they were enough to have drownd a whole world in a flood of the wrath of God: I also had my thought turnd to think of the death of Christ & his sufferings, & fear my sins to be procuring cause of his sufferings, as if there had been no other persons sins but mine to do it, and I

---

[14]   Mt 9:12, Mk 2:17, Lk 5:31.
[15]   William Hamilton (1689–1769) – minister, Douglas.
[16]   Lk 22:20.
[17]   Insertion ['Aug 1']: McCulloch.
[18]   William McCulloch (1691–1771) – minister, Cambuslang.
[19]   Ro 8:13.

thought my sins alone were enough to procure them all: and found my heart filld with grief & much broken down at that sight & sense of all my sins, ~~especially~~ original & actual, my unbelief & going about to establish my own righteousness & not submitting to the righteousness of Christ as the cause of his sufferings. The Devil quickly perceivd that I had got an awakening that was like to prove effectual, & immediatly fell upon me, & cast in this thought as a dart into my mind That I would be damnd for these sins of mine justly as I had been the cause of Christs Sufferings: this put me into great confusion & had almost driven me to despair [ ]²⁰ tho' alas if I had thought right of it, I might easily have answered, That none would be damned for whose sins Christ suffered. But a merciful God kept me from sinking into despair, & put it into my heart That I must seek him else I would never win out of the state where I was, but ly there continually groaning & never get further. And after Sermon I accordingly set my self to seek him; & wrestled [ ]²¹ with the Lord by prayer, That he would give me Christ to save me from my sin & from that Eternal wrath which I saw I justly deservd by my sins. Next morning early I went out to the fields & prayd that he might not take away [220/–] the convictions he had given me, but go on & wound me to the bottom of my Soul, ~~that Christ might~~ and lead me to Christ as my only Physician. Next day being appointed to be observed but the Manse by the Societies for Prayer in Camb. before the 2d Sacramt there, I came in at the door of the Hall in the Manse, the Minr was giving out that line Ps. 65:1 to be sung, Praise waits for thee in Zion Lord &c: which gave [ ]²² a strange knell to my heart, for I was struck with a conviction that I had never praisd God nor prayd to him all my life: & how should I now praise or pray in that meeting for prayer: & the Minr looking to me as I entred, I apprehended that he knew what sort of person I had been, and this put me into great confusion. I then began to put up my petitions to God, that he would teach me how to pray & praise him: and the Lord was pleased to give me more [ ]²³ kindly sorrow for sin [. . .] sin than what I had the day before & may say I had never in my life formerly had any good sorrow for sin at all: all the remarkable sins of my former life were brought fresh to my remembrance, & there many Psalms sung that day, and every one of them I got a deeper wound, and more affecting Sense of my Sin, and particularly when the Minr calld for one (James Millar)²⁴ to pray, I was much grievd to hear that he would not come, & praise God, & when he came, in time of his prayer I still a more humbling Sense of Sin than before & when a woman crying out about the close of it, I thought I found Satan casting in wicked thoughts into my mind, and thought he had

²⁰ Insertion ['which was the thing he was aiming at']: McCulloch.
²¹ Insertion ['a good part of that night']: McCulloch.
²² Insertion ['came with']: McCulloch.
²³ Insertion ['of a']: McCulloch.
²⁴ James Miller – weaver and elder, Cambuslang.

got hold of me & was pulling me away, & cryd out in my heart, Lord Jesus
Save me from the Enemy of my salvation. I continued with them till about
one o'clock in the morning, & hearing a very young person about the close
give out the 80 Ps. 14 vs. to the close to be sung, Look down &c: I was in
great distress thinking my self to be cut off from all claim to Christ, by what
I heard, & was greatly ashamed to look about me among the people. Next
morning my distress of Spirit continuing I would have gladly have spoke to
a Minr after family worship in the Manse, but durst not [221/–] fearing he
would know that I was just a hypocrite. And I went on under that apprehension
that I was an hypocrite, & mourning for that & my other sins for about 20
days thereafter. I came back to Camb. next Sabbath with a great load of a
sense of sin again my Spirit. At hearing a Minr (Mr McC) Lecture, these
words, the corruptions of the heart are as an army drawn up in battel aray
fighting against God, gave with a power that came along, gave me a very deep
wound, finding it to be so indeed in my own heart: and I was willing to
submit to any thing that might be the will of God if he would take the
corruptions that were in my heart out of it. At ~~having~~ joining in singing the
51st Ps. as a mMnr (Mr McC) appointed to be sung in the Manse after sermon
where there were a great deal of people in distress, my soul tremble was great
& might justly say with David, My sins I ever see. On Munday after ~~the
Sacrament~~ I went to Bothwell where the Thanksgiving was after the
Sacrament there, & heard a Minr (Mr Steel of Dalserf)[25] preach, but in such
a legal strain, that by the time he had done, my heart was as dead as a stone:
but hearing another (Mr Henderson)[26] preach in a more Gospel way, at
hearing of the name of Christ, my heart again took a beating & I fell under
a shaking & trembling as a before [ ],[27] at which I ~~Secretly~~ was glad: & after
Sermon would have gladly spoke to him that preachd first [ ][28] about my souls
case, but could not get freedom to do it, & when I was coming by the Kirk
end coming away, that word came onto my mind, Wo wo to them that speak
peace to my people when there is no peace,[29] which made me conclude that
if I had gone & spoke to that Minr he would have spoken peace to me while
God had not yet intended peace, & made me see that I must only fly to Christ
for that healing virtue that is in his blood: and I carryd the lively impressions
of that upon me all that night. On the Fast before the Sacrament at Camb.
hearing a Minr preach (Mr Robe)[30] when he said God has made many of you
poor in the world, that your poverty might be scorge to whip you in into
Christ, but in stead of that, many of you have made it a whip to whip

[25] William Steel (1706–60) – minister, Dalserf.
[26] Richard Henderson (d. 1769) – minister, Blantyre.
[27] Insertion ['under a Sense of Sin']: McCulloch.
[28] Insertion ['being of my acquaintance']: McCulloch.
[29] Jer 6:14, Jer 8:11.
[30] James Robe (1688–1753) – minister, Kilsyth.

yourselves into hell: ye seek after no more by your meat & wages. And what is your wages, a poor two pence & day for a woman, what woman wilt then be content to sell thy soul for a two pence; this heightned my distress to a great degree, so that I was almost driven to despair [222/–] In hearing another Minr (Mr Curry)[31] preach read his Text, he that hath the bride is the bridegroom,[32] tho words of it made so great impression on me that I would have given 10,000 worlds if I had had them, to have had Christ to be the bridegroom of my soul: I went away sorrowing & seeking for Christ but found him not. I came & joind the meeting for Prayer at Camb. on ThursDay thereafter, but could get nothing, but only a deeper sorrow for sin. At Close an old grave man (Robert Wright)[33] praying & say O Father O Father, as he did, but I never did or could say so. I went & prayed by my self that night, that he would help me to pray & say so: but could not attain to do so: and the devil suggested to me, That I would never God to be my Father, nor be able to call him so: I replyd, That he was never let into the Secrets of heaven to know whether it would be so or not. On Fryday seeing two persons (Sergeant Forbes & Ingram More)[34] who had never seen one another before, very lovingly embrace one another at first sight, I threw my self down in great anguish, at the thought, These children of God know one another at first meeting, & love one another so dearly, but alas for wretched me! I know not them & they care not for me. After that going in that night to a Society for prayer, I had a great deal of tears for my Sin: I had sorrow of heart [ ][35] before; but I never got weeping for it till now. I did not that evening go to sermon, but thought I would be made to cry out among the people, which I was very unwilling to do, but that it would be better for me to go to a Secret place by my self & there mourn for sin; But alas, when I did go apart, I found my heart turn'd harder than it had been: & there I pleaded that I might not take sleep to my eyes nor slumber to my eye lids, till I got an Interest in Christ: & accordingly I slept none that night but spent all that night in prayer by my self & with others. On Saturday at the Sermon I got little or nothing sensibly: at night when joining & hearing some others pray (Serjeant Forbes) my distress turn'd so great that I could not hear what was said: upon which I went to a place by my self, & while I was praying with all the earnestness I could, It was said to me, He will come but not yet, This word coming with such life & power, that it made my drooping heart to flighter. Upon that Satan suggested, like one whispering into my ear that I had sin'd that [223/–] unpardonable Sin against the Holy Ghost, & that tho I had been mourning

---

31 John Currie (d. 1758) – minister, New Monkland. Son of John Currie (d. 1741), minister of Old Monkland.
32 Jn 3:29.
33 Robert Wright – lay person, Cambuslang.
34 Sergeant Daniel Forbes – lay person, Edinburgh and Ingram More – elder, Cambuslang.
35 Insertion ['and mourning']: McCulloch.

for some sins I would never get mourning for that sin, or never get it forgiven. I could make no answer to this, but cryd out to the Lord, What shall I do to be saved. It was answered, Believe in the Lord Jesus Christ & thou shalt be saved. I replied, It is not in me to believe, I neither can nor will believe, till thou work it in me & enable me to believe: but to this I got no answer: I continued praying some time after that: & then came to the Brae to hear sermons. When a Minr (Mr McC) at the entry of publick worship, gave out those words again (as before in the Manse) Ps. 65.1. Praise waits for thee on Zion Lord &c: these words pierced me thro' the heart more sharply than any two-edg'd sword could ever pierce thro' my bodily heart. After the Psalms were sung, I was very deeply affected with the Prayer: & found my heart drawn out earnestly after Christ, [ ][36] and an acceptance of him upon the terms of the Gospel. While the Tables were a serving, I felt much of the same frame, & would gladly have been at the Lords Table, but I knew I could not be admitted [ ]:[37] and therefore beg'd the Lord that he might make up that loss another way, that he might bellow with his own liberal hand, what he knew I needed and long'd for & give me a sight of my sins & a sense of his mercy. At night when I was in a barn with many others, I fell under a sense of my sin of unbelief, by it self to such a degree that I was made to shake & tremble; I was then made to see that all my life formerly, I had not believed Gods word, but perverted doubted denyd the truths of it in my heart; and particularly that I had never believd the Gospel report concerning Christ: and at day-break going apart for prayer by my self, that sense of unbelief continued and increased with me. On Munday morning hearing a Minr (Mr Webster) on that text, Fear not little flock &c:[38] As I went along with closs attention, I could get hold of nothing thro' the power of my unbelief, & my Soul distress was great: and next discourse (by Mr H—n) it rose to that degree that I could hear nothing & I was all along out of one swarf into another, but I got crying refraind with much ado hoping still to get all conceald & that no body should know of it & a secret pride of heart made me resolve that I would not be like others [ ][39] [224/–] I came in to the Manse after Sermon & was spoke to by a Minr (Mr Webster)[40] tho not the one I wanted: before he came to me while I sate in the Garret, Satan cast all my sins, as many at least, as he could muster up, into my mind with violence, & upbraided me with them, & then added those will keep thee out of heaven, that thou shall never get there. ~~Thou~~ [ ][41] art guilty of greater sins than those, those are not the tenth part of them. When I was coming out of the Manse, that word

---

[36] Insertion ['to a closure with him']: McCulloch..

[37] Insertion ['none being there from whom I could get a Token']: McCulloch.

[38] Lk 12:32.

[39] Insertion ['that did cry']: McCulloch.

[40] Alexander Webster (1707–84) – minister, Tolbooth/Edinburgh.

[41] Insertion ['I ansed, I am']: McCulloch.

came into my mind When I died sin revived:[42] & I ~~accordingly~~ [ ][43] felt as it were the company of two armies fighting within me: I had felt it so before but not so strongly as then: the one struggling to draw me to love this and the other idol, & the other to love Christ and his ways & the interest of his kingdom. My bodily trouble was such that next Lords day I was not able to go to the Kirk: but I still continued engag'd in the Spiritual Warfare, looking to Jesus the author and finisher of faith.

   Some short time after this, I fell under a temptation that all I had met with was but delusion, & was hereupon brought under great distress: but next day at Secret Prayer I got my heart pourd out before the Lord with much sweetness: but quickly after Satan suggested to me with great vehemence That I had sold my part of heaven for the pleasures of Sin, as Esau did his birth right & that there was no place for repentance: this put me into great confusion & anguish of Soul [ ][44] & I fell into a swarf & continued so for about an hour. And about an hour after that again having for some time recover'd out of the swarf, while I sate at the fire side, these words came into my heart, Fear not, for I have drunk the cup of the Fathers wrath, but you shall have a cup of consolation to your soul. This came with such great power & light, That the light that shin'd into my soul, was vastly brighter than the light of the sun at the clearest time that ever I saw it shine, especially at the third time, that those words came to me for they were thrice impressed upon me, tho at the first & 2d time they came with less power & light, & I could not then get it believed that it was Christ was speaking to me: but at the third time I firmly believed it to be so. I had my eyes shut before when those words came all the three times [225/–] but after the third time, when this marvelous light shone into my heart, I opened my eyes to see if it might be the light of the sun that shin'd in this manner but I saw the house was still dark, [ ][45] the day being misty & the sun not shining, This Glorious light continued shining still into my heart for about the space of an hour. And I then got such a discovery of the glory of Christ & my heart was so filld with love to Christ, that if every hair of my head had been a heart, it was too little to give him. Then my spirits were lifted up to sing, as in Rev. 5.12.13 Worthy is the Lamb that was slain to receive power & wisdom & riches & strength, and every— these words I uttered with great joy: & I invited all about me [ ][46] to help me to praise my God & Saviour for redeeming love: I then invited all the beasts of the Earth & fowls of the air, all that was under the heavens to help me praise him for what he had done for me who had been the chiefest among sinners. But all this I did

---

[42]   Ro 7:9.
[43]   Insertion ['that night as I went home']: McCulloch.
[44]   Insertion ['& made me cry out which occasioned many persons to come in where I was']: McCulloch.
[45]   Insertion ['but']: McCulloch.
[46]   Insertion ['& all men']: McCulloch.

in my heart without speaking any thing to any one about me. At length
looking about to my Mother, who was weeping, I askd her why she wept,
whether it was for Sins or for me. She answered Have I not good cause to
weep for you? I told her, no, she had no cause to weep for me, but ought
rather to rejoice that ever she had born me, & that ever Christ had choosd to
look by the great ones of the Earth, & to cast his love on me the chief of
sinners. A friend asked me if I could go to the door with her: I answered yes,
I was able to go to the door [ ]⁴⁷ & accordingly, tho e're these words came to
me, & sometime before, I was not able to go or stand or sit on the chair where
I was without two persons supporting me, one on each side of me, I now
went to the door with her with great vigour: then she askd me how I was, I
told her I was better than ever I was: she askd me if I had got any comfort;
yes I told her, I had got great comfort: She askd me what it was? I told her ~~I
would tell her~~ upon condition She would praise my God for what I had got,
I would tell her, but upon no other terms. She said That ever since she ~~was~~
knew any thing, she desired to praise God [. . .] [. . .] [. . .] [. . .] [. . .] [. . .]⁴⁸
she had been aiming at it [226/–] but did not know if ever she had praised
him aright: that she thought she had got an honest heart, but she did not deal
honestly with it which was the cause she oft walked in darkness: but that she
would go & praise God for me, as God would enable her: I then told her
what I had not with & how it came; at hearing of which, she fell into a flood
of tears & was not able to stand it longer, but got away from me. In this frame
in a good measure I continued for near four days. [During which when I
would have retird to the fields for secret prayer, I was so overjoyd that when
I saw a place to pray in, I knew not how to run fast enough to it.]⁴⁹ till on
Sabbath just when I was sitting in the Kirk, thinking on heaven, & that I
would be admitted to enter into the Holy of Holies, & how happy I would
then be: but as soon as a Minr (Mr Wm Steel of Dalsorf) came up and ~~sate
down~~ into the Pulpit, whenever I saw his face these thoughts and & that sweet
frame I had then and so long before ~~immediatly~~ instantly vanishd & wore
off. & I immediately fell into great distress, which being observed by some
about me, I was straightway carried out of the Kirk, and after I was out of
the Kirk–door, I fell under great terror ~~at the thoughts of my provoking God
to hide~~ under the hidings of Gods face. And being carried in to a house, Satan
threw in these words into my mind like a dart with a hasty violence, This
light thou had was but a delusive light, thou shalt never see it again, & God
will never have mercy upon such a sinner as thou: Another Minr ( ) coming
in to see me, as He came in I thought all the Legions of hell were about me,
going to drag me to hell, all my great sins were cast in my teeth; Christ hid

---

⁴⁷ Insertion ['as well as even I was ']: McCulloch.
⁴⁸ Illegible text due to worn tail edge.
⁴⁹ Text bracketed by McCulloch.

his face, & unbelief made me think it would be as the Devil had said: The Minr (Mr Linen)[50] said Ye are calling to the Lord Jesus Christ to come & save you, & he will come save you if you be seeking him with a sincere heart: at that I immediatly fell into a swarf & heard no more he said: & lay in that swarf for about an hour, & after I came out of it, these words came into my heart with power, Ps. 40.6,7 No sacrifice nor offerings&c:[51] Upon which I felt my heart drawn out in love to Christ [227/–] that when all would not do, he came & satisfied for his people. Then I felt a vigour in my body also, & went by my self to prayer, and beggd the Lord might open that Minrs eyes & let him see that he was not labouring faithfully for these souls he had the Charge of. I went to the Kirk in the afternoon to hear the same Minr, & immediatly when I entred the door I fell into the old confusion again: but resolvd I would if possible sit & hear him out, & heard him preach on 1 Tim. 5.10 well reported of for good works, if she—but heard with much pain of heart to think that tho I had done these things in the Text that were in themselves good, yet I had laid too much stress upon them & not done them from right principles & ends & in a holy manner; & to hear these things pressed, if I mistake not, in such a legal strain: & that there was little or nothing of Christ in the Sermon. On the Evening retiring to secret Prayer, the same words as before, Fear not for I have drunk the cup—came into my mind after with as great light & greater than before, which filld my heart with love to Christ and such joy in him that I was made to get up to my feet instantly & to leap for joy & the whole barn where I was was all shining: I was filld with wonder at the manifested glory of Christ to poor sinners, & that he had manifested so much of it to me a wretched sinner: from wondring I fell to prayer, & from prayer to wondring again: & in that manner I spent the whole night there. In the morning these words were impressd on my heart, Do not forget thy [ ][52] brethren nor thy mothers sins while thou art at the Throne with me, plead for them, plead and it shall be granted thee. So I pled for all my friends, my brethren, & spiritual Mothers sons [ ],[53] (for I have no brethren or mothers sons according to the flesh) and particularly while I was pleading for Cambuslang, that if there were any delusions among them, he would take them away, & make true Christianity appear, that the wicked might not open their mouths so wide against them, but that it might [228/–] appear that it was the work of his Holy Spirit & no delusion: and it was answered, I will purge away the dross from among the gold & make it to shine forth as bright gold; and that he would spare the Minr there, as a Son of the Church & add more souls to his Crown. I came away out of the place overjoy'd, but I was

50   Thomas Linning (also Lining or Linen) (1657–1733) – minister, Lesmahagow.
51   Ps 40:6–7, Scottish Psalter (metrical).
52   Insertion ['friends nor']: McCulloch.
53   Insertion ['of the Church']: McCulloch.

no sooner come away; but all my former fears & doubts return'd, & was made to conclude that all was nothing but delusion I had met with. I went to a Minr (75)[54] and told him the matter, who gave me but little comfort, but said, If this be the way of the working of the Spirit of the Lord, it is strange. He ask'd me if I was capable to know, if the shocking terrors I had been under, were the wounds of a friend, or if I thought they were the wounds of an Enemy? I told him, I could him, that I took them to have been the sharp arrows of the Almighty piercing my soul with convictions of sin, & therefore I took these to have been the wounds of a Friend: but I was then under such doubts & fears at the time, that I durst not then add that he had often taken me into the mount of communion with himself, & shew'd me his kindness & love. I told him also that I had cast my self at his footstool & was minded if I perishd to perish at his feet. He told me that if I had put on these Resolutions & would keep by them, that there was no fear of me, for there was never any that perishd at the feet of Sovereign mercy. And advis'd me to go to Secret Prayer, as an excellent mean of Relig. I did so but continued in distress that week. On Sabbath next (being the preparation Sabbath before the Sacrament at Douglass. In hearing a Minr (11)[55] saying That there were several places that were now watered from Heaven, as the Return of Prayers, & [ ][56] that the wrath of God was hanging over my head and would press me down to hell immediatly. That Minr at night, asked me if I was not willing to accept of Christ in all his offices. I told him, if my heart deceived me not, I was heartily willing to receive him in [229/–] all of those offices, as a prophet to teach a priest to save me by the merit of his sacrifice & power & intercession & as a king to rule over me. On Saturday hearing a Minr (26)[57] preach on that Text, Ye who were sometimes alienated & enemies[58]—I fell under such a Sense of the natural Enmity & deep corruption of my heart, which I could not get remov'd, that I could not forbear crying out some, tho I strove against it what I could. On Sabbath Evening, hearing that Minr (26) on that Text, Behold I come quickly &c:[59] Satan suggested to me That the whole Congregation saw Christ wearing a Crown of thorns & knew that it was I that had put it on his head, at which I cry'd out most bitterly thinking there was no mercy for me that had done so by my sin. I continu'd in great distress for about ten days after, & was willing to be put into any state [ ][60] if I might have Christ, within which was all I was seeking; when one day when I was at Secret Prayer at home, these words came into my mind, Is.51.21,22. Therefore

---

54 Identified in McCulloch's index as 'Wm Bogle 75'.
55 William Hamilton (1689–1769) – minister, Douglas.
56 Insertion ['I apprehended']: McCulloch.
57 William McCulloch (1691–1771) – minister, Cambuslang.
58 Col 1:21.
59 Rev 22:7, Rev 22:12.
60 Insertion ['if it had been even to go to hell it self']: McCulloch.

hear now thou afflicted & drunken but not with wine &c: These words came
with such power & life, & joy & love, that I could do no nothing but cry out,
but Glory to God in the highest for what he had done to me. And this frame
continued with me in a good measure for about a month after when I began
again to fear, that the Lord might leave me to my self, & suffer the corruptions
of my heart to break out, to his dishonour & the discredit of Religion, & that
might prove eternally ruining to my Soul: & after I had continued so, like a
person bound & fetterd, for about eight days, incapable to pray or read with
any composure, that word came into my heart, Ps.84.11, for God the Lords
a Sun & Shield, he'll grace & glory give, I will withhold no good from them
that uprightly do live. These words came with such power ~~that~~ & filld me so
with the love of Christ, that I thought that if every hair of my head had been
a life, I could have most willingly have given them all up to the greatest
torture that men & devils could inflict, for ~~the sake of Christ~~ his sake. [230/–]
~~Some time after that~~ About Janry 1. 1743., the Devil suggested to me, That
God was about to bring some dreadful stroke upon me, and therefore I must
either go out of the Place ~~I liv'd in, or murder~~ [ ][61] my self, & so prevent it,
for that I was going to hell forever, and that stroke would send me there. I
was so far left to my self, that I rose up from prayer immediatly & went into
the house: And the Lord in holy justice for complying with the Devils
suggestion & my other sins left me to go mourning under the hidings of his
face for a long time, & such was my anguish, that I was made with Job to
curse the day in which I was born, & to pray that the Sun might not shine on
it:[62] but I had it to notice, that [ ][63] ~~some co God was displeased with me
for it~~ there was not a brighter Sun shine day for a long time than it was. In
that distress I was driven such a length by the Devil, that I was brought to
downright atheism, & could not believe that there was a God: till one night
looking up to the Stars twinkling in the Sky, I ~~thought~~ began to say within
my self, If there be not a God in the Heavens, what could have put these Stars
there: & from the Stars I looked at the spires of grass about me, & wondred:
& from these, to my own body, & was made at the thought of the frame of
it, to ~~cry out I was~~ say with David I am fearfully & wonderfully made:[64] &
within a little I was made to cry out, Where is the God of all consolation
now gone! I went to Secret Prayer, but he ~~seemed to me~~ continued still to
hide his face & to cover himself as with a thick cloud that my prayers could
not pass thro.' I earnestly pleaded that he might bow the Heavens & come
down for I had much need of pity. Next Sabbath hearing a Minr (76)[65] preach

61   Insertion ['I was praying in, or murder']: McCulloch.
62   Job 3:1–4.
63   Insertion ['when that day came']: McCulloch.
64   Ps 139:14.
65   The duplicate account in Volume I:154 more accurately notes identification code as (85) – Mr
     Thomas Wharrie [MacQuarrie] (1679–1761) – minister, Lesmahagow (see Volume I, p. 168).

on that text Rom.3.24,25, Being justified &c: When he said that when Christ came to judge the world he would owne or receive none but such as had the Image of his Father stamped on them, tho I could not then see the Image of God on me, yet I was made to believe that he would yet Christ who was the image of the Invisible God would form his [231/–] form me after after his own image: & as he went on in preaching much of the Grace of God, I could do nothing but cry out in admiration in my heart, O free Grace! free rich Sovereign Grac! & went away rejoicing. But next Lords day tho' I heard that Minr (76)[66] on the same subject, I could get no hold laid on any thing for my comfort, apprehending my self to be but a hypocrite. But in time of his prayer at the Close, these words (tho' not utter'd by him) came into my heart, Hos.2.19,20. I will betrothe thee unto me—which filld me with great joy in Christ & love to Christ him. And indeed I never felt any thing of comfort or joy at any time, but I felt love to Christ going along with it. That week I felt my heart so warm'd with the love of Christ, that I would have given never so much for any person to talk to me on that subject. Next day hearing a Minr (75)[67] on that text, Wherefore, we receiving a kingdom &c:[68] Where he spoke much of the Love of Christ, particularly in his conquering purchasing a kingdom that cannot be moved, the kingdom of heaven & taking possession of it in their [ ][69] name: I found my heart filld with much of the love of Christ, & could not but bless him for directing his servant to speak on that subject, & giving me to believe & hope that he would receive me in due time to be for ever with him in his heavenly Kingdom.

[232/– through 239/– blank]

---

[66]   The duplicate account in Volume I:154 more accurately notes identification code as (85) – Mr
        Thomas Wharrie [MacQuarrie] (1679–1761) – minister, Lesmahagow.
[67]   Identified in McCulloch's index as 'Wm Bogle 75'.
[68]   Heb 12:28.
[69]   Insertion ['his peoples name']: McCulloch.

[244/-]¹ Mary Scot about 24

Reverand Sir, Befor Mr Whitfild came to Glasgou my time was spent in
nothing but madnes & vainity I would have stay'd at home on Sabath fornon
dresing my self for to go to Church afternons & prepared not my self by
prayer if some aufull despencation had not mov'd me to it such as thunder
or ye like, And qn I went to Church it was only to se & be seen, But took
littel head to qt I heard, as for outbreakings the world neither then nor since
could not nor canot charge me with ym

I reading Mr Whitfilds 2 leters to Bishop Tillitson² I was much afected
with ye last, so I had a strong inclination to hear him or he came, The first Text
I heard him preach on was The Lord our Righteousness,³ And acording to
his useuall freedom he said he could say, That ye Lord was his Reighteousnes,
which I was strongly afected with, & stayed so closs with me That I durst not
be qt I had bene before, Prayer then was a pleasure to me [243/2] I stay'd no
more on dresing my self as formerly I heard nine sermons of him in Glasgou &
fouer in Paisly I could no more take up with carnall mirth I was so Ompresed
with sprituall things & the medetation of yt I had heard or Read,

Then after yt i went to Cambuslang on a Monday I heard Mr Macolloch
on thes words, Thy shal look on him whom yy have perced & shal mourn,
But I was not afected with it, which made me to doubt if I was among thes
number fer qoum he was perced, Yet I atendedcloss at Cambslang, & heard
Mr Maculoch on yt Dispisest thou ye Riches of his Rom 2,4 In that sermon
he had a ofer of Christ which I was enabeled to Imbrace & Resolved to go to
yr first sacrament I could get so I went to Kinkintiloch, and heard Mr Rob
on ys words, Rom, ist 17 for yrin is is ye Reighteousnes of God Reveled from
faith to faith about ye end⁴ of ye sermon he discharged all from coming to ye
Tabell yt had not Imbreced Christ, which put me to a great confusion Because
I was jealeoues I had not done it, I went to ye Tent & sate yr all yt Satarday at
Lenth on persuaded me to go to ye church But againe I went yr [242/3] their
ye last Table was sereving, on Mondy I went to heare but could not ~~with~~ I was
confused, i came home in ye same condition, &c till Mr Whitfild came again

---

¹   In the original document the pages of this account are bound in reverse order, the text
reads sideways, and is in the hand of the respondant (Mary Scot). Page sequence has been
corrected to read in the intended order.

²   First two letters contained in: George Whitefield (1714–70) – evangelist (1714–70) – evangelist,
*Three Letters from the Reverend Mr. G. Whitefield viz., Letter I. To a friend in London, concerning
Archibishop Tillotson: Letter II. To the same, On the same subject: Letter III. To the inhabitants of
Maryland, Virginia, North and South-Carolina, concerning their negroes* (Philadelphia: Printed
and Sold by B. Franklin, 1740).

³   Jer 23:6, Jer 33:16.

⁴   Ro 1:17.

ye 2d year I felt no alteration to ye better he preached in ye highchurch yard on Isa, 53 who hath belived our report &c[5] But I gote as I thought no profet of it my hart was so full of coruption, yet I went after him to Cambuslang & stayed yt 2 days their that he was yr I was full of coruption unbelif & Rebelion against God, I came home so full of Rebelion yt I thought I had sined ye sin unto death, so I was for a long time I thought self & unbelif had Botled my hart against Christ, I continued so all yt sumer my hart I thought was fitted, with wickednes, 1742 Agust in hearing Mr Potter[6] on ys words Acts 20, 28, feed ye flock of God which he hath purchaced with his own blood, I though yr was such power came along with words, that I thought lightned me of a Burden of guilt I foremerely was Burdened with, At ye end of ye sermon 68, salm 18 Thou hast asended on hie Thou hast lede captivity captive Thou hast Receved gifts for men Even for ye Rebelioues[7] Thes. 2 texts or places Lightned me mightely for 3 or 4 days, I went to hear Mr Maculuch[8] on a Sabb hebr 7, 25, wherfor he is abell to save to ye outermost all yt come unto god throu him for he ever lives to make Intersesion [241/4] Ther was so much power came along with The whole of yt sermon That enabeled me to Belive That he was as willing as he was abel But losing my feeling I lost my Beliving ys next day even tho I had been convinced formerly of ye evil of unbelif.

And That sin of unbelif went a prodigeus lenth even to doubt of ye Being of a God, On that condition I went till I heard Mr Whitfild[9] on ys words, While yet a coming ye Devel throu him doun & Tare him[10] which was plainly my cace as he in yt sermon signified to me which I thought eased me a litel That even thes who are coming to Jesus are so temped as I was, Throu y' winter I was in great Darknes when I saw my coruption I knou yt I was But in Darknes I could not, I went in ys darknes till ye spring of ye year, And yn yr was a power put forth so yt I was enabeled to belive & I thought coruption was more subdued in me Then I heard Mr Stirling[11] on ist Epehes i3 i4 & he speaking of ye Love of God in sending his son in ye work of mans Redemption I was so Impresed with ye thought of yt Redemption That I thought my Bands was Loused my couruptions I thought got a fatell wound for several days I walked sencably under ye Light of His countenance I thought ye joy of ye Lord was my strenth I thought then I could have died I could

5   Isa 53:1.
6   Michael Potter – Professor of Divinity at the University of Glasgow (Robe, *Narratives of the Extraordinary Work at Cambuslang*, 82; D. Macfarlan, *The Revivals of the Eighteenth Century, Particularly at Cambuslang. With three sermons by the Rev. George Whitefield, taken in short hand. Compiled from original manuscripts and contemporary publications* (Edinburgh: Johnston & Hunter, 1847; Richard Owen Roberts, Publishers, 1980), 221).
7   Ps 68:18.
8   William McCulloch (1691–1771) – minister, Cambuslang.
9   George Whitefield (1714–70) – evangelist.
10   Lk 9:42.
11   James Stirling (d. 1773) – minister, Glasgow/Outer High Kirk.

have all ye days of ys week sabath days[12] And this sweet frame continued with me for four or five days after & I could then say The lines are fallen to me in pleasant places & I have a [240/–] goodly heritage. And I can truly say from my Experience That the Lords Service is a reward to it self, tho there were no reward after this life. I could then say The Lord is my portion saith my Lord therefore will I hope in him.[13]

---

[12] From this point on, the handwriting and spelling are markedly different from all that precedes it.
[13] La 3:24.

[245/-] b.q.   A Young Woman of 23 years[1]

In the former part of my Life before the year 1742, so far as I can now look
back upon it, my way of behaviour & temper was quiet & peaceable, but I
scarce had any form of praying in Secret till I was about twelve years old,
when I fell under some concern about Salvation, and would have prayd often
& went much, for a time, at the thoughts of my being liable to perish. A
~~Grandfather~~ [ ][2] observing me weeping & much cast down, asked me what
I wept for, but I did not incline to tell him what was the reason of it: he told
me, I might have as good a life as any of my neighbours, if I would take it.
After that, I became more easy, and was no more troubled about my Soul-case
as I had been. But falling in with some frolicksome persons, I became as vain
& frothy as they. [ ][3] I fell under some concern again about Salvation, & often
thought of turning Serious & Religious, & changing my way; but this went
no further with me than some weak Resolutions to grow & to do better; but
still I put it off for the present, & thought it was time enough yet for me to
turn grave & thoughtful. About 20, when a near friend of mine was dying,
I fell again under concern both for his Salvation & my own, and for some
time after he died, was much harassd with black & horrid temptations, but I
got no [246/-] sensible relief or outgate from them, but they just wore away
by degrees. And I turn'd more and more worldly & vain, and drew up with
young persons of that way, and still sought after this and the other vanity
in dress that I might be even with them: and I laid Secret Prayer aside, if it
was not at some happening time, and found my self very backward to any
thing of that kind.

And thus I continued till the Awakening brake out in Cambuslang In
Febry 1742; About two or three weeks after it began, I came to that place on
a Thursday, & heard a Minister (14)[4] preach, but do not now remember his
Text: but I got my mind much stay'd in hearing that Sermon, which I could
never say of my hearing any sermon before that: but I got not then a Sight
of my Sins, or of the remedy of Sin. Only I felt my heart drawn out much
in compassion & kindness to any I saw there in distress about their Souls
condition. And in joining with the congregation, in singing these words,
which that Minister gave out,

---

[1]   Bessie Lyon – the shorthand text in McCulloch's 'Index of persons' names who gave the
     foregoing accounts to Mr. McC' states: daughter of John Lyon, cooper in Blantyre. Taught
     to read the Bible, got Catechism to heart, and retained it pretty well.
[2]   Insertion ['Friend']: McCulloch.
[3]   Insertion ['Some time after']: McCulloch.
[4]   John McLaurin (1693–1754) – minister, Glasgow/Ramshorn.

> That Man who bearing precious seed,
> In going forth doth mourn
> He doubtless bringing back his sheaves
> Rejoicing shall return[5]

I felt a kind of heart melting, & was made to burst out into a flood of tears.

Next Lords day, I came & heard Sermon there, [247/–] but found my heart very hard, and not touched with kindness & sympathy to these in distress as on the Thursday before, and when I came into the Manse after sermon, I felt my heart very hard and averse to any thing that was good. It was much the same way with me in hearing sermon there on the Munday after; but coming in to the Manse after sermon, & hearing a Minister (26)[6] give out these words in the 6th Psalm to be sung,

> In thy great indignation
> O Lord rebuke me not[7]

I fell under such a dread of Gods wrath & fears he would rebuke me in his indignation, that I was made all to shake & tremble, & to cry out in great agony among the people there present. I went away in great distress, & continued under great Concern, coming to Camb. & returning from it almost every day. Some of these I walkt out the way with, were one day saying, There were none that were affected with this work, but these that had been ill folk, & had lived wickedly, & therefore they doubted if it was of God, while they spoke so, these words came into my mind with some power, Christ came not to call the righteous but sinners to repentance, upon which I was made to believe more firmly that it [ ]⁸ was from heaven. Another time, I was tempted to think that it was not the Lord was dealing with me, but that I was only striving to work up my own heart to some concern; & therefore I resolved I would not take any pains that way [248/–] but only go to Camb., without any thoughtfulness, & see if I would be affected with the Sermon there; and yet I found my heart so engag'd, that I could not forbear praying within my self almost all the way as I went. One night when I was in my bed, I was awaked suddenly with these words, spoken to me as one man would speak to another, Thou'rt a fool for ever going to Cambuslang: at which I started & got up quickly out of my bed, & knowing it was the Evil One, I spake out & said to him, Thou art both a Liar & the father of lies, & fell to my prayers to God, & was much composd again. About this time, coming to Camb. & hearing a minister (26) on that Text, In whom the God of this

---

⁵ Ps 126:6, Scottish Psalter (metrical).
⁶ William McCulloch (1691–1771) – minister, Cambuslang.
⁷ Ps 6:1.
⁸ Insertion ['this work']: McCulloch.

world has blinded the minds of them that believe not &c:[9] I then got a Sight and Sense of my Sins that was very affecting to me; and from that time I got a sense of my ~~natural~~ enmity & averseness to God & all that was spiritually good, which I had never got before; and next day (Friday) when I was at home at my work, I was made to see my present danger of perishing in a very affecting manner, & apprehended my Condition, like that of one on the top of a high tree, having nothing to take hold of & the wind blowing fiercely upon him: & I thought I would not only go to Hell when I died, but that I would be sent just alive into the Pit of perdition, & just saw my self lost and undone at present. And while I was in this distressed condition, it was strongly suggested to me, to say, I would not be beholden to God [249/–] for mercy; but this I refusd to do, & rejected it with abhorrence: but my distress continuing, a Minister (1) was sent for, who gave me good Exhortations, but I could lay no hold on any thing comfortable he said. Shortly after this, hearing a Preacher (33)[10] discoursing much of Unbelief, in his sermon at Camb. I got a deep conviction of the evil of that Sin, which I had never got a sense of before, tho I had several times before that got an affecting sense of multitudes of my other sins. And that same day, as I was going home, I sate down by the way, & read the third chapter of Zechariah, which first cast up to me upon opening the Bible, and was much easd of the burden of Soul-distress I was under, & comforted in reading it, & particularly with that passage about the taking away the filthy garments from Joshua & appointing him change of raiment;[11] I had not however such a clear understanding of it then as afterward when I heard a Minister (26) lecture on it. ~~On reading this chapter~~ [ ],[12] I fell on the ground before the Lord, & earnestly beggd of him, that he would give me grace to serve him, & keep me from sinning against him; for that nothing would satisfy me but that, & I was willing to undergo any thing he saw fit, if he would help me to do so.

Some time not long after this, coming to Camb. & hearing a Minister (14) preach concerning the Israelites being enjoind to have their door posts & lintels sprinkled with the blood of the Paschal Lamb, & shewing how we ought to have our hearts & Consciences sprinkled [250/–] with the blood of Christ the Lamb of God that takes away the sins of the world. I was under great concern to have my heart & conscience sprinkled with that precious blood, and it was comfortable tidings when he further said, That one might

[9]   2 Co 4:4.
[10]   Andrew Arrott (1683–1760) – minister, Dunnichen, and brother-in-law of John Willison (1680–1750). He joined the Secession/Associate Presbytery in October 1742 (Arthur Fawcett, *The Cambuslang Revival: The Scottish Evangelical Revival of the Eighteenth Century* (London: the Banner of Truth Trust, 1971; The Banner of Truth Trust, 1996), 196; Scott, *Fasti Ecclesiae Scoticanae*).
[11]   Zec 3:4.
[12]   Insertion ['One day being at home']: McCulloch.

have his soul sprinkled with it, & yet not know of it at the time. After Sermon
I came into the Manse, where hearing an old grave man (56)[13] give out the
91st Psalm to be sung, as these words were a reading & singing

> He that doth in the Secret Place
> Of the Most High reside
> Under the shade of him that is
> The' Almighty shall abide[14]

I found my heart drawn out after God, and burning in love to Christ, tho' yet
there was still a contrary party within me drawing it back ~~from~~ again. And
when that good man in his Prayer said, O for the wings of faith to fly above
the world & all the things of it, I was made earnestly to join in that Petition,
& found my heart mounting upwards towards Heaven, but yet corruption
was pulling me back & weighing me down again. Next day, a Minister (1)[15]
coming to see me, asked me, If I was wanting to be an open Professor? I said
no; I wanted to serve him with the hidden man of the heart, saying, O that
he would give me to trust under the Shadow of Christs wings, and that he
would never leave me nor forsake me. One day hearing part of a Psalm sung
in the Manse, these words as they were a singing were applied to me with
much sweetness, & power,
      If they my laws break & do not not

> Keep my commandments,
> I'll visit then their faults with rods
> Their sins with chastisements
> Yet I'll not take my love from him
> Nor false my promise make &c:[16]

[251/–] Another time as I was hearing the Exhortations in the Manse, inviting
sinners to come to Christ, polluted in their blood & filthy as they were, &
he would wash & save & freely justify them: In time of these Exhortations
& Prayers after them, I was much troubled, that I found so much of selfish
principle within me mingling with my duties, & that I could not get free of
it, when I would come to Jesus Christ: but in singing that Psalm with the rest,
I was enabled to plead with God against this selfish disposition, with much
earnestness, in these words of the Psalmist, then apply'd to me.

> How long take counsel in my Soul
> Still sad in heart shall I

13 Robert Wright – lay person, Cambuslang.
14 Ps 91:1, Scottish Psalter (metrical).
15 Richard Henderson (d. 1769) – minister, Blantyre.
16 Ps 89:31–3, Scottish Psalter (metrical).

How long exalted over me
Shall be mine Enemy?
O Lord my God consider well
And answer to me make &c:[17]

About the beginning of May 1742, I came to Camb. and heard a Minister
(17)[18] on Saturday Evening, preach concerning the trembling Jaylor, &
making large offers of Christ to the Hearers: but I found my heart unwilling
to receive him or to come to him on his own terms, at which I was much
grieved & distress'd. Next morning before Sermon began, these words Hos.
6. 1, 2, 3 Come let us return to the Lord, for he hath rent &c: were applied to
me with some comfort as I read them. And so also that word that cast up to
me in my Bible, Then they that feared the Lord spake often one to another
&c.[19] gave me much relief & comfort. That day in hearing a Minister (17) on
that Text, Sir we would see Jesus,[20] I found strong desires raised in my heart
to see him; [252/–] but I continued in much darkness, & so also in hearing
another Sermon after that; and much unwillingness to come to Christ still
prevaild, which was a great grief of heart to me. And thus it continued with
me for about 10 days after, when after I had heard Sermons on a Tuesday,
I came into the Manse, much cast down, and distressd with a Sense of my
Ignorance, Unbelief, Selfishness & averseness to come to Christ & to close
with him on his own terms, and that I could not heartily bless God for Jesus
Christ, (which was one of the Marks a Minister that had been preaching (14)
had given of true believers; and that I could not bless him for any Spiritual
favours. While I sate in the Hall in a deep Sense of my Sins, & was thinking
of going away home in a worse Condition than ever I was, I was urged by
one whom I knew not, to rise and come & speak to a Minister (14) in the
Closet: I was averse to do it, having nothing to say that was good to that
Minister; but when I came to him, he asked me about the condition I had
been in formerly, & that I was in at present & the grounds of my weeping
& distress, I told him I thought I was now turnd worse than ever, & that I
had often been at the point of returning to my old carnal life & to go back
to Spiritual Egypt again; & that I could not be thankful for Christ or my
Spiritual mercies: he told in a great many Instances, what reason I had to
be thankful that the Lord had not given up with me altogether, that he had
not suffered me to return to my sinful ways, that he was yet dealing with
me by Convictions making new offers of Christ, & keeping the door of
mercy [253/–] still open, with many things to that purpose. After he had
been speaking in this strain for some time, another Minister standing by,

---

[17]   Ps 13:2–3, Scottish Psalter (metrical).
[18]   William McKnight (1685–1750) – minister, Irvine.
[19]   Mal 3:16.
[20]   Jn 12:21.

turning his face to me, said, Gods mercies I will ever sing: these words, as he repeated them, came with such a mighty power to my heart, and filled with me with so great joy, that I could not refrain crying out aloud for joy, before all present in the Closet; at the thoughts of Gods wonderful mercies to me, that he had been shewing me mercy, when I had been sinning against him, & mercifully keeping me back from turning away quite from him. Now I was affected with my great Ignorance of God, & his ways; now I was made heartily thankful for his mercies toward me; & above all to bless God for the mercy of mercies Jesus Christ his unspeakable gift [].[21] Now I was made heartily willing to come to him & to close with in all his offices, and to accept of him on any terms, and to be eternally indebted to him & the riches of free grace in him; & to hope that I should sing of the mercies of God for ever in Heaven. This frame continued with with me in some measure for some days; but much of a Sense of the evil of heart-Corruptions, came to be my Exercise, and as the Love & joy abated I found my Corruptions more strong & my darkness increasing. And while I was much bowd down on Sabbath after, I was again quickened & revived by that word, If thou, Lord, mark iniquity, O Lord, who shall stand.

About the End of May 1742, hearing a minister (33) on that Text on a Munday at Camb. I write unto you [254/–] little children because your sins are forgiven you for his names sake,[22] I found my heart sweetly agreeing to it, that God forgives sins for his own names sake. Some time after that, hearing another Minister (46)[23] on Saturdays night in the Kirk of Camb: on that Text, What think ye of Christ?[24] I was in hearing of it, filled with a deep sense of my own vileness & filthiness by Sin, & of Christs Glory and Excellency, and with great love to him & joy in him.

At this first Sacrament at Camb. in 1742, I found Corruption very strong, & got nothing sensibly at the Lords Table: but being much cast down at the thoughts of this after that occasion was over, as I was reading Guthries Tryal of a Saving Interest[25] where he shews how persons should covenant with God before they communicate, how they should bless God for sending & giving Christ, & Christ for coming and giving himself for his Elect, & the Holy Spirit for applying Christ to Souls; the Lord was pleased to enable me to do so, & in doing it, to give me much comfort.

---

[21] Insertion ['& my heart with just burning within me with love to Christ']: McCulloch.

[22] 1 Jn 2:12.

[23] McCulloch's records makes identification difficult, but (46) is likely to be John Lawson (d. 1757) – minister, Closeburn and Dalgarno.

[24] Mt 22:42.

[25] William Guthrie, *The Christians Great Interest: Or a Short Treatise, divided into two parts: the first whereof containeth, the tryal of a saving interest in Christ. The second, pointeth forth plainly, the way how to attain it: wherein somewhat is likewise spoken to the manner of express covenanting with God. By W. Guthrie, minister of the Gospel in Scotland* (Kings Arms in Poultry: printed for Dorman Newman, 1681).

At the 2d Sacrament there I felt the power & strength of Corruption much broken, compar'd to what it had been. At the first Sacrament at Camb. in 1743, while a Minister (41)[26] said, I see there are severals of you that are under great distress of Soul, & ye cannot tell, ye dare not tell, what is the ground of your distress, none but God & your own Consciences know it: These words were brought home to my heart & comforted me at the thoughts that there were others in such distress as well as I, and that tho I durst not, I could not tell it [255/–] to man, yet that the Lord knew it, & could help me under me. In hearing another Minister (13)[27] on these words, on Sabbath Evening, But now I go my way to him that sent me, & none of you asketh me, whither goest thou. But because I have said these things unto you, sorrow hath filled your heart, Joh. 16. 5, 6. I felt my heart greatly affected & melted within me in time of that Sermon. I would gladly have gone straight away to Heaven to Christ: & sorrow fill'd my heart that I must stay a while in this Sinful World.

At the Sacrament at Blantyre in 1743, hearing a Minister (26) on Saturday on that Text, The Lord is my portion faith my soul,[28] Lam. I thought at hearing the Text, that I could have said the words of the Text as my own words, but in hearing the Sermon on it, I was in great distress at the thoughts that I had too much made the world my portion: but on Munday hearing that Minister on these words, Christ in you the hope of Glory, what was said was made relieving and comforting to my Soul.

To draw to a close: vain frothy company was formerly agreeable to me: now I have not that pleasure in any Company that appear to be of that temper & way; but when they fall into any thing of that kind, I'm (I) choose gladly [ ][29] to withdraw from them. Before March 1742, I usd to make lies to excuse my self when I was challengd by others for any thing I did or said amiss; but since that time to this (Mar. 9. 1744.) I durst never knowingly offer to do so, because it is dishonoring to God, & wounding to my own Conscience. & when I at any time stumble out with my thing that is not [256/–] true, it is a grief of heart to me afterward. In my former life before March 1742, I could allow my self to neglect Secret Prayer; & have little or no uneasiness for such neglects; but since that time, I cannot allow my self to neglect it, even tho I find my self much out of a due frame for going about it; because I know it is a commanded duty, & the neglect of it brings on carnal Security, & I have sometimes felt Sensible Soul advantage in that duty. I cannot approve the way of Self-commendation & have good reason, for I have no good at all to say of my Self, but every thing that is Evil. But yet I would fain say something to the commendation of free-grace if I could; and I think I may venture to say this,

---

[26]   Thomas Gillespie (1708–74) – minister, Carnock; founder of Relief Church in 1761.
[27]   John Willison (1680–1750) – minister, South Church, Dundee.
[28]   La 3:24.
[29]   Insertion ['glad of an occasion to'; alter 'I' to read 'I'm']: McCulloch.

to the praise of the Lord's free-grace, That I now for these two years past find it better with me when I am at my worst; than ever it was formerly when I was at my best. When Temptations press upon me, some suitable passage of Scripture usually is brought into my mind, tho not oftimes with great power, yet so as usually to break the power of the Temptation [ ],[30] & to fence my heart against yielding to it. Wherefore when others about me would have been speaking of Good, I had no fear to put in my word: but now I often dare not put in my word with others, fearing least I should speak of what is good in a hypocritical manner. I often want the Lords gracious & sensible presence with me, but I am never without some desires & longings after it weaker or stronger: & I am made sometimes earnestly to long for Heaven that I any be freed from Sin & be there with Christ for ever

To his name be all Glory & praise. Amen.

---

[30] Insertion ['in some measure']: McCulloch.

[257/–] b.f. A Young Woman of 19 years.[1]

As to the former part of my Life, I livd much in the same manner as other
morally honest people do, with some outward profession of Religion. I
sometime minded Secret Prayer & sometimes neglected it. I usually went to
the Kirk on Sabbaths being oblig'd to do so by my Parents: but I little minded
what I heard, but came away just as I went there: and if I could get any little
note to bring home to my Father, I thought all was well enough. I could not
endure to hear persons talk about things serious, but shund it as much I could.
My Father kept up Family Worship twice in ordinary days and three times on
Sabbaths; & that was a great weariness to me, & I reckon'd all that time lost
to me, & would gladly have been absent from such occasions but durst not.

And thus matters continued with me till the Awakening at Cambuslang in
the Spring 1742, when I went and heard there every Sabbath day, & often also
on week days: and fell under some [258/–] Concern in hearing Sermons &
seeing the people in distress there: and my concern about Salvation increased
particularly one Sabbath in May 1742 after I had been hearing sermons there,
so that I was made to say within my Self, Oh what is this! What a poor
wretched sinner I am I that still come & go this way so long? Shall I go away
without Christ this night also? Oh I cannot think of going away this night
without Christ. And thereupon ~~another~~ I resolvd I would go into the Manse
& see if I might meet with him there: but after staying at worship there, till
it was about ten o' clock at night, another young Woman & I resolvd upon
going home to Glasglow together: but we were got but a very little way
from the Manse, till that other young Woman who was walking on a small
space ~~before~~ [ ][2] me, cry'd out, Oh what shall I do! lost and undone! Upon
hearing her cry out so, I ran back to hold her up or lift her up: and the minute
I got hold of her, I was struck to the heart my self, with a Sense of my Sin: &
cry out as fast as she Oh lost & undone What shall I do. No particular word
[259/–] of Scripture was then brought to my mind, but my Conscience was
immediatly awakned, & I was made to see that I was in a lost and perishing
condition, & a deep Sense of the Evil of Sin as dishonoring to God was set
home upon my ~~heart~~ Conscience,[3] but this Conviction of Sin at this time
was only in a more general way. The other young woman return'd to the
Manse; but a man who was going to Glasglow with a Lass going along with
him, persuaded me to go with him to Glasglow, and as we went out the way,

---

1   Jean Walker – daughter of Archibald Walker, shoemaker in Calder. Taught to read the
    Bible, got part of the Catechism to heart, and retained it.
2   Insertion ['behind']: McCulloch.
3   Textual overwrite, 'Conscience' superimposed upon 'heart'.

was laying out many comfortable Promises before me, but I could lay hold
on none of them: I could not think that God would ever shew mercy to such
a sinner as I had been. I was afraid however, that the concern I was under,
would wear off before I & that I would turn as bad as ever I had been, and
so Religion would suffer on my account, if any should notice the concern
I was in: and therefore I thought I would conceal it, as much as possible: &
essay'd to do so when I came home; but it would not conceal within me: for
a little after I sate down, my Soul-distress was so [260/–] great, that I could
not forbear crying out, & these about me were obligd to take hold of me for
some time. I went next day to Cambuslang but got nothing by way of Relief:
but my convictions increasd, and came to be more particular from time to
time. And my distress was sometimes so great under them, that when I have
been walking on the Street, I been ready to think I would have sunk thro'
the ground. I continued about five or six weeks in great distress before I got
any Relief: in which time I could sleep or eat little: I essayed to work some,
now and then, but my mind still lay another way. I would almost constantly
have inclind to read or pray, if I could have got it done. One night after I had
been in great distress, and had gone to bed, I dream'd I was just hanging over
the mouth of hell, and ready to fall in; & while I was struggling to get up, &
could not, & crying to the Lord for help, I thought he pulld me up & set me
in his way: and when I awak'd I conceivd some hope he would do so: but I
could take little comfort from it because it was but a dream.

[261/–] One day I was hearing a Minister ( ) in the North-West Kirk of
Glasgow, I felt my heart glowing with love to Christ, & joy springing up in
my Soul, and that night, while my Mother was about Family Worship, that
word was pressd on my heart, I have loved thee with an everlasting love:[4]
upon which I Was made to believe that it was so, & at the belief and thoughts
of Gods Eternal love to such a poor unworthy Sinner as I, I was made to rejoice
greatly []^5 and found my heart inflam'd with love to him. I then also got
a very humbling Sense of my Unbelief, & was made to see that Christ was
ten thousand times more willing to receive me than I was to come to him.
And from that day to this (Nov. 9. 1743) which is about 5 quarters of a Year,
I could never once doubt of his Love to me.

The 2d Sacrament Occasion at Cambuslang drawing bear, I long'd much
to be a Partaker there: And in order to I went to the Minister ( ) in whose
quarter I livd to be examind & to get a Line to obtain a Token: & after he
had askd me many Questions, he sent me to the Elder of that Proportion
where I livd to get a Line [262/–] from him as to my outward behaviour,
who readily gave me one, with which I returnd to the Minister & got his
Line for a Token at Cambuslang, and upon producing it got a Token there.

---

4   Jer 31:3.
5   Insertion ['& could not refrain crying out aloud for joy']: McCulloch.

I found all the Sermons there brought so powerfully & closly home to me, as if there had been no other but my self to hear. I was enabled by faith to embrace Christ as offered in the Gospel, & got a more affecting Sense of Sin at the Lord's Table, & was filled with joy and peace in believing.

After this, I was enabled by grace, to live much above the world, & got my heart in a good measure set upon things above. And last Winter I have been often so overjoyd when I was walking on the Streets, or about my work, that I scarce knew where I was, & there seem'd to be scarce any thing of me out of Heaven but the Body. At other times Sin makes my life a burden to me; and because I cannot live here without Sin, but am daylie offending him & coming short of his Glory in all I do, I have often made to long for death to free me from a body of sin & death, & for Heaven where I shall serve & enjoy him for ever, without any sinful imperfection & without any interruption.

[263/–] When I wak'd in the morning, I often use to be greatly vex'd at my self, that I should have slept so long, & that I was not up long before praising God for what he had done for my Soul; & would have got up quickly to that Exercise.

At the Sacrament-Occasion in Glasglow in the Spring 1742, as it drew near I fell under a deep sense of my unworthiness, and thought I was not worthy to eat of the Crumbs that fell from the childrens Table: & tho I knew yet I knew the Lord was calling me to come to his Holy Table, and durst not stay away. When I came there, that word came into my heart with power, Fear not, for I have redeemd thee[6] from thy sins & iniquities, & then the Love of Christ was so shed abroad in my heart, that I was quite transported with it. And tho I could not doubt but the Lord had forgiven me, yet I could not forgive my self for often & so greatly offending him, or never will. And I would have been glad if I had had 1000 tongues to praise him & to recommend Christ to others, & if I had had 1000 Lives, I thought I would have been willing, if he enabled [ ][7] me, to lay them all down for his sake, & all too little for him who had done so much for me.

[264/–] I attended both the Sacrament Occasion at Cambuslang in 1743. And could say of both, that they were a Bethel to my Soul. I sate down under Christs Shadow there, & his fruit was sweet to my taste. He shed abroad his Love richly in my heart. He gave me an Earnest of Heaven & made me long for the full Enjoyment. And still the more he gave me to see of his Glory by the eye of faith, the more I was made to abhor my self in dust & ashes, on the account of my Sin & unworthiness.

These are but a few kinds of the many things I could say to the thro' Grace to the Commendation of Christ & his love to poor unworthy me: but I hope

---

[6]   Isa 43:1.
[7]   Insertion ['and called']: McCulloch.

to spend an Eternity in loving admiring & praising him in another way than I am now capable. ~~May~~ And I hope it will not be long to that time. Even so come Lord Jesus. Amen.

[265/–] a.z.[1]

It pleased God to preserve in a great measure outwardly blameless before
the world all my Life hitherto, sometimes living at home with my Father &
sometimes at service. My Parents brought me up, as they did all their other
Children, in a religious manner. I all along from my Infancy kept up a form of
praying in secret, and now and then read my Bible, and attended on Publick
Ordinances, but rested in these things.

When I was about 17 years of age, I fell under strong ~~Convictions~~ Awakenings,
a little before the Sacrament was to be administred in the Parish, and was much
excited by the motions of the Holy Spirit striving with me, to a Concern to
prepare for the Lords Supper, particularly by that Word that awakned me
one night while I was sleeping, Awake thou Sleeper, and call upon God, and
go forward: at that I immediatly sate up in my bed, but comply'd no further
but ~~sate~~[2] lay down again. But this Awakening had not abiding effects, but
after that Sacrament Occasion [ ],[3] I just return'd to my old Course again.

In hearing a Minister (26)[4] in December 1741 preach on that Text, We
then as Workers together with him beseech you also that ye receive not the
Grace of God in vain: for he saith, I have heard thee in a time accepted, & in
the day [266/–] of Salvation have I succoured thee: behold now is the accepted
time, now is the day of Salvation;[5] I fell under deep Convictions of my Sin
& misery: & was made Sensible that my Original Sin alone, tho I had had no
actual Sin, was enough in justice to damn me for ever. [ ][6]

A Weekly Lecture being set up in the Parish on Thursdays, about the first
of February 1742, I had such a thirst after the Word, and such an earnest desire
to get leave to hear it, particularly on Thursday Febr. 11th, that I sate up a
good part of the night before, spinning at my Wheel, to make up the time
at my Work, that I was to spend next day at the Weekly Lecture, that so my
Master and Mistress might have no ground to complain that I neglected my
Work with them by my going to such Occasions: tho' this was not what they
required of me, but on the contrary bade me oftner than once, go to my bed.

On Sabbath the 14th of Febry hearing a Minister (26) preach on that Text
Joh. 3.3,5, on which he had been insisting for a long time before, —Except

---

[1]   Catherine Jackson – daughter of James Jackson, elder at Cambuslang. Sister of narrative
    respondants Janet Jackson (I:15–25 and II:273–81) and Elizabeth Jackson (I:67–72).
[2]   Textual overwrite, 'Lay' superimposed upon 'sate'.
[3]   Insertion ['was over']: McCulloch.
[4]   William McCulloch (1691–1771) – minister, Cambuslang.
[5]   2 Co 6:1–2.
[6]   Insertion ['and from that time my Convictions of actual Sins went on from day to day']:
    McCulloch.

a man be born again he cannot see the kingdom of God, my Convictions & Soul-distress in time of Sermon increasd to a very high degree. After Sermon, I went with my two Sisters to a friends house near by the Kirk. And while I sate there weeping in great Agony of Soul bewailing my wretched & Sinful Condition, [267/–] apprehending that there was no thing but the blackness of darkness in hell fire for ever for me, and that I was ready every moment to fall into it, a Preacher ( ) and another person now an Elder ( ) came to the Place where I was, and spoke several things suitable to my Case. But for what followed that night before I went home, I refer to the following Account of it, writen by the Minister, next morning, & drawn up from his own Memory, and that of the other two persons just now spoken of, which is all true so far as I can remember, and the truth of it can yet also be attested by many others who were then present.

The Preacher ( ) ask'd her, what particular sins lay heavy upon her Conscience at the time? She in answer bitterly bewaild her despising Gospel Ordinances dispensd in the Parish, that she had gone to hear the Seceders, and that she had gone astray like a lost sheep. She also deeply bewaild her Unbelief, that she had received Gospel grace in vain, mispent much precious time; that she had been a Lover of pleasures more than a lover of God; that she had neglected to comply with that Call she had met with, to prepare for communicating in this Parish; and that she had grudged [ ][7] at the Conduct of Divine Providence in giving (what she thought) an Effectual Call of her Sister and passing by her self.

[268/–] After some little time, she was brought accompanied by the two Persons mentioned & her two Sisters, to the Ministers Closet, weeping bitterly all along as she walkt with them thither, and for some considerable time after she was there. After She had sat down beside the Minister, at his desire, he ask'd her, What it was that aild her?, She cry'd out, Oh! What shall I do, what shall I do? What shall I do? It was some time e're he could get in a word for her weeping and crying; at length he replied, Believe on the Lord Jesus Christ, and thou shalt be saved.[8] She still bitterly weeping, cry'd out, Oh! but my Sins are so great he will not receive me: my Sins, Oh! my Sins are great and hainous. He answered, Come let us reason together, saith the Lord, tho your Sins be as Scarlet, they shall be white as snow; tho they be red as crimson, they shall be as wool. Oh no! cryd she in anguish, He will not accept of me, He will not accept of me. [I][9] but he will, said the Minister: If you be willing to come to him and accept of him; I assure you in his name, he is willing to accept of you: Whatever you have been, whatever you have done, come to him, and he will not reject you. When

---

[7]   Insertion ['in her heart']: McCulloch.
[8]   Ac 16:31.
[9]   Aye.

there is a Willingness on both sides, [269/–] he is willing, and you, I think, are willing, what should hinder the concluding of the blessed Bargain, the match between Christ and your Soul; Come then to him & I assure you [ ]¹⁰ he will in no wise cast you out. At this she stopt her weeping a little, & seem'd to be somewhat calm'd for a small space. Some considerable time after this day, being asked what she was about during this Pause? She said, She was aiming, in dependance on Grace, to believe in Christ, and to comply with these gracious Calls & Invitations. But within a little, she bursted out in tears & weeping, crying out, Oh my Sins! my Sins! He will not receive me, He will not receive me, I'm the chief of Sinners. The Minister reply'd, are you a greater Sinner that the Apostle Paul? he was the Chief of Sinners, as he calls himself, yet he obtained mercy, Christ forgave him all his Sins, & received him into favour; and he is set forth as a Pattern & Instance of the Riches of the free grace & mercy of Christ, to encourage others to believe on him to the End of the World: come to him then, and ye shall obtain mercy, as the Apostle Paul did. She again crying out, Oh, but he will not receive me, he will not accept of me: my Sins! my Sins! Yes, he will accept of you, said the Minister: What greater Evidences would you have of his willingness to accept of you: he shed his precious [270/–] blood, his hearts blood, out of love to such as you, and his blood can cleanse you from all your Sins, be what they will, & fetch out the deepest stain of them on your Soul: he hath made peace by the blood of his Cross: the blood of Christ, who thro' the Eternal Spirit offered himself a Sacrifice without spot to God, will purge your Conscience from dead works, to fit you for serving the living God. She hereupon stopt her crying & calm'd a little, and said mournfully, Oh! but I cannot believe in the Lord Jesus Christ that I may be saved. Will you, said he, cry out to him with that poor man in the Gospel, Lord, I believe, or Lord I would believe, help thou my Unbelief. She immediatly fell to repeating these words, and did with her whole heart aim at the Exercise of faith in Christ, and was in some measure helped to it (as she told afterwards) and then refrain'd her weeping a little: but, unbelief again prevailing, she in a short space, cry'd out again, Oh! He will not accept of me. [I]¹¹ but he will, said the Minister, himself assures you he will; whosoever will let him take of the water of life freely. But she going on weeping bitterly, Come said the Minister, Shall we pray for a Pull of Gods Almighty Arm to draw you to Christ. O yes, yes, said she, and got up on her feet. Some of the Company said she would not be able to stand (for that was the Posture design'd) in time of Prayer: There is no fear of that, [271/–] said one standing by, I will take care of that, said he, & so took hold of her arm: And the Minister began the Prayer, with Adorations of the Love of God in giving the Son of his Love for a perishing World of Elect Sinners,

---

¹⁰ Insertion ['himself assures you']: McCulloch.
¹¹ Aye.

& the wonderful Love of Christ in giving himself, &c: And quickly came to her Condition in particular; and ~~quickly~~ within a very little, while he was going on in Prayer, she told the Person who was supporting her, He (meaning Christ) says to me, He will never leave me nor forsake me, repeating it over & over; and immediatly after, she said to that person again, He is telling me, He hath cast all my Sins behind his back. The Minister shortly concluding Prayer, she then repeated to him the Promises before mentioned that God had spoke in to her heart; and brake out adoring and admiring Christ in the Glories & Excellences of his Person, and the Wonders of his Love and free Grace, and complaining of her late Unbelief, crying out with melting admiration, Oh! I would not believe 'till I felt his Power; but now his Love hath conquered my heart: he has pardon'd my unbelief, he hath drawn me with Cords of Love and bands of a man: I thoughts my Sins were so great and many, that he would not pardon them; but now He hath cast them all behind his back; His thoughts are not as my thoughts, nor his ways as my ways.

The Minister seing a good deal of People, by that time, gathered into the Room, and [272/–] particularly some young Women of her Acquaintance, all of the Company being greatly affected, several of them weeping & crying out almost all this time; said to her, pointing at some of them, You see that there are several Daughters of Jerusalem there, that will be, it's like, saying in their hearts to you, What is thy Beloved more than another Beloved: Have you any thing to say to commend Christ to them? She immediatly turn'd to them, and said in the most moving and feeling manner, My Beloved is white and ruddy, the chief among ten thousand, yea he is altogether lovely. O Sirs, will ye come to Christ. O come and trust him. If ye cannot cry to him, O long after him, Oh! will ye at least sigh & sob for him. I can now say, My Beloved is mine & I am his.

At this time, there was a great Stir among the Affections of these present. The joys of some were plainly transporting, & almost too strong for them to contain, and others also greatly rejoiced in spirit. And there was a sound of weeping among others, that might be heard at a considerable distance.

After some time had been spent thus, the Minister said, Compose your selves, Sirs, and let us praise God; and turning to the lately distressed but now comforted Person, [273/–] ask'd her, If we should Sing the 103d Psalm at the beginning, and if she would join in it? to which she cheerfully agreed, and the first eight verses of that Psalm, were accordingly sung by the Company, in which she joyfully bare a part; and some others of the Company sung with much of the same frame. After that Exercise was over, the Minister said to her, I suppose you have been singing with pleasure; She answered, That she had never sung in that manner before, and said she had never known Christ before this Occasion.

She then rose up with great Vigour of Body & liveliness of Spirit, and turn'd about first to her Sister, who, in the judgment of Charity was supposd to have been converted some weeks before, and (like old Jacob embracing his son Joseph) fell upon her Neck & kissed her; and own'd her obligations to her for her Prayers ~~for her~~ & good Advices. ~~to her~~ And after that, she went and shook hands with all the Company, commending Christ and the sweetness [274/–] of his Love and the Riches of his Grace to them; and inviting every one whom she took to be a Stranger to Christ to come to him; and begging such as she took to be acquainted with him, to help her to praise him for his wonderful Love and Grace to her that had been the chief of Sinners, but now had obtained mercy.

After this the Minister a Preacher and another Person prayed; and the Company was dismiss'd. And all this, for her first coming into the Room, to the Close, lasted above three hours. During all which time, the gracious Power & Presence of God, was very sensible and remarkable to these of the Company who had been before acquainted with it: and a deep Concern about Salvation also fell upon others of them, that had formerly been Strangers to any thing of that nature. And this Account being set down by the Minister next morning, as was said before, & read over by him to a General Meeting of the Socities for Prayer in the Parish that met at his House that day, they were greatly affected in hearing it.

[275/–] a.z.

On that Lords Night after I had first received Comfort in the Ministers Closet, I went home with much joy, and after some time going to bed, I fell asleep for a little time, & awaked again in a great fright, finding nothing of that sweet frame with which I lay down: but within a little, that Word, Fear not for I am with thee,[12] shin'd into my heart with sweet Divine Rays, and immediatly quieted & comforted me. And much of this frame continued with me till Thursday thereafter; when many doubts & fears about my Souls condition arose in my mind, but these were banished from me by that word coming into my mind with great sweetness, Truly our fellowship is with the Father & with his Son Jesus Christ.

On Munday next my Master being to go in to Glasgow, desir'd me to go along with him to an Associate Minister ( ) there, saying, my doing so might do much good, & be a mean of bringing that Minister to a good Opinion of the Work here. I thought if it might be for the Glory of God & the good of Souls, I was willing to go, & speak to him, & it was with these hopes I was prevaild on to go. My Mistress desir'd me to keep all close, & let no body know [276/–] any thing of my going till I came back: at her desire I did so, and did not so much as tell my Parents, who liv'd hard by, of it. My Master before I went out with him, told me, There would be Exercise [worship][13] in that Ministers house, and therefore I

---

[12] Gen 26:24, Isa 41:10, Isa 43:10.
[13] Text bracketed by McCulloch.

took my Bible along with me, in order to join at it. I went to Secret Prayer before I went, but was much straitned, and had little access to God in it. By the way, when we were a pretty good distance from my Masters house, he askd me, If I had told my Father of my going to Glasgow? I told him I had not: he answered I might I might have done it. My masters Son ( ), who had also been awakned shortly before, and another young man ( ) who had been greatly comforted went along with us, with the same view, I believe, with my self. But while we went on, especially when we were got near, to Glasgow, I found my self in a very dark dead & lifeless frame: My Master left us in a house in the Bridge-gate, bidding us stay there, till he went to that Ministers, to see if he were ready to receive us, telling us he would come back for us. However he came not, but after we had tarried about an hour, one came and bade us, Come away to that Ministers house: [277/–] When we came there, we were straight brought into a Room where that Minister was and so many men with him, That the Room seem'd to be full. He ask'd me several Questions, but I was so dash'd seeing him & such a Company with him, and apprehending I was come where I ought not to have been & where I had no business, and at the same time finding the Lord withdraw his gracious presence from me; that as soon as I entred the Room, I in a manner lost my Sight and my Senses, and was so fill'd with Confusion, that I do not remember a word either of what he asked or what I answered. Only I mind that after he had spoke for some time to me, he said, It is all Delusions: at hearing which, I was just ready to fall down on the Ground, but my Master took hold of me & held me in his arms for a little. And while he was holding me that word came into my mind with much sweetness, I will be thy God and the God of thy people,[14] ~~which~~ and I immediatly told all the Company, what the Lord was telling me. I was afterward told by the other two young men that went with me, that at this time, that Minister was retird to another Room with them: We were however all sent away, and nothing like worship was there while we were present. But when the other two told me [288/–][15] by the way that that Minister had askd me If I had seen Christ with my bodily Eyes & that I had answered, Yes [ ][16] I was so filled with grief & confusion at the thoughts that I had so much dishonoured God by uttering that Word, that I knew not what to do with my self, and I would gladly have gone where none might see me & mourn before the Lord. But the other two obliged me to go home along with them. But by the way going in to the Kirk, while one ( ) was praying there, That word came into my mind, Daughter be of good

---

[14]   Possibly Ru 1:16.
[15]   Primary pagination numbers 278–87 omitted by McCulloch.
[16]   Insertion ['tho' I did not remember that I had said so']: McCulloch.

cheer, thy sins are forgiven thee:[17] at which I was again much composd, and made indeed to be of good cheer, & put into a disposition for the service of God. But for several days after I came back to my Masters, I was often vex'd & griev'd that I had so greatly dishonoured God, when last at Glasgow; but at length I was again comforted by that word spoke in to my heart, There is forgiveness with thee that thou may be fear'd. And for a considerable time after this, the Lord gave me much composure of spirit and stayedness of mind on him in his service.

But doubts & fears and darkness as to my Interest in Christ again return'd, and I could not lay claim to one of all the promises of the New Covenant, & was just ready to give up all for lost, till that word came into my mind [289/–] I said I am cast out of thy sight, yet will I look again toward thy holy temple, which revivd my fainting hope, made me look to God in Christ with hopes of favour & mercy, & gave me comfort & peace in believing. And this continued for some time; but falling again under great damps of Spirit, and not being able to discern true grace in my heart thro' the prevalence of corruption; That word came into my mind one day as I was about my Work, I am crucify'd with Christ nevertheless I live, yet not I but Christ that liveth in me,[18] upon which I felt the former power of sin and corruption much abated & broken, and my heart deadned to all things here below, and rising up in fervent desires after Jesus Christ.

For some time before the first Sacrament-Occasion at Camb. in July 1742, I was under great discouragement, finding little of that liveliness and Spirituality I had sometimes had formerly, I durst not think of communicating at that time; but came however to the Minister with some others, to get some Instructions & Directions as to my Duty: But after hearing these, when he offered me a Token, I refusd it, thinking I had not got a Token from God to go to his Holy Table: But when I was returning home, under great uneasiness of mind [290/–] at the thoughts of my unfitness for a Communion Occasion, that Word came into my heart, My Grace is Sufficient for thee,[19] which made me resolve upon coming to the Table of the Lord, & tho' I was Sensible I was most unprepared, yet I was led to led to rely upon that Sufficiency of Grace that is in Christ, to prepare me for that Holy Ordinance.

In time of the Action Sermon on that Text, Yea he is altogether lovely, this is my beloved & this is my friend,[20] the Lord was pleased to give me very much of heart-brokenness for sin, & to draw out my heart in love to Christ, I had also much of the Lords presence at his Table. On Munday hearing a Minister (12)[21] preach on these words; Let the same mind be in you that was

---

[17]   Mt 9:2.
[18]   Gal 2:20.
[19]   2 Co 12:9.
[20]   SS 5:16.
[21]   George Whitefield (1714–70) – evangelist.

in Christ Jesus,[22] I ~~felt~~ saw much of God & Christ in that Sermon, and was made earnestly to desire to have the mind of Christ in me, but at the same time was humbled to find so little of it in my Soul.

Going to see a Person ( ) about that time who was sick, as I went along thinking of him, that word came into my mind, with respect to that sick person, A Man greatly beloved:[23] and while I was wondring at that Word, it was immediatly added, For my own names sake have I loved him.

[291/–] At the 2d Sacrament at Cambuslang in August 1742, in hearing a Sermon by a Minister ( ) on that text, He that hath the bride is the bridegroom,[24] I was made to believe that Christ was the bridegroom of my Soul, & had my heart drawn out after him above all things, & had much heart-brokenness for dishonouring him. At the Lords Table, there was much of a Sweet Savour of God and Christ on my Soul. On Munday hearing a Minister ( ) on that Text, Pray without ceasing,[25] I felt my heart melted down with the love of God, and an earnest desire raisd in my Soul, that he Lord might enable me to the Duty exhorted to.

That harvest I fell under great darkness & deadness of spirit and continued so for a considerable time, till one day after I had been at Secret Prayer, while I was thinking I need never essay that Duty again, for the Lord would not hear me, I had so greatly sinned & offended him; that word came into my heart, In a little wrath have I hid my face from thee for a moment, but with everlasting loving kindness will I have mercy on thee,[26] upon which I was made to see & believe, that the Lord had justly hid his face from me for my sins, & that tho' my hasty & unbelieving spirit was ready to [292/–] think the time he had hid his face from me long, yet it was but wrath for a moment, I got also the Love of Christ shed abroad in my heart at that time, & was made to believe that Gods love toward me was from everlasting and would continue to everlasting.

In Winter ~~thereafter~~ following [ ][27] ~~after I had fallen under reproach~~ [ ],[28] tho' it was very unjust and undeserved, yet reproach was like to break my heart, at the thoughts that Religion should suffer thro' such unjust Reports: as I was one night weeping & mourning in my bed on this Accout, and wishing that no body had ever got notice that I had met with any thing of God, that his ways might never have been evil spoken of by any for my Sake, that word came in to my heart, Be still, & know that I am God,[29] upon which I got

---

[22] Php 2:5.
[23] Da 10:11, Da 10:19.
[24] Jn 3:29.
[25] 1 Th 5:17.
[26] Isa 54:8.
[27] Insertion ['some having forg'd a false Story against me to my prejudice']: McCulloch.
[28] Insertion ['will']: McCulloch.
[29] Ps 46:10.

my fretting troubled heart stilled & calmed, & melted into godly sorrow
for my offending him by my impatience, and was made to resign my self to
his, to order any Lot for me in the World that seem'd good to him, and that
might be most for his Glory. About 14 days after that, when I was thinking
of the harsh and unjust Treatment, I had met with such reports, that word
came into my mind with great power, Thou must endure hardness as a good
soldier of Jesus Christ,[30] which made willing [ ][31] to undergo any [293/–]
Sufferings of hardships Holy Providence might order for me, and to follow
Christ thro' good report and bad report.

Sometime in January 1743, hearing of the Lords dealing bountifully with
the souls of some others in their meetings for Prayer in the Parish; I thought
that we in the meeting to which I belongd had surely dishonoured God some
way beyond others, when there was generally such deadness among us as had
been for some time. And while I was much cast down with these thoughts,
one morning before we were to meet for Prayer, as I was earnestly wishing
and praying, that the Lord might favour our Meeting that day with a reviving
visit of mercy & Love, tho I should not share in it, that word came into my
heart with much Power, If thou wouldst believe, thou shall see the Glory
of God. Accordingly at night when we met for Prayer, there were several
persons in the Meeting, that were so filled and overcome with the Love of
God, when at Prayer or Praises, that they could not speak or converse for
some time after it, but were taken up in admiring the free Love of God in
Christ. I earnestly wish'd & pray'd that the Lord might give me if it were but
one minutes Enjoyment of what I saw the rest [294/–] were favoured with;
but it did not seem good to the Lord to grant my request at that time: but
taking my Bible to read, before I read any, these words came into my heart,

> This Word of thine my comfort is
> In my affliction[32]
> and immediatly after, came in that other word,
> My Soul wait thou with patience
> Upon thy God alone.[33]

upon which my heart was composd to a patient waiting on God till his
good & appointed time should come, for a Visit of Love to my Soul, &
was enabled in the mean time to praise him for that gracious Visit he was
giving to others: especially when that word came into my heart, while one
( ) was praying for us all, I charge you that ye stir not up nor awake my
Love till he please. And after this while I was imployed in my turn to pray,

---

[30]   2 Ti 2:3.
[31]   Insertion ['thro' grace']: McCulloch.
[32]   Ps 119:50, Scottish Psalter (metrical).
[33]   Ps 62:5, Scottish Psalter (metrical).

I got great Liberty to bless & praise the Lord for his great Goodness to the rest of the meeting that day.

A little after this, going to Paisley-Sacrament in Company with some others, I was under much discouragement by the way, thinking that there was none of the rest like me, and that I was not worthy to go in company with them; On Saturday morning I was a little revivd by that word coming into my heart,

> Yet God is good to Israel
> To each pure hearted one[34]

In hearing Sermon on Saturday, I got much [295/–] of brokenness of heart for sin, as that whereby I had dishonoured God. And in time of the Action Sermon on Sabbath ( ), I had my heart filled with the Love of God & Jesus Christ. And so also in hearing a Minister ( ) preach on that Text on Sabbath Evening that day, Truly our fellowship is with the Father, and with his Son Jesus Christ.[35] On Tuesday morning following, I was awaked with that word, As ye have received Christ Jesus the Lord so walk in him,[36] upon which I was confirm'd in the belief that I had received Christ Jesus as my Lord, & was made to resolve by grace to walk answerably to my Priviledges and Engagements to his Service.

At Glasgow Sacrament in April 1743, I got nothing sensibly till at the time the 2d Table was a serving, when I began to say in heart, This Work is not far on, but alas! I have got nothing, it seems there is nothing prepared for me here—; when these words came into my heart, Can a Woman forsake her sucking Child that she should not have mercy on the fruit of her womb? Yes she may, yet will I not forget thee,[37] saith the Lord: this cheer'd my heart & raisd my Expectations: And after that while a Minister (26) serv'd three or four Tables, I had my heart melted into sorrow for Sin at the thoughts of Christs Sufferings & of his Love, & got my heart filled with love to him. And on that Sabbath Evening, hearing a Minister ( ) preach on that Text, I will never leave [296/–] thee nor forsake thee,[38] I was greatly confirm'd in the ~~faith~~ belief, that it would be to me according to that word that had been made so sweet to me at my first Acquaintance with the comforts of Religion.

To come to a Close. I bless the Lord, that ever since the time just now mentioned, the thoughts and desires of my heart, ~~do~~ are mainly and ordinarily carried out after Spiritual and Eternal Blessings. Tho my heart is sometimes much deader in reading & hearing of the Word [];[39] yet I often long for

---

[34]   Ps 73:1, Scottish Psalter (metrical).
[35]   1 Jn 1:3.
[36]   Col 2:6.
[37]   Isa 49:15.
[38]   Heb 13:5.
[39]   Insertion ['than at other times']: McCulloch.

Opportunities of attending Gospel Ordinances, before they come, both on Sabbaths & Weekly Lecture days, and prize them more than my necessary food; and I bless the Lord, he has often made them by his ~~Blessing~~ grace, reviving strengthning & comforting to my Soul. The World & the things of it bulks little in my eye; but it is very afflicting to my Spirit, to find my thoughts so oft wandring from God in the time of holy Duties, after meer vanities. I find vastly more pleasure in enjoying the Light of Gods countenance for a very little time, than in [ ][40] all my life before. What I chiefly want & desire is more and more communion with Christ & conformity to him, his law & image, while I live, to be made like him when he appears, and to be for ever with him in Heaven.

To him be glory for ever, Amen.[41]

[297/– through 300/– blank]

---

[40]   Insertion ['all worldly pleasures']: McCulloch.
[41]   Ro 11:36.

[301/–] b.k. A Woman of 20 years.[1]

I was kept in the former part of my life, before the last year, from things outwardly gross & sinful before the world. I usd often to neglect Prayer, but sometimes minded it, especially when my conscience checkt me for any thing that was against the light of it, as making a lie to excuse a fault. I would thereupon have gone to my knees, and beg'd pardon of it, and I reckon'd that my doing so, was enough to take away that. When I read or thought on the penitent thief on the Cross, I thought I would also repent of my sins when I was going to die & so get mercy as he did. Yet these words Many are called but few are chosen,[2] Strait is the gate & narrow is the way that leadeth to life & few there be that find it,[3] would have sometimes come into my mind & made me somewhat uneasy for a time. But this would have soon worn off again. I usd always for ordinary, since my childhood to go to the Kirk on Sabbath to prevent the clamours of Conscience that would have risen by neglecting it. And the Effect of all my Religion, was in short only to make me a proud Self-conceived Hypocrite.

[302/–] And thus it continued with me, till I came to Camb. in the Spring 1742 when seeing some young persons at the East end of the Ministers House in great distress, some of them about my own age or younger, I began to think this with my self; These persons seem to be taken up in earnest about the things of another world, and the Eternal Salvation of their Souls, tho as young as I, and I have only been taken up about the things of a present world: and hereupon I fell under some Concern about my Soul. Some short time after this coming again to Cambuslang, and hearing a Minister (26)[4] preach on that Text, 1 Joh. 5.11. He that believeth not on the Son hath made God a liar, because he hath not believed the record that God gave of his Son,[5] while he was shewing the Evil of Unbelief as it was a giving the lie to God, & other things of that kind, I was made to see the hainous nature of the Sin of Unbelief: I had never thought of the Evil of it at all; now I was made Sensible that it was the greatest of all sins that ever God pardoned: [303/–] and hereupon I fell under great distress: and continued so till the Close: when hearing the Minister pronounce the Blessing, at dismissing the

---

[1]   Janat Park – the shorthand text in McCulloch's 'Index of persons' names who gave the foregoing accounts to Mr. McC' states: daughter of Gavin Park, now living in Carmunnock, but formerly a packman in England. Taught to read the Bible, got the Catechism to heart, and retained it.

[2]   Mt 20:16, Mt 22:14.

[3]   Mt 7:14.

[4]   William McCulloch (1691–1771) – minister, Cambuslang.

[5]   1 Jn 5:10–11.

people, [The Grace of our Lord Jesus Christ, the Love of God the Father, the Communion of the Holy Ghost be with you all Amen][6] I thought these words were made a mean of taking a great part of the burden of distress that was on my Spirit, off me, while I was made to think, That the Lord had sent forth his Servant to bless his People in his name, I hop'd that he would bless me with Christs imputed Righteousness, without which I now saw, there was no real Blessing or Salvation. After this I fell under a Conviction of many other Sins as particularly my Pride, Self-conceit hypocrisy and breach of the Sabbath-day. And there was scarce a sin could be nam'd, but I found it stirring in my heart. And while I was under these Convictions, I thought much & oft of the Punishment of Loss, (What a dreadful thing it was to loss the favour [304/–] and enjoyment of God for ever) but not of the punishment of Sense. And my convictions at length rose to that height that I thought there was no mercy for me. But while I thought so, that word came often into my mind, The Chief of Sinners:[7] I knew that word was spoken by the Apostle Paul of himself, and that yet he obtained mercy: & therefore tho I was sensible that I was the Chief of Sinners, I found some glimmerings of hope break in, that I might likewise obtain mercy.

There was one thought that yielded me some comfort when I thought of Hell, and that was, That God was glorify'd in the punishment of the damn'd there: and therefore, that if God should condemn me to everlasting Separation from him, he would be glorified in my Condemnation. I had also another thought as to this matter, That tho the Damn'd would not glorify Gods Mercy, yet they would glorify his Justice: but this I came afterward to see was a wrong thought, for that tho Gods Justice would be glorifyd in them, yet they would not glorify his Justice.

[305/–] While I was one day thinking on the sadness of my own condition, that word cast up to my thoughts, Come unto me all ye that labour & are heavy laden and I will give you rest, which gave me some Encouragement, & made me to believe that Christ was willing to receive all them that came to him in ways of his own appointment, & I desird to be made willing to do so. And about this time, or shortly after, these words came with power and light into my mind, I will take away the heart of stone, & give you a heart of flesh,[8] & these, Thy people shall be willing in the day of thy power;[9] which gave me some Comfort, believing that he that had made these Promises was able also to perform them, and that he would accomplish them to me.

There were many Temptations from Satan with which I had to conflict, which would be tedious to mention, tho my memory could serve me to

---

[6]   Text bracketed by McCulloch.
[7]   1 Ti 1:15.
[8]   Eze 11:19, Eze 36:26.
[9]   Ps 110:3.

~~mention~~ name them all, as it does not. One Temptation with which I was sorely assaulted, tho but for a short time, was, That I was not Elected: but while I was tossed [306/–] with these thoughts, that word struck into my mind suddenly, Him that cometh unto me I will in no wise cast out: upon which I was made to believe, that Christ was willing to rescue all that came to him, in his own appointed way, be who they would: & this brake the force of this Temptation.

There was another Temptation that was one of the most dreadful & afflicting of any that ever I laboured under: and that was to Downright Atheism, or to think there was no God. It was urg'd upon me with great violence for about three or four days, That there was no God: tho I argued against the Temptation from the works of Creation & Providence, & tho I rejected it with detestation, yet it was still born in upon me. But tho' I could not get rid of it; yet the Lord was pleased to give me great comfort and joy, while he enabled me to resist it & his Glory, his Wisdom Power & Goodness & other perfections appeard Shining in every thing about me. And these two passages of Scripture, were then cast into my mind with much power, Mic. 6. [307/–] I will wait for the God of my Salvation, my God will hear me. Rejoice not against me, O mine Enemy, when I fall I shall arise, when I sit in darkness the Lord shall be a Light unto me. I will bear the indignation of the Lord because I have sinned against him, until he plead my cause and execute judgment for me: he will bring me forth to the Light & I shall behold his righteousness.[10] And these words of our Lord to Thomas, Be not faithless but believing.[11] These two Passages of Scripture came to me with that power that this Temptation with which I was afflicted immediatly vanished, & I was never troubled with it since that time to this [Nov. 15.1743.].

When the Sacrament-Occasion in the Parish where I livd drew near, I was much tossed between a sense of Duty & a desire to obey that Command of Christ on the one hand, Do this in remembrance of me,[12] & on the other hand, fears that if I should come to the Lords Table, I would afterwards backslide & prove a Scandal & reproach to Religion: but these words coming into my mind,

> [308/–] Wilt thou not who from death me sav'd
> My feet from falls keep free.[13]

I was made to hope that God who had done so much for me, would preserve me from falling away, and so was encouraged to resolve to come to his Holy

---

[10] Mic 7:7–9.
[11] Jn 20:27.
[12] Lk 22:19, 1 Co 11:24, 1 Co 11:25.
[13] Ps 55:13, Scottish Psalter (metrical).

Table. But at that Occasion both when at the Table & in [ ]¹⁴ Sermons, Satan attack'd me so hard with his Suggestions & Temptations, that I could scarce get hearing one full Sentence. Only on Munday when a Minister ( ) preaching said, These that could say, that God had Sensibly answered them might have hope, this gave me some comfort; for I could often say before this, that the Lord had fullfilld that word to me, Before they call I will answer, & while they are yet speaking I will hear.¹⁵

At the first Sacrament out Cambuslang in Summer 1742, on Munday the Lord was pleased to shew much of his Goodness to me, especially while I heard a Minister ( ) on that Text my God shall supply all your wants;¹⁶ and tho I cannot say I then got all wants supplied, I got good hope thro' grace that he would supply them all in his own good time.

At the 2d Sacrament at Cambuslang in Harvest 1743, ~~on hearing a Minister~~ ~~( )~~ [309/–] the Lord was pleased to enable me to offer up to him at his Holy Table, that sacrifice he had said he will not despise, a broken heart. On Sabbath Evening, hearing a Minister ( ) preach on that Text, Now lettest then thy servant depart in peace, for mine eyes have seen thy Salvation,¹⁷ when he said, These to whom Christ has manifested himself formerly, tho: they might now be under the hidings of his face or in darkness, yet some time or other he would lift up upon them the light of his countenance: just as he spoke these words, the Lord was pleased in a very sensible & remarkable way, to lift up the light of his countenance on my Soul,¹⁸ and to give me a deep & humbling sense of my sinfulness before him & my unworthiness of the least of his mercies, to shed abroad his Love in my heart, and to give me assurance of his Love & favour; and to grant me much of a grateful frame for his great mercy toward me.

[310/–] To conclude. That which I find my heart & desires run mainly & for ordinary after, is that I may get more grace, that I may love Christ more and hate sin more. I can say thro' grace, with the Psalmist, I joyd when to the house of God, go up they said to me; I have great delight in hearing the Gospel preach'd, as it is the great appointed mean of Salvation, & as Christ there manifests his Glory, & often meets with his People. Sometimes I find as great concern on my Spirit for the Salvation of others as ever I had for my own. The body of sin & death is ordinarily a great burden to me, & the thoughts of Death has sometimes been sweet to me in hopes of being then freed from it. There's a word has often been a great Comfort to me, He that cometh will come & will not tarry,¹⁹ which I understand of his coming to

¹⁴   Insertion ['time of']: McCulloch.
¹⁵   Isa 65:24.
¹⁶   Php 4:19.
¹⁷   Lk 2:29–30.
¹⁸   Ps 4:6.
¹⁹   Heb 10:37.

manifest himself to his people, coming to deliver his Church & coming to judgment. To the first two of these comings, I can by grace always, & to the last of them sometimes say Amen, Even so come Lord Jesus.

[311/–] c.g. A Marry'd Woman; aged 38[1]

~~In August 1743~~ My Father brought up all his Children (of which 7 came to be men & women) & me among others agreeable to the Engagements Parents use to come under for their Children at their Baptism. He gave good evidence of his being a good Man himself; & was not wanting to give both good advice & example to his Children. Many a time he us'd to rise out of his bed to Prayer in the night time. He took care to have us all train'd up to read the Bible. And each of us had our times for some form of prayer. But however it was with the others, all was but meer form with me. In my younger years []² I seem'd at times, particularly about Sacrament-Occasions, to have some desire after Good, & some concern to be good, but after such Occasions were over, I return'd again to my former carnal security & worldliness. And thus matters continued with me, 'till the year 1743, when I was about 38 years of Age, having been then married to John Hamilton for about 14 years, & born him four children, 3 of which are at this time (Dec. 6.1749) still alive: It pleased God, that at the Sacrament at Blantyre that year viz. in August 1743, hearing a sermon on Saturday on that Text []³ Lam. The Lord is my portion saith my soul, therefore will I hope in him;⁴ and another on Munday on these words [],⁵ Christ in you the hope of Glory,⁶ I fell under much thoughtfulness & anxious concern about my Soul-~~concerns~~ []⁷ I was made very uneasy at the thought of my then wretchedness, That my soul could not say to the Lord, Thou art my portion, & That Christ was not formed in me the hope of Glory: & long'd to be able to call God my Portion.

[312/–] On that Munday Evening, after I went home, while I was thinking on what I had been hearing in Publick, & lamenting, That nothing I heard took any due inpression on me, & particularly, That I knew not Christ, a kind of a great horror of Darkness, came upon me, I mean an inward darkness & confusion of mind & thought with dreadful apprehensions, as to the sad & dangerous state I was in, while I knew not Christ savingly, nor the way of Salvation by him: & I earnestly desire'd & beg'd of the Lord, That he would awaken me out of my Security, & bring me savingly to know him in Christ, & that he would draw me to

---

¹ Margaret Smith – the shorthand text in McCulloch's 'Index of persons' names who gave the foregoing accounts to Mr. McC' states: spouse of John Hamilton in Lettrick.
² Insertion ['& even after I was some years married']: McCulloch.
³ Insertion ['by Mr McCulloch']: McCulloch.
⁴ La 3:24.
⁵ Insertion ['by Mr McCulloch']: McCulloch.
⁶ Col 1:27.
⁷ Insertion ['Matters']: McCulloch.

himself with the Cords of Love & bands of a man, To which the Answer was sent to my heart, That the work was begun, & the Cords of Love were let down. The Second Sacrament at Cambuslang approaching, & while I was resolving to attend there, & desiring the Lord might there shew me the Evil of Sin, Satan, suggested that it was to no purpose to go to any more such occasions, for that the day of grace was over with me, & that if I saw the Evil of Sin I would despair. But the Lord gave me to hope that he would yet bring me thro' all my Difficultys. I heard a sermon there [ ]⁸ on that Text, The Lord thy God in the midst of thee is mighty, he will save, he will rejoice over thee with joy, he will rest in his Love, he will joy over thee with singing.⁹ I was much affected with the many sweet & awful things I heard in that sermon. On that Munday Morning, when I awaked, & while I reflected on several Truths I had read & heard from the word, these were so brought home to me, That I was made to see, That all that ever I had done was Sin, in the Sight of a holy God, as to my sinful frame & way of doing, & that I had broken all the commands of God, in thought word & deed, & the commandment came and sin received & I died. On the Thursday after, the Lord gave me a Sight & Sense of Original Sin [ ]¹⁰ That I had the Seeds all Sin in my nature, & that I was justly liable to the wrath of God on the account [313/–] of it, & my mouth was stopt before him, & I was made sensible, that all my own righteousness was but as filthy rags, & that God would be just, perfectly just, if he should have cast me out of his sight & cast me into hell for ever, on the account of my Original & Actual Sins, & therefore was made to justify God in all that he threatned & inflicted for Sin, & to condemn my Self as justly deserving it all. But while my Conscience & heart was thus burdened under a Sense of Sins of my nature & life; the Lord was pleased in Mercy, to relieve my almost fainting perishing Soul, with that word that was then brought in to my heart with much power, authority & sweetness, I even I am he that blotteth out thy transgressions & will not remember thy sins,¹¹ for my own names sake &c: Many other gracious words were also at that time in like manner brought home to my soul, such as, Thy Maker is thy husband, the Lord of hosts is his name,¹² Tho' after my skin worms consume this body, yet in my flesh shall I see God,¹³ To him that overcometh will I give a white stone with a new name writen upon it which no man knoweth but he that receiveth

---

⁸ Insertion ['By Mr Gillespy']: McCulloch.
⁹ Side margin note: 'Zeph.3.17'.
¹⁰ Insertion ['& made me to see']: McCulloch.
¹¹ Isa 43:25.
¹² Isa 54:5.
¹³ Job 19:26.

it.[14] [ ][15] And I was at this time, made with all my heart & soul to accept of the Lord Jesus Christ in all his Redeeming offices, and to devote & give up my whole Self, Soul, Body & Spirit, to him to be forthcoming for his glory, & to be Saved by him in his own way, & to be wholly & for ever his.

Soon after this, Satan charg'd me ~~with~~ & upbraided me with the breach of all the commands of Gods Law: I was made to take with the charge & to owne that all this & much more than the Enemy knew, was true; but was made to fly to Jesus Christ, as my alone City of Refuge, & to take Shelter in his merits & mediation.

For about two years and a quarter after this, I was much troubled & persecuted by the wicked ~~temptations~~ [ ][16] of Satan, & firy darts, of blasphemous thoughts cast into my Soul, putting all into confusion there, & urging me to throw away all I had met with in dutys, as Delusion. Yet, all along, the Lord mercifully supported my drooping soul by secret yet powerful supports, & several gracious words now & then brought home to my heart, that greatly relieved me, as particularly, that word, For [314/–] a small moment have I forsaken thee, but with great mercies will I gather thee. In a little wrath have I hid my face from thee, but with everlasting loving kindness will I have mercy on thee, saith the Lord thy Redeemer.[17] And when my Soul Enemy tempted me much to make away with my self, or threatned to destroy me, the Lord made me reject such motions toward Self-Murder with abhorrence, & made me hope that he would protect me, by that word, No plague shall near thy dwelling come, no ill shall thee befall![18]

At length at a Sacrament-Occasion in Cambuslang in 1745, when hearing a Sermon on that Text [ ][19] I will betroth thee unto me for ever, yea I will betroth thee unto me in righteousness & in Judgment, & in loving kindness & in mercies &c: Hos.2.[20] in which Sermon, there were many Invitations to Backsliders to return, & I knew my self to be one of these, & was made sensible that these Invitations were directed to me in particular; & was powerfully brought to fall in with them: In that Sermon, it was said, that Sometimes when a poor soul would aim at returning to God, & closing with a Promise, Satan & the unbelief of the misgiving heart, would knock down with a Threatening: this I had very often found in sad Experience, before this, in many Influences: but while the Speaker, exhorted to come upon that gracious Call, at the Close of of the Bible Rev. 22.17 The Spirit & the Bride

---

[14] Rev 2:17.
[15] Insertion ['I know that my Redeemer liveth, &c: and']: McCulloch.
[16] Insertion ['suggestions']: McCulloch.
[17] Isa 54:7–8.
[18] Ps 91:10.
[19] Insertion ['by Mr Gillespy']: McCulloch.
[20] Hos 2:19.

say comes and let him that heareth, say come, [ ]²¹ & whosoever will, let him take the water of life freely: I was made willing to comply with this call, & in some measure enabled by grace to do so.

A short while after this on hearing a Sermon at Kilbride Sacrament, on these words, Phil. What things were gain to me these I counted loss for Christ, yea doubtless I count all things but loss for the excellency of the knowledge of Jesus Christ my Lord &c:²² While the Speaker was shewing in [315/–] many Instances what things these were more a person might account gain to him in his unregenerate State, that afterward he would count Loss for Christ, to know him & be found in him, I found all these to agree to what I had found. And particularly when he came to say, That the person who formerly to think that all Sermons almost were alike, would come to see a vast difference, & how comes he to do so? It is by the Spirit of the Lord, said he, teaching him to see that difference; This I was made to see in a way sensible manner, as to several Sermons I had heard, formerly, & some also at that same Occasion, & I was made to hope that it was by the Spirit of the Lord teaching me, That I was made to see that difference, & to prize these Sermons, that tended to abase Self & exalt the Saviour, before these of a very different strain; & I was led after this, to be more in reading the Scripture & in Prayer for help & relief from Christ, sensible that I could not help or relieve my self, & that he was just such a Saviour as I stood in need of, able to save to the uttermost them that come to God by him & who alone Could bring me & enable me thus to come to God.

Sometime after this, one Evening when reading in Durham on the 53d chapter of Isaiah, 10 verse, He shall see his seed his seed, he shall prolong his Days, the pleasure of the Lord shall prosper in his hand, while I read his Sermon on that Text,²³ & particularly his Exhortation there taken from Mat.11.28 where our Saviour says, ~~He shall see his seed, he shall prolong his Days, the pleasure of the Lord~~ Come into me all ye that labour & are heavy laden & I will give you rest to you Souls, I was enabled to comply with that Call in some measure of Sincerity; & also with the Call that follows there, we as Embassadors for Christ, beseech you to be reconciled to God,²⁴ & to take hold of Gods Covenant & strength, to throw down (in affection resolution & endeavour) the weapons of sin & rebellion against God, to renew my acceptance [316/–] of Christ on his own Gospel Terms, & to devote my self entirely to him to be for the Lord & not for another. But some days after

---

²¹ Insertion ['& let him that is athirst come']: McCulloch.

²² Php 3:7–8.

²³ James Durham. *Christ Crucified, or, the Marrow of the Gospel, evidently holden forth in LXXII sermons, on the whole 53. chapter of Isaiah wherein the text is clearly and judiciously opened up* (Edinburgh: Printed by the heir of Andrew Anderson, 1683).

²⁴ 2 Co 5:20.

this, I lost sight of what by grace I had now [ ]²⁵ in closing with Christ &c:
& unbelief again got up head & provaild: however I resolved that by grace I
would still follow on to know the Lord in ways of his own appointment, &
cast my Self at the feet of Christ, and if I perished I would perish there. But
in a few days after that, on a Sabbath Evening, reading in Durham on Isaiah
chap 41.53d. the Lord on a sudden opened up the Eyes of my understanding,
to see the alone way of salvation by Jesus Christ, and my heart was brought
to love it & approve of it, & delight in it, so entirely, that tho any of the ways
of Salvation I had been often thinking of in my own mind, had been possible,
I would have rejected all these ways of Salvation, & chosen the Gospel way
of Salvation, by the imputed Righteousness of Christ, & the Sanctifying of
his Spirit, before all others whatsoever. After this for some time I was much
taken up in reflecting with wonder at the Lords way of dealing with my Soul,
& comparing it with the word. At Blantyre, I heard the Minister there, with
much satisfaction, on that text, where 'tis said, The people spake of stoning
David, but he encouraged himself in the Lord his God;²⁶ & was helped to
endeavour also to encouraged my Self in God as my God: & in hearing him
on another Sabbath on that Text, Thou art my hiding-place,²⁷ —was helped
[in that time of general Danger in these Lands, from the High-land-men
under the Pretender]²⁸ to seek for shelter & protection in God reconciled to
me in Christ.

[317/– and 318/– blank]

---

²⁵ Insertion ['been helped to do']: McCulloch.
²⁶ 1 Sa 30:6.
²⁷ Ps 32:7, Ps 119:114.
²⁸ Text bracketed by McCulloch; 'The Pretender' was the moniker given to Charles Edward
Stuart (Bonnie Prince Charles) who challenged King George II for the Throne of England
during the Jacobite Uprising of 1745–46.

[319/–] b.m. A Young Man aged 21.[1]

When I was a Child and Boy, I was more frequently taken up in some kind of Secret Prayer, than when I came to more years. As to my outward behaviour all along my life, I believe no body could charge me with anything vicious, & I had no challenge against myself for outward misbehaviours before the world in my former life, & if I could keep fair before men, I was very little concernd for any more. I made no account of the inward disposition of my heart. In my own opinion of my Self, I was, as to Spiritual Concerns, rich, increased in goods, & stood in need of nothing; and did not know that I was poor and miserable, blind & naked, & standing in need of all things. I usd all along to go to the Kirk on Sabbaths, but it was only out of Curiosity, & because I saw others go there: and when I heard the word preach'd, it came in at the one ear & went out at the other: and I understood but little of what I read in my [320/–] Bible or heard preach'd, if it had it not been something of moral Duties between man and man, as justice, honesty, charity and the like: but as for Gospel Truths & Spiritual duties we owe to God, I understood very little of that kind at all.

But in all my Life I never found any thing I read or heard come home with any Power to my Conscience or heart, till on a Fast day in the Parish, a little after the great Hurricane on the 13ᵗʰ of January 1740, when hearing a Minister (26)[2] preach on that Text Fire, hail snow, vapour, stormy wind, obey his word,[3] that sentence he had in his sermon, Will neither the voice of God in the Tempests in the air, nor in the threatnings of devouring fire & everlasting Burnings awaken you, [‡][4] came home to me with a powerful Impression, & made me see it as a message sent from God to me, & made me see that I was lying dead in Sin & Carnal Security. Yet I was not then made fully sensible of the need I had of a Saviour: and this Impression wore off in a little time.

[321/–] For some time after this, I had some more concern, but I came afterward to be as bad as before, or rather worse. And Till one day a little after the Awakening brake out in Camb.[ ][5] when I was reading my Bible or at

---

[1]   Andrew Falls – the shorthand text in McCulloch's 'Index of persons' names who gave the foregoing accounts to Mr. McC' states: son of Robert Falls in Cambuslang. Taught to read the Bible when a child, got the Catechsim to heart, and retained it mostly.

[2]   William McCulloch (1691–1771) – minister, Cambuslang.

[3]   Ps 148:8.

[4]   Bottom margin insertion: ['‡ N.B. On the very day when that great Tempest or Hurricane happen'd that had been the Text who shall dwell with devouring fire who shall abide with everlasting burnings. Isai.']

[5]   Insertion ['Febry 1742']: McCulloch.

Secret Prayer, that word that had been before sent ~~came~~ to me, came home to me again, with with fresh Power, Will neither the voice of God in the Tempests of the Air, or in the Threatnings of devouring fire & everlasting burnings awaken you: Whereupon I was made sensible ~~of my being~~, as before, that I was dead in Sin & Carnal Security: and another word that followed not long after, & that also came with power, further confirm'd me in the persuasion that this was indeed my State, "[ ]⁶ Thou art yet in the gall of bitterness and bond of iniquity.⁷ And now I was made to see my guilt of not improving aright my first awakening when the words above mentioned came to me in the year 1740: & I continued uneasy in my mind about my Soul State after this: And [322/–] some little time after hearing a Minister (26) preaching in the Kirk-yeard of Camb. & giving several marks of Unregenerate persons, when he said, [ ]⁸ things go outwardly well with him in the world, then are usually easy & think all is right: I found this ~~to be~~ applied to me with Power; and was made sensible that this had been indeed my Case, and that it ~~had been~~ was a sign of my being truly in an unregenerate state. I was very uneasy in mind at that time, but neither cry'd out fainted or swooned at that or at any other time. Nor had I ever any Visions. Immediatly after this Word in the Sermon struck my heart, that word, (tho not utter'd by the Minister) came in with power, Then shall ye know if ye follow on to know the Lord;⁹ upon which I was made to hope that there was yet hope concerning me, and that if I followed on to know him & seek him I would find him; & I found a great weight taken off my Spirit, & went home that night with much composure.

And at a meeting of a Company of Young People that night, I could not [323/–] forbear telling them, That I could never say, That I had a Right to Christ before that day. And what made me think I had a Right to him, was, that whereas formerly I always thought there was [ ]¹⁰ something in my own Duties to recommend me to God; that day, when that word came in, Then shall ye know, if ye follow on to know the Lord,¹¹ there came such a Divine Light along with it to my mind, That I was made to see, That it was only for the Sake of Christ & his Righteousness that I must be accepted, and was persuaded at that time that I was accepted of God in him. I then was helped to a reliance on Christ, & had some sensible Love to him & joy in him, & wanted to have many engagd to praise him on my behalf.

I continued in this frame from some Days: but afterward began to doubt whether it was the Lord was graciously dealing with my heart or no? But while I was much disquieted with such thoughts, that word came in to my

⁶ Insertion ['I perceive']: McCulloch.
⁷ Ac 8:23.
⁸ Insertion ['When']: McCulloch.
⁹ Hos 6:3.
¹⁰ Insertion ['or must be']: McCulloch.
¹¹ Hos 6:3.

heart In God still hope & rest, which came with such Influence, as made me to believe [324/–] that this Awakning, at that time, was the work of God upon my Self & others: and my Soul was thereupon made to hope and rest in God thro' Christ. But sometime shortly after this, hearing some call it a Delusion of Satan: & I was in fear at that time that it might be so with my Self & others: but that word coming in with power & light, Fear not, be not afraid, It is I: which Scatter'd my doubts and fears, & made me believe that it was the work of the Spirit of the Lord, and not a Delusion.

On a Thanksgiving Day in May 1742 hearing a minister (26) preach on that Text, The Lord hath done great things for us whereof we are glad,[12] I could then say with respect to my self in particular, The Lord hath done great things for me whereof I am glad; for I was then made clearly to see by Scripture Evidences, the reality of a Saving Change on my Soul: I saw that I had thro' grace got hatred of Sin, as displeasing to God and wounding to Christ, & I now & for some time past, had a great desire after the Word, & came to hear in order to meet Christ in it, & often found it sweet to my taste things I had been quite a stranger to in the [325/–] former part of my life before Febry 1742.

At the first Sacrament at Camb. that year, I met with nothing sensible 'till Sabbath Evening, when hearing a Minister (12)[13] on that Text, Thy maker is thy Husband &c:[14] I found it to be a new Reviving to me. And when he said He was sent to take a wife for his Masters Son, asking, If there was any there that wanted to take Christ for their Husband, & bidding them come, & he would marry them to Christ, after which he laid out the Terms, & I found my heart made sweetly to agree to those Terms & found the Evidences he gave of these that were married to Christ wrought in my heart.

To draw to a close of this short account. I now find a remarkable alteration in the habitual bent of my heart from what usd to be before my Awakening in Feb. 1742. I now find no pleasure in several things wherein I took pleasure before, & I have now much pleasure in things wherein formerly I had none. Formerly [326/–] my chief pleasure was having things in the World go well with me: in this I find but very little pleasure now: formerly I could take no pleasure in Spiritual things or exercises: now I find my chief delight is not in things here below but in things above, & I can heartily say with the Psalmist, That One day in Gods courts I have found to be better than a thousand elsewhere.[15] And I think I can say, That I would rather choose to endure affliction with the People of God, than to enjoy the pleasures of Sin which are but for a Season. If I ~~might~~ were to say, with Job, O that the

---

[12] Ps 126:3.
[13] George Whitefield (1714–70) – evangelist.
[14] Isa 54:5.
[15] Ps 84:10.

Almighty would grant me my desire,[16] it would be, That I might depart & be with Christ: & that while he is pleased to continue me here, he would give me grace to glorify his name. I usd to say sometimes when I went away from a Sermon, ~~How~~ (according to a note of a Sermon I heard lately) How well he preach'd! but now I oft go away with that, How ill have I liv'd: Sin is now become the chief burden & grief of my Soul: but in the hopes of being delivered from it, I think I can heartily say with the Apostle

Thanks be God thro' Jesus Christ Our Lord.

[16] Job 6:8.

[327/–] a.r. A Married Woman of 29 years.[1]

I liv'd a kind of moral Life all along from my Childhood: & usd to pray by my self sometimes once sometimes twice a day, & to go to the Kirk on Sabbaths, to see if I might get any good by doing so: but never got any sensible benefit, except one time hearing a Minr ( ) at a Sacrament Occasion in Kilsyth several years ago, on that Text My Soul thirsteth for the living God:[2] at which time, I was a little grieved & uneasy about my Souls condition: but this soon wore off again. I cannot say, that ever I could discern the Presence of God in Prayer, or other duties, except only that I sometimes felt more enlargement & more desires after God than at other times.

About the beginning of March 1742 I came to Camb. & heard a Minr (26)[3] preach on that Text, If any man be in Christ he is a New Creature old things are past away, behold all things are become new:[4] I was then made to see that I was not in a safe State, for that Old things were not passd away with me, & that all things were not made new with me. Upon this I turn'd very uneasy, & was much grieved, that I had mispent much precious time, and that I had not been religious in good Earnest as I ought to have been: and had so much dishonoured God by my Sins.

[328/–] And particularly, that I had slighted & neglected Christ in the Gospel, and that many a day when he has been knocking at the door of my heart I did not open to him. I came often to Camb. & heard sermons there, & got more & more discoveries of the Evil of Sin & of my heart-plagues. And my heart-trouble continued for some weeks before I got any Out-gate [‡][5] ~~And that was~~

At the Barony Sacrament in Summer 1742, when I was sitting in the Kirk between Sermons, these words came suddenly in my mind, Whom have I in heaven but thee, O Lord, & there is none on Earth I desire beside thee:[6] at which I felt the uneasiness I had been under instantly went off and I felt great Love in my Soul to God as my Portion & Christ as my Saviour: and could then ~~express~~ speak these words as expressing the real inward sense of my own heart. And much of this frame continued with me that day and the next: and after that I fell back into my former uneasiness, thinking I had lost

---

[1]   Agnes Burnside – the shorthand text in McCulloch's 'Index of persons' names who gave the foregoing accounts to Mr. McC' states: spouse of James Rob, tenant in Shettleston. Taught to read the Bible, got much of the Catechism by heart, and retained it.

[2]   Ps 42:2.

[3]   William McCulloch (1691–1771) – minister, Cambuslang.

[4]   2 Co 5:17.

[5]   Text insertion (found on p. 148), beginning at the symbol '‡' to the bracket ']'.

[6]   Ps 73:25.

all I had got, & thinking I had done something that had offended Christ, but I was not sensible what it was. But got my heart again composd after some time when at Prayer.

[329/–] ‡ One night when I was very uneasy & found my Corruptions very strong, and my unbelief greatly prevailing, & found great difficulty to believe, and thought if I could be helped to believe in Christ, I would be saved: that word came into my mind, Is there no balm in Gilead, is there no Physician there:[7] which was accompanied with a great love to Jesus Christ and a longing desire after him. And next Munday after that, coming to Camb. I heard a Minr ( ) preach on the same words, and then I found greater Love to Christ than before, & found all that Sermon was very desirable to me, & had much joy in hearing it, and Christ in the offers of himself was precious to my Soul: and this continued with me till night.][8]

I find my chief desires for ordinary are after more & more Love to Christ and more hatred at Sin: and my chief ~~grief and~~ fear is lest I should offend him. And my chief delight is in serving God, & if I could serve him as I would, ~~I would~~ think it my chief happiness. And my chief uneasiness is that I cannot get my heart sincere enough before God as I would: & long much to be with Christ in heaven.

[330/– blank]

---

[7] Jer 8:22.
[8] Text from the symbol '‡' to the bracket ']' to be inserted on p. 147.

[331/–] b.h. A Young Woman of 20 years.[1]

I have Reason to be thankful for Restraining Grace that kept me from any thing gross before the World: And when I heard of any gross Outbreakings of others, I thought if people knew my heart, they would think me as bad as these. And when I read in the Larger Catechism[2] of the inward punishments of Sin in this World, such as hardness of heart, blindness of mind &c: I thought these punishments had indeed remarkably fallen on me. I liked well to read good Books and hear Sermons, but I thought I got no benefit at all by them, but rather turn'd still more dead stupid & hard hearted: yet I thought I would still wait on & ly at the pool-side of ordinances, & possibly I might sometime or other meet with a case of grace. I had a form of Prayer all along, but ~~my~~ it did not deserve the name of Prayer, I was so dead & stupid in it. I thought when hearing Sermons, that if I could always sit still & hear there would surely be a change wrought [332/–] on me: but I had no thought of the Righteousness of Christ, & that I must be Saved by that. When Ministers gave the Marks & Evidences of Gods Children I could lay no claim to any of these, but I thought that at the Close of the Sermon, there might be some word dropt to Sinners, & I would wait on to hear that, and I saw clear ground to apply that to my Self: but when I got it, it had little or no Effect upon me; I did not take the right way to get it have any gracious Effect on me: I looked no further than the word, and so came of it, I came away more hardend than when I went there. Only I heard one Sermon by a Minister ( ) at Dumblain Sacrament on these words It is finished,[3] and was very much affected in hearing it, tho yet I was sensible I was none of these that could lay claim to that Redemption which Christ finished & perfected for his people. I also usd oftimes to take much delight in singing of Psalms, in the Congregation & in the Family, when yet I knew I could not praise God for any Spiritual & Saving mercies I had received.

[333/–] About five or Six years ago, when I heard Mr Edwards Narrative of the Surprising work of God at Northampton read;[4] I was very glad to

---

[1]   Margaret Richie – the shorthand text in McCulloch's 'Index of persons' names who gave the foregoing accounts to Mr. McC' states: daughter of James Richie in Gorbels. Taught when a child to read the Bible, and got the Shorter Catechism.

[2]   *Larger Catechism of the Westminster Assembly* (1647).

[3]   Jn 19:30 or Jas 1:15.

[4]   Jonathan Edwards, *A Faithful Narrative of the Surprising Work of God in the Conversion of Many Hundred Souls in Northampton, . . . In a letter to the Reverend Dr. Benjamin Colman . . . Written by the Reverend Mr. Edwards, . . . And published, with a large preface, by Dr. Watts and Dr. Guyse* (Edinburgh: reprinted for J. Oswald in London; and sold by Messieurs J. Paton, J. Davidson, J. Traill, G. Hamilton, A. Duning, in Edinburgh; and by T. Lumisden and J. Robertson: also at Glasgow by J. Barrie, 1737).

hear that there was such a Work of Conversion in these far distant Places: & I thought that if I were there, I might perhaps get a Case of Grace among others, & I was busy from time to time contriving Methods how I might get there.

When I was a Child I got many merry songs by heart, & took much pleasure in singing them over: but two or three years ago, I strove all I could to put them out of my mind, because I found they carried away my thoughts from things of far greater concern to me, & I liked rather to be sad and thoughtful than merry & frolicksome.

Some years ago, there was much talk of Wars that many apprehended we would have in this Country. I then thought they were happy in such a Case that had an Interest in Christ and had him to fly to: but for my Self, I was sure I had no interest in him: & this occasiond some thoughtfulness to me, but any concern I had that way soon wore away again.

[334/–] I found in Experience very often in my life matters so ordered in Providence, that any thing I set my heart much upon in the World, I was sure to be depriv'd of that or cross'd in it. But I thought after many instances of that kind, that if I could secure the one thing needful & get an Interest in Christ, that would Satisfy me & never fail me or be taken from me. But then I knew not how to come by that, or what way to take to attain it.

I got many good Instructions and advices from my Parents; and particularly to improve the time of youth, & to study to be early Religious: & one thing I mind my Father often told me, That he heard once a Minister say in his Sermon That Conversion was rare after 20 years: but I thought with my Self I am not yet 20 years, it may be I may yet converted. And indeed it was about that time of my life when I came to perceive a remarkable Change on my Self.

When I read Mr Whitefields Journals before he came to Scotland, I was glad that God had raisd up so [335/–] remarkable an Instrument of good to many: & that many elsewhere were getting good by him as a mean: & I thought that if I might hear him, I might get good also: but I looked more to the Instrument than any thing else. When he came to Glasgow I was impatient to hear him, hoping he might be an Instrument of awakning me out of my Security, and bringing me to see my lost State by Nature that I was in. I went and heard him preach his first Sermon on these words, If our Gospel And this is the name whereby he shall be called even the Lord our righteousness,[5] and was made Sensible of the vanity and insufficiency of all righteousness of my own [ ]:[6] and while he made offer of Christ to all sorts of Sinners among the Hearers, I would gladly have received him, but could not get my heart brought up to do so as I would. I continued to hear him from day to day while he continued to preach at Glasgow, & thought every Sermon I heard greater than another. I found my heart still continue hard &

---

[5]   Jer 23:6.
[6]   Insertion ['and the Sufficiency of Christs righteousness']: McCulloch.

could not melt or mourn [336/–] for Sin as I saw I had reason: I now say my
Sins in their hainous & aggravated nature & endless number: And above all,
my neglcting the great Salvation, & rejecting ~~the gra~~ Christ in his Gospel Calls
& offers. And that word haunted me much. Prov. Because I have called & ye
have not answered, I have stretched out my hands & ye have not regarded,[7]
I also will laugh at your calamity & mock when your fear cometh;[8] and so
did that other word, If our Gospel be hid it is hid to them that are lost.[9]
Which encreased my Concern & distress. I heard that Minister speak much of
Regeneration & Conversion: and my great Concern was to experience what
it was to be born again, & to be renewed in the Spirit of my mind, & what it
was to sorrow after a godly sort. My distress of Soul was such as debarrd my
eyes in a great measure from the rest & sleep. I inclind however to conceal it
from all as much as I could, & for that end, I sate up often reading and praying
after the rest of the Family were gone to bed.

[337/–] I was also thus imployed oftimes when I was at my Work, and none
were present to observe me. And one day when I was thus taken up, that word
was impress'd on my mind, Behold the Lords hand is not Shortned that he
cannot Save, nor his ear heavy that he cannot hear, but your iniquities have
hid his face from you:[10] I was thereupon made Sensible of Christs Sufficiency
& willingness to Save, but was made to grieve for my Sins, especially my
Slighting Christ in his Gospel offers, whereby I had provokd him to hide
his face from me. Another day when at my Work, that word, The blood of
Jesus Christ his Son cleanses us from all Sin:[11] but I cannot now remember
what effect it had upon me.

At the Sacrament in Glasgow in October 1741, hearing a minister () Lecture
on the Fast day & speaking concerning the Children of Israel coming up
out of the Land of Egypt & eating the Passover with bitter herbs which he
explaind as signifying that godly for Sin with which persons should keep
the Gospel Passover: which I was made [338/–] earnestly to desire. Hearing
another Minister () on the Text How Shall I put thee among the Children[12]
I saw that to very applicable to my own case. Hearing another () [][13] on the
Title of Christ, The Wonderful Counsellor I was greatly affected with what
he said from it concerning Christ: And when he came to shew who were
allowed & invited to come to the Lords Table I listned eagerly: And when
he spoke of these that were burdened under a Sense of Sin and were longing
to be relievd from it by Christ, I found that well agreeing to my Condition

<hr />

7   Pr 1:24.
8   Pr 1:26.
9   2 Co 4:3.
10 Isa 59:1–2.
11 1 Jn 1:7.
12 Jer 3:19.
13 Insertion ['preach the action Sermon']: McCulloch.

at that time: ~~but I~~ which gave me some little ease & encouragement. But I could not go to the Holy Ordinance, having made no preparation for it.

But some time shortly after this I fell into as bad a condition as ever I had been in. I thought the Righteousness of Christ could never be imputed to so great a Sinner as I had been, who had so long slighted and despisd him in his Gospel offers. But hearing a Preacher ( )[14] in the Gorbal Kirk on these words, Which hope we have as a sure & stedfast anchor of the Soul entring into that within the [339/–] vail,[15] I was then made to see, that Christ by his Obedience & Death had brought in a perfect sufficient and everlasting Righteousness: able to justify & Save even the greatest of all Sinners that came to him to for it, and laid hold of it by faith. And was made to praise him in my heart for making a Revelation & discovery of this Righteousness to me. And I became consciously concern'd & impatient, to ~~get~~ be found in Christ not having my righteousness but his, even the righteousness that is of God by faith.

On the Thursday thereafter when I was at my Work, these words in Hos. 14.1. O Israel return unto the Lord for thou hast fallen by thy iniquity: and so on to the 7ᵗʰ verse: all these words came into my mind, & were so powerfully & sweetly impressd on my heart, that & filled me with such love to Christ and joy in him, that I scarce knew whether I was in Heaven or on Earth, and so ravish'd my heart, that for some time I could do nothing but praise the Lord Jesus my gracious Deliverer.

[340/–] In my younger years, I had got not only the Shorter Catechism,[16] but a good part also of the Larger by heart: and many of these Questions in the Larger Catechism[17] were now made very useful to me, When they came into my thoughts as they did often, particularly the answer to that Question 25 Wherein consists the sinfulness of that Estate whereinto man fell? The Sinfulness of that Estate whereinto man fell, consists in the guilt of Adams first Sin, the want of that Righteousness wherein he was created, & the corruption of his nature, whereby he is wholly disabled & made opposite to all that is Spiritually good, and wholly inclined to all Evil and that continually. This account of Original Sin I felt in sad Experience, to agree exactly to what I was by nature, when I lookt back on my former temper and way, & what I was still in my Self. I was therefore now made the more concernd, to look after a real change of heart by grace, & to take heed that I did not rest in any thing short of a saving Interest in Christ & a Saving work of grace in my Soul, and Several Questions with their Answers in the Larger Catechism, ran often in my thoughts & were matter of serious Meditation to me [ ][18] &

---

14 According to Scott, *Fasti Ecclesiae Scoticanae*, the preacher mentioned is most likely John Corse (1715–82).
15 Heb 6:19.
16 *Shorter Catechism of the Westminster Assembly* (1647).
17 *Larger Catechism of the Westminster Assembly* (1647).
18 Insertion ['on that subject']: McCulloch.

made useful for clearing up this matter, in some satisfying [341/–] measure
to me, particularly these relating Effectual Calling and Justification. Many
other Answers to Questions in the Larger Catechism, were made very Sweet
& very useful to my Soul, in these times & since especially these relating to
Christs Exaltation in his Resurrection Ascension & Sitting at the Right hand
of God and Intercession there: as that he arose again from the dead on the
third day, whereby he declard himself to be the Son of God, to have satisfied
Divine Justice, to have vanquished Death & him that had the power of it,
& to be Lord of Quick & Dead: & that he did all this as a Publick person
the Head of his Church &c: That he in our nature and as our Head, ~~visibly~~
triumphing over Enemies, visibly went up into the Highest Heavens, there to
receive Gifts for men, to raise up our affections thither, & to prepare a Place
for us, where himself is & Shall continue &c: That as God-man he is advabced
to the highest favour with God the Father, with all fullness of joy, glory, &
power over all things &c: That he makes Intercession by his appearing in our
nature continually before the Father in Heaven, in the merit of his obedience
& sacrifice on Earth, & so on to the End of that Answer.

One Sabbath night after the rest of the Family were gone to bed, when I was
at Secret Prayer, the Lord was pleasd to give me much more Enlargement of
heart [ ],[19] than I think ever I had been acquaint with before: and while I was
going on in Prayer, that word Hos. 2.19 was born on upon my Spirit, with a
strong & sweet Impression, I [342/–] will betrothe thee unto me, I will betrothe
thee unto me, yea I will betrothe thee unto me forever &c: which filled me
with love to Christ & joy in him, and admiration at his condescending grace
to such a Sinner & poor worm. But this frame was very soon interrupted &
removed by Satans being loose upon me, & permitted to attack me with his firy
darts, & to afflict my Soul with wicked Imaginations & hellish Suggestions:
I wishd if possible, that I might fall asleep, if so be I might by that means get
free of these wicked thoughts: accordingly I did fall asleep, but within a little
awaked in great horror, and under a terror that Satan would appear to me in
some ~~bodily~~ [ ][20] shape: and as I was essaying Prayer, that Word Eph. 6. came
into my mind with a heavenly Impression, Take unto you the whole Armour of
God,[21] —and above all things take to you the Shield of faith whereby ye may be
able to quench all the firy darts of the wicked one:[22] whereupon I was enabled
to See That it was indeed Satans firy darts that were giving me this trouble, &
was helped to very lively actings of faith in Christ as having overcome all the
Powers of darkness & foiled them all in his death on the Cross, & thereby also
purchased & secured Victory over them to his followers.

---

[19]   Insertion ['in that duty']: McCulloch.
[20]   Insertion ['visible']: McCulloch.
[21]   Hos 6:13.
[22]   Hos 6:16.

When I heard that a Seceding minister ( ) was speaking contemptuously of these that were thought to have been awakned by means of some Sermons preach'd at Glasgow in Septr 1741 by a Stranger Minister ( ) I was much concern'd about the matter, & prayd earnestly That if that [343/–] was indeed the Lords work on these persons, he might make it evident that it was so: & one day as I was at my Wheel, thinking on this subject, these words came in with power to my heart, These People have I formed for my Self & they Shall ~~praise me~~ shew forth my praise:[23] & this was immediately followed by that other word He [ ][24] shall build the temple and bear the Glory:[25] which satisfied me that it was indeed the Lords work.

That Winter before the awakening brake out at Cambuslang, I was so much & oft taken up in praying for a Revival or Religion, that I seemd in a great measure to forget my Self & my own concerns: And one day while my heart & thoughts were much running out that way, there were several passages in the 102nd Psalm that were impress'd on my heart with great sweetness, tho' I did not know at the time they came into my mind, where they were to be found, such as

> vs 13 Thou shalt arise and mercy have
> Upon thy Zion yet.
> The time to favour her is come
> The time that thou hast set[26]

—And so on to the 19th verse

> And so also these words Ps. 147.3[27]
> God doth build up Jerusalem
> And he it is alone
> That the disperst of Israel
> Doth gather into one.

And the first time I came to Cambuslang after The Awakening appeard there, these two Psalms and these same Passages in them, were appointed to be publickly sung by the two Ministers (&) who then preachd.

[344/–] I was very often in doubts & fears about my own Condition, & the reality of a work of grace on my heart, & under Apprehensions that I would fall away; and very often after it had been so with me, the Lord was pleasd to give me most of near access to him and communion with him: and

---

[23] Isa 43:21.
[24] Insertion ['Christ']: McCulloch.
[25] Zec 6:13.
[26] Ps 102:13, Scottish Psalter (metrical).
[27] Ps.147:2, Scottish Psalter (metrical).

particularly [ ][28] by speaking in these words with great power & sweetness to my Soul, I will strengthen thee yea I will help thee, yea I will uphold thee with the right hand of my Righteousness,[29] & this was followed with that Seasonable word of Caution, Be sober, be vigilant, for your adversary the Devil goes always about seeking whom he may devour.[30] At another time, that word was applied to me, I will never leave thee nor forsake thee,[31] To which I was made to reply immediatly with my whole heart, Into thine hands I commit my Spirit; for thou hast redeem'd me O God of truth.

One day coming out to Cambuslang, I was helped to sweet meditations by the way, in Is. Who is this that cometh up from Edom, with dyd garments from Bozra, Glorious in his apparel traveling in the greatness of his strength? I that speak in Righteousness, mighty to save:[32] I was made with delight to see that even the Justice of God was more glorified in the Salvation of Sinners, by reason of the Completeness & infinite worth of Christs Satisfaction, than it could be in their Eternal Ruine, & endless sufferings

[345/–] I frequently attended at Cambuslang in 1742, and was sometimes there allowed near access to God, & sometimes I was under many doubts & fears about my Souls State.

And the 2nd Sacrament there in 1743, I felt the Word preachd come not in word only but in power in the Holy Ghost & with much Assurance: And was enabled in the most solemn & hearty manner, to dedicate & devout my whole Self entirely to God in Christ, & to accept of God the Father as my Reconciled God & Father in Christ; to accept of Christ in all his offices on his own Gospel terms, as my alone Lord & Saviour; and the Holy Spirit as my alone Sanctifier, Guide and Comforter. And to take the Bible, & all the Servants of the Lords present as witnesses against me at the day of the Lord, if I had not done so, with my whole heart. And his enabling me to do so, by his grace, I still take to be an Evidence, That the Lord has made with me an Everlasting Covenant, well ordered in all things & sure; and this is all my Salvation and all my desire, whatever Lot he may see fit to order for me in the World. In his name be Eternal Praises. Amen.

[346/– blank]

---

[28] Insertion ['one time']: McCulloch.
[29] Isa 41:10.
[30] 1 Pe 5:8.
[31] Heb 13:5.
[32] Isa 63:1.

[347/–] a.x. A Woman of 18 years of Age[1]

I was thro' Divine mercy, all my life kept from things outwardly gross before the world, and in complyance with my Parents Orders when I was a Child, I usd to make a fashion of praying twice a day: but it went against the Grain with me. When I came to years, I usd to pray more seldom: but did not lay it aside altogether: yet I had but little list or Inclination to it, my heart being drawn away after the vainities of a present world. I usd however all along my life, when I could get access to go to the Kirk on the Sabbath days: but I think it was much owing to Custom that I did go, and when I was there, I took but little heed to what was said, but Suffered my mind to wander after worldly vanities. And I never felt any thing like the presence of God in reading or hearing of the Word or [ ][2] any other duty. I sometimes thought of Death, but I thought I was but young & had time enough before me, And never laid to heart what would come of me when I died. When I fell sick, I thought what would come of me if I died then? But when I recovered I soon forgot these things.

I came to Cambuslang several times in the Spring 1742, & fell under some Concern, but it did not come to any great height, till one day about the middle of May, being a Thursday, [348/–] that I came in, after hearing Sermon on the Brae, into the Manse, to hear the Exhortations & prayers there, and while a Minister (26)[3] was Exhorting in the Hall there, and speaking about Prayer, and Peoples being asleep in Sin, & shewing it, by their careless drousy and unconcernd way of praying, not regarding much whether God heard them or no, & sometimes falling asleep in time of prayer, and not hearing or noticing what they themselves said. While he was speaking to that purpose, I felt my Conscience awakening upon me, & flying in my face, for my guiltiness this way: for this was truly what I had been often guilty of, frequently falling asleep in time of the Prayers in the Family, where I was, & sometimes also in time of my own Prayers: And I thought I had been sleeping & dreaming all my days, and I thereupon fell immediatly into great distress of Soul, not knowing what to do, or what to say or think; for I thought I was undone & that there was no mercy for me. I was under fears of being turn'd into Hell for my Sins; but what I was chiefly griev'd for, was that I had so long been dishonouring God by my Sin, and that I had slighted so many gracious Calls & Invitations to come to Christ.

---

[1]   Mary Colquhoun – the shorthand text in McCulloch's 'Index of persons' names who gave the foregoing accounts to Mr. McC' states: daughter of James Colquhoun, tenant in Old Monkland. Taught to read when a child, got the Catechism to heart, and retained parts.

[2]   Insertion ['prayer or']: McCulloch.

[3]   William McCulloch (1691–1771) – minister, Cambuslang.

I continued in distress that night and for some weeks before I got any Relief. I came over to Cambuslang frequently & heard Sermons [349/–] there of Exhortations & Prayers in the Hall, and [ ]⁴ to join my self to any Company I had access to, where there was any worshipping God; to read my Bible, & retire often to Prayer by my self: and got more & more Convictions from time to time of my Sin, & all the Evils that ever I had done became bitter to me: and the Corruption of my Nature was very grieving to me. While under these Convictions my distress was so great that I could work very little, tho I now & then essay'd it, sleep almost quite departed from me, & I could eat none but with reluctancy. I could have wish'd, if it had been the will of God, to have been out of this world, because I could do nothing but sin in it, & yet alas! I saw I was not prepared for better.

Among other things for which I was grieved, one was that I had all along lived in the neglect of the Holy Ordinance of the Lords Supper, and had never essay'd to obey that Command of a dying Saviour, Do this in remembrance of me. I now resolvd to take the first Opportunity of waiting on God in that Ordinance, & accordingly did so at the first Sacrament at Cambuslang, which was in July 1742: but got nothing sensibly, till the Munday after that Sacrament, when in the time I was hearing a Minister (12) preach, these words, (tho not uttered by him) came into my mind, when I was under great fears, that at the Lords Table I had eat & drank damnation to my Self, Fear not for I am with thee.⁵ [350/–] which banish'd my fears in some measure but not altogether, & was made to hope that the Lord would be ~~with me~~ not utterly cast me off: but tho I was a little easd by this word unbelief very soon prevaild, & my fears returnd again.

I continued a long time again, under doubts & fears, till one night when I was out in the Yeard at Secret Prayer, in great distress of Soul, that word came into my heart, Come unto me all ye that labour & are heavy laden & I will give you rest: upon which I felt a Power coming along enabling me to obey that Command of coming weary and heavy laden as I was to Christ, & was made heartily willing to accept of him in all his Offices, & to rest and rely on him alone for Salvation; and was relievd at the time of that burden of doubts & fears, and had my heart enlarg'd in love to Christ.

One Morning when I awak'd out of sleep, these words were brought into my mind, & impress'd on my heart with great Power

> My heart & flesh doth faint & fail,
> But God doth fail me never
> For of my heart God is the strength
> And portion for ever.⁶

---

⁴ Insertion ['usd']: McCulloch.
⁵ Gen 26:24, Isa 41:10, Isa 43:5.
⁶ Ps 73:26, Scottish Psalter (metrical).

And upon this, I felt my heart drawn out in Love to God ~~and~~ in Christ, & was made to rejoice in him as my alone portion. [351/–] That night before when I was lying in my bed, I was awaked with the most delightful sound, as of a great Company of People Singing Psalms: and lay listning to with great ~~delight~~ [ ]⁷ after I awaked for about the space of an hour. And was sorry when it ceasd. But tho' I thought the Sound was as the Company Singing had been round about me in the place where I was, and did not stop as we usually do, when we sing Psalms, but went on in one continued Song of praise, yet I could not understand any of their words.

One night at Secret Prayer, that word came into my heart Ho every one that thirsteth, let him come to the waters, &c:⁸ I found these words refreshing to my Soul, for I had been earnestly thirsting after Christ and could not find him.

At the Sacrament at Camb. in August 1743, I found it to a most sweet and comfortable time to me: especially on the Sabbath all day over when I got my heart filled with the Love of Christ: and in time of the Action Sermon, these words came into my heart (tho not uttered by the Speaker) My meditation of him shall be sweet & I will be glad in the Lord: & I found it to be indeed so with me that day; & much so also on Munday thereafter.

[352/–] I now for ordinary find my desire chiefly running out after Christ and holiness: and am thro grace, brought in some measure to submit to whatever he orders for me from time to time. I have no [. . . . . . .] for the riches or great things of the world, and have little relish for any of its pleasures. My heart Evils are a burden to me. I take much delight in reading the Bible & Prayer, & hearing of the Gospel. My great fear is that I may be lost to my Self & fall back to my former ways, & my daylie Prayer & desire is that I may be preservd from every thing dishonouring to God & Religion, & that he may ~~preserve me to the [. . . .]~~ keep me from every evil way & work & preserve me to his heavenly kingdom. To his name be praise.

[353/– and 354/– blank]

---

⁷   Insertion ['pleasure']: McCulloch.
⁸   Isa 55:1.

[355/-] a.p. A Young Woman about 18 years[1]

I was all along, thro mercy, kept blameless before the world in my outward behaviour. I usd from my Childhood to pray evening & morning, & read the Bible by my self oftimes, & went to the Kirk on Sabbath days to hear Sermon, and endeavour'd to abstain from all vices; and thought my self in a fair way for Heaven. One night about a month before the Awakening began at Camb. I found much of a heart-melting, & would gladly have gone out to the Yeard for Secret Prayer, but I was so timerous I durst not adventure to go out by my self alone, & one whom I desir'd to go out with me, not complying with the motion I made to her, I did not go: which has often been matter of grief to me since. But all this time I had never got a sense of my lost Condition by nature without Christ, till I came to Camb.; in the Spring 1742, and as I came there from time to time, I got Convictions of my sins both of heart and life, & was deeply grieved, that I had been so long alienated from the Life of God, & rejected Christ, & dishonoured such a holy God by my Sins. I gave my Self much to Secret Prayer, & read my Bible & other [356/-] good Books whenever I could have Opportunity. My inward distress was such that I often slept very little & could eat but little. But I never cry'd out in publick, that any could notice, nor did I ever swarf, and tho I often felt a great agony within my Soul, I felt no bodily pains. And in this Condition I continued for about six weeks, ~~about~~ without meeting with any Relief; till one day when I was at Secret Prayer, that word came into my heart, Fear not, for I am with thee; this word came with such great Power, that I was made to believe it was from the Lord: formerly I thought any Exercise I was under, was not of a kindly sort, nor like any other of the people of God: but now I was persuaded that it was indeed the Spirit of the Lord that was dealing with me, & was made to hope that the Lord would be with me.

I got a Token in order to communicate at the Barony Sacrament, & in time of a Minrs (65)[2] Sermon on the Fast-day, the Lord by his Spirit, set home many gracious words (tho' not uttered by that Minister) on my heart, with great power & sweetness, and gave me such manifestations of his Love that I had never met with any thing like it before: and this sweet frame continued with me [][3] all the following days of that Solemnity.

---

[1] Ann Montgomery – the shorthand text in McCulloch's 'Index of persons' names who gave the foregoing accounts to Mr. McC' states: daughter of Mathw Montgomery, shoemaker in Glasgow. Taught to read the Bible when young, got the Catechism by heart, and retained it mostly.

[2] Colin Campbell (1718–88) – minister, Eaglesham.

[3] Insertion ['most part of']: McCulloch.

[357/–] After that Communion-Occasion, I long'd much for another; & shortly after got liberty to go to the Sacrament at Paisley: but there I was all the time under great hardness of heart: I came home from it much discouraged, and continued two days under great Agonies of Soul, because I had not met with Gods gracious presence there: And was made to see that I was lost & undone, unless I got on a better Righteousness than my own. And I was helped to renounce all trust in my own Righteousness, & was made to believe that Christ clothed me with his Righteousness: and every time I went to Secret Prayer, I was made to believe that Christ was pleading my Cause at the Right hand of God, & was standing with out-stretched arms of mercy ready to receive me; and found him allowing me much communion and nearness to him. And this frame continued with me for a considerable time.

Not long after this, I came to the 2d Sacrament at Camb. in August 1742, and had great manifestations of the Love of God to my Soul, on Sabbath & Munday, (which were the only days I had access to attend there). On Sabbath when I was hearing Sermons at one of the Tents, that word [358/–] came into my heart with great sweetness & delight, Arise my Love my fair one and come away.[4] Upon which I came quickly & cheerfully to the Table, & met with much of the Lords presence there. My heart was even almost overwhelmed under the Sensible Out-lettings & Manifestations of the love of Christ to my soul: and this frame continued with me next day; and for a long time after. All the harvest following, much of it remain'd with me, & every day almost I was still getting some new manifestations of the Love of God.

And so also all the Winter ensuing the Lord favoured me with much sweet Communion & fellowship with himself, especially in the duty of Secret Prayer: tho' I cannot say, I met with so much of his gracious Presence in Publick Ordinances, as I had the Summer before. And in the Spring & Summer 1742, I also met oftimes with the Lords gracious Presence in Secret duties, tho' I do not meet with that measure of Love & joy that I usd to have, except at some particular times.

My heart-Corruptions are a daylie grief to me, & I endeavour to apply to Christ to cure me of them: but many a time when I find them so strong, I am made to think that I have not yet met with a Saving Change: at other times I got some Victory over them, & then I am made to hope the Lord has begun a good Work in my heart, & will perfect it at the day of Christ; to whom be glory for ever, Amen [359/–] and I find my heart main desires for ordinary running out, above all things in the world, after the Enjoyment of Christ in his Ordinances here, & for ever hereafter in Heaven; to him be glory for ever. Amen.

[360/– blank]

---

[4]   SS 2:13.

[361/–] a.n. A Young Woman of 23 years.[1]

I had my Lot in Religious Families since I was a Child, & was kept free of any thing gross before the World, all along: & usd to pray for ordinary twice a day; & always when I had access went to the Kirk on Sabbath days, to hear what the Lord would speak to me by his Servants; & usd to read the Bible by my Self. But never felt the Word of God coming with the Power of God to my heart till I came to Camb. in the Spring 1742: & there some time I think in March, hearing a Minr (26)[2] on that Text, He will not break the bruised Reed, nor quench the smoaking flax &c:[3] I fell under some Concern about my Salvation, & was under some trouble about my lost State by Sin; but in the Evening, I felt it like to wear off again, yet something of it still remain'd with me, that night and next day it increasd on me, & I found my Spirit much vex'd & grievd for my Sin, & sent for an Elder to speak with him as to my Souls ~~State~~ Case; and got a humbling Sight of all my Sins, sins of life & sins of heart, Original & actual sins. I had some fears of Hell, but what chiefly [362/–] troubled me was a sense of Gods anger & displeasure against me for my sin, and that I had thereby dishonoured & offended him. I continued till about July following under soul trouble for sin before I got any Relief or Comfort: and was all that time, very often at Secret Prayer, and as earnest as I was enabled to be; I also came to Camb. to hear Sermons, almost every day but Sabbath when I went to the Parish-Kirk I belong'd to: & almost every time I came there I was getting more and more Convictions of the Evil of Sin, & discoveries of particular iniquities: and when at any time I miss'd new Convictions when I came to Camb. I was much grieved that it was so. I was sometimes made to cry out in publick under fears of the anger of God whom I had dishonoured by my sins so greatly: but never swarfd but once: but had no bodily pains or Convulsions.

The first Outgate I got my Soul-distress was one night when I was sitting by my self, much cast down under a sense of Sin, when these words came into my mind

> Those that are broken in their hearts
> And grieved in their minds
> He healeth & their painful wounds
> He tenderly up-binds[4]

---

[1] Bethea Davie – the shorthand text in McCulloch's 'Index of persons' names who gave the foregoing accounts to Mr. McC' states: daughter of John Davie, weaver in Mid-Quarter Barony. Taught to read the Bible, got the Catechism, and retained it mostly.
[2] William McCulloch (1691–1771) – minister, Cambuslang.
[3] Isa 42:3, Mt 12:20.
[4] Ps 147:3, Scottish Psalter (metrical).

[363/–] which settled my troubled heart a little, and gave me peace love and joy in God. And something of this frame lasted with me for two or three days.

Another time when I was hearing Sermon in the Barony, (19)[5] that word, tho not uttered by the Minister, came in to my heart, Thou wilt keep him in perfect peace whose mind is stayed on thee.[6] I then got my heart stayed on God, & had much of holy peace & composure of Soul.

I now find my heart set upon Jesus Christ above all things: the vanities of a present world have not now that room in my heart they usd to have. I find great delight in reading my Bible & hearing Sermons. I have sometimes a Concern & uneasiness about heart Evils, but am not so cast down altogether as sometimes I have been. And desire to trust in the merits of Christ for all the Hopes I have of Heaven.

[364/– blank]

[5] John Hamilton (d. 1780) – minister, Barony/Glasgow; translated to St Mungo's in 1749.
[6] Isa 26:3.

[365/–] a.y. A Young Woman of 18 years[1]

My manner of life from my Childhood was free of ~~any~~ gross Stains before the world. When I was a Child, I was often urgd by my Parents to pray, and in compliance with them, I would have made a fashion of it sometimes once & sometimes twice, & []² oftimes not at all. When I came to more years, falling in Providence into a Religious Family, I usd for ordinary to pray once or twice a day. I usd all along, when I could have Liberty, to go to the Kirk on Sabbath-days: but it was only in a formal way: & when I was there I usd often to give but little heed to what was said. And I never knew what it was, 'till last year, to meet with the Presence of God, in praying reading or hearing the Word.

In hearing a Minister (12)³ preach at Glasgow in June 1743, on that Text Who hath believed our report, & to whom is the arm of the Lord reveald, I fell under a Concern, but could not well tell what aild me: but hearing that Minister a little after at Camb. on that Text, Gen. Make haste flee for thy life, escape to the Mountains,⁴ When he said, flee to Christ flee for your life lest ye be consumd: these words came with great power to my heart.

[366/– through 372/– blank]

---

1   Catherine Tennant – the shorthand text in McCulloch's 'Index of persons' names who gave the foregoing accounts to Mr. McC' states: daughter of David Tenant, maltman in Glasgow. Taught to read the Bible and got the Catechism mostly to heart.

2   Insertion ['but']: McCulloch.

3   George Whitefield (1714–70) – evangelist.

4   Gen 19:17.

[373/–] a.q. A woman of about 24 years of age.[1]

My Life & conversation before the World was not stain'd with gross out-
breakings. I usd to pray by my self when I was a Child, & when I came
to more years, I sometimes minded it, but often neglected it. I usd to read
the Word by my self, & to go to hear it preach'd on Sabbath Days, to see
if I might get any good by it: but did not much attend to what was said:
But never felt it come with any Power to my heart, till I came to Camb.
in the Spring 1742; and hearing a Minr Sermons often there, (26)[2] I fell
under more Concern than ever before, about my Salvation: & when I
heard & saw so many there so much affected, my Concern was thereby
increased; yet I thought I was so stupid that there was none like me. My
Concern was greatly heightned in hearing a Minr (11)[3] on that Text, Him
that cometh unto me I will in no wise cast out.[4] Next morning after that,
these words came into my heart like a sword, while I thought What a
wretched Sinner am I who will not come to Christ, having such an offer
made to me! And then I fell into great distress of Soul, at the thoughts of
my Sin whereby [374/–] I had so greatly offended and dishonoured God,
& losing and mispending so much precious time. I came very oft after that
to Camb. & every time I came, I got more and more Convictions of Sin, &
more love to the Word, so that I could have been content oftimes to have
stayed all night on the Brae, and to have continued hearing Sermons, and
joining in Prayers & Praises there. My Corruption of Nature, my unbelief
and hardness of heart were particularly affecting to me. I was sometimes
constraind to cry out some in publick, but it was but little, but I never
swarfd, or fainted or had any bodily pains.

I continued in this distressed Case, all the Spring and Summer, till a little
before Harvest, that these words came into my mind,

> A broken Spirit is to God
> A pleasing Sacrifice
> A broken and a contrite heart
> Lord thou wilt not despise.[5]

---

[1] Janat Moffat – the shorthand text in McCulloch's 'Index of persons' names who gave
the foregoing accounts to Mr. McC' states: daughter of Alexander Moffat, shoemaker in
Shettleston. Spouse of John Paton, bleecher. Taught to read the Bible, got the Catechism
by heart, and retained it mostly.
[2] William McCulloch (1691–1771) – minister, Cambuslang.
[3] William Hamilton (1689–1769) – minister, Douglas.
[4] Jn 6:37.
[5] Ps 51:17, Scottish Psalter (metrical).

I had then some measure of heart-brokenness for Sin, tho I was afraid that it was not of the right kind: but now, I was made to hope that this brokenness of heart the Lord had wrought in me was such as he would accept thro' the merits of his Son; and this gave me a great deal of ease at the time: but I wanted still to have more of this heart-brokenness for Sin.

I bless the Lord, I have got some Love to Christ, & am grieved that I cannot love him more [375/–] and serve him better: and this is my chief Concern when I rise up and when I ly down & my great grief is that I am so often offending him.

[376/– blank]

[377/1] A. D. a young man about 20 years of age.[1]

My Parents set me to pray by my self when I was Child, but I often neglected it especially at night, hasting to my bed, and when I did mind it my heart was not in it: I also continued to keep up some form of it after I came to years; but I cannot say that ever I found any thing like the presence of God in that or any other duty, till one Sabbath day that my Brother & I were at home reading that part of the Bible together, about Christs Sufferings, at the thoughts of which I burst out into tears & ran away to my knees & pray'd: but this wore off in a little. It pleased God in his mercy to keep me all along free of many things that ~~could be called~~ are called gross before the World: only I was a little voguish among my Commorades when young, & one time I was drawn away by some Companions to drink till I was the worse of it: and I usd sometimes to let an Oath fly & to prophane Gods holy name. I usd all along to go to the Kirk on Sabbath days, but not on other days, but it was but in compliance with my Parents orders & for fear of their anger if I had not done so. But I never felt the word come home to my heart with any power when I went, only there were some Sermons I heard with more delight than others: but all the while I never got any sense of my lost condition by nature, [378/2] till May 1742, at Cambuslang. I came out in Febr. to that place a little after the Awakening brake out there; & hearing a Minr (26)[2] give out that Ps. to be sung in the Entry, When Zion's bondage God turn'd back &c:[3] my heart was much affected at the thoughts that God was now reviving his Work after such a long time of deadness. I had also some Concern on me in the time of Sermon, but I found no abiding Effect follow, but that I was made more diligent in duty than I had been before; & prayd the Lord might send me Convictions as he had done to others; & was persuaded that this was indeed the Work of God on Souls. I usd after that all along thro' that Spring, ~~not only~~ to come out & hear Sermons at Camb. not only on Lords days, (except once) but oftimes on Week days also; wishing and praying often as I came along that that might be the day of my Awakening. But it did not prove so till on a Thursday in May, after I had been hearing two Sermons on the Brae ( ) and got nothing, I went in to the Kirk where another Minr (26) preached on that Text Is. He feedeth on ashes, a deceived heart leadeth him astray, so that he cannot deliver his own soul, nor say, Is there not a lie

---

[1]   Duncan Alge – the shorthand text in McCulloch's 'Index of persons' names who gave the foregoing accounts to Mr. McC' states: journeyman weaver in Glasgow. He was, along with his brother, put to school by parents, taught to read and write some, got the Catechism, and retained it mostly.

[2]   William McCulloch (1691–1771) – minister, Cambuslang.

[3]   Ps 126:1.

in my right hand.[4] In hearing that Sermon I found my self struck thro' the heart by the power of God coming along with what was said, which appeard to be all leveld against me in particular. He spoke much of Covetousness & worldly mindedness [379/3] as being Spiritual Idolatry: and this had been my great predominant sin: & when he said the Spiritual Idolater, the Covetous worlding (the person particularly aim'd at in the text) could not say with the Psalmist []⁵ Lord, I am continually with thee;⁶ but he might justly say. O World, I am continually with thee, when I am going to sleep at night, & when I awake in the morning, and all the day long, I am continually with thee, & thou art continually with me. These words in a particular manner were made to pierce me to the heart, & I saw I was just the person described, & fell into great distress of soul, at the thoughts that I had been so much taken up about the World, & had neglected God so much: []⁷ & that I had been all along feeding upon such ashes & base husks, & had been led astray from God by a deceived heart: but tho my distress was great I did not at this time or at any other, cry out openly among the people, nor did I ever swarf or faint, or find any convulsions or bodily pains, but I have frequently been made to burst out into tears thro anguish of heart, tho I kept all as quiet & secret from the notice of others as possible. I went home that night in great heaviness of spirit & uneasiness of heart, & went to Secret prayer; & confess'd this my great guilt of too great eagerness after the world & deceiving my own soul []:⁸ & had great freedom in pouring out my heart before him. And after this my Convictions of sin went on from day to day.

[380/4] In hearing several Sermons on the Brae at Camb. Brae before this, I had concerning the evil & danger of the Sin of Unbelief (26), I had got some Sight and Sense of that Sin: but now I got a deeper and more affecting Sense of this Sin at that Sermon in the Kirk at Camb. than ever before. I was then made to see that I justly deserved hell, but I can not say that I was then or at any time else terrifyd with the thoughts of hell. After this I found the Sermons at Camb. more agreeable to me than before, but continued for some weeks in great heaviness under a sense of my sins [].⁹

One Sabbath after this coming home from Camb. a person by the way observing an appearance of sadness & concern upon me, askd me, If I was yet got into any Society for Prayer, I answered no: the person promised to take me into one & did so soon after. At one of these meetings I was desird to pray,

---

⁴ Isa 44:20.
⁵ Insertion ['Nevertheless O']: McCulloch.
⁶ Ps 73:23.
⁷ Insertion subsequently marked out for deletion: ['& at the sight of the other sins of my past life']: McCulloch.
⁸ Insertion ['and other sins']: McCulloch.
⁹ Insertion ['but often I went home with a sad heart fearing I would not profit under the Gospel so clearly dispensd']: McCulloch.

& did so, but with some confusion. At another occasion, I was urg'd to pray, but would not, I was under so great fear lest I should utter something that was not right; but when I came home was much vexed that I should have had so much of slavish fear on me, that I refusd to confess God before men. I went however & spent most of that night by my self in Secret Prayer; and pleaded that the Lord might take away slavish fear & gave me a door of utterance to pray with others when called. I was never left to despair, but was under such a terror this night, that I was never nearer it than now.

[381/5] This night or early next morning, that word was pressed on my heart with some power, God forbid that I should glory in any thing save in the Cross of our Lord Jesus Christ:[10] I sometimes thought this word came from the Lord to me, to shew me that I ought not to put the gift of praying before others, on which my mind had before been much running, or anything else, ~~before~~ in the room of the knowledge of Christ and him crucifyd. But I oftimes doubted if it was from God to me at all, & my unbelief in this matter so far prevaild, that tho I thought I had read these words somewhere in the Bible, yet I did not seek to find it out there.

My Master with whom I learn'd my Trade at this time, took me out into the fields, & gave me many good counsels. A Friend asking me if I had got any at the Sermons at Camb. I said I did not know well, but I was made more diligent in duty, & had a greater thirst after the Word than ever I had before.

Going to a Sacrament Occasion at Kilmaronnock about the middle of June, I did not think when I went of communicating there, & so did not ask for a Token: but in hearing the Minr (37)[11] preach the Action Sermon on these words, In him shall all the Seed of Israel be justify'd & shall glory,[12] I felt my heart so filld with the Love of Christ, that I was much vex'd at my self that I had not applied for a Token,

[382/6] that I might have gone to the Lords Table: and I was so eager to get there, that tho I knew I could not be admitted without a Token, yet I had almost ventured to go & sit down there without one. On the Munday, hearing a Minr (71)[13] preach on that Word I had met with before, God forbid that I should glory in anything save in the Cross of our Lord Jesus Christ,[14] to which was added in his Text, tho not as the words came to me first, by whom the World is crucified to me & I unto to world;[15] I was made to rejoice much to hear a Sermon on the same words that had been sent to me, not long before this: and tho' I could scarce then think they came from God to me; yet now I was made to believe that it was indeed so: & found what

10 Gal 6:14.
11 William Brown (1702–61) – minister, Kilmarnock.
12 Isa 45:25.
13 James Baine Jr (1676–1755) – minister, Killearn.
14 Gal 6:14.
15 Gal 6:14.

was said brought home to my heart: I was then made to glory in a crucified Saviour & in what he did & suffered for perishing Sinners; and thought the latter part of the Text very much suited to me, who had been such a Lover of the World, & wanted & wished for nothing so much, as that by virtue of the death & sufferings of Christ on the Cross, the world from thenceforth might be crucified to me, & I to the world.[16] That night I join'd with several others in prayer with great delight & Enlargement, & continued joining prayer & praises with them till next morning.

Hearing that there was to be a Sacrament at Camb. in July 1742, I resolv'd by grace to attend it: And coming out there & hearing a Minr (16)[17] preach on Saturday on that Text Luke 2. Fear not for behold I bring unto you glad tidings &c.[18] [383/7] I was made to burst out into tears of grief that I had so long neglected that Ordinance of the Lords Supper & of joy that there was a Saviour provided for lost Sinners such as I. In hearing another Minr (12)[19] on that text, I will pour out a Spirit of grace and supplication, & they shall look &c:[20] the Lord gave me a heart to look to a crucified Saviour, & to my sins as what had procured the Lord of Glory to be pierced, & tho I had formerly endeavoured to keep my weeping secret from the eyes of others, yet at this time I was made to mourn & weep so as I could not get it concealed. After those Sermons, I went away with haste to Glasglow & got a Line to get a Token, & came back with it to Camb. that Evening & got one, & spent all that night in prayer by my self and with others. On Sabbath I communicated but did not get all that I thought to have got: I delighted however much in the Work of the day. And so also on Munday.

In harvest 1742 being in Kilmaronnock, I set apart a day for humiliation for my sins, being then free from business: & in the Evening of that day, others came & join'd in prayer with me. After that chapter Jer. 31. had been read in the meeting, a Woman askd me what I thought was the meaning of a passage in it: I told what I thought; but I & she have her thoughts of it. I was afterwards sensible she was in the right, & I in the wrong, as to the meaning: Next Sabbath a Minr hinted a little at the matter, & spoke of some wresting the Scripture & wished persons might have right ends in resorting to such meetings. For my self I could appeal to the Witness & judge of all, I had no carnal ends in it. [384/8] but was much cast down to think that such things should be suspected. In the afternoon, hearing that Minr preach on Isai. 61. To proclaim the acceptable year of the Lord,[21] where he shewed, that the year referr'd to was the year of Jubile, & that this year present was indeed

---

16 Gal 6:14.
17 Alexander Webster (1707–84) – minister, Tolbooth/Edinburgh.
18 Lk 2:10.
19 George Whitefield (1714–70) – evangelist.
20 Zec 12:10.
21 Isa 61:2.

an acceptable year of the Lord, a Spiritual Jubile to many souls: to which I heartily agreed, & found my heart enlarg'd in joyful blessing of God that he had made it a year of jubilee to my Soul & to the souls of many others.

In May 1743 being at Camb. on a Lords day, & hearing a Minr (26) preach from these words, We were children of wrath as well as others,[22] & insisting at large on our Original guilt & corruption; I was greatly affected with the Sense of it in my Self. I had got some Conviction and sense of heart-corruptions about a year before, when first awakened, & many times after that; and some few days before I heard this Sermon, I had sad Experience of the power of it, feeling my heart rise against one who was disputing with me & contradicting what I said; I thought I had got anger & such Corruptions much mortified & subdued, but finding them stir with such vigour, I was much cast down, & went & mourn'd to Secret [ ][23] them before the Lord: And coming & hearing this Sermon, I was greatly afflicted & humbled for these corruptions of my heart & sin of my nature, beyond whatever I had been formerly before. And hearing another Sermon (26) shortly after that, on the Text before the [385/9] Sacrament in May 1743, on that Text, By one mans disobedience many were made sinners,[24] I got still a further humbling sight & sense of my Sinning in Adam when he sinned, & being made thereby liable to wrath, & yet more by the pollution & corruption of my nature derived from him: & I wanted still have further humbling discoveries of this kind made to me. I came to the Lords Table there, with that in my view, as a great part of my Errand, that I might get my strong corruptions subdu'd & weak grace strengthned, & hope the Lord gave me my request in some measure; for I do not find my corruptions quite so strong as they were. Hearing a Minr (13)[25] preach on that text on [ ][26] Sabbath Evening there, Joh. 16. Several Expressions he had were brought home to my heart with sweetness & in a suitableness to my Condition then, & what had been my Exercise for some time before, such as, That there were two armies in a Believer fighting against one another, an army of Grace, & an army of Corruptions: that as Jonathan climbd up between two sharp rocks; so the believer had to climb to heaven, between the two sharp rocks of presumption & despair: that one thing that made the believer long to be away to Christ in heaven was that then he would be free of the Canaanites of Corruptions that now dwell in his heart: and this was what made me also long to be there. [386/10] On the Munday I found some Expressions in that Ministers Sermons come very pressingly on my heart, particularly when he said, Exhorted young people to open their hearts to Christ, & added, That if they would not do so, Christ would one day tell

---

[22] Eph 2:3.
[23] Insertion ['and bewaild']: McCulloch.
[24] Ro 5:19.
[25] John Willison (1680–1750) – minister, South Church, Dundee.
[26] Insertion ['the Communion']: McCulloch.

them, when they knockt at the Heavens gates to get in saying Lord, Lord open to us, I will open heaven to you, as you opened [ ]²⁷ to me such a day at Cambuslang. This made me earnestly look & cry to God in my heart, That he would open my heart to himself, for I found I was unable to do it my self, & found some love to Christ stirring within me.

On the Sabbath after that Sacrament, hearing a Minr (26) Lecture concerning Peters denying his master, & shewing, That Peter did not deny Christ to be the Son of God or the true Messiah, but only that he did not know him; & so persons might deny Christ tho they did not deny his being the true God or alone Saviour, or such fundamental Truths, if they deny'd their acquaintance with Christ, & the power of his Grace on their hearts, or too much conceald his loving kindness to their souls. These words I found applied to me in particular, with ~~such a~~ power [ ].²⁸ And I could not forbear going to the Minr after Sermon, & acknowledging with [ ]²⁹ grief of heart That I had been guilty of Peters Sin in denying his master, who gave me some suitable Exhortations & told me I might come some other day if I pleasd & declare what Christ had done for my Soul: And this I have now given some few hints of. May it tend to his Glory, & to his name be praise.

---

27 Insertion ['your hearts']: McCulloch.
28 Insertion ['and I saw I had been too much a hidden Disciple']: McCulloch.
29 Insertion ['tears and']: McCulloch.

[387/–] a.m. A Young Woman of 20 years[1]

I was along kept from cursing, swearing, lying and such vices [].[2] I had no pleasure in loose company, and was in mercy kept from them. I usd all along from my Childhood to pray once a day or ofter; yet a little thing would have made me sometimes to neglect it. I usd also to read my Bible by my self and to go to Church on Lords days out of some desire to hear Sermons, but cannot say that ever the Word came home with power to me till last year in March 1742, that I came to Camb. & heard a Minr (26)[3] preach there, on that Text, A bruised Reed will he not break, the smoking flax will he not quench:[4] I heard that Sermon with a great deal of pleasure, but cannot say that any thing I then heard pierc'd my heart: I went away however in some Concern, & came back in a few days again, & thought I then felt my heart harder then ever it had been, & that every one about me was more concernd than I. I frequently came & heard at Camb. & was under a good deal of concern, tho [388/–] I thought it was nothing so great as I would have had it, & conceald it from all about me, but frequently usd to go & pour out my complaint before God.

One day I came to Camb. hearing a Minr (26) preach on that text, While the Strong Man armed keeps the house all his good are in peace:[5] when he spoke of the various ways whereby Satan kept sinners in carnal security with a false peace, particularly, by Suffering them to make as many good resolutions to mind their life as they pleasd, but keeping them by his wiles & temptations from putting these Resolutions in practice, & keeping them from seeing their lost & undone State without Christ: I thought that I was just the person he spoke of, for I had had many purposes of turning better & yet all these purposes came to nothing; & my distress of Soul turn'd then so great, that I could scarce refrain crying: tho yet I got it refraind, & never cryd out nor swarfd then or at any other time: but by endeavouring with all my might to refrain crying, I felt my body much [389/–] pain'd sometimes, & my heart as it were ready to leap out of my mouth, I was never under any fears of Hell, but all my grief was that I could not be griev'd enough for sin, ~~and could not~~ as dishonoring to God, & wounding to Christ, and grieving to the Holy Spirit, & that I could not get a heart to love Christ as I would

---

1   Isobel Moffat – the shorthand text in McCulloch's 'Index of persons' names who gave the foregoing accounts to Mr. McC' states: daughter of James Moffat, shoemaker in Mid-Quarter Barony. Taught to read the Bible, got Catechism, and retained in mostly.
2   Insertion ['for ordinary']: McCulloch.
3   William McCulloch (1691–1771) – minister, Cambuslang.
4   Isa 42:3, Mt 12:20.
5   Lk 11:21.

have had it. When I heard Sermons, it was not the terrors & threatnings of the Law that affected me, but the slighting and neglecting of Christ & Salvation, that I had been guilty of so long. At the Close of this Sermon the Minr (26) appointed the 13th Psalm to be sung, How long will thou forget me Lord &c:[6] At the singing of which I was so affected that I had almost cry'd again out, but got it refraind till after Sermon that I was by my self, & then my heart was ready to burst.

At hearing a Minr ( ) on that text at Camb. He hears the cry of the poor & needy: When he said, It is better to cry out now then to cry for ever in hell, I could not allow my self to cry out for all that: but when he added, I hope there are some crying in their hearts to God, that are not crying out with their voice, I was sure I was one of these.

[390/–] One Sabbath in Harvest 1742, ~~hearing~~ being in the Barony Kirk, at singing of the 8th Psalms at the Entry of publick worship, I was greatly affected, especially at these words, Then said I What is man that he, remembred is by thee,[7] I was then made to admire at the patience of God toward me, that he had [. . .] cast me into Hell long e're then. The Minr (19)[8] that day preachd on that text, He will speak peace to his people & to his Saints, but let them not turn again to folly. He had been preaching on it before, when I was not present: & now he said, He would address himself to three sorts of persons, Those that never had any peace spoke to them from God, and that no concern to obtain it: those that knew not whether ever God had spoke peace to them or no: & those that could say on good grounds that God had spoken peace to them. When he spoke to the first sort, I thought I was one of them, for that I had never had any suitable Concern upon me for peace from God and my Soul-distress was then very great at this apprehension: & was glad that there was yet a Call to me to seek after [391/–] this peace & any possibility to obtain it, & my heart was earnestly crying to God for it. I thought also that I was among the second sort, for tho I could not deny I had had some Concern for peace with an offended God by Jesus Christ, yet I knew not if ever God had spoke peace to me or no: but now O how precious would ~~have~~ such an Intimation have been to my Soul. In singing the 4th Psalm at the Close, especially these words,

> Upon my heart bestow'd by thee
> More gladness I have found
> Than they even then when corn & wine,
> Did most with them abound.[9]

6   Ps 13:1, Scottish Psalter (metrical).
7   Ps 8:4, Scottish Psalter (metrical).
8   John Hamilton (d. 1780) – minister, Barony/Glasgow; translated to St Mungo's in 1749.
9   Ps 4:7, Scottish Psalter (metrical).

I felt my heart fill'd with such a joy in God, thro' Jesus Christ, as far excelld any joy ever I had found, in creature Enjoyments, or than be found in any thing below the Sun.

Next Sabbath hearing a Minr (19) Lecture on Christs Sufferings, & speaking of the Crown of Thorns put upon Christs head, and how they then smote him with a Reed on the Head, driving the Thorns into it, & how the Blood gushd down from his Sacred Head, I found my heart like to burst at the thoughts of my Sins whereby I had pierced him in that manner, or made him be pierc'd.

After that I fell into a Fever, and in the [392/–] time of it, that Word came into my mind,

> He took me from a fearful pit
> And from the miry clay
> And on a Rock he set me feet
> Establishing my way.[10]

I was then in the Rage of the Fever & cannot now refect distinctly what Effect it then had upon me: but only it stuck much in my mind, & when I recover'd I found some Comfort when it came fresh into my heart. After Recovery from this Sickness, that Word also came into my mind with some Comfort,

> The troubles that affect the just
> In number many be
> But yet at length out of them all
> The Lord will set them free.[11]

A little while after this, That word was darted into my mind all on a sudden,

> All that fear God come hear I'll tell
> What he did for my soul[12]

These words came with much power & sweetness, but at first I knew not what to make of them, not knowing that they were in the Bible: but at length finding them there, I was much overjoyed, & knew not how to praise God enough for what he had done for my Soul. I had along conceald all I had met with from all the world, except that I had told a little of my trouble to a Minr (19) when I was sick. But now I told something both of my troubles and comforts [393/–] to one of my Acquaintances.

One night I was going to bed, these words came into my heart,

---

[10]   Ps 40:2, Scottish Psalter (metrical).
[11]   Ps 34:19, Scottish Psalter (metrical).
[12]   Ps 66:16, Scottish Psalter (metrical).

> Those that are broken in their hearts
> And grieved in their minds:
> He healeth & their painful wounds
> He tenderly up-binds[13]

I never thought my Grief for Sin was so great as it should have been: but I was made at this time to bless God that I felt some brokenness of heart for sin, & to hope for healing from the same merciful hand that had wounded.

One day I was reading my Bible, and was much discouraged at the thoughts of my being such a vile & Sinful Creature, & that there was none like me, and that I would never get good at all, these words, tho' I was not then reading that place where they are, came into my mind, Why art thou cast down O my Soul,[14] these were the only words that came with power, but having read that place formerly, I also remembered the words that follow, Why art thou disquieted within me, Trust in God &c:[15] upon which I was made to rejoice That I was in any measure cast down for my Sins, tho' not so much as I would, and that I was yet in the way of mercy.

One night when I was in my Bed, These words came with power into my heart, Tho' [394/–] your Sins be as crimson & Scarlet I'll make you white as wool: if ye be willing and obedient ye shall eat the good of the Land.[16] I was hereupon made to believe that God was able & willing to forgive my Sins, tho I had not been under so great distress for them as many others, & made to rejoice on the belief that he had done ~~or would do~~ so, & thought I would never doubt of it after that: I knew I could not obey his commands by any power of my own: but I believed that he that had made me willing to obey, could also enable me to obey his Calls, & trusted he would ~~do~~ help me to do so in some measure of Sincerity.

The Minr of the Parish (19) coming thro the place where I liv'd, I was very desirous to speak to him, but did not know what I would say, when that word came into my mind, Let your Light so shine before men, that others seeing your good works may glorify your Father which is in Heaven,[17] which I took to be a Call to tell him some things I had met with & did so: & found a great desire in my heart to glorify God in a course of Holiness, and a greater hatred of Sin & care to avoid it.

One day, I found vain thoughts crowd into my mind, & could not get rid of them at all, & was afraid God had forsaken me altogether; but these words being pressd on my heart, settled my mind & made me to rejoice in God

---

[13] Ps 147:3, Scottish Psalter (metrical).
[14] Ps 42:5.
[15] Ps 42:5.
[16] Isa 1:18–19.
[17] Mt 5:16.

[395/–] He will not chide continually
Nor keep his anger still
With us he dealt not as we sinn'd
Nor did requite our ill.[18]

One night while I was alone, these words Believing we rejoice, came into my mind, but more faintly; but afterward that same night while joining in Family Worship, as he[19] read in the Chapter that fell in of course that night, while he read these words, Seeing him who is invisible, the former words came into my heart suddenly & fully, Whom having not seen we love, in whom tho' now we see him not, yet believing we rejoice with joy unspeakable & full of glory: and at that instant, I was enabled to behave in Christ with a lively faith, & felt my heart warm'd with Love to him, & fill'd with unspeakable joy in him.

One morning when I was rising, these words came in to my heart, If any man be in Christ he is a new creature: old things are pass'd away, all things are become new: I thought this was just I: for I now felt that all old things I had been formerly inclin'd to, were pass'd away, & all things were made new to me; I had got new desires, & hopes, new delights & joys, new fears & griefs: and the Bible & every thing in it was become new me.

[396/–] One Sabbath morning, I was thinking of going to the Kirk, but the morning being foul, and being but very weak thro' the trouble I had been under both in body & mind, some about me were disuading me from going, thinking it might be prejudicial to my health. But these words coming into my mind, Wait, I say, upon the Lord,[20] determin'd me to go, hoping I would get strength to go. And to my great surprize when I came, these were the very words, the Minr (19) read out for his Text: and I was much delighted to hear that Sermon, and much edify'd by it.

Being for several Lords days unable thro' bodily weakness & indisposition, to go to the Kirk; I was one night much cast down at the thoughts of my Loss this way. But that word being press'd on my heart, For I reckon that the Sufferings of this present time are not worthy to be compared with the Glory which shall be revealed in us; I had much joy in the prospect of the Glory to be revealed, & got my mind & will brought up to a pliableness to the Will of God, whatever afflictions he might see meet to lay upon me, & was made to bless him for the tokens of his favour he was pleasd to allow me in Secret Duties, when I was in Providence kept from attending him in publick Ordinances.

[397/–] One day, when I was not well, sitting by my self, that word came into my mind, In all their afflictions he was afflicted, the angel of his presence saved them, in his love and in his pity he redeem'd them, & he bare them &

---

[18]   Ps 103:9, Scottish Psalter (metrical).
[19]   Insertion ['my Father']: McCulloch.
[20]   Isa 40:31.

carried them all the days of old: which fill'd me with much comfort: & the thoughts of Christs being afflicted in my afflictions lightned my trouble so that I did not feel it.

One day reading on a Book, which spoke of Returns of Prayers & Sensible Manifestations, I was much cast down at the thoughts that I knew scarce any thing at all of that, as I then thought: but within a little after ~~after~~ when I had been at Secret Prayer, that word came in to my heart, You hath he quickened who were dead in trespasses and sins: by which I was much comforted, being made to believe that God had quickened me from that death in Sin I had been under, which was the great Blessing I had often been essaying to pray for.

One morning, these words were pressd on my heart, What things were gain to me these I count loss for Christ, yea doubtless I count all things but ~~loss~~[21] for the Excellency of the knowledge of Christ:[22] I then found it to be so indeed with me: the things I had been much taken up with in my former life, I now lost all relish and value for them, & counted them but loss dung & dross compar'd with Christ: & I continue to do so still.

[398/–] One time when I was much troubled at the thoughts of my unbelief, & thinking that I had no faith, or that any sort of belief, I had, was but a false belief: But that word coming into my heart [ ][23] Ye believe in God, believe also in me;[24] put away my heart trouble at these thoughts, & made me to see that I had some Faith, & got some new strength and increase to ~~my faith~~ it.

One morning, that word came in to my heart,

> Yea that most holy law of thine
> I have within my heart.[25]

I was amaz'd to think, Could it indeed be so, that I had Gods laws in my heart? And that word followed, That of I could win sincerely to ask this Blessing, he was both able & willing to put his Laws in my heart: and trusted in him to ~~daylie~~ enable me to do so.

One day when I was in affliction, that word came in to me, Knowing that in Heaven ye have a more enduring substance,[26] which reconcild my mind to my afflicted Lot, in hopes of that better and enduring Lot of endless blessedness in Heaven: And I thought that if it were not for these afflictions ~~in Heaven~~ on Earth, I might forget what manner of person I ought to be in all holy conversation & godliness, in the views of the approaching dissolution of all things here below.

---

[21] Insertion ['loss and dung']: McCulloch.
[22] Php 3:7–8.
[23] Insertion ['Let not your heart be troubled']: McCulloch.
[24] Jn 14:1.
[25] Ps 40:8, Scottish Psalter (metrical).
[26] Heb 10:34.

One day going to hear an Examination, I was putting up my Petition to the Lord [399/–] that he might keep my mind from wandering after vanity in the time of it, & that word came in, He will keep them in perfect peace whose minds are stayed on him:[27] & I accordingly got my heart much composd at that Occasion. And the same word often return'd after that, & was accompanied with the like Effects.

One Sabbath[28] hearing a Minr (19) speak preach much to the Commendation of Christ; at which I greatly rejoiced: and that word coming in to my heart made me still more to rejoice, Let the heart of every one rejoice that seeks the Lord.

One day when I was at my Work, I found a great weight on my heart, which made me very uneasy: But these words coming into my heart with powerful sweetness

> My head thou dost with Oyl anoint
> And my Cup overflows.
> Goodness & mercy all my Life
> Shall surely follow me:
> And in God's house for evermore
> My Dwelling Place shall be.[29]

The weight was immediatly taken off my Spirit, & I was so filled with joy, that I could scarce refrain crying out, & hastned to go out to the fields, where I might give vent to my joy in praises to God.

One day, hearing tell of some miscarriages that some had been guilty of who seemd to have had some awaknings not very long [400/–] before, I was so much affected with the news of it, that I slept home that night: but next morning that word came into my heart, Cast thy burden upon the Lord & he shall sustain thee,[30] upon which I felt the pressure of Spirit I had been under taken off, and was made to trust in God to carry me thro,' being persuaded that he was able to keep that good thing that I had committed to him to the day of Christ.

One Morning, I could not get my mind set on Spiritual things as I would have had it, which was very vexing to me. But that word There remaineth a rest for the people of God, coming in, comforted & relievd my restless heart much, in the hopes of that everlasting rest, & made me more patiently submit and resign to the holy will of God, as to whatever [ ][31] he might fit to exercise me with while here.

---

[27] Ezr 7:12.
[28] Insertion ['Day']: McCulloch.
[29] Ps 23:5–6, Scottish Psalter (metrical).
[30] Ps 55:22.
[31] Insertion ['troubles']: McCulloch.

On Friday before the Sacrament at Camb. in May 1743 when I was at home, thinking of coming & joining at that Occasion, that word came into my heart, My Soul wait thou with patience

Upon thy God alone——.[32]

which engag'd me to resolve to wait with as much serious composure on God in that Ordinance as might be, to see what ~~the Lord~~ he would do for me or to me, in a way of mercy.

On Saturday I had much delight in hearing the Sermons there; & as I came away, these words came in, Return to thy Rest [401/–] O my Soul.[33] I knew no other rest for my Soul but Christ, & to him I desird to return as my quiet rest. I had also great delight in hearing Sermons on Sabbath & Munday, but cannot say that I met with any thing more at that Occasion, sensibly & immediately from the Lord.

And now when I reflect on the ordinary bent of my heart & course of my Life, I desire to acknowledge it to the praise of free grace, that tho other things beside Christ have but too much room in my thoughts; yet I find my heart run out after Christ above all things, & how to get more Communion with him & more likeness to him, to be under his conduct & care, & the Influence & guiding of his Holy Spirit. Sin is my daylie trouble & grief, and I long to be perfectly free of it, & to be with Christ in Heaven; to whom be Glory and Dominion now & ever Amen.

[402/– blank]

---

[32]   Ps 62:5, Scottish Psalter (metrical).
[33]   Ps 116:7.

[403/–] b. a.[1]

My Parents brought me up in a Religious way both by Precept & Example.
When I was young, I had more of inclinations to what was Religious like,
than when I came to more years. As to my outward behaviour, I do not know
what any that observ'd me, may have thought of me, but I suppose none
among whom I liv'd, have any thing to ~~say~~ object as to my Character in the
World. In my younger years I was more given to Prayer than afterwards when
I came to age, and was led away by Company to follow after many youthful
vanities. I usd however all along to attend Publick Ordinances on the Lords
days; but it seems I went there out of no good design, when I made so little
good use of ~~it after~~ any thing I heard. When I was between 10 and 14 years of
age I took much delight in Secret Prayer, but afterwards was gradually drawn
away, and seem'd in a manner to forget God entirely. I had very little care
about my heart, and when I should have been growing more wise, I became
more foolish, and thoughtless what would become of me when I died.

   And thus it continued with me, till March [404/–] 1742, that I became
a little more thoughtful about Soul-Concerns, and prayed some after; &
continued to do so for some time. In the beginning of Summer thereafter,
I came to Camb. on a Thursday, and heard two sermons without meeting
with any thing beyond ordinary. In hearing the third sermon that day by a
Minister (26)[2] on that Text Keep back thy Servant also from presumptuous
Sins, let them not have dominion over me:[3] where he spoke of several
sorts of presumptuous sinners, particularly these that once seem'd to have
had some good dispositions in their younger years, but afterward came to
give loose reins to their lusts & full swing to their Corruptions; these were
presumptuous sinners in a high degree, and were fast tumbling down to hill
to Hell, and in the high way to the great Transgression, the unpardonable Sin,
& utter Apostasy from God, if infinite mercy did not speedily take hold on
them: or words to that purpose. This came home with an awakening Power
to my Conscience, & I was made sensible that I was just the Man pointed
at. I then fell under great Concern, & saw my self lost and undone for ever
without an Interest in Christ, & was much afraid that Death would snatch me
away before I got out of my sad State, and could get no rest for a considerable
time. [405/–] At first, tho' I saw that I had offended God [ ][4] yet the chief

[1]   John M'Alay (McAlay, Malay, or M. Alay) – the shorthand text in McCulloch's 'Index of
     persons' names who gave the foregoing accounts to Mr. McC' states: gardener in Glasgow,
     age 27. Taught to read and write, and got the catechism to heart.
[2]   William McCulloch (1691–1771) – minister, Cambuslang.
[3]   Ps 19:13.
[4]   Insertion ['& had some sense of Sin']: McCulloch.

ground of my Distress & trouble was fears of Hell and Eternal misery: and if it had continued so with me, I think I would have run quite to despair; and as for I could neither eat nor drink nor sleep not work as I usd to do, but was in a great measure put from all these things. But some time after in that Summer, in hearing some Sermons, particularly one in the High-Church yeard (12)[5] I was made chiefly to grieve for my Sins, both of the heart and life, as dishonouring to God, and particularly that I had mispent so much precious time, that I had been so stupid and unconcern'd under Ordinances, and had rejected so much offers of Christ & the great Salvation, & followed after lying Vanities, & forsaken my own mercies.

When the Sacrament-Occasion ~~Glasgow~~[6] drew near [⊗][7] I made some preparation in order to come to the Lord's Table: but got nothing sensibly there, or in hearing the Sermons. And after that Occasion was over, I was under great uneasiness for two or three weeks, at the thoughts that I had been an Unworthy Communicant there: and was made impotunate with the Lord, in pleading, that if that was the case, I might get forgiveness from him, thro' that precous Blood that cleanseth from all sin.

[406/–] At the Sacrament-Occasion at Glasglow in October 1742, I attended in the College-Kirk: but cannot say that I met with the Lords gracious Presence in a sensible way, till just as I came from the Table, hearing a Minister ( ) speak of the Sufferings of Christ, and his Love in his Sufferings, I found my heart melted under the Sense of Sin that procured these Sufferings, and warmed with the Love of Christ, who had evidenced such wonderful Love in Suffering & dying for saving poor perishing Sinners, such as I.

[⊗[8] According to the Ministers ( ) desire signified in publick, that these who had never communicated before & inclined then to do it, should come & speak with him at his House privately, I did so & he examind me as to several things, and told me, That in the view of approaching God in that Holy Ordinance, I must bid an Eternal farewell to all my sins & lusts, and that when I came to the Lords Table, I must set me self by faith, as under the Cross of Christ, & behold him in his Sufferings out of Love to an Elect world, & labour to have my heart suitably affected with the thought of them & receive him by faith in all his offices as my Prophet Priest and King: which I accordingly essay'd to do in dependance on grace.]

I have sometimes in Secret duties been so raisd above this World and every thing in it, that I regard neither the pleasures nor profits of [407/–] it, so be I might have an Interest & place in Christs favour & Love: I find the motions of lust and corruption stirring too oft in my heart, but I use in such cases to

---

[5] George Whitefield (1714–70) – evangelist.
[6] Insertion ['Barony that Summer']: McCulloch.
[7] Insert text found at the corresponding sign ⊗ further down this page.
[8] Insert text at the place indicated two paragraphs up this page.

cry to the Lord ~~in my heart~~ for strength against them, that they may not be allowed to have dominion over me, & endeavor thro' the Spirit to mortify the deeds of the flesh that I may live. Before I was awakned last year, I was much set upon the World, & gathring more & more of it; but now I do not for ordinary find my thoughts run much that way. I am not afraid of worldly poverty, but desire to rest content with whatever Lot God shall order for me. I do not want to be rich in this worlds goods, but to be rich in faith, & to be an heir of that kingdom he hath prepared for them that love him, & undervalue all things compared with Christ & an Interest in him. I see so much sin in all I do, that I need pardon of sin in the best duties ever I essayed to perform: yet I find a byass in my corrupt nature tending to make me lay some weight on these my defiled duties, & a great difficulty to be entirely deny'd to them all; but I think I have been enabled to renounce all my own Righteousness & to submit to the righteousness that is of God by faith, and to build all my hopes of pardon acceptance with God & Eternal Life on the perfect Righteousness of Jesus Christ: to whom be Glory for ever Amen.

[408/– through 410/– blank]

[411/–] b.g. A man of 21 years of age.[1]

I liv'd all along a moral and civil life as to my outward behaviour among
men: but as to my Duty toward God I was very negligent and careless: and
tho I had some kind of form of praying in secret, from my Childhood, yet it
was but a very heartless and lifeless form. I also for ordinary usd to go to the
Kirk, but it on Sabbaths, but it was more for to see and be seen than for any
other thing. Only I was for about two years mostly a Hearer of the Seceding
Ministers: & for that time I heard them, I thought I turn'd more hardned and
obdurd than ever: yet I then thought that I was well enough & fair enough in
the way to Heaven sinc I was following them. I had never any concern about
my heart either while I followed them or before, or never felt any thing I heard
in Publick Ordinances come home with any warmness life or power to my
heart, till I came to Cambuslang in the Spring 1742; when I fell under some
concern to see so many persons in distress about their Souls; & I thought,
what a stupid crea- [412/–] Creature must I be who am so unconcerned
when so many young Persons, that cannot be guilty of near so many sins
as I, are thus mourning & crying out under a Sense of their Sins. And one
Sabbath when I was hearing a Minister (26)[2] there, speaking concerning a
great many different Cases, I thought, What a Strange Creature am I that he
never touches on my Case, and immediatly after that he spoke some words
which I cannot now remember that came home with a knell to my heart.
Another Sabbath some time after that, hearing a Minister ( ) there preach on
that reading these words Eph.2. At that time ye aliens & forreigners strangers
to the Covenant & promises, without God and without Christ in the world,
&c.:[3] these words as he read them, by a power that came along with them,
struck my heart, and made me say within my Self, And have I been all this
time living a stranger to God, without God & without Christ in the world:
Surely then there is no help for me. I saw my Self to be such a great Sinner.
At first it was chiefly fears of Hell that startled me, but I afterwards came to
get a more affecting Sense of Sin as dishonouring to God who had been so
merciful & long suffering toward me, than as it exposed me to Hell.

[413/–] That night with much difficulty I got about 4 or 5 miles on my
Road home, and when several persons who had gathered together in the
House where I was, ( ) and some of them persons in distress of soul, were
imployed in Prayer & Praises, I fell under such distress, that I was afraid my

---

[1] Charles Cunningham – the shorthand text in McCulloch's 'Index of persons' names who
     gave the foregoing accounts to Mr. McC' states: shoemaker in Glasgow, born in Gorbels.
     Taught to write, read the Bible, and got Catechism to heart.
[2] William McCulloch (1691–1771) – minister, Cambuslang.
[3] Eph 2:12.

head would have gone wrong, and was made to cry out most bitterly under a Sense of Sin and fears of wrath. A Sense of all my Sins in general press'd my Spirit, but there were some of them that star'd me much more in the face than others, and the sins & corruptions of my heart affected me most of all. I continued in very great distress till Wednesday thereafter: & that day hearing a Minister (12)[4] in the High-Church-yeard, preaching concerning the Pool of Bethesda, which he explained as signifying the Blood of Christ, to which he invited poor sensible sinners to come, & dip their polluted Souls by faith in it; I found my self somewhat lightned of the load of guilt that press'd me, while I essay'd to comply (thro grace) with these Calls & Invitations, but that night after, unbelief often prevaild, and when it did so, my former burden returnd.

[414/–] Next day I came & heard him at Cambuslang, but unbelief prevaild so much, that I thought I was as bad as ever again. Next day while I was hearing him there, that word (tho not uttered by the Speaker) Ho every one that thirsteth, come to the waters, and he that hath no money come buy wine & milk without money & without price:[5] and these words followed me all that night: next day while I was in the fields there, at Secret Prayer, these words were press'd upon my heart, Arise and shine, for thy light is come, & the glory of the Lord is risen upon thee:[6] these words came with a beam of light into my Soul, & discovered much of the glory & beauty of Christ, & his suitableness to my necessities, beyond anything I had seen before: & I was made to rely on him for all I stood in need of; and ~~raisd~~ got my affections raisd toward him which vented it self in joyful praises to him for his own Excellency, and for what he had done for my Soul in giving me a Sense of my Sin & my lost Condition without him, and for sending me such a gracious word, with such power at this time.

[415/– through 418/– blank]

---

[4] George Whitefield (1714–70) – evangelist.
[5] Isa 55:1.
[6] Isa 60:1.

[419/–] b.b.[1]

I had a Religious Education, and usd to pray in Secret when a Child, sometimes, and when I came to serve my Apprentiship: but very often neglected it. But after that, getting a house of my own, I minded it more frequently. And when I came to be married, I for ordinary kept up family Worship twice a day, and pray'd also by my self, but not so often as I did with my family. I was never guilty of any gross vices before the World, except that I fell into a way of profane Swearing, when I was young, for about a month: but one day hearing a gross habitual Swearer (Swearer) saying of me to another, in my hearing, Hear how he swears! I was immediatly so struck with the word, that for two or three days after, I could do little but mourn & beg pardon of the Lord for what I had done. After that I always took care to behave soberly, and never was guilty of any gross Outbreaking before the World. I always usd to go to Church on Sabbath days, when I could go, for I though I could not get any good if I absented my self from Publick Ordinances, & I thought that some time or other I would get good there: [420/–] but still I returnd as empty of all good when I came home as when I went there.

And thus it continued with me 'till hearing of the Awakening at Camb. in the Spring 1742, ~~when~~ I went out there to see & hear, and to try if I might get some good to my Soul. However I was under some Prejudices against the Work there, because I had a greater liking to the Seceders & their way than to the Church. I came out there ordinarily every Sabbath-day for a considerable time, but got nothing sensibly: only I was struck with amazement to hear so many people crying out so as they did there, and thought, That surely these Cryers must be greater Sinners than the rest that did not cry: But one Sabbath in April hearing a Minister (26)[2] preach on that Text, Ps. 68.18, Thou hast O Lord ascended up on high, thou hast led captivity captive, thou hast received gifts for men, yea even for the rebellious also that God the Lord might dwell in the midst of them:[3] in the afternoon hearing him chiefly insisting on the latter part Yea even for the rebellious also [][4] &c: my pride of heart and contempt of others that cry'd began to fall, and I began to conclude that I was as great a Sinner as any of [421/–] them all: and where as before this I thought I was a very good Christian, now I saw all was wrong with me, & began to mourn for

---

[1] Charles Thomson – the shorthand text in McCulloch's 'Index of persons' names who gave the foregoing accounts to Mr. McC' states: shoemaker in Glasgow, age 31. Taught to read the Bible, got the Catechism to heart, and retained it mostly.
[2] William McCulloch (1691–1771) – minister, Cambuslang.
[3] Ps 68:18.
[4] Insertion ['tho' I cannot now remember the words that struck me']: McCulloch.

my losing & misimproving my precious time & the Seasons of Grace I had enjoy'd, & triffling about Soul-Concerns as I had done hitherto.

And thus things continued till ~~about~~ the 17th day of June 1742, when ~~Mr Whi~~ hearing a Stranger Minister, who came first to Camb. that day, discourse on the Brae there that night, after Day-light was gone, a little after I had been bewailing my Sad Case, some sentence he spoke, (which I cannot now distinctly remember,) struck me to the heart, so that I fell into a swoon, (tho I did not cry any) a horror of great darkness coming over me, and continued for some small space, during which time I heard nothing. But my ~~senses~~ understanding remaind with me. And in the middle of this Swoon, my bodily eyes being shut, I thought I saw a clear light all at once shining about me, as when the Sun shines bright at noon, and apprehended that I was in a very large Room []⁵ there was represented to my mind, a very large Scroll of Paper, let down as from the Roof [422/−] above, filling the breadth of the room & one end of the Room upwards, & the Scroll brought so near me, that the lower End of it was just at my feet, and it appeard to be all printed over in large distinct lines & letters; but when I thought I essayed to read ~~it, I could~~, the lower part of it next me, I found I could not read one word of it: only it was impress'd on my mind, that was a Scroll containing all my Sins, that were all marked & recorded before God. And after a little the Scroll was drawn up again, & I recovered out of my Swoon [].⁶

[423/− through 426/− blank]

---

⁵ Insertion ['I thought I saw a deep dark pit on both sides of me, which I took to be Hell, & thought I was just ready to tumble into it: and']: McCulloch.
⁶ Insertion ['& the former darkness returnd']: McCulloch.

[427/–] b. x. A Married Woman aged 28 years[1]

I had the mercy of good Education & Example from my Parents, in my younger years. I usd to go always to Church on Sabbath-days, & was traind up to pray in secret twice a day & continued all along my life to do so for ordinary. And sometimes I met with much Sweetness in prayer & reading & hearing of the Word: and this together with outward blamelesness before the world, in a good measure, made me think I was in a good way. But in the years 1740 & 1741, & for some years before, I fell under great deadness lukewarmness & worldly mindedness: sometimes I would scarce have gone to Church. Once in a month, and when I went there, what I heard was but as a sounding brass & as a tinkling cymbal: and there was much carelesness and indifferency in performing that and other duties also of Gods Worship.

Hearing of the work at Cambuslang, I went there, a little after it began, about the beginning of March 1742, & heard a Minister (26)[2] preach on these words, If any man be in Christ he is a new Creature,[3] and heard many marks of the new creature given, from which I concluded that I was none, & thereupon felt a great weight upon [428/–] my spirits, & sin became very burdensome & grievous: & [][4] that word uttered by the Speaker in his Sermon, where God says, my Soul shall have no pleasure in them that draw back, I was made to chatter as a Crane; & sense of dishonour done to a holy God, & affronting the majesty of Heaven by my sins, made me often to say in my heart in much anguish, Whither shall I fly from thy presence. I continued in this condition for many days with a heart as hard as a stone.

One Morning I went to Secret Prayer but found no relief: I could pray none: & Satan and a deceitful heart told me, that I was good enough already; yet I was sensible it was otherwise: and not knowing what to do, I took up my Bible, & having beggd the Lord might direct me to some suitable passage of his Word, & bless it to me, & opening my Bible, I read the 60th chapter of Isaiah, & was much affected in reading of it, particularly the 1st, 19th, & 20th verses, Arise shine for thy light is come & the glory of the Lord is risen upon thee,[5] The Sun shall be no more thy thy light by day, neither for brightness shall the moon give light unto thee; but the Lord shall be unto thee an everlasting light, & thy God thy glory: thy Sun shall no more go down neither shall thy

---

1   Mrs Wier – the shorthand text in McCulloch's 'Index of persons' names who gave the foregoing accounts to Mr. McC' states: from Hamilton; taught to read and write, got the Catechism to heart, and retained it.
2   William McCulloch (1691–1771) – minister, Cambuslang.
3   2 Co 5:17.
4   Insertion ['at']: McCulloch.
5   Isa 60:1.

moon withdraw it self; for the Lord shall be thine everlasting light and the days of thy mourning shall be ended.[6] I felt the load that was upon my spirit [429/–] hereupon taken off: I felt the love of Christ shed abroad in my heart; and was so filld with joy in him, that I scarce knew where I was, & my tongue was made as the pen of a ready writer in blessing the Lord for his Love & for bringing me out of the fearful pit & from the miry clay.

But alas! Satan soon got in with his Temptations & told me that I was but a hypocrite: and I was made to go some days in darkness & could see no light. I went to Cambuslang, & at the Entry of Publick worship, the Minister (26) who was to preach, appointing the 34th Psalm at the beginning to be sung.

> God will I bless all times his praise
> My mouth shall still express
> My Soul shall boast in God, the meek
> Shall hear with joyfulness[7]

I was made to sing these words with great joy & to believe & apply them to my self, or rather got them powerfully applied to me and my Joy was further encreasd in hearing of the Text read, from 1 Joh. 5.10, He that believeth on the Son of God hath the witness in himself, & he that believeth not God hath made him a liar &c: I was in hearing the Sermon on that Text, made sensible of the great Evil of unbelief, which I had never seen before; but was helped to act faith on Christ and the promises. But when [430/–] I was going home, Satan & unbelief made me think that none of these promises were to me. I went to God in Prayer several times, & begg'd he would discover my true State to me: and at length he was pleased to answer my Petition with these words, I am faithful who have promised, and am able to perform my promise; I will not take my loving kindness from thee nor alter the word that is gone out of my mouth. On which I was made to believe these promises, & was filled with much love to God thro Christ & joy in him.

I have many a time since that, fallen into deep distress of Soul under Sense of Sin & manifold temptations & discouragements, & the Lord has been pleased mercifully to pity in such Cases, and to relieve and comfort me with several gracious Promises suited to my particular distress at the time, brought into my heart, such as, I will never leave thee nor forsake thee,[8] The ransomed of the Lord shall return and come to Zion with songs and everlasting joy upon their heads they shall obtain joy and gladness & sorrow and sighing shall flee away &c:[9] And these and other Promises applied to me, were always accompanied with much love to God & joy in him.

---

[6]   Isa 60:19–20.
[7]   Ps 34:1–2, Scottish Psalter (metrical).
[8]   Heb 13:5.
[9]   Isa 35:10.

[431/–] I can now say, that for these two years past & more (to the glory of Gods free grace be it spoken) I find my heart in the prevailing & habitual bent of it set upon things spiritual & heavenly. Whereas formerly the thoughts & cares about things worldly things usd ~~usually~~ [ ]¹⁰ to ly down and rise with me, Gods testimonies are now become my Song in the house of my pilgrimage [ ]:¹¹ And I can say in a good measure, my fellowship is with the Father & with his Son Jesus Christ; my meditations of him is sweet & I am glad in the Lord: Oh how love I thy law, it is my meditation all the day. I see a glory in Christ, & a perfect suitableness to all my wants. I am content to be resign'd to his holy will & pleasure, yet I cannot but frequently long to get out of this imbodied state & to [ ]¹² ever with the Lord.

To him be praise everlasting, Amen.

[440/– blank]¹³

---

¹⁰   Insertion ['ordinarily']: McCulloch.
¹¹   Insertion ['& my first & last thoughts daylie.']: McCulloch.
¹²   Insertion ['be']: McCulloch.
¹³   Primary pagination numbers 423–39 omitted by McCulloch.

[441/–] c. b.   A Man about 40 years.[1]

In my Childhood, I got some kind of form of Prayer, tho I understood little what I said. After that I liv'd for some time in a house where there was much outward plenty, but no form of Religion, and there I laid my form of Prayer much aside. After that during my five years Apprenticeship, I seldom minded it, except for about a year or some more, when I was much hamper'd as to outward necessaries, and in straits I would oft have calld on God, and durst not go one night to bed, till I had pray'd. After my Apprenticeship was over, when I came to the Age of Manhood, I was quite carried away with youthful vanities & follies or worse, & then I laid aside Prayer altogether. After I was married, I sometimes prayed by my self & with my Family, and at sometimes I fell under such Terrors of the wrath of God, that I would have been afraid the Earth under me would have opened its mouth & swallowed me up & sent quick to Hell: but these terrors wore off in a little while, & left me just where I was again. I was kept sober & just in my dealings with men, & kept free of many gross Out-breakings, ~~only~~ yet I would sometimes in passion curse & swear, & sometimes [442/–] drink to Excess, & boast of making others of the Company drink, while I continued fresh. I went to Church on Sabbath days, for ordinary, except that for about a year or so in 1741, upon some disgust, I stayd at home on Sabbaths & went no where to publick Worship.

In Febry 1742, hearing of some people at Cambuslang that were crying out, some saying that God was there, others that the Devil was there; I put my Bible in my pocket on a Week day, saying I should see what was among them 'ere I came home. When I came there, I was persuaded the Lord was among them, especially by seeing many of them that had been under Convictions & were got out of their distress expressing so much brotherly love to one another, & instructing & encouraging one another. I heard Sermon that day there, but found nothing remarkable at that time, but only that I found some kind of fright upon my spirit, but could give little account for what. I went home & came in a day or two after, & brought all of my Family that could come along with me to Cambuslang, which happened to be on a Saturday, and two of them & I stay'd there till Thursday thereafter. On Sabbath night, when I could not get in to the Manse for the great Crowd of people, I stood with some Concern at the End of the Manse without, & then went into the Yeard and pray'd, & as I came back toward the Manse, I found a Son of my own (a Boy [443/–] about 13 years) bursting

---

[1]   Archibald Smith – the shorthand text in McCulloch's 'Index of persons' names who gave the foregoing accounts to Mr. McC' states: mason in Kilbride. Taught to read the Bible and write some, got the Catechism to heart, and retained it mostly.

out into tears & crying out under Convictions, at which I was glad: but intending to carry him away to some house, away from the Manse, & to endeavour to have him still'd, as I was taking him away, a word I had heard a Minister say in his Sermon, a little before that at Cambuslang (26) struck in upon my mind & over aw'd me, That these who endeavoured to stifle Convictions in themselves and others, were acting the part of the Devil. Upon this I brought him back to the Manse, and about two in the Morning, he got some Outgate. Another in my Family also fell under Convictions, at which I was glad, but much surpriz'd to see that Person who had been much more blameless & religious-like than I, in former life, in so great distress. On this I was amaz'd & fill'd with indignation at my own stupidity & unconcern'dness. I thereupon not only attended close on the Sermons there, but was much & oft in Secret Prayer: and the Lord gave me both a Sense of my lost Condition by nature & by actual Sin, & a Sense of my particular Sins both of heart & life from my Childhood to that time, which were brought fresh to my remembrance & embitter'd to me, not only as exposing me to Hell, but mainly (especially after they had continued for some time) as offensive & dishonouring to God. [444/–] I wanted however to have still more strong Convictions than I had: but that which first quitted me from seeking after that, was hearing a Preacher (36)[2] say in the Kirk or Manse, The most affecting sight of Sin that ever he had, was to see his hands reeking in the heart-blood of Christ: but however that was not necessary: the lowest needful was to see ones Self in a lost State without Christ, and that he only was able to help. This was what I could not deny the Lord had given me.

I went on in the diligent use of the means of grace under Convictions for some weeks, often going & conferring with this & the other Person that I thought knew something of Serious Religion from Experience, to see what they thought of my Case, & get directions & advices in duty. At length hearing a Minister at Cambuslang (12)[3] on these Words, Go to Joseph,[4] from which he exhorted Persons in Soul difficulties & straits, in stead of going to men for Relief, to go to Christ himself in all their Troubles. After that, I went less to men & essayd to go more to Christ: and some time after that when I was at Prayer, that Word came into my mind, with such Power, that I was made to believe it would be, according to that Word, to me and mine, Thou shall be Saved & thine house.[5] If my heart do not deceive me, I had before this Word came, accepted of Christ in his Gospel offers, in all his Offices [ ][6] (particularly at hearing the Sermon on the Text abovementioned) & thro' his merits, I look for the accomplishment of the Promise.

[2] James Nasmyth [Nasmith] (1683–1774), minister, Dalmeny.
[3] George Whitefield (1714–70) – evangelist.
[4] Gen 41:55.
[5] Ac 16:31.
[6] Insertion ['several times']: McCulloch.

[445/–] At Secret Prayer & other duties I had several time after that some Promises applied to me with much sweetness, such as The Lord heareth the cry of the poor & needy; He will hear the prayer of the destitute, and will not despise their prayer &c:[7]

In May 1743, intending to attend the Sacrament-Occasion at ~~Blantyre~~ Cambuslang; but having at that time considerable Wages coming in to me every day I followed my Imployment, I began to cast up in my own mind, what might be the Sum I would lose by attending at that Sacrament-Occasion as I proposd, & finding it rise to something considerable, I was tempted to resolve rather to stay away & follow my work: but putting up a Petition to the Lord against this Temptation, & that the Lord would carry me there & keep me from thinking of the world when I was there on the several days of that Solemnity; I was then made to hope he would do so: & found the Lord sensibly granting me my desire all the time of it, taking the world quite out of my thoughts, & filling my heart with love to Christ, give me much joy in hearing the Word, & peace in believing. And this sweet frame continued with me in a good measure, for about half a year thereafter, that is, till about Martinmass 1743. For about two weeks after that I lost that desireable frame; but coming to Camb. & hearing a Minister (26)[8] preach on a Text I have now forgot, as he was exhorting to a patient waiting on God in the way of Duty, that the Old Testament Church waited 4000 years for the Coming of Christ, before he came, yet he came at length in the due and ap- [446/–] pointed time; so the particular Souls might think the time of their waiting for his coming to them in Visits of grace & mercy long & tedious, yet he would come at the set time & the best time, adding, The Lord is a God of judgment, blessed are all these that wait for him: I then found these last words carried home to my heart with such power, as remov'd the uneasiness I had been under for two weeks before, upon finding these sensible comforts withdrawn I had so long enjoy'd, & raisd & settled my heart in a patient waiting for Christ in the exercise of faith & hope.

From my Awakening in the Spring 1742, to this time (July 9.1744) I find a very great difference & alteration from ~~my Condition~~ the way & manner it was with me before that. Formerly I had no Sweetness in the duties of Gods Worship; but now I for ordinary long much for the Sabbath before it comes (which I did not use to do before) & when it comes I find great pleasure & sweetness in the duties of it, and particularly in praising God, & hearing Christ preachd, & being helped to rely on him along for Salvation. At some times, my heart has been brought to a submission to Gods will, if he should in holy justice cast me into Hell for ever; providing he would keep me from being a reproach to his Religion, while I am here. Sometimes when I walk out

---

[7] Ps 102:17.
[8] William McCulloch (1691–1771) – minister, Cambuslang.

the way by my self, I find my Soul as it were carried out of me, in wonder & admiration at the thoughts of free grace & redeeming Love, so that for some time I do not know where I am. A body of Sin & death within me, is matter of much grief to me, & I long often to be delivered from it. Thanks be to God thro' Jesus Christ who has promised deliverance   Amen.

[447/–] a.w. A Woman of 42 years.[1]

I had no sort of form of Secret Prayer, till I was about twelve years of Age, when I had my Lot among people that had some Religion, who advisd me to set about it, and I did so, & continu'd to ~~do so~~ [ ][2] for some time; but removing elsewhere I turn'd more careless & unconcern'd about it, tho' I did not leave it off altogether: and I was all along kept moral & civil in my outward behaviour. I us'd also to go to Kirk on Sabbath-days, tho' I think it was often only to see & to be seen: only I kept sometimes at home because I could not read, & I was much ashamed that I could not make use of my Bible in the Kirk, as others about me did. And therefore I set about learning to read, when I was about 18 years of age, having never learn'd to read any before that: and it was one of the Terms of my Agreement with these whom I serv'd, that I should always get a Lesson every day: and by following it out in that manner, I came to be capable to read the Bible, and got part of the Catechism[3] by heart, and retain part of it still.

[448/–] But tho I sometimes fell under some more Concern about my Salvation, than at other times, as particularly at Sacrament-Occasions; yet this Concern soon wore off again, and I never got a Sight & Sense of my lost and perishing Condition by nature & by actual Sins, till one Sabbath in Summer 1742 after I had been hearing Sermon at Camb. brae, & had got nothing that touch'd me all day, & was just going away ~~home~~ off from the rest of the multitude homewards, before the last Psalms were sung; I heard the Minister (26)[4] read that Line of the 119th Psalm (being the first Line of that portion of the Psalm he appointed to be sung,

I thought upon my former ways: which came home to me with such a Power, that I could not forbear crying out under a Sense of my Sin & lost Condition, by Sin, and was just ready to drop down, but got hold of a Chair near me, & got leave to sit down on it. At that instant, on hearing these words, I was made indeed to think on my former ways to purpose. The Sins of my former Life were presented to me in their horrid nature, & star'd me in the face, so that I was filled with dread & confusion. [449/–] I then thought that I was the chief of all the Sinners on the Brae: more & more sins still were set before me, as the rest of the Lines were Sung: I join'd in singing two or three of the first Lines; but was not able to go on in joining in singing the rest, my

---

[1] Margaret Clerk – the shorthand text in McCulloch's 'Index of persons' names who gave the foregoing accounts to Mr. McC' states: spouse of John McGlass, day-labourer in the Glasgow burghs.

[2] Insertion ['mind it']: McCulloch.

[3] *Shorter Catechism of the Westminster Assembly* (1647).

[4] William McCulloch (1691–1771) – minister, Cambuslang.

heart was so overwhelm'd, partly with a sense of my Sin as dishonouring to God, & partly with fears of perishing.

And thus it continu'd with me for about 14 days. My Convictions of Sin & Danger went on from day to day: and my Distress under under them was so great, that I could work none: & I ate but very little, & sleep in a great measure departed from my eyes: and very often I thought there was no Mercy for me. I could scarce do any thing at all, but run to my knees every now & then, & hear Sermons at Camb. & read my Bible.

The first Relief I got was one morning when I was lying in my Bed, half sleeping half-walking, when that Word came into my mind, as if one had spoke to me (Song.2.10) Arise my Love my fair one & come away, which easd my troubled heart a little, and persuaded me that it was Christ who was speaking to my heart, & got some faith to depend and trust in him, believing that tho' I was the chief of Sinners, yet he was able & willing to forgive me.

[450/–] I continued much easier in mind, till ~~Thursday~~ [ ]⁵ thereafter, when hearing a Minister (12)⁶ at Camb. on those words, The Summer is past the Harvest is ended, & we are not saved;⁷ I fell into great Confusion & distress, thinking I was now in a worse condition than ever, and that there would never be a better of it. And as the Psalms began to be sung before the next Sermon, my fear and grief at the thoughts of my Sin threw me into a Swarf, in which I continued all the time of that Sermon. I was carried up to the Manse when I recovered, & down again, & heard that Minister (12) preach a third Sermon, but was in much confusion. And in the time of it, while I was looking clearly up, I [ ]⁸ thought I saw with my bodily eyes, Christ as hanging on the Cross, and a great Light about him in the Air, and it was strongly impress'd on my mind; that he was Suffering there for my sins. And at the same time while I lookt at this Sight, a Woman who was sitting beside me, before I spoke any thing to her of it, said to me, Do you see yon great Light, pointing at the Place where I beheld it. I withdrew my eyes from it two or three times, & lifting them up, saw the same again: at length after several minutes, it vanish'd & I saw it no more: & do not or never did desire to see it again, & never laid any stress of my Salvation upon my seeing this Sight.

[451/–] However, that night and for two days after that, my mind was wholly set upon Christ and Heaven, and entirely taken off every thing ~~tha~~ in the World, not so much as having all that time one thought of my own Children, and found much Love to Christ in my heart. That Sabbath following, while I looked up, I thought I saw the Sun Moon and Stars in the Sky: and looking down I thought I saw a great darkness betwixt my eyes & the Ground.

---

⁵   Insertion ['Friday']: McCulloch.
⁶   George Whitefield (1714–70) – evangelist.
⁷   Jer 8:20.
⁸   Insertion ['verily']: McCulloch.

On the Munday after the first Sacrament at Camb. some words in a Ministers Sermon (12) struck me with such fear, that my distress threw me into a Swarf, but continued to hear what was said in the Sermon: and while I was in this Swarf, that word, tho not then uttered by the Minister, came into my mind, Fear not for I am with thee,[9] and I was then enabled to lay hold on Christ in a way of believing. Betwixt Sermons I had great freedom & enlargement in Prayer: and heard the next Sermon ( ) with much Satisfaction. But that might when I went home & was in bed slumbering, I was awaked with a noise like one ~~talking~~ speaking [ ][10] sharp & bitter words to me that piercd me like swords; & put me into a great terror: yet I understood nothing of what was said, but after I got praying, the terror wore off. I took this to be the Evil one seeking to affright me.

[452/–] Next day I found much of last nights terror on my Spirit, & could neither read nor pray, but was in a dead & stupid frame. Lying down on my bed, after I had shut my eyes & opened them again, I saw a great darkness before me, & felt a straitness in my throat that I was like to be strangled. Getting out of my Bed I fell down on the floor in a Swarf, & continued so for some time. In the Evening going out to the fields, I got some liberty in Prayer & reading the Bible, & the terror went off gradually. Next morning that word came into my mind, Believe in the Lord Jesus Christ and thou shall be saved,[11] & at the same time I was helped to trust & rely on Christ and him only for Salvation: but unbelief within a little prevailing, I went to prayer, but thought it would be the last Prayer ever I would put up, my distress was so great, and my hopes so very low. But returning again to that duty & getting more liberty in prayer & being helped to more reliance on him, I was encouraged to go on in the practice of that and other duties, for a considerable time.

At Eastwood Sacrament, I got my longing Soul satisfied, by the sensible presence of Christ, and the Refreshings of his Grace: and ~~this~~ much of this frame continued with me for a good while after. At Cathcart Sacrament [ ],[12] I was helped to much of a desirable frame, but after it I fell into great deadness, & was much straitned in Prayer: but the Lord was [453/–] pleased to give me much of enlargement in that duty again: & sometimes I have had so much of a Spirit of Supplication pour'd out on me, that I could have been glad to have continued whole nights at that Duty.

I have been many a time when under convictions & distress for Sin, in great bodily pains and distress: I have born several Children, but have been in as great ~~pain~~ bodily pains under my Convictions, as at bearing any of my Children.

---

[9] Gen 26:24, Isa 41:10, Isa 43:5.
[10] Insertion ['loud']: McCulloch.
[11] Ac 16:31.
[12] Insertion ['in May 1743']: McCulloch.

These pains usd to begin at my left side, when I fell under distress of Spirit for Sin: & if I had not got my Cloaths loosd when I found my ~~Spirit~~ Side rising, I had been in hazard of my Life: And the Pains would have proceeded from my Side to all the other parts of my Body. My Bones especially would have been all sore and pain'd, as if they had been bruisd by beating.

I now find for ordinary, my heart and affections running out after Christ and Spiritual things. I find a vast Change in my self now from what usd to be formerly. I know not if I have met with a Saving Change or not, but I would not for a thousand Worlds go back to the State I was formerly in. My heart-Corruptions are a great burden to me. And I long very oft ~~to be~~ for the coming of Christ, & to be dissolvd & to be with ~~Christ~~ him for ever.

[454/– blank]

[455/–] a.f. A young woman unmarried aged about 20 years[1]

I was all along kept, thro' mercy, from what is reproachful before the World, & had but too great Commendations from these among whom I lived, which has often been matter of grief to me, to think how little I deserv'd them. My Parents pressd me to the Duty of Prayer when I was young; and tho' I complyd with their Direction for a while when I was a Child: yet I came afterwards much to neglect it. I have in these early times of my life, found something within me, at times, pressing me to go away & pray, which I really think now upon Reflexion, was from the common motions of the Spirit of the Lord: yet I many a time neglected to comply with them, & put it off to some other ~~more~~ time: & I came at length to lay aside praying altogether for a long tract of time. Yet for all that I always all along since I was capable, usd to go to the Kirk on Sabbath days, & took good heed to what was said. But I may say, I went I knew not for what: to be sure, I was not seeking to be better, when I went there, and yet pray'd none. I also read the Bible & other good Books oftimes with great delight. [456/–] I livd a sober quiet life my self, & liked good people because they were sober & quiet too. However I often think that unless I had been kept under by many afflictions and troubles I had not been so sober & quiet as I was. When I was about 14 or 15 years of age, I was admitted to the Lords Table; but made but very little preparation for it, but only that I prayd some little: and therefore it may well be thought, that I got nothing there: only I had some kind of heart-meltings, & shed abundance of tears both at the Table & before & after I was there: but I returnd [ ][2] just to my old ways again: only I said a prayer now & then for a fashion. But I had no concern about my heart & the Evils of it or any care to have it made better.

At length about 4 or 5 years ago, hearing a Preacher ( ) on that Text, God is a Spirit, & they that worship him, might worship him in Spirit and truth:[3] when he said about the Close, O that ye would now live as ye will with ye had done, when death comes: I found that word come to me with some power, so that I said, Alas for my way of living, I'm sure when I come to die I'll wish I had livd another way than what [457/–] I have done. I must certainly change this way of life. Hearing another Minr ( ) that day (which was a Fast day before the Sacrament at Carmunnock) on these words Let the wicked forsake his way & the unrighteous man his thoughts &c:[4] I was glad to think

---

[1] Elizabeth Finlay – the shorthand text in McCulloch's 'Index of persons' names who gave the foregoing accounts to Mr. McC' states: daughter of John Finlay, tenant in Carmunnock. Taught to read the Bible and got the Catechism.

[2] Insertion ['in a few days']: McCulloch.

[3] Jn 4:23.

[4] Isa 55:7.

there might be mercy for me yet. From that time I set about Prayer, and was much taken up in it; and tho' I had formerly been very timorous & durst not go out of the door my self alone after it turn'd dark, now I frequently went out to secret prayer in the fields after it was dark: & had much delight in the duty: And on Saturday Evening, I often thought O how shall I get ready for the Sabbath day: and when I was obligd to stay at home on a Sabbath, I was as busy in Secret Prayer as I could be. And when I went to the Kirk, I was much in Prayer before I went, & heard Sermon with great delight: but I cannot say I got any thing else. When I was at my Work, my heart would have been like to break for sin, for the offence & dishonour I had done to God by it. And in this way I continued till next Sacrament Occasion the following year.

[458/–] At that Occasion, I had much melting of heart for Sin: especially in time of the Action Sermon ( ) on that Text, The Master is come & calleth for thee:[5] I had a great Inclination to go to the Lords Table, but had nothing to clear my way but only that I had a desire to be of the number of these whom the Master called. When I was there, I promised to God, as I had done before I came, That wherein I had done iniquity I would do so no more. But soon after this Sacrament Occasion was over, I broke all these promises: I did not trust to the righteousness & strength of Christ, but to my own, & so came of it. I soon turn'd carnal & secure again, & took great pleasure in carnal mirth jesting & sporting: I kept up a form of prayer, but was very dead in it: when I met with any thing like the presence of God in it, I was pleasd: & when I did not, tho I was not satisfied, yet I was not so dissatisfied & uneasy as I should have been.

And thus it continued with me till the Awakening brake out at Camb: some short time after which, I came & heard a Minr ( ) preach there on that text Gird [459/–] thy sword upon thy thigh O most mighty:[6] but got nothing sensibly. In the Evening I stayd & heard a Preacher ( ) & several others pray, & found a great melting on my heart, tho I could not well tell for what. ~~Several~~ days after that, being at home, I fell under great Concern about my Souls State, and felt, as it had been, a great weight on my heart, & went out to Secret Prayer, and was very earnest in it. Next Weekly-Lecture-day I came to Camb. again very much weighted under Sorrow for sin, but that word came into my mind by the way & relievd me a little, ~~I fainted~~

> I fainted had unless that I
> Believed had to see.
> The Lords own goodness in the Land
> Of them that living be.[7]

---

[5]   Jn 11:28.
[6]   Ps 45:3.
[7]   Ps 27:13, Scottish Psalter (metrical).

When I came there, hearing a Minr (26)[8] on that text, By him we are justified from all things from which we could not be justified by the Law of Moses:[9] I had such great sorrow of heart & grief for sin upon me, that I was not able to stand, but fell just down upon the ground. As I was coming away home, that word came into my mind, There is no Condemnation to them that are in Christ Jesus, which refreshd me a little: [460/–] but I got little or no comfort by it, because I could not apply it to my Self or think that it belongd to me. Next day after I had been at Prayer, when I was at my Work, that word, Daughter be of good cheer, thy sins are forgiven thee,[10] came in with great power all on a sudden on my heart: & with light & clearness that I was as certain it came from God & was certainly belongd to me, as ever I was that I saw the Sun shining at noon-day. And I ran away with joy to the Barn, & pleaded the Lord might keep that Promise for me that he had sent me. But the light & power that came with this word very soon died away: yet after it did so, I got great liberty & freedom to trust in God, & resolvd I would do so, tho he should slay me.

[461/– through 462/– blank]

---

8   William McCulloch (1691–1771) – minister, Cambuslang.
9   Ac 13:39.
10   Mt 9:2.

[463/–] b.g.[1] A Woman of 44 years of Age.[2]

I was from my Childhood all along kept aiming at the Duties of Religion: But when I now look back on my past life, I think I have Reason to conclude that I was all along a stranger to true & real serious godliness: for tho' I shunn'd what I took to be Sinful, it was not out of any real hatred of sin, but because I thought it would bring misery upon me here or hereafter or both. And in performing Duties, it was not out of Love to Christ, or out of a single regard to the Glory of God, but only from Self-love, & a view to my own happiness, or some advantage or other to Self, that I went about them. And thus it continued with me, till I came to Cambuslang in March 1742, & heard a Minister (26)[3] preach on these words, He that believeth on the Son hath everlasting life:[4] he that believeth not on the Son, is condemn'd already:[5] While he repeated these words of the Text, He that believeth not is condemn'd already,[6] and added, The sentence is already past, I found [464/–] a Power bringing home these words and applying them to my Conscience, convincing me that I was the person that did not believe on Christ, & that the Sentence of Condemnation was past already against me; formerly I took my Self to have been a Believer in Christ: now I was convinc'd I had never believed in a Saving manner: and I found my Self cut off from all pretences to faith, by everything that I heard said afterward in that Sermon. I hereupon fell under great distress of Spirit; but did my utmost to refrain crying, because I now saw I had been but a hypocrite, & was made to apprehend God was now about to manifest my hypocrisy openly, and was ashamed any should see me in that distress, & so covered & hid my face, ~~& got my voice kept in.~~ like a condemnd person, as I then indeed saw my Self to be. At night both the Kirk & Manse was full of people, I would gladly have gone into the Manse, but my pride of heart was then so pull'd down, that I thought my self [465/–] unworthy of going in & sitting among the rest of the Lords people there: & so I just sate down in the Close of the Manse by my Self & bemoan'd my own sad condition. And while I sate moaning there, I heard a Minister saying to these within, your iniquities have hid Gods face from you,[7] which came

---

1 Duplication of title code 'b.g.'
2 Christine Lamont – the shorthand text in McCulloch's 'Index of persons' names who gave the foregoing accounts to Mr. McC' states: daughter of James Lamont, tenant in Rosneath. Taught to read a little when a child.
3 William McCulloch (1691–1771) – minister, Cambuslang.
4 Jn 3:36.
5 Jn 3:18.
6 Jn 3:16.
7 Isa 59:2.

home with power to me without where I sate, & I was made Sensible this was indeed my Case. Some Man from within looking out & seing me & hearing me moaning said to the Minister, There's a Woman in distress in the Close: the Minister bade him bring her in: the Man came and ask'd me if I would come up & offered to give me help: I told him that I was not in such distress but that I could go up my Self: I did so: & when I came in the Minister askd me, If I had got any Convictions: I told him I had. Then said he, be sure you guide them tenderly, cherish them, & take heed that you do not stiffle them, or if ye do, remember that I am free of your blood: these words were made to pierce my heart with a sense of my great guilt this way in stiffling my Convictions often since my Childhood which many Instances of which were now brought fresh to mind.

[466/– through 470/– blank]

[471/–] a.h. A Young unmarried Woman aged 17[1]

My former life was but very course. Till I was about ten years of age, I scarce ever so much as said Lord help me, except when forc'd to it by my Parents; and after that coming from them among Strangers, they took but very little care of me as to any thing that belong'd to my Soul. I would now & then have gone to my knees to Secret Prayer, but I had no delight in it. I usd for ordinary to go to the Kirk, but when I was there, I took no heed, but would have slept a good part of the time, and minded nothing almost of what was said when I came away. And one year I never went to the Kirk at all, but would have ~~just~~ stay'd at home & just loitered & slept away the time. I had however at some times a pleasure to read my Bible, especially passages about Christs Sufferings. At other times I read it for nothing but that I might have it to say That I read it as well as my Neighbours. I thought when I heard of any persons that [ ][2] repented on a Death-bed, ~~I thought~~ I need not trouble my Self to become good now, I'll just be like these persons, while I live, and I'll get repentance as they did, at my latter end. [472/–] I had a wicked way of swearing: I could scarce speak a sentence without profane swearing: And lying was habitual to me: but I was in mercy kept from [ ][3] uncleanness & stealing:

At length when I heard of the Awakening at Camb. in the Spring 1742, I said to some about me I'll away to Camb. It may be I may get a Cast among the rest. I went & heard ~~about~~ there several times in March & was surprizd to see people in such distress and crying out there, & thought many a time, it seems I must have a sad sort of heart, when I cannot be affected with that which affects others so. But [ ][4] I cannot say, That ever I was effectually touch'd at the heart, till one day hearing a Minr there (26)[5] preach on the Brae, one Sabbath on these words, While the strong man armed keeps the house all his goods are in peace.[6] In that Sermon while he said, Secure carnal Sinners, fast asleep in their Sins, wonder much what makes people cry out so, in a Sense of their lost condition, & reckon them mad that do so: but better acquaintance with them [ ][7] would make them cease to wonder. Its just on this case, said he, as if you should see a company of people on the top of an

---

[1]   Jean Wark – the shorthand text in McCulloch's 'Index of persons' names who gave the foregoing accounts to Mr. McC' states: daughter of John Wark, weaver in Provanmill, Barony. Put to school when a child, taught to read the Bible, got the Catechism by heart.

[2]   Insertion ['livd ill but']: McCulloch.

[3]   Insertion ['outward']: McCulloch.

[4]   Insertion ['tho I had some concern']: McCulloch.

[5]   William McCulloch (1691–1771) – minister, Cambuslang.

[6]   Lk 11:21.

[7]   Insertion ['and their way']: McCulloch.

hill dancing to Musick playing beside them: if you stand [473/–] and look at them at a great distance, you would think by their motions That they were all mad: but approaching nearer & nearer to them, ~~and~~ when you come up to them, you would be so far from looking on them as mad, that you would admire their regular motions, & the delightful musick, & would fall to & dance as fast as any of them, yourself. So said he, you that now in your hearts look on others as sort of mad people, when you hear them cry out under a Sense of their Sins, & in longing after a Savior, & listning eagerly to the Word & complying with the Calls of it; & the motions of the Spirit of God, & praying & reading with such earnestness: & speaking of the joys they have in the light of Gods Countenance [ ];[8] would ye but draw nearer & nearer, till ye come up close to them: ye would [ ][9] be as much taken up in these things as they. This affected me much, & made me concern'd to do so. And some time after in hearing the same Sermon, [ ][10] that Citation Awake thou that sleepest arise from the dead and Christ shall give thee light[11] came home with power to my heart, & was the first word that ever came to me in that manner: he added it might seem ridiculous to speak to a dead [474/–] man in the grave & bid him rise; because it was impossible for him to do so: & said he, it is as impossible for you that are dead in trespasses & sins here before the Lord, to rise up from under the power of that death; yet Christ who gives the Command, to arise, can with the Command give power to obey it, and cause you to arise from the dead & give you ~~the~~ light, the light of life. By this time, I was fallen into great distress of Soul, under a Sense of my Sin & my lost condition, & thought them to be so great that it was impossible for Christ to pardon them. And my Agony of Soul [ ][12] immediatly threw me into a swarf, & I continued in it, as I was told afterward, by some about me, for about half an hour; during which time I heard none. ~~And~~ I do not mind what were my thoughts while in that Swoon: but the first thing that came in my thoughts after I came out of it, was, Lord thou hast forsaken me & will never take hold of me again. I continued in distress & heard the rest of that & other two Sermons & came in to the Manse after Sermons & lay all night in the Church-yard by my Self: Next day, I heard a Sermon (26) on that text, Come let us return to the Lord &c:[13] & was in so great distress in time of it, that if I had not had a sister to help me, I believe I would not have been able to come into the Manse that night after it. I stayd [ ][14] also at Camb. & ~~heard~~

---

[8]   Insertion ['& their holy walk']: McCulloch.
[9]   Insertion ['change your thoughts of them and']: McCulloch.
[10]   Insertion ['I was struck to the heart with']: McCulloch.
[11]   Eph 5:14.
[12]   Insertion ['was so great that my heart was like to leap out of me, & forced some low cries from me but much against my will and']: McCulloch.
[13]   Hos 6:1.
[14]   Insertion ['that night']: McCulloch.

~~Sermon,~~ went [475/–] home early and came back again to Sermon; & went home on Tuesdays night, still getting more and more Convictions of Sin, & a Sense of the particular evils of my heart life: my Swearing profanely was especially grievous to me: but I had got such a habit of it, that I was afraid God would never shew me mercy & that I would never get the wicked practice forsaken. I got it not quite broke off altogether, but would sometimes, 'ere I knew what was I saying, rapt up a profane Oath; but it would scarce have been half out of my mouth, till I would have checkt my Self & ~~been~~ not known what to have done to my Self in way of revenge [ ].[15] [ ][16] From Sabbath morning till Tuesdays night, I think I scarce tasted meat or drink: I prayd much of the Sabbath night in the Kirk-yard: on Mundays night I slept some, but when I awak'd, I thought I was in the midst of hell. On Wednesday when I was at Secret Prayer, the Devil ~~while~~ suggested to me What need then pray so [ ],[17] I'm as sure of thee as if I had thee: I went on however in prayer, at that time. I had never had any thought of hell before this while I was in trouble of mind: but now I thought I need not need trouble my Self to get an Interest in Christ, for that I would go to hell among the Wicked. I went & prayd however on [476/–] Thursday: but when I was essaying to do so on Friday, Satan prevaild so far by his suggestions as to raise me from my knees, & I then resolvd I would never again pray or open my mouth to God, for it was needless, I thought. I had gone the day before to divert my Self among a Set of loose wicked people nearby, that made a mock of the Work at Camb. & told me, that no doubt I would be one of the Cambuslang Converts. I told them if they would let me alone, I should never go back again to that place. I also went back to their company on Friday to put away the uneasy vexing thoughts I was under: but when I came in from them, I fell a weeping when I met with more jeers from my Mistress.

On Saturday I went to a young Woman ( ) nearby, who had been in great distress under her Convictions, & had got some Outgate: who gave me many a good Counsel at that and other times, & particularly, That I should not regard the Scoffs & jeers of mockers. One Sabbath I came to Camb. & heard Sermon & was in great distress in time of it: & a word then came into my mind, ~~The Lord J~~ 'tho, not uttered by the Minr, The Lord Jesus shall be revealed from heaven in flaming fire, taking vengeance on them that know him not & that obey not the Gospel:[18] and this word haunted my mind almost constantly, for about 14 days after that: but I think it came not from the Spirit [477/–] of the Lord but from Satan seeking to drive me to utter

[15]   Insertion ['but blessd be God I have at length utterly forsaken it']: McCulloch.

[16]   Insertion ['My unbelief grieved me greatly & I thought it was the greatest Sin ever I had committed. And the sins of my heart were more afflicting to me than ever before.']: McCulloch.

[17]   Insertion ['for I am thy Master']: McCulloch.

[18]   2 Th 1:7–8.

despair, & he had almost gaind his point, for [ ][19] when I was going home, I thought when I was going thro' Clyde, no matter tho' I should fall down into the water never to rise again: It was not however fears of hell, that was the ground of my trouble, but that God was angry with me, & that I had so greatly dishonoured him by my sin. I did not ~~however~~ after this go back to the Company of those mockers in order to put away my Convictions: but set about Prayer again, & took great delight in reading my Bible: & wrought also as I was able in the day time, but oftimes slept little at night. Another word also came into my mind, Many will say to me in that day Lord Lord &c:[20] this I thought came from the Holy Spirit bi its tending to lead me to repentance, & forsaking all iniquity.

I continued in great distress for about 8 weeks before I got any Sensible relief: At length one night I was at Secret Prayer, the Lord gave me great enlargement of heart in that duty, & that word came into my heart Come unto me, all ye that labour & are heavy laden & I will give you rest: I had been thinking I was one of those that betrayd Christ: but now I thought, if I could get faith to believe on him, he would yet Save me for all that, and I thought it pleasd the Lord then to give me some faith, so that I could [478/–] say, Lord I believe help thou mine unbelief.[21] And that other word also then came in to my heart, If thou love me, deny thy Self & take up thy cross & follow me:[22] I then said within my Self, I'll fly to the Blood of a Redeemer for the pardon of my past guilt, & resolve by thy grace to forsake all known sin for the time to come, & that if I could get a heart to seek & follow Christ, I should be easy whatever the World might say or think of me. And all this was accompanied with some measure of joy in Christ.

But in a little while this went off, when I thought, I had been, like Peter, too self confident, when he said, Tho' all men forsake thee yet will not I.[23] And now I was afraid that it was only Satan that had been deluding me, & that I had been building on a sandy foundation: Upon this I fell back into my former distress: and continued so for about 20 days before I got any relief, and it was by means of that word of Scripture coming into my heart, Look unto me all ye ends of the Earth & be ye Saved;[24] which I did not then know to be a Bible-word, & it was long 'ere I could get it. But it came with so much love to Christ that I cannot express: Some time after that, that word came unto my heart, If thou wilt draw near to me I will draw near to thy cry. I went not to prayer at that time, but at night I went out [479/–] about 10 o'clock, and continued with other two young Women ( ) in the fields till

---

[19] Insertion ['next day']: McCulloch.
[20] Mt 7:22.
[21] Mk 9:24.
[22] Mt 16:24, Mk 8:34, Lk 9:23.
[23] Mt 26:33.
[24] Isa 45:22.

6 o'clock in the morning, taken up mostly all that time in Prayer, & Singing of Psalms, which some of ~~them~~ us had by heart. And that night I felt much of love to Christ in my heart.

I went to the Lords Table at the Barony Sacrament: but got nothing there, but only a great deal of grief for sin, whereby I had offended such a gracious God & Saviour. But after I had been there, I fell into great grief & sorrow, that I had gone to that Table, thinking I had been thereby betraying the Son of Man with a kiss, & had profan'd that holy Ordinance: & in this distress I continued till Wednesday thereafter, when that word came into my mind

> O Lord my God if it be so
> That I committed this
> ~~If [...]~~ if in my hands
> Iniquity there is.[25]

This I thought was made useful to bring me to repent & mourn for that guilt of unworthy communicating, I was afraid I had brought upon my Self: and I continued long greatly bowed down under a Sense of that iniquity of my hands & heart.

At the first Sacrament at Camb. July 1742, I [480/–] found much Sweetness in hearing the Word especially on the Sabbath forenoon, when that Word came into my heart Man liveth not by bread alone, but by every word that proceedeth out of the mouth of God;[26] ~~which made me~~ I long'd to feed on Christs broken body & shed blood, & felt strength conveyed to my inner man by the power of his Spirit coming along with his word. At the Table I got little Sensible: but after it, while hearing that word My Soul is exceeding sorrowful even to death[27] coming into my mind, ~~that~~ I was much grieved that I could not be more sorrowful for what I was & I had done in offending him []:[28] and immediatly I found my grief turned into joy.

One day hearing a Minister preach, (12)[29] that Citation, Come let us reason together saith the Lord, tho your sins be as scarlet & crimson I'll make you white as wool,[30] came with powerful delight to my Soul: & made me wonder at the condescending love & grace of Christ in the Promise to such a poor wretched Sinner as I.

One night after I had been much despisd & reproachd in the house where I was, & much cast down; when all the rest were gone to bed, I went out & sate down at the house-end by my self alone: and heard a pleasant sounds as

---

[25] Ps 7:3, Scottish Psalter (metrical).
[26] Mt 4:4, Lk 4:4.
[27] Mt 26:38, Mk 14:34.
[28] Insertion ['and procuring his sorrow']: McCulloch.
[29] George Whitefield (1714–70) – evangelist.
[30] Isa 1:18.

of a multitude Singing the 103rd Psalm, which I took first to have been on this side & then on that side, at length [481/–] looking up, and yet seing nothing, I took it to proceed from above; & that it was the voice of these that had been gathered together to the Lord. And found my heart & voice joining together with them. I went in to my bed, but after some time, went out & sate down there, and sate & heard the same heavenly sound, and joined in it as before.

To close: I now find my heart much deadned to the World, & all the profits and pleasures & every thing in it. And for ordinary I find my chief desires going out after Christ & communion with him: & can say That there is none in heaven or earth I desire in comparison of him: And my great grief is, that I cannot get serving God as I would: and that I cannot get my corruptions subdued, & my thoughts captivated to the obedience of Christ. I have not assurance of Eternal Life, but blessed be God, I have some hopes of it, since he took a dealing with my Soul, & desire to rest entirely on what Christ did & suffered as the Surety of the Elect, as the only ground of all my hopes of blessings here & hereafter

To him be Glory World without End Amen.

[482/– blank]

[483/–] c.r. A married man of 51 years[1]

I was much neglected in my Education in my Childhood & youth: I was taught to read a little in the Bible, but very indistinctly: I was addicted to all Evil, & indulg'd my self in the open practice of many vices, as cursing & swearing and breaking the Sabbath, gaming &c: and yet I usd to pray now & then by my self, & kept the Kirk for ordinary on Sabbath days. When I was about 22 years of age, I fell under dreadful ~~atheistical~~ unbelieving apprehensions (whether proceeding from Satan or my own heart I know not) relating to the Bible: I heard that the Turks had their Alkoran, the Papists their Traditions, and all Sects pretended to what they received for their Rule to be from God, & yet all was but from man; & I thought, So also might the Bible which I & others I liv'd among, be, for any thing I knew to the contrary. I was much perplex'd about this matter but kept all within my my self, fearing that if I should mention such thoughts to any, I would be taken for an Atheist, & I did not know but the Laws of Man might take hold of me & put me to death. Whereupon I began to search the Word of God, that I might see what was in it before I proceeded any further, or ventured to make my thoughts known to any: and while searching it, I met with that passage 1Pet. Holy men of God spake as they were moved by the Holy Ghost;[2] and in reading that, I rested there, believing it to have been to, and so I concluded my self to be a Believer.

David Logan Collier in Camb. c.r.[3]

[484/–] Soon after this I apply'd to an Elder in the Place where I liv'd, who gave me a Token to come to the Lords Table: and before I came there, I enter'd into some kind of Personal Covenant with God, the nature of which was, that I would endeavour to keep a Conscience void of offence toward God & man, that is, that I would not defraud steal cheat or over-reach any man, & would study to keep my self from all filthiness & pollution of the flesh. A little after this I went into the Army, ~~and~~ where I was kept free of gross fleshly pollutions, & did not cheat or defraud any, but now & then would have let a profane Oath fly, according to the wicked custom that prevaild there. Yet I was an object of mockery to the rest of the soldiers, because I would not run to the same excess of riot with them

---

[1]   David Logan – the shorthand text in McCulloch's 'Index of persons' names who gave the foregoing accounts to Mr. McC' states: collier and retired soldier situated in Cambuslang.

[2]   2 Pe 1:21.

[3]   Bottom margin note made by McCulloch.

in profane Swearing, & cursing drunkenness, and whoring, as they did, and on that account they could scarce endure to see me.

{[485/–] through [490/–] blank}

[491/1] John Aiken Weaver in Cambuslang Aged 22.[1]

I was put to School, & taught to read the Bible & got my Shorter Cat. by heart & retain it still. I was put in my Childhood to pray in Secret by my Self, and in the after part of my former life, I sometimes kept up a way of praying in Secret, & sometimes neglected it but when I did neglect it, I usd to have some checks for it. I usd all my life when I had access to come to Kirk on Sabbath days. I have always been kept sober & civil & free of any thing the world could challenge, except that I have been drawn away by others to break some fruit yeard. When I was a boy I would sometimes have sung Psalms in the fields by my Self, & prayed 7 or 8 times a day by my Self: but when I usd to go to prayer, it was always when I met with some difficulties, & not of delight in the duty it self: Sometimes the Lord has cast in a good thought in my mind, but it has within a little vanishd away again. As one day going to Glasgow I thought, O if I could call the Lord my God, all would be right. but still I found the word read & heard to be but as a dead Letter to me, & never came with Spirit & life to me as I have found it to be of late.

The first time ever I heard the word as a joyful sound was ~~about M~~ on a Sabbath about Martinmass 1741, in hearing a Minr preach upon that text, Joh.3.3,5 Except a man be born born of water & of the Spirit, he cannot enter into the kingdom of God:[2] In hearing which I was greatly affected, & that was the first time I found the call of the Gospel come home to me in particular, [ ][3] & after that I could not omit seeking a Blessing on what I was to hear before I came out, which I had never usd to do before. I became very uneasy about my Soul Condition, & continued to be so to the degree that for about a Quarter of a year thereafter, I scarce ever slept above 3 hours in a night, [492/2] [ ][4] I was greatly grieved under a new [. . .] [. . .] [. . .] [. . .][5] yet had not heartily believd it & complyd with the Call of it for want of peace with God thro Jesus Christ. I never almost had any dread of hell upon me, but what troubled me was the offence & dishonour I had done to God by my sins, which every day were brought as fresh to my mind, ~~as~~ even all the sins I had almost ever been guilty of, as at the time when I committed them. And I was made to pray earnestly that I might be born again, & that I might get my peace made with God thro Christ. And all that Quarter of a year I was

---

[1]   This partial duplicate account is an earlier version of the version found in Volume I: 277–81.
[2]   Jn 3:5.
[3]   Insertion ['And that day I thought either the minister or I was changed & I said so in the family after I came home and was changed <. . .><. . .><. . .>']: McCulloch.
[4]   Insertion ['from that day forward']: McCulloch.
[5]   Illegible text due to closely cut and worn head-edge. The duplicate account in Volume I ((p. 277) reads: '. . . that I had heard the gospel so long, and . . .'.

often taken up in Secret Prayer, and did not choose to be in company but to be much by my self alone at prayer meditation. And every day I was getting some new sight of Gods merciful dealing with me. And while I was praying to be born again, one day, I found my heart just melted down to a willingness to give up my self to God to do any with me he pleasd. Another day at prayer, I found my heart so filled with love to Christ, that I thought if I had a thousand hearts I would give them all to him. Another day at Prayer retiring to pray for one of my Acquaintance who I heard was dangerously sick, after I had been praying for some time for him, I came to pray for my self, & was then first seiz'd with fear & trembling, & then a great light light appeard [ ]⁶ to shine round about me, and at the same the light of the knowledge of the glory of God in the face of Jesus Christ shind into my heart & filld me with joy, & sense of my Interest in Christ, so that I could not forbear crying out [ ]⁷ My Lord & my God. And this was the first time that ever I got a sense of my Interest peace with God thro Jesus Christ. And one night when I was on the Road going to the East Country in company with another Person, I dreamd'd I saw a great multitude of people about Cambuslang Kirk, & told that person so next morning. He made answer, Yes there will be a General meeting there very soon. And this I think was in the first week [493/3] of Janry 1742, which was about 6 weeks before the Awakening brake out on Feb, 18. Some little time after [ ]⁸ I dreamd again that I saw the Kirk-yeard full of people & my self at the standing at the Out-side of them. And this I saw made out in some Weeks after. I now found my heart mere tender than usual & much affected when I read or heard of spiritual things, & tears of joy would have rushed out when I read or heard of the success of the Gospel. I then got a hearty concern for to pray for Ministers, the destruction of Satans Kingdom, & the advancing of Christs Kingdom thro' the world. Idle & vain discourse became distasteful to me, & I always kept silence when I heard it, which I seemd to be very ready to join in before. I became watchful over my heart, & jealous and afraid of my self that I would turn back to my former state & way of life. [ ]⁹

I had not been at the Weekly Lecture on Thursday Feb. 18, nor did I go to the Manse on Friday, but on Saturday morning about 4 o'clock, I got up & went in to a barn for prayer, and while I was at that duty, that word came into my mind with great life & joy & power, & filled me with the light of Gods countenance & filled me which I was sure could not proceed from the

---

⁶ Insertion ['not to the eyes of my body which were shut, but to the eyes of my mind']: McCulloch.
⁷ Insertion ['with all my might']: McCulloch.
⁸ Insertion ['the work began']: McCulloch.
⁹ Insertion ['I never cryd out in publick, nor had I any visions, nor had I any swarfs.']: McCulloch.

Devil, My soul wait thou with patience upon thy God alone[10] [ ][11] After that I found what it was to have union & communion with God, & had much joy & peace, & the spiritual food came to my Soul, with as much appetite for it & refreshment by it, as my outward food came to my body. [ ][12] I came to the Kirk & heard Sermon, & stayd there & at the Manse till next morning.

I got much good at Family Worship in my Masters & particularly in singing of Psalms in which I had great delight, & was sometimes ready to cry out for joy, I never knew what it was in my former life, to join in prayer or in seeking a blessing, at meat, as I did now. [494/4] [Ø][13] For about 6 weeks after this I usd to retire or 6 times a day to Secret Prayer, & had daylie communion with God in that & other duties, and following my work, I behovd to be sending up short ejaculations of heart to God, and I thought I got just all I desird of God, & was just satisfied.

[‡][14] One night [ ][15] hearing a Minr (Mr McC)[16] preach on that text, There the wicked cease from troubling there the weary are at rest,[17] I was lifted up with joy, in the Views of that everlasting rest after the toils & labours of this mortal sinful life were over, that I thought I was just at the gates of Heaven already. [‡ I scarce ever heard a Minr (Mr McC) preach but I got some sensible good by it.]

I came at length to have many ups & downs, at one time rejoicing & within a very little in a moment cast down again. One night [ ][18] I dreamd that I was just led thro' the world, & then taken up to heaven, and then next morning, reflecting on this dream, these words in the 107th ps. came into my mind came with great light & power, & relieved me of the fears I had been under, & made me willing to die at that time, at the thoughts of which I had oft had a reluctancy before, Then are they glad because at rest & quiet now they be, so to the haven he them brings which they desird to see.[19] Many times, when I came from the Preaching I would have been strongly tempted to think there was not a God, which would have grievd me exceedingly, but within a little again before I got home, I would have been rejoicing, & mounting up in ardent desires as on eagles wings to heaven. —One night after I had been

---

[10] Ps 62:5, Scottish Psalter (metrical).
[11] Insertion ['I thought the letters of that Verse shind as if they been printed in Gold Letters']: McCulloch.
[12] Insertion ['I found one predominant evil that had stayed in my heart & I could never get it overcome, but now I found the power of it broken & got the victory over it.']: McCulloch.
[13] (Ø) Insert corresponding text from p. 214.
[14] Mark indicates that bracketed text preceded by identical mark in middle of this paragraph is to be inserted here.
[15] Insertion ['on the harvest night to the Shearers']: McCulloch.
[16] William McCulloch (1691–1771) – minister, Cambuslang.
[17] Job 3:17.
[18] Insertion ['after I had been much tossd with fear that I would fall back again to former ways']: McCulloch.
[19] Ps 107:30, Scottish Psalter (metrical).

~~under~~ greatly perplexd ~~at the~~ with fears of falling away, being out in the fields with another at prayer []²⁰ these words came into my mind, Our God for evermore he will even unto death us guide²¹ [495/5] this promise came with power & revivd me so that after I had ended that Prayer, & was going away I behovd to return to prayer, on which I was much enlarged. And in these times, I got always every day new arguments to plead with God in Prayer.

At the 2d Sacrament at Camb. when at the Lords Table, I had much of heart-melting for sin, & I got so much of love to Christ that I was even sick of love to him.

I now for ordinary take much delight in hearing the Gospel & meet with much comfort in Publick Ordinances: but in Secret duties it is not just so well with me as ~~sometimes~~ it was last Spring & Summer: for then ~~I could~~ when I had lost Spiritual sensible comforts, I could not settle half an hour till I recovered joy in the Holy Ghost again: but now tho I do not find so great joys as sometimes, yet I find a more steddy peace in believing. I now find that for ordinary Christ is the great Object of any chief thoughts desire & delight, & it was not so before Nov. 1741. I found before that at some times, some flashes of good but they quickly pass'd away, & seem to have come only from the common Operations of the Spirit, but now I find much of an abiding spiritual frame, (tho not so much as I would,) & a suitableness of heart to spiritual things.

[Ø²² One night coming from hearing a certain Minr I heard some by the way coming home speak very bitterly against him, at which I was much movd: & going home I went to prayer about this very thing, and that word came into my mind, with some ~~power~~ distinguishing power, What God has cleansd that call not then common or unclean,²³ & this was immediatly followed with that word, How long wilt thou pervert against the righteous man. This easd me of the trouble I was in about him, & after that I had a greater liking to him than ever.]

---

²⁰ Insertion ['after he went on:']: McCulloch.
²¹ Ps 48:14, Scottish Psalter (metrical).
²² [Bracketed text for insertion on p. 213 at the corresponding Ø symbol].
²³ Ac 10:15, Ac 11:9.

[496/6] Alexr Bilsland Shoemaker in Glasgow mryd aged 47.[1]

I was put to School when I was young & taught to read and write: & got the Shorter Cat. by heart & retain it still. I got also the Proof Cat. by heart, but have now much forgot it. I was much given to Secret Prayer when I was young. But when I came to years I very often neglected it. And so it was also with me as to family prayer, after I came to have a house of my own. I usd all my life to go to the Kirk on the Sabbath days ~~& thought~~ in order to hear the word. I usd often to mispend my time at a bottle, & sometimes would have a drank to Excess, ~~yet I thought~~ but afterward would have been much displeasd with my self for it. And I thought I had a liking to the people of God & to his ways, & reckoned that all was well enough with me. Yet I never felt the Word come home to me with power, so as to convince me of my lost Condition, or to draw my heart to Christ, Till ~~about~~ at hearing the Action Sermon [ ][2] by a Minr (Mr McLaurin)[3] before the Sacrament in Glasgow in Octr 1741, when he mentioned our being naturally full of wounds & bruises & putrifying sores, I felt a Divine Power bring home those words to me as what was my case in particular, & was made to see my self all covered over pollutions & spiritual sores ~~& of~~ both by Original & actual sins, & got my heart melted down, under a Sense of it, and continued much affected all day. After that I forsook my old Companions that I usd to be entangled with and set about praying in Secret & in my family that I had much neglected, & attended carefully on publick Ordinances, & got more & more discoveries of the evil of my former ways, & of my lost State by nature, & attended diligently to the Word. [497/7] But I got no Outgate till the next Sacrament Occasion at Glasgow,[4] hearing a Minr (Mr McLaurin) preach on the ~~Sacrament~~ Sabbath before, when he cited these words in Heb. How much more shall not the blood of Christ who thro' the Eternal Spirit offered himself a Sacrifice without spot to God, purge &c:[5] at hearing of which I felt the Power of God bringing up my heart to embrace Christ in all his offices, & got clear discoveries of Christ in all his offices as an All-sufficient Saviour, and as not only ~~willing~~ able but willingness to save me, & felt his willingness in making me heartily willing to receive him. And at the same time had much of heart brokenness for sin & spiritual joy in him. And on Saturday when hearing a Minr (Mr Robe)[6] saying, Any of you that

---

1   This partial duplicate account is an earlier version of the version found also in Volume I: 76–90.

2   Insertion ['on that text – & the work of faith with power']: McCulloch.

3   John McLaurin (1693–1754) – minister, Glasgow/Ramshorn.

4   Side margin note: 'April 1742'.

5   Heb 9:14.

6   James Robe (1688–1753) – minister, Kilsyth.

are sensible that you have got your hearts brought up to embrace Christ on his own terms see you stay not away ~~from~~ at which I felt a power came along that melted my heart, & made me willing to come to the Lords Table: On the Sabbath morning before I went out, that word came into my mind ~~with Power~~ My flesh is meat indeed & my blood is drink indeed,[7] which came with so much power, that I could not forbear crying it out, in hearing of my Wife. At the Table I was helped to feed by faith with much brokenness of heart for sin on Christs broken body & shed blood, & found it to meat indeed & drink indeed to my soul. And on the Munday I found what was said come with power to me & got faith to apply it to my self. Next Sabbath after the Thanksgiving Sabbath, coming out to Camb. before I got near I heard the 45th Ps. I was greatly melted, & warmd: hearing a Minr (Mr McC)[8] preach on that text, If any man be in Christ he is a new creature,[9] I ~~got my~~ found every word he said brought home to me, & was melted greatly both with sorrow & joy, particularly when he said [498/8] a believer could no more live without Christ, than the streams could subsist without the fountain. And I continued in this frame for several weeks, attending at Camb. on the Lords days, & on Thursdays and another days also, & found more & more light and strength. Going home the first Sabbath that word came into my mind, with a Light shining into my heart along with it whereby I plainly knew it was from the Lord, The Spirit of God moved upon the face of the waters,[10] whereby I was ~~fill~~ further confirm'd (tho I was not doubling before, but heard many others doubling of it) that the Spirit of the Lord had been moving upon the face of the waters of the Sanctuary at Camb, & I had felt it to be so as to my own Soul that day. One day after that, when I was meditating on what I had heard at Camb. & on some other texts, that word came into my mind with power, The fig-leaves begin to appear,[11] & my Wife searchd the Bible & found it, & was made to believe that the Lord was doing good to my Soul; & within a little that word came into my heart, Pray ye the Lord of the harvest to send forth labourers into his harvest,[12] ~~after w~~ upon which I was made more & more to believe that it would be a harvest time for Souls, wherein many would be brought in to Christ, & was made to pray more earnestly that the Lord might be with his Ministers, & enable them to labour for the good of Souls. One ~~day~~ [ ][13] I had been at Camb. & that day had been but a dull day with me, & after I was gone home, & going to Secret Prayer, that word came with a powerful impression upon me, as if it had been writen or

---

[7]   Jn 6:55.
[8]   William McCulloch (1691–1771) – minister, Cambuslang.
[9]   2 Co 5:17.
[10] Gen 1:2.
[11] Mt 24:32, Mk 13:28.
[12] Mt 9:38, Lk 10:2.
[13] Insertion ['Thanks day']: McCulloch.

engraven on my Soul, What if God willing to shew his wrath & make his power known, endured with much long-suffering the vessels of wrath filled for destruction?[14] The distress [ ][15] was not so great at first as it came to be afterwards, which increased gradually upon me.[16]

[14] Ro 9:22.
[15] Insertion ['hereupon']: McCulloch.
[16] Parital duplicate account ends abruptly. The remainder of this narrative can be found in Volume I, p. 78.

[499/–] b.s. A Young Women of 16 years.[1]

In till my former life before the year 1742, I had no pretences to Religion, nor any thing like it. I endeavoured still to carry warrily that men might have nothing to upbraid me with: but I had no dread nor fear of God in my heart, nor did I carry as under his all-seeing eye. I was full of pride & vanity & self-conceit: if I had got good cloathes, or could dress my self clean & neat enough, I then usd to go to Kirk on Sabbaths; and when it was otherwise, I choos'd rather to stay at home: and when I was there, I took no heed to what was said, for I thought it enough that I was there. I very seldom usd to pray any at all, and when I did pray, I ~~thought~~ had no sense of the evils of my heart, or life; yet I thought the Lord would no doubt hear & save me. I was so stupid that I scarce thought I was a sinner at all. Once indeed, when I lookt to the Elements at the first Sacrament Occasion ever I was at, the tears came running down my cheeks, but I scarce could tell for what, only I then thought I was a great Sinner: but this wore quickly away, & I went on in my vain careless way, having seldom any thought at all about Soul-Concerns.

[500/–] At hearing a Minister (12)[2] in June 1742, in the High-Church-yeard of Glasgow, I was so far affected with several things he said, that after that I durst not go to bed one night, ~~till~~ without some form of prayer, which formerly I usd generally to neglect altogether. But I came not to get a sight & sense of the Evil of Sin or my danger by it, till the Sabbath of the first Sacrament in Cambuslang, in July 1742, when I was on the Brae there, hearing one Minister (12) I fell into a careless slumbering sort of way: & continued so till hearing another Minister [ ][3] after him, I was awakned with these words he was citing, Rev. 21.27. And there shall in no wise enter into it [ ][4] any thing that defileth, neither whatsoever worketh abomination or maketh a lie. this struck my conscience with great power, & my making a lie frequently to my mother, to excuse my self, & other Instances of that kind, were brought fresh to my mind; & now I found my hope of heaven was quite cut off. On the Evening of that day hearing a Minister (12) on that Text, Thy Maker is thy Husband,[5] when he said, You that have not Christ for your husband, ye have the Devil for your husband, & you sleep all night in the Devils arms; I found

---

[1]   Margaret Carson – the shorthand text in McCulloch's 'Index of persons' names who gave the foregoing accounts to Mr. McC' states: daughter of John Carson, sailor in MacCairn parish in the Highlands. Taught to read the Bible, got Catechism to heart, and retained it mostly.

[2]   George Whitefield (1714–70) – evangelist.

[3]   Insertion ['whom I knew not']: McCulloch.

[4]   Insertion ['into heaven']: McCulloch.

[5]   Isa 54:5.

my heart so fill'd with confusion & amazement at the thoughts that this was my condition, that I was rendered in a manner stupid. After Sermon, going into the Kirk & hearing a young Lad give out a Psalm to be sung, (Ps.23.1.) I thought there is a young Lad, who it seemd could say The Lord was his [501/–] Shepherd &c: but for me, my hope was perished from the Lord, & was thereupon made to cry out, among the people present. After this I got more & more of my Sins brought to my remembrance from time to time, all the remarkable sins I had been guilty of since I was a little Child, & set home on my conscience in a very affecting manner: And was almost quite reducd to despair. And thus it continued with me [].[6] I had great fear of Hell, at that time, but my chief grief was that I had so greatly offended God. I thought however that my Convictions were not deep enough, & wish'd & prayd that I might never take or get comfort or relief till he was pleased to give it himself. On the next Saturday that word came into my mind, Believe on the Lord Jesus & then shalt be saved, not believe and thou shalt be damnd; upon which I was immediatly made to say with heart & mouth Lord, I believe help thou my unbelief, and was instantly made to rejoice, finding a Secret Power coming with the word, causing me to believe in Christ, and was made to hope & for the time to be persuaded that he would save me.

[502/– through 506/– blank]

---

[6]   Insertion ['about a week']: McCulloch.

[507/−] b.p. A Woman about 26 years.[1]

In my Childhood, I usd sometimes to ~~pray in~~ make a fashion of praying in
Secret, & sometimes neglected it & ofter than I minded it. I went also to the
Kirk ~~for ordinary~~ then & all along for ordinary, but did not well know for
what end; I design'd to attend to what was said, but my mind was often running
after other things. And oftimes when I came home, & heard some persons
speak of Sermons & the good some got by them sometimes, I wondered much
at my own ignorance of any thing of that kind. Yet there was one time when
I was a Child, hearing a Minister (78)[2] preach, that one word he had in his
Sermon, affected me much, This is the condemnation that light is come into
the world, but men love darkness rather than light because their deeds are
evil.[3] This word stuck with me, & made me very uneasy for two or three
days, & put me often to my knees, but not understanding my self what was
dealing with me, and the people about me mocking at the Concern they saw
me under, the Concern wore off after two or three days, & I returnd just
where I was again. Yet for some Sabbaths after that, when I thought on that
word, it would have sent me to my prayers again. [508/−] ~~But still~~ As to my
Outward behaviour, merciful Providence kept me from any thing gross or
reproachful before the world: but I had no Concern about my heart: none
knew ~~what~~ [ ][4] I was but my self, & I knew not my own Case my self neither.

And thus matters continued with me till I came to Cambuslang in April
1742: and hearing a Minister (26)[5] on that Text, There are some of you that
believe not,[6] I fell under more Concern than I had ever been before. Next
Sabbath being at home at my own Parish Church, and a young Lass (83)[7]
that had been awakned at Cambuslang crying out, in time of Sermon in great
distress, the Minister (25)[8] ordered her to be taken out, thinking, as he said
afterwards, that she would be the better to be taken out, ~~because of~~ to prevent
her fainting: at seeing & hearing of that Girl & the Minister speaking to her,
I was under much Concern & in great Confusion.

Next Thursday I came back to Camb. & heard Sermons but got nothing
sensibly. Next Sabbath I came there again & heard Sermons without at the

---

[1] Margaret Barton – the shorthand text in McCulloch's 'Index of persons' names who gave
the foregoing accounts to Mr. McC' states: daughter of Williiam Barton, tenant in Calder.
Taught to read the Bible when young, got the Catechism to heart, and retained it mostly.
[2] John Wilson (1683–1746) – minister, Carstairs.
[3] Jn 3:19.
[4] Insertion ['how sinful']: McCulloch.
[5] William McCulloch (1691–1771) – minister, Cambuslang.
[6] Jn 6:64.
[7] Catherine Jackson – lay person, Cambuslang.
[8] James Warden (1695–1745) – minister, Cadder (Calder).

Brae, but was [509/–] not much affected. After sermons at the Brae were over, a Minister (26) went in to the Kirk, & preached there; what was his Text I know not, for it was read out before I got in to the Kirk: but there was one word he had [ ][9] that struck my heart with power, & that was, That our hearts were black as Hell, and ugly as the Devil, and I was made sensibly to see that my Heart was indeed so; & thereupon I fell into great distress, and tho I did not cry out at that time, yet I was made often that night both to cry out and faint at the sight and sense the Lord gave me, of the horrid blackness & ugliness of my heart by Sin. And this was the first word that ever ever effectually reachd my heart & Conscience, and by means of which the Lord made me sensible that that was indeed the Condition I was in. After that Sermon, I essayd to get into the Manse, but while I was getting up upon a Chair to hearken, at a Window, when I could not get in, I fell down on the Ground, but was taken up again by some about me: but the Throng was such, that there was no getting in to the Manse: and therefore after hearing one pray in the fields near the Manse, I went home. [510/–] As I went home, a young Woman in Company with me, was often talking about Spiritual things, but my grief was so great that I could speak none, which she observing at length forbare. I continud in great distress from day to day, from that time for about six or seven weeks, and once at Dinner with others in the family, fell down from the Seat where I was sitting. I came back to Cambuslang shortly after this awakening, & heard a Minister (10)[10] preaching on that Text on a Thursday, Come to me all ye that labour & are heavy laden & I will give you rest;[11] I was in much distress in time of that Sermon; but could not think that I was one of these weary & heavy laden Sinners he was speaking of: and therefore that I could not expect that rest Christ promised to such. After Sermon, my distress continued or rather increased in the Manse. Some Minister there spake to me: but I got no relief, at that time nor any time after I went home, till the Sacrament Occasion in the Parish where I livd. And for the space of 6 or 7 weeks from my first Awakening, my distress of Soul was so great that I could neither eat nor drink nor sleep but with much reluctancy: nor could I apply [511/–] my self to work any to any purpose, tho I essay'd it sometimes as I could. The chief cause of my grief & sorrow, was that I had offended God so much by my sins, that I had neglected the offers of Christ and the great Salvation so long: and that tho I had usd to attend Gospel Ordinances I had done it in such an unconcern'd way: that I spent so much time on Sabbath mornings, before I went to the Kirk, in taking care of my body, & had taken so little care about my Soul: and that I had such a hard & impenitent & unbelieving heart: & I thought then that if ~~ever~~ there was a hypocrite in all

---

[9]   Insertion ['in his Sermons']: McCulloch.
[10] Sir William Hamilton (d. 1749) – minister, Bothwell.
[11] Mt 11:28.

the world I was one: and I thought that if I dy'd in the condition in which I then was, that I would surely go to Hell: yet the fears of Hell were never so heavy to my heart, as the grief I had for offending God: and when I saw or heard of others being under such Terrours of Hell, I suspected my self still the more, because I had never had much of any thing of that kind.

And thus I continued till the Sacrament Occasion in the Parish where I livd. I was under such agony & distress, that I durst not think of communicating, especially [512/–] when among other things the thoughts of my being guilty of unworthy communicating when I was at the Lords Table once before, lay so heavy on my heart. My Distress rose to a great height on the Fast day & Saturday: but I got no relief, till on Sabbath hearing a Minister (12)[12] at the Tent without, when he said Ye are not your own ye are bought with a price.[13] These words came with great Power by the Spirit of the Lord to my heart, & filld me with great joy at the full persuasion that I had at that time, that I was not my own, but Jesus Christs, and bought by him with the price of his own most precious blood: and my Soul was so filld with love & gratitude to him, that I was much taken up in praising him, & would have gladly had all the Christians I saw there to praise him on my account. And much of this frame continued with me for two or three days after; that when I was joining with the rest at Family Prayer [ ];[14] that I started up a little from the Seat on which I was leaning, yet could not well tell for what. But for about two or three weeks after, I fell under a damp on my Spirit, & was made to doubt of the reality of the work I had been under: [513/–] But after that space again, in time of Family Prayer, that word came in to my heart with some power (tho not utterd by him that was praying,) Seek & ye shall find, knock & it shall be opened to you. Accordingly I went out, immediatly after Family Prayer was over, to a place by my self, and found my heart much refreshd in that duty: And after I had come in from it, I could not forbear going out to it again, and found more of the presence of God, & thro' that day, I found my heart much melted down under a Sense of Sin, & of the Love to Christ.

But in a short while after this, I fell under great doubts & fears again for some weeks, till one day hearing a Minister (12) at Auchinloch say, that it was great presumption for any to rest in the faith of Adherence, & not seek after the faith of Assurance, that my trouble encreasd to a much greater height, when I thought, What would come of me then, that had never, as I then thought, got the length of the faith of Adherence?[15] But in speaking with an Elder (84)[16] after Sermon, on that subject, I attaind to much composure of mind by means of what he said.

---

[12]   George Whitefield (1714–70) – evangelist.
[13]   1 Co 6:19–20.
[14]   Insertion ['a deadness came on my spirit']: McCulloch.
[15]   'Assurance' superimposed over 'Adherence'.
[16]   John Wark – elder, Glasgow/Barony.

[514/–] In a very short time after this, being at the Sacrament-Occasion at Campsy, & hearing a Minister (20)[17] preach, and a Woman standing before him among the people, and crying, O What will I do? that Minister looking to her said, I'll tell thee, what thou shall do Woman, Fly to Christ, & he will save thee: What should thou do but fly to Jesus Christ: at hearing this, O I thought they were in a happy condition that were helped to fly to him: but for me I could do nothing. I then felt my heart very hard & full of unbelief: and was in great distress of soul, all that day, till about twelve o'Clock at night when I was at Secret Prayer, that I got my heart loosed, & poured out before the Lord. A word (tho not uttered by in the Sermons) had come in to my heart while I was hearing that day, but with far less power than ordinary, Fear not for I am with thee:[18] but the Power with which it came was so small, that I could not venture to think it was to me, and got but very little comfort by it. But I have reason to bless God, for giving me that day a very deep & humbling sense of my sins against a gracious God in rejecting so many offers of Christ & Calls of his Gospel, & for my Unbelief, which I then found so strong in my heart. [515/–] I was from that time under much deadness till the first Sacrament at Kilsyth in Summer 1742, when towards the Close of the Action Sermon (20) that word the Minister uttered, came into my heart with power, Awake thou that sleepest, arise from the dead, and Christ shall give thee light:[19] upon which I was made to see and believe & feel, that tho I was dead & dark, yet Christ could give me light & life, & was doing so: & this frame continued with me till Munday, when the Minister ( ) just when the people were to be dismissd, told them they might all be divided into two sorts, these that had received Christ, & these that had not, and that all of them would go home either with the devil or with Christ in their heart. This damp'd me much; yet I was made to hope, tho I had not the Assurance of it, that I had received Christ or some light & life from him at that Occasion.

I attended the Second Sacrament there, that year: & tho' I got no ravishing joys, yet I met with some reviving & quickening to my Soul.

[516/–] I continued on so, till about Martimass 1742, when hearing a Minister (25) examine the people, for the two first days of it, I felt every word he said brought home to my heart with such power, as filled me with joy, to hear the method of Salvation opened up, and so much spoken to the commendation of Christ and his grace, & felt my heart melted under a Sense of his Love, and drawn out in love to him. [†][20] But about 20 days after that, hearing that Minister examine other two days, I felt nothing of the power or

---

[17]   James Robe (1688–1753) – minister, Kilsyth.
[18]   Gen 26:24, Isa 41:10, Isa 43:5.
[19]   Lk 11:36.
[20]   Insertion ['† and my heart was made to close with him in all his Offices as my Prophet Priest & King, as an Alsufficient Saviour & as my Saviour & Lord, as I think I had also done several times before that.']: McCulloch.

presence of God in attending to what was said, but it was all to me like idle tales. But reflecting on what I had met with on the first two days, & comparing that with what I then found to be the Case, I was made to see much of the condescending mercy of God to me in two such different dispensations, to make me sensible of his Fullness & my own emptiness, & that Gospel Ordinances were either sweet or tastless as he was pleased to countenance them or not, and that all Ordinances were nothing without his presence.

[517/–] But the last of these two days, being under much discouragement, I ~~stayd~~ inclind ~~to stay all night~~ to speak to that Minister, and it being late, I was prevaild on to stay there all night. Next day when I came home, some of my Relations were very displeasd that I did not come home the night before, & chided me much. With which I was much discouraged. Within a little after that, being sent in to Glasgow, & talking there with one that had been in deep Exercise, & had got many Outgates from her distresses, I fell under further discouragement at the thoughts that my Exercises had not been so deep & sharp as hers; and this added to what I had met with from my Relations, made my distress great. But while I was in this condition going home, by my self, these words Rev. 3.20 came into my heart, To him that over cometh will I give to sit with me on my Throne, even as I overcame & am set down with my Father on this Throne.[21] This affected me and raised my heart a little; yet I could not apply the Comfort in the Promise to my self, because I thought the promise was to him that Overcometh; which I took to be overcoming Corruption & all Enemies [518/–] of Salvation, which I reckoned could not be said of me. But after a little falling down to Secret Prayer, these words Ps. 45 in meeter came in to my heart with a wonderful power & sweetness

> O Daughter hearken & regard
> And do thine ear incline.
> Likewise forget thy fathers house
> And people that are thine.[22]

Upon which I was filld with joy wonder and praise to the Lord for his condescending goodness to me in Christ, in sending these words with such power at that time [ ][23] when I had been under such Vexation for meeting with so much anger from some of my Relations in the family, & to wean my heart from ~~what evil in~~ [ ][24] things of that kind

I forgot to notice in the due place, the Lords Goodness to me at the Second Sacrament at Cambuslang in the year 1742. I had been under great deadness & darkness on Saturday, & all along till toward the Close of the Action; while

---

21   Rev 3:21.
22   Ps 45:10, Scottish Pslater (metrical).
23   Insertion ['and by them to comfort me']: McCulloch.
24   Insertion ['too much concern for']: McCulloch.

a Minister (20) was serving a Table, these words, tho, I think, not uttered by him, came into my heart with great power, Ps. 27. in Meeter

> One thing I of the Lord desir'd
> And will seek to obtain
> That all days of my life I may
> Within God's house remain[25]

which filld me with love to Christ & joy in him, & made me wonder at his grace in determing me to seek after that as my One thing, & making such a change to the better in my frame so suddenly & surprizingly. And much of the like [519/–] sweet frame continued with me on Munday in hearing the Sermons, & after I went home, and so also in meditating on what I had heard at Cambuslang Sacrament, & in Secret prayer in the fields on Tuesday.

One time in the Spring 1743; after I had been in great distress under a sense of my neglecting the calls of Christ, & the offers of grace & salvation by him; as I was standing at a house end, & looking about me & noticing the works of God; I thought now the grass is springing, the birds are singing, all things are reviving, after the winter, all things are obeying [ ][26] their Creator but I, I am daylie & hourly dishonouring him, I am withering & declining in Religion if ever I had any. While I was thinking after this manner, & ~~meditating~~ [ ][27] for these things, that word came into my heart, Thou shalt revive as the corn,[28] thou shalt grow as the lilly, thou shalt cast forth thy roots as Lebanon.[29] These words came with an overcoming Sweetness, & filled me with joy in God, & I found my poor drooping withered Soul greatly revived, & this frame lasted with me in a good measure for two or three days after.

[520/–] To draw to a Close of this account, tho I might mention many more particulars, I forbear, & shall only mention some things that are more general.

Since my Awakening in the Spring 1742, to this time, the Spring 1744, I have often been in that Condition, that I could neither pray nor read or hear the word or meditate upon spiritual things with delight, but with great deadness darkness and confusion: yet when it has been so it has always been the grief & burden of my Soul. But before the Spring 1742 it was not so.

In the former part of my Life, I thought I had some regard & esteem for good people more than to others: but since Spring 1742, I think any Love I had for them was none or next to none; but now I feel my heart drawn out to them all the meanest & weakest of them as well as others, if I can see any thing of the image of Christ in them, and I love them dearly, both because

---

[25] Ps 27:4, Scottish Psalter (metrical).
[26] Insertion ['and praising']: McCulloch.
[27] Insertion ['mourning']: McCulloch.
[28] Hos 14:7.
[29] Hos 14:5.

I think God loves them & they love him. And this I find to be a constant & abiding thing with me, since that time, whatever be my frame otherwise; tho when my frame is desirable, my love to them is stronger.

[521/–] I have it also to remark, That since Spring 1742, even in the deadest time & in the worst frame I have been in, I could not allow my self to neglect the duties of Gods Worship, as praying, reading & hearing of the Word; but I would have thought with my self, It is indeed so bad & so bad with me, I'm altogether out of frame for duties, What will I do then? Shall I neglect them? That was what I could not allow my self to do, or endure to think on, but still I would essay them. And I would rather steek 20 Prayers (tho' that was also a grief to me) than neglect one, when I had a fit season & opportunity for it. But it was quite otherwise with me in the former part of my life.

As for good frames & manifestations of the Love of God, they are very desirable, and what my Soul [ ]³⁰ earnestly pants after, & desire more & more of: yet it is neither the performance of duties nor good frames, nothing either done by me or wrought in me, I desire to rest on [522/–] as the ground of my hope of the pardon of Sin peace with God & eternal life. I cannot say I have a full assurance of these blessings; tho I have sometimes had much of a persuasion of my interest in them: but I bless God I am not without some hopes of them: and all my hope of them, I desire to build entirely on what Christ has done & Suffered & is still doing in Heaven for his people.

To him be Glory now & ever. Amen.

³⁰ Insertion ['cannot but']: McCulloch.

[523/–] b.t. A Young Woman about 20 years:[1]

It pleasd God in mercy to keep me in a great measure outwardly blameless before the World, tho indeed in the former part of my Life before 20, I was not so grave & composd as some others, but much given to the vanities & frolicks of Youth. My Mother traind me up to pray in Secret when I was a Child, but after she died, which was before I came to the age of a Woman, I neglected it much. I went however for ordinary to Church on Lords days. When I was about 16, I was admitted to the Lords Table: I pray'd some before I went there, but knew nothing of the Duty of Self-Examination. After that Occasion, retiring to Secret prayer, I aim'd at giving my Self away to God in Christ, in way of personal Covenanting; & at accepting Christ as my Prophet Priest & King, & took all Creatures about me to witness that I had done so: And after this for some time I was pretty oft at Secret Prayer, & went twice again to the Lords Table in a short time after this. But what Concern I had been under wore gradually off, and for about three years after this, I liv'd almost altogether without any thing that was serious like, & as if I had never been to die, seldom using so much as a form of Secret Prayer. Only I went to the Kirk on Sabbath days for a while; after that I sometimes came to the Kirk & sometimes went to hear the Seceding Ministers: at length I left the Kirk altogether & joind only with the Seceders, & continud to do so for about half a year. One day hearing one of their Ministers (54)[2] give it as a Mark of Unregenerate Persons that while the strong man arm'd [ ][3] kept the palace of the heart his goods were in peace;[4] I thought this was my Case & was somewhat affected at the thought of it: but this [524/–] soon wore off: hearing that Minister preach concerning Regeneration, I was much surpriz'd at that Doctrine. I thought Could not a person be good enough, without that change of nature he spake of. A little while after that I came out to Cambuslang on a Thursday in Mar. 1742 out of Curiosity, to see the People that had been reported to be awakned lately there. I heard Sermon in that place both from the Tent, & at night in the Kirk, but was not touchd with what I heard. I was however somewhat affected to hear & see severals crying out in distress in time of Sermon, & after it in the Manse, & thought I was a Sinner as well as they, and needed a Sight & Sense of my Sins, & secretly wishd & prayd the Lord might send it: but got it not then: but all the way almost as I went

---

[1] Janat Lennox – the shorthand text in McCulloch's 'Index of persons' names who gave the foregoing accounts to Mr. McC' states: daughter of John Lennox, gardener in Glasgow. Taught to read the Bible when young, got the Catechism to heart, and retained it mostly.

[2] James Fisher -Associate Presbytery minister, Glasgow.

[3] Insertion ['the devil']: McCulloch.

[4] Lk 11:21.

Home that night to Glasgow, that word haunted my thoughts, We have seen
strange things to day. Next Lords day I came & heard a Minr (26)[5] at Camb.
on that Text If any man be in Christ he is a new Creature,[6] Several Marks
he gave of these that were not made new Creatures or born again, ~~were ver~~
came very closs to me, particularly That these that never spent an hour all
their life in serious thoughtfulness about their Souls Salvation, their lost &
perishing state by nature & the Gospel method of Recovery by Jesus Christ,
were yet in an unregenerate condition, by which I was made clearly to see
that I was in a natural state, & was then made to resolve [ ][7] to be more
taken up about Religion, & to take time to than ever seriously to think on
Soul-Concerns. I went into the Manse after Sermon, & my Concern increas'd
at seeing the Persons in distress there: I tarried at Cambuslang also the next
two days after that [†][8] When I returnd to Glasgow I went only once to
hear the Seceding Minister there again; when he preachd on that Text,
Humble your selves [527/–][9] under the mighty hand of God & he shall lift
you up,[10] & endeavoured to shew, That no Revival of Religion was to be
expectd, or that God would never return to a people or person in a way of
mercy, till they first humbled themselves; this was what I could not agree
to; for I thought that the work must begin on Gods part, & that if God was
pleasd to humble a Person or People by his preventing grace, that that was a
Sign of his merciful return to them already. After this I went no more back
to hear the Seceding Ministers, but came & heard very oft at Cambuslang,
and sometimes in the Kirks, at Glasgow: I wanted much to have such Strong
Convictions & powerful Awakenings & deep distress for Sin, as I saw many at
Camb. under, & often prayd for these things; & would have been glad of any
thing that would have brought me into the Case of some distress'd persons I
saw; and sometimes I would have wishd that the Devil might be permitted
to appear to me in the most frightful shape & terrible manner, if that might
be a mean to alarm & terrifie me with a sense of my danger by Sin. I could
not get my heart affected either with my Sin or misery as I would have had
it: I thought I was the most stupid & hard-hearted wretch in all the world,
and that there had never been such a great Sinner on Earth in former times
nor was there any such above at present. I usd often to compare my self with
Manasses, with Paul before his Conversion, & other great Sinners mentioned

---

[5]   William McCulloch (1691–1771) – minister, Cambuslang.
[6]   2 Co 5:17.
[7]   Insertion ['thro grace']: McCulloch.
[8]   Insertion ['† And on one of these two days as I sate in the Hall in the Manse & read my
      Bible, that Passage affected me much Rom. But they being ignorant of Gods righteousness &
      going about to establish their own &c: which I was made to see was my Case']: McCulloch.
[9]   In the original document this account was misnumbered and bound out of order. Page
      sequence has been corrected so that [525/–] and [526/–] now follow [530/–].
[10] 1 Pe 5:6.

in Scripture; but I thought I was a far greater Sinner than any of them, for that they had sinned ignorantly, ~~but I had~~ or at least had not sinned against so clear light as I had [528/–] done; and when I saw or heard of some in the present Age running on to all excess of Riot & committing many outwardly gross sins, I thought, they were but sinning in the darkness of ignorance, & that their outward gross sins were nothing to my inward heart-abominations, committed against so much light & knowledge. And that which most of all galled me, was that I had kept up such a profession of godliness while I was a stranger to the power of it; that I had rejected so many Gospel-offers of Christ, & had never sincerely closd with him on his own gracious terms. I was often made to fear while I walkd in the fields, that the Earth would open under my feet & swallow me up quick, or that the Heavens would rent above me & the sword of Gods Justice & vengeance would come down upon my guilty head, & destroy me in a moment. My distress put me [ ][11]

About the middle of April 1742, hearing a ~~Stranger~~ Minister (13)[12] preach on that Text Is there no balm in Gilead &c:[13] When he was giving the Reasons why this balm was not applied to poor sinners for their healing, one reason of it he said, was, That they were not willing to be wounded deep enough with the arrows of Conviction, but sought to get them pulld out: I then earnestly beggd of the Lord he might wound me with these arrows, tho it were never so deep; & appeald to him that I was was willing, if he saw it needful for driving me out of my Sins in to Christ, to submit if it were to be rent into ten thousand pieces. But after that Sermon was over, I began to think, Others are getting Convictions that were not seeking after them, I have been long & earnestly seeking them, & cannot get them, what need I vex my self this way to get, what I am never like to get, it seems I [529/–] am one of these whom God pass'd by from Eternity, & has judicially hardned for former sins, & sworn that I shall never enter into his rest: & since I must be damn'd it shall not be for nothing, I'll take my fill of the pleasures of Sin in this World, & I'll never read nor pray nor hear Sermons nor mind Religion more. But as I went home that night, I began to think of the Excellences of that Balm of Gilead, which the Minister that preachd that day had explaind to be the Blood & Righteousness of Christ, I found my mind & heart, as I thought of it, much composd and sweetned; & I began to conceive some hopes of Mercy; & to say within my self who can tell but the happy time is yet coming, when God may graciously visit my Soul: & thereupon I put on a solid form and settled Resolution, that I would still go on to read & pray & hear the word, & wait upon God in his own way.

---

[11]   Insertion ['from meat & work in a great measure & sometimes also from sleep, at other times I felt my self very heavy & drousy, & thus I continued about a month.']: McCulloch.
[12]   John Willison (1680–1750) – minister, South Church, Dundee.
[13]   Jer 8:22.

For a months time, I conceald my Case from all. At length when I told a
certain person of it, He askd me What would please me, if I had my choice?
I told him that I was willing to Suffer any thing the Lord pleasd provided he
would give me a new heart. He said, he did not like that [ ][14] for that looked
as if I wanted to bring a price with me in my hand to purchase his favour, or
to get some blessings from him: but that I should come to God just as I was;
guilty and filthy, & to be sensible that I could do nothing and give nothing
& ~~then~~ to beg that he would freely give & do all. This I often essayd to do,
pleading that for his own names sake, he would give me the new heart &
new spirit, that he would convince enlighten & renew me, & enable me to
close with Christ as offered in the Gospel. Two Scripture texts frequently
haunted my mind, I cry & shout but he shutteth [530/–] out my Prayer,[15] I'll
bear the indignation of the Lord because I have sinned against him.[16] I was
kept crying to him, & got my mind fram'd to a quiet & patient waiting upon
him. I found my self made to thirst both after Justification & Sanctification,
but to desire Holiness more than Happiness; I was made heartily willing to
close with Christ in all his Offices, & felt my need of him as a Prophet and
Priest; but above all things as a King, to overcome my strong Corruptions &
to subdue me wholly to himself by the power of his Spirit and grace.

Sometimes when under great fears; while I was lying prostrate before the
Lord, my Sins appeard so heinous that I durst not ask the pardon of them;
but that word darting into my mind when in this Case, Salvation is freely
offered to all, would have made my heart cleave to Christ. At other times I
would have got more enlargement in prayer, & tho I was submissive as to
Temporal mercies; yet I knew I was allowed to be importunate as to spiritual
& saving Blessings; and was sometimes so instant in asking them, that I would
have protested before the Lord, That I would not go away out of the Place
where I was, till he would give me some token for good, something to shew
at least that he notic'd me as one of his own; and usually he did so by giving
me some heart melting for Sin, or some Scripture Word sent into my heart
with sweetness. But after I had been sometimes very earnest this way, it would
have been suggested to me, what needs all this ado about Religion, cannot
you behave like other good Christians, who content themselves with praying
morning & Evening, & are as merry & pleasant thro' the day as any other.
To this I was made to reply, that either these were [525/–] only Christians in
name & profession but not indeed & in truth; or if they were sincere, they
were such as had got their Covenant Interest in Christ secur'd and clear'd
~~which~~ to their Satisfaction, which was far from being my Case.

---

[14] Insertion ['way of speaking']: McCulloch.
[15] La 3:8.
[16] Mic 7:9.

At Cathcart Sacrament May 1742, in hearing the Action Sermon (2)[17] on a Text relating to the love of God in giving his Son, I got a lively & affecting view [][18] of all Mankind by nature as running away from God after the devil, & God as on a Throne of Grace calling after them & inviting them to return to him; & the thoughts of the Love of God shewed in this matter was so affecting to me, that I was sometimes almost ready to cry out among the people, Be astonished O Heavens at this! Yet I did not feel the love of God shed abroad in my own Soul at that time. When the Elements were brought forward & laid on the Table, I was much affected, & said in my heart, These are to be the Symbols of Christs broken body and shed blood, broken & shed for others, but not for me. Here's to be a feast of love for others but nothing for me! for at that time I durst not think of communicating.

About the middle of May 1742, ~~where~~ as I was coming out to hear at Cambuslang, The devil & my own corrupt heart joining together, made me reason falsly to this purpose, I have never yet got these convictions of Sin I ought to have, I have been seeking them & have not got them, I cannot work them in my self, man cannot help me, & unless the Spirit of the Lord work them in my heart, I can never have them. Well, since it is so, if I perish, I'll have this for my Excuse at the great day, that I could not get them tho I sought after them, & so the fault will not be mine that I got them not. [526/–] But in hearing a Minister (24)[19] that day at Camb. on that Text, O Israel thou hast destroyed thy self but in me is thy help,[20] that Minister was directed to answer my false & even blasphemous reasonings, whereby I would have excusd my self & laid the blame of my perishing on God ~~himself~~, [][21] that I was the cause of my own misery, & that if I should perish for ever, I would only have my self & my own sins to blame, & that my mouth would be stop'd at the great day, for that I could not say I had sought Convictions & converting grace from him with that earnestness I should & might, else he ~~had~~ would have given them. And that Text that came much in my mind, made me apprehend there was something wrong in my askings which I yet saw not, Ye ask & receive not because ye ask amiss.[22]

At the Sacrament at Carntalloch in June 1742, when at the Lords Table, I got little remarkable, but liberty to pray for the Ministers, & some composure followed that day: but next morning, it was impress'd on me that I was making a Christ of my duties, upon which I resolvd thro' grace, I would not rest in any duty except I met with Christ in it.

[17] George Adam (1698–1759) – minister, Cathcart.
[18] Insertion ['by faith']: McCulloch.
[19] John Warden (d.1764) – minister, Campsie; son of John Warden (1671–1751), minister, Gargunnock (Macfarlan, *Revivals*, 242; Scott, *Fasti*).
[20] Hos 13:9.
[21] Insertion ['and made to see']: McCulloch.
[22] Jas 4:3.

Hearing a Stranger Minister at Cambuslang a little after & Seeing many people in distress about me, I was much grievd that I could not be affected as they were, and at length burst out in tears, on this account. After Sermon coming into the Manse, where there were many in distress, just as I entred there, these words were darted in upon me (Ps.

> Unto thy people thou hard things
> Hast shewd & on them sent
> And thou hast caused them to drink
> Wine of astonishment[23]

which was very shocking and affecting to me, & made me cry out before all present.

[531/–] At the Sacrament-Occasion at Calder in June 1742, hearing a Minister (12)[24] on that text How shall we escape if we neglect so great salvation,[25] the words of the Text struck a fear on me, & when he said, God had prepard a great Feast at Calder, but it was for children & not for dogs, adding, Thou Dog touch it if thou dare, my fears of a rash approach increasd: but I had come to that Occasion resolving against hope to believe in hope, & so I hopd still that tho I was but a dog, yet I might allowed some crumb of mercy that fell from the childrens Table: & so then adventured to go forward to the Lords Table: the Minister then Exhorting at ~~that Table~~ [ ],[26] (12) said, Can any of you now say with Thomas, My Lord & my God![27] I then felt my heart made to say so [ ],[28] & these words Ps. 18.2. came into my heart with great love & sweetness, & I was made to express them as my own, The Lord is my rock, & my fortress & my deliverer, my God, my buckler & the horn of my salvation & my high tower: and toward the close of his Exhortation he said, Some of you now will be longing to be in heaven & loth to come down from the mount, & to return to the world again: this I found indeed to be the case with me at that time.

At the first Sacrament at Camb. in July 1742, I expected great things; but found my self very dead & lifeless: only that word being pressd upon my heart in time of the Action Sermon (tho not utterd by the Speaker) My God shall supply all your wants,[29] my hopes were a little reviv'd: I got nothing sensibly at the Table: after I came from it, I was much grieved, thinking Now he has sent me empty away, I may now go mourning to my grave: but that word

---

[23] Ps 60:3, Scottish Psalter (metrical).
[24] George Whitefield (1714–70) – evangelist.
[25] Heb 2:3.
[26] Insertion ['it']: McCulloch.
[27] Jn 20:28.
[28] Insertion ['with much love & joy']: McCulloch.
[29] Php 4:19.

came[532/–] back again & again [ ]:[30] I essayd to lay hold of it, but found no comfort. On Munday I heard a Minister (16)[31] preach much comfort from that text, but I could apply none. But at Secret Prayer next day after I went home I got my heart pourd out before the Lord & at coming away from that duty these words came into my heart with much sweetness (Ps. 35.9,10.)

> My Soul in God shall joy and glad
> In his Salvation be
> And all my bones shall say, O Lord
> Who is like unto thee[32]

And for a year after this, I found that word My God shall supply all your wants, my daylie comfort, and I was never in want of any mercy spiritual or temporal, but I found the Lord accomplishing that promise in supplying it.

A little time after this, going to the Sacrament at Campsy & examining my self, tho I durst not say that I lovd God directly & immediatly, yet I could say I lovd his Ordinances & his people & all that had his image, & that Word coming into my mind, If ye love me keep my Commandments,[33] I thought that since I must shew love by keeping of his Commandments, I must certainly obey that command Do this is remembrance of me. Accordingly I went to the Table, but got not what I was looking for at it. But while I sate & heard a Minister (20)[34] serve a Table & say, Poor Communicant, What are thou seeking there, Will not ordinances satisfy thee, will not Ministers Satisfy thee, will not being let down at the Lords Table among his children Satisfy thee? I found these words come home to me with much sweetness & suitableness to my Condition: for I could & did appeal to him who knew all things, that neither Ordinances nor Ministers nor any thing in the world, nor even Heaven it self [ ][35] would not Satisfy me without Christ & the Enjoyment of him

[533/–] At the Second Sacrament at Camb. in August 1742, On Saturday while hearing Sermon, that word (tho not utter'd by the Minister then preaching) was brought to my mind with some power, I have loved thee with an everlasting love,[36] which I endeavoured to take hold of. At the Table, I found my self at first somewhat straitned: but within a little, I got liberty & enlargement to pray for the People in the place where I was, for all the Lords Servants there, & for spreading of the Gospel thro the world, & Saving Efficacy to go along with it: and last of all when I was going to plead for something to my self, before I got leave to think on any promise, to plead

---

30 Insertion ['My God shall supply all your wants']: McCulloch.
31 Alexander Webster (1707–84) – minister, Tolbooth/Edinburgh.
32 Ps 35 9–10, Scottish Psalter (metrical).
33 Jn 14:15.
34 James Robe (1688–1753) – minister, Kilsyth.
35 Insertion ['as a state of happiness']: McCulloch.
36 Jer 31:3.

upon, that word was brought in to my heart with great power & sweetness, I am thy salvation,[37] which filled my heart with much love & joy in God, & I wanted if possible to have men & angels & all the Creatures engagd in glorifying and praising him. And much of this sweet frame continued with me for a long time after.

In Winter 1743, I was much & long under fears of Hell, & while I was under many terrible apprehensions of it, I would frequently have beggd of the Lord, with the greatest earnestness, That if he had so determin'd in his Eternal Purpose to pass me by, & that I was to be sent in holy Justice to Hell for ever, that he would grant me that favour, that I might not be allowed to blaspheme his Holy Name there, as I understood from the word: the damn'd ~~in Hell~~ do: for this of all other things in Hell appear'd to me to be the most dreadful.

[534/–] To come to a Close, I think I can say safely as in the sight of God, that for above two years past before this (June 6.1744) The chief thing in all the world my heart has been ordinarily running out after, is to get the power of Sin subdue'd by the Spirit and grace of God, to get the images of God renewed on my Soul, to get conformity to Christ and Communion with him. 'Tis my habitual desire to live under a sense & belief of Gods All-Seing Eye being ever upon me. I bless his name he has given me to see & feel such an emptiness in my Heart, that nothing in all the world can Satisfy but himself. I desire that his name may be honoured from the rising of the Sun to the going down of it, & that all the Ends of the Earth may see the salvation of our God. My heart within me has sometimes been ready break & faint in longing for the full & eternal Enjoyment of Christ in Heaven, when the ~~Eternal~~ [ ][38] day shall break & the present interveening shadows shall flee away. Mean time I desire to wait his pleasure [ ][39] To his Name be Glory for ever. Amen.

---

[37] Ps 35:3.
[38] Insertion ['Everlasting']: McCulloch.
[39] Insertion ['& to aim thro his grace, at perfecting holiness in his fear']: McCulloch.

[535/-] a.s. A Young Woman of 23 years[1]

When I was a child I was put to School to learn to read; but I was so much set upon my diversions, & so much neglected, that I learnd little more than to read the Catechism;[2] and when I came to more years & went to Service, I could not find leisure to learn to read, tho I much desir'd; but I came to by following the Minister with my eye on my Bible, as he read that portion of Scripture, he was going to Lecture on, on the Sabbaths, I came gradually to learn to read, more than by any other way. I never pray'd any by my self alone till I was about 14 years of age, when I was in the Kirk on the Lords day, hearing a Minr. (10)[3] praying That God would set up his Worship in every Family and his fear in every heart, and that there might not be a prayerless person in all that Congregation, from that time I inclind to pray at I thought it a sad thing that I should be one of the prayerless persons in the Congregation, & resolv'd to try it when I went home: but did not know how to fall about it; but going out to a Dyke-side by my self, I essayd it twice but could get nothing to say; upon which I wept much; but the third time, I got some Expressions put into my mouth, & some freedom: & for some days [ ][4] after that, I thought I was come to that, that I could pray well enough. [536/-] After this I sometimes pray'd once a day but often neglected it and a very little matter would have made me neglect it. And because I was all along in Providence kept from outwardly gross things before the World, I thought there was no fear of me, & all would be well with me. When any thing vex'd me I would have said, O that I were dead, that I might get out of this ill world; but then I did not know where I would have gone to if I had died, whether to Heaven or Hell: but I thought I would be made to know it when I was dying. But I had never any serious Concern about my heart, nor the necessity of its being chang'd. When I would have read of the wickedness of the heart, I would have said within my self, I'm sure my heart is not wicked. When I would have thought of Christs coming into the World to save sinners, and of his coming to call, not the righteous but sinners to repentance, I would have said to my self, Well, it seems Christ came to save me, for I am a Sinner; & that unless I had committed some sins, Christ would never call me or save me. And by many such foolish and Sinful reasonings, the devil,

---

[1]   Margaret Borland – the shorthand text in McCulloch's 'Index of persons' names who gave the foregoing accounts to Mr. McC' states: resident in Bothwell, daughter of James Borland, tenant in Shawfield.

[2]   *Shorter Catechism of the Westminster Assembly* (1647).

[3]   Sir William Hamilton (d. 1749) – minister, Bothwell.

[4]   Insertion ['two or three years']: McCulloch.

the strong man armed kept quiet possession of my heart; & all his goods were in peace.[5]

~~But~~ And thus it continued with me till one Sabbath in the Spring 1742, that I came [537/–] to Camb. & heard a Minister (26)[6] preach on that Text, Joh. —he that believeth not on the Son shall not see life, but the wrath of God abideth on him:[7] where he gave many marks of these that believe not on the Son of God, & that are under the reigning power of unbelief; & shewed that all these are in their natural State: and shewed their great misery, how the wrath of God abides on them: I was then made sensible by the marks given, that I was yet in Unbelief & in my natural unrenewed condition, but knew not how to get out of it. And when he said, All you that are in this condition, whatever ye do, wherever ye go, & wherever ye are, even in that very brae where ye are sitting, the wrath of God is still hanging over you, and abiding upon you; I found these words brought home to my heart with ~~such a~~ power, and affected me much, & made me very uneasy: My uneasiness return'd every now & then as I went home, at the thoughts of my sad condition: & after I got home, I would frequently have taken my Bible and read that Text, & bursted out into tears and weeping at the thoughts of being an Unbeliever, & being under the wrath of God wherever I was, and not knowing how to get out of my natural State.

About three weeks after that, coming to Camb. on a Thursday, while I stood at the Stair-head in [538/–] the Manse, where I had come to hear the Exhortations ~~there,~~ after the Sermons were over, that Word spoken by a Minr (14)[8] who was then exhorting in the Hall, pierc'd my heart like a Sword, Awake thou that sleepest, arise from the dead and Christ shall give thee light,[9] I then thought I was both dead ~~in sin~~ and asleep in sin, & that there was no mercy for me: and I continued as I went home and for about 20 days after that, in great distress: and during that time, I often felt such a great heat within me, that I thought I would have been burnt up with it. I ~~had~~ was not without fears of Hell, but what made the greatest impression on me was a sense of the dishonour I had done to God by my Sin, that I had triffled away so much precious time, & given so little heed to the Calls of God in his Word & when I was hearing Sermons. I then thought I could pray none, and tho' I often essayd it; yet I was afraid to go about it, or to take Gods holy name in my polluted lips. I could not apply my self to work; & could ~~not~~ eat but little, my sleep oft departed from me, & one morning I awaked with a great Fright, thinking all was in a flame about me.

[5]   Lk 11:21.
[6]   William McCulloch (1691–1771) – minister, Cambuslang.
[7]   Jn 3:36.
[8]   John McLaurin (1693–1754) – minister, Glasgow/Ramshorn.
[9]   Eph 5:14.

~~One night~~ The first Relief that came to me was one night after I had been thinking on that passage [ ]¹⁰ in Isaiah, 1.19,20. If ye be willing and obedient ye shall eat the good of the Land: but if ye refuse & rebel, ye shall be devoured [539/–] with the Sword, for the mouth of the Lord hath spoken it. While I thought on my many Rebellions against God, & ~~my d was wondring at Gods pa~~ my danger by them, that word Lam. came into my mind with light shining into my heart, It is of the Lords mercies that we are not consum'd; which gave me some ease & comfort at the thought of Gods wonderful patience toward me, that he had not consum'd & cut me off long 'ere now.

About a Week after this, one morning when I was at home reading a Chapter, at the fire side, which happened to be the third Chapter of Jeremiah, when I came to these words, vs 14 Return, O backsliding Children, saith the Lord, for I am married unto you; & I will take you one of a city, & two of a family, & I will bring you to Zion:¹¹ these words came to me with great comfort; & I was persuaded that it was the Lord who was thereby speaking to me: and I now found the great heat that was within me that had been so long like to burn me up, taken away: but yet the great & heavy burden I had long felt upon me, & that was like to crush me, was not yet taken away. But a little after this again I fell into doubts & fears.

About eight days after this, While I sate on a Seat, with my wheel before me, but was unable to work, & felt such a Load on my Spirit, & such a weight on my heart, that I was not able to stir, that word of Ps. 143.7

> Haste Lord to help my Spirit fails,
> Hide not thy face from me¹²

came into my mind, expressing the frame [ ]¹³ of my heart [540/–] at the time, after which that word came into my heart immediatly with great Light, Whatsoever thou shall ask the Father in my name he will give it thee. This came with such Power, as instantly took away that great Load I had so long been groaning & sinking under; & lifted up my hands as high as they could reach; & made me to bless & adore him for his wonderful goodness to my Soul, & fill'd me with great Love to Christ & joy in him. And tho I have often been much troubled with doubts & fears & other Exercises since that time; yet that insupportable Load that had been lying long on my Spirit before this, never return'd again.

As this joy & Love abated, my fears that all I had met with was but a delusion increased: & I was thereupon much vexed and grieved in spirit. But sometime after I had been greatly cast down under such apprehensions, I was awaked out

---

¹⁰ Insertion ['which I read']: McCulloch.
¹¹ Jer 3:14.
¹² Scottish Psalter (metrical).
¹³ Insertion ['and desires']: McCulloch.

of sleep in the midst of the night with these words Is. 53. He was wounded for our transgressions & bruised for our iniquities, and the chastisement of our peace was upon him, & by his stripes we are healed:[14] These words came with great power & comfort to my Soul, being made to believe that God did not impute sin to me, but that he had laid the punishment due to them all on Christ: and I found my heart melted under a sense of the Love of God & Christ in this matter; and was made to look to him whom I had pierced, & to mourn for Sin in a more kindly manner than ever ~~before~~ I had done before.

[541/–] I attended at the first Sacrament at Camb. in Summer 1742, & found it to be a sweet time as could be to my Soul. Particularly in hearing a Minr (12)[15] preach the Evening Sermon on Sabbath on that Text, Thy Maker is thy Husband:[16] When he said, You that have been married to Christ before, would now renew your acceptance of him: ~~I found my heart made~~ Are there any of you that are pleased with the Terms of the Contract, & are willing to be married to Christ, come and I'll marry you to him just now; I thought, Willing! Who would not be willing: And I found my heart drawn out to an acceptance of him on his own terms, & to an ardent Love to him. And next day if I could have met with that Minr would have told him that he had married my Soul to Christ. And this frame continued for some time.

But after a while, doubts again arising, I was much cast down. And I thereupon earnestly wish'd That the Lord might give me to know in whom I had believ'd: And One morning about that time, I was awaked out of sleep with that word, as if one had spoken it to me, Look the 37th Psalm & 7th verse: I did so & found these words

> Rest on the Lord & patiently
> Wait for him do not fret
> For him that prospering in his way
> Success in Sin doth get.[17]

Which in reading ~~them~~ came with great power, composd my mind, & gave me much comfort.

[542/–] But after this, falling again under doubts & fears, that Word came into my mind, and by the power that came along with it, settled my troubled heart, Fear not, for I am with thee, I am thy God, I will help thee yea I will strengthen thee, yea I will uphold thee with the right hand of my righteousness.

I inclin'd much to be at the 2d Sacrament at Camb. in Aug. 1742: but when I had but little prospect of being allowed to go there, and was much perplexed

---

14   Isa 53:5.
15   George Whitefield (1714–70) – evangelist.
16   Isa 54: 5.
17   Ps 37:7, Scottish Psalter (metrical).

that it should be so; that word came into my mind & much composd me, whatsoever might fall out

> My Soul wait thou with patience
> Upon thy God alone
> On him dependeth all my hope
> And Expectation.[18]

I got [ ][19] liberty to go there on Saturday; but coming on Sabbath; I heard the Action Sermon with much of a desirable frame: and was very desirous to get access to the Table, but could not for want of a Token: and about the Close, When a Minr (26) ask'd Are there no more Lovers of Christ here to come forward to his Table? I found my heart greatly affected with that Word & would have given never so much to have had ~~have~~ access [ ][20] but could not see any from whom I could ~~receive~~ be provided with a Token: and one beside me seing my uneasiness, bade me sit down & settle my self; God would accept of the Will for the Deed.

[543/–] At Kilsyth 2d Sacrament in Octr 1742, just as I came there, which was not till Saturdays Evening, that Psalm was a singing in the Kirk, Ps. 90.

> O let thy Work and Power appear
> Thy Servants face before
> And shew unto their Children dear,
> Thy Glory evermore[21]

in Singing of which I was filled with great joy in the hope & belief that it would be so at that Occasion. And when the Minr (26) who preachd that Evening, urg'd the Hearers much to a present Acceptance of Christ, ~~telling th~~ & not to delay doing so 'till they would go home, telling them, That now, even then, was the accepted time, I was made very earnest and willing to do so. The Comunion Sabbath ensuing was a delightful time to me. And when I attended that night in the Manse, there, and heard a Minr (20)[22] in his Exhortations, telling some persons there under Concern, That when God was pleasd to send in a Word with the Power of his Spirit into their hearts, & to comfort them, they should not doubt & disbelieve & put it away from them; for that was to believe the Devil rather than God. I was hereby much comforted & encouraged to give due regard to what the Lord might be pleased to make known of his will in that manner.

[18] Ps 62:5, Scottish Psalter (metrical).
[19] Insertion ['not']: McCulloch.
[20] Insertion ['to come to it']: McCulloch.
[21] Ps 90:16, Scottish Psalter (metrical).
[22] James Robe (1688–1753) – minister, Kilsyth.

[544/–] On Munday morning, that word came into my heart, Herein is love not that we loved God but that he loved us. I had been much filled with the Love of God on the day before: & at this word, I was made to rejoice at the thought that it was not I that had loved God, but he that loved me & had given me to love him.

Some time after this I fell under great distress of Soul at the thoughts of my former great Sinfulness, squandring away my precious time, and that I had been so long led captive by the Devil, & my lusts & walked according to the course of this world: but that word, While we were yet Sinners, in due time Christ died for the ungodly, came into my heart with such power, as much calmed & comforted me; for as he died for Sinners in the due & appointed time so I & not sooner; so I thought if the [ ]²³ & appointed time for bringing me home to himself had come sooner, he would have done it.

One time last Winter I fell under great Concern about the people in the Parish where I live, seing many of them so unconcern'd; & that word coming into my mind increas'd my Concern for them, The great day of his wrath cometh and who shall be able to stand: which I understood as referring to the day of judgment, & that none would then be able to Stand that got not on Christs imputed righteousness. While I continued to plead for them with God, that word came into my mind, It is not meet [545/–] to take the Childrens bread & cast it to dogs;²⁴ but I was helped to plead, True Lord, yet the dogs eat of the crumbs that fall from the Childrens Table: and that Word came for Answer, If they will come to me, I will write my Laws in their heart minds²⁵ & put my fear in their heart.²⁶ I insisted no further but only that the Lord might enable them to come to him.

One time I was under fears of falling away when that word Ps. 22

> And I was cast upon thy care
> Even from the Womb will now²⁷
> And O send thy light forth & thy Truth
> Let them be guides to me.²⁸

made me [ ]²⁹ hope that God would mercifully do so. guide by his Light & truth in his holy way.

A Paper in print, that came from Edinburgh, proposing that Societies for Prayer should keep that 18ᵗʰ of Febry 1743 as a Thanksgiving-day, for the Revival of Religion in the West of Scotland the year before: and many

---

²³ Insertion ['set']: McCulloch.
²⁴ Mt 15:26, Mk 7:27.
²⁵ Heb 8:10.
²⁶ Jer 32:40.
²⁷ Ps 22:10, Scottish Psalter (metrical).
²⁸ Ps 43:3, Scottish Psalter (metrical).
²⁹ Insertion ['pray and']: McCulloch.

in these Societies in the Place where I liv'd, saying, They might keep it that knew any thing of that Work, but for their own part, they did not know but it might be all Delusion. This vex'd me much when I heard of it: but that word coming into my mind

> Still trust in God for him to praise
> Good Cause I yet shall have:
> For of my Countenance he's the health
> My God that doth me save.[30]

This banishd my anxiety, & made me to trust & hope in God, and to wait for his Salvation.

[546/–] With difficulty I got attending at the Sacrament Occasion at Glasgow in April 1743: On Saturday morning, that word came to me Ho every one that will, let him come & take of the Water of life freely.[31] The work there was very delightful to me: and on Munday morning, that word was sent into my heart, As ye have received Christ Jesus the Lord so walk in him, which made me very concern'd to walk humbly.

At Camb. Sacrament in May 1743, hearing a Sermon [ ][32] (74.)[33] on that text, Blessed are they that know the joyful sound.[34] — I found almost every Word of it brought home to my heart, & was greatly comforted. And on Munday morning that word was impressed on my heart, Whom he loveth he loveth to the End, which came with great delight & love to God, & I was persuaded of Gods love to my Soul, & made to wonder at the riches of his free love to such a vile worthless Sinner, & at the thoughts of his loving me to the end.

At Blantyre Sacrament in Summer 1743 in hearing a Sermon (26) on Munday on that Text, To whom God would make known what is the riches of the Glory of this mystery,[35] which is Christ in you the hope of glory: the Lord made it the sweetest Sermon to me that ever I heard, while I was made to see Satisfying Evidences of Christs being in me the hope of Glory. [547/–] I also heard another Sermon that day by a Minr ( ) on that Text, Be ye followers of God as dear Children,[36] with much of the like frame.

To conclude. Tho the World cannot observe any great alteration in my behaviour from what it usd to be formerly, because I was all along kept from any thing outwardly offensive to men: yet I find a very great Change in my self, even as great a difference as between Light and darkness: formerly my mind usd always to be running out after this and the other thing in the World:

---

30 Ps 43:5, Scottish Psalter (metrical).
31 Rev 22:17.
32 Insertion ['on Sabbath']: McCulloch.
33 Robert Donald – elder, Old Monkland.
34 Ps 89: 15.
35 Col 1:27.
36 Eph 5:1.

now I care no more for it, than if I had nothing ado with it: and tho I likd to hear the Gospel before, yet it never made any impression on me, but went in at the one ear & out at the other: now I hear it with great delight & often feel it powerfully applyd to my heart; & I now for ordinary am taken up even when about my Worldly business in meditating upon passages of the Word I have been reading or hearing. Formerly I had no Love to Christ, tho I foolishly imagin'd I had, now I find my heart often warm'd with his Love, tho' yet it is my grief I have not much more love to him; & long to be freed from sin whereby I am daylie offending him, & to love and enjoy him perfectly and for ever in Heaven: To him be all Glory & praise now & ever. Amen.

[548/– blank]

[549/–] c.e. A young woman of 25 years[1]

When I was in my childhood, & till I was about 12 years of age, I usd to pray by my self, only on the Sabbath, after that I began to pray once a day some times. At 17 or 18 I had a desire to come to the Lord's Table, and while a Minister ( ) preachd on Is. 55.1. Ho every one that thirsteth, come to the waters &c: I found these words & what was said on them make some impression on me; but delayd going at that time to that Ordinance. Next year when the Sacrament was to be dispensd in the place I had a greater desire than before to go there: but there was a person I had some ill-will at in my heart, & I did not know if in that case I should go or not. However I went, but repented as I was going, fearing I would partake unworthily: yet I went forward [ ].[2] Next morning I was awaked with these words in my mouth How durst thou go to my Holy table? I then resolvd I would never go there again, and [550/–] that I would never be present where it was administered, lest I should be engag'd by any thing I might then hear to come to it. That next year, I went about duties in a cold rife manner. Next year after that, I broke my resolution & came to the Lord's Table, & thought I met with something of the Lords presence & some melting of heart. I went on in the performance of duites at least as to the outward part, ~~One night~~ I could not find any thing of the life and power of Religion on my heart, but was kept from gross out-breakings. One night being in great deadness & darkness at prayer, these words came into my mind, I will lead the blind by a way they know not, I will make darkness light & crooked things straight before them these things will I do & not forsake them,[3] which easd me a little of the confusion that was on my mind. But all this while I think I never got my heart truly humbled for sin: worldly crosses were more affecting to me than sin. One day full of discontent, that word was cast into my mind, It is better for me to die than to live; but it got no [551/–] place in my heart; but was put away by another word coming in The Lord knows how to deliver these his own that are tempted. And all this while I was never truly thankful for any mercy.

About the beginning of March 1742, I went to Cambuslang, and heard Sermon there [ ][4] frequently, and after that, and thought I felt more than

---

1   Margaret Brownlie – the shorthand text in McCulloch's 'Index of persons' names who gave the foregoing accounts to Mr. McC' states: daughter of James Brownlie, smith in Hamilton. Taught to read the Bible when young, got Catechism to heart, retained it.
2   Insertion ['And that word that was then brought to mind Did not our heart burn within us while he talked to us, was I thought accompanyd with some motions of love to God.']: McCulloch.
3   Isa 42:16.
4   Insertion ['for the first time and']: McCulloch.

ordinary measures of the power of God coming along with what was said. One Sabbath in that Spring, hearing a Minister (26)[5] preach on that text Joh. 3 ult—He that believeth not on the Son shall not see life but the wrath of God abideth on him.[6] I fell under a sense of the wrath of God in some measure: but neither cryd nor fainted nor trembled then or at any other time. Afterward hearing that Minister (26) on that text, Thou hast a name to live & art dead; I felt what was said, make some impression on me, & was made to fear I was one of these that had a name to live & was dead;[7] tho I could not change my self with seeking after a name to live. That Evening hearing a Preacher, give out these words in Ps. 149 to be sung by the people,

> [552/−] Let Israel in his maker joy
> Unto him praises sing
> Let all that Zions children are
> Be joyful in their king.[8]

At hearing of which read, I got more tenderness & more love & comfort than I usd to have: but it did not last.

Hearing a Minister discourse at Camb. without a Text, he said, Methinks I hear some of you complain of a hard heart, & longing to have it softned: and ye propose to get it done this way and that way; but it is nothing to thee what way deliverance comes, but to want on the Lord to bring it about any way he pleases; adding, Wait I say, upon the Lord. These words came home to me, as if they had been directed to me in particular, and I was then made to wait on God to send me deliverance in what manner he pleasd.

At the first Sacrament at Camb. in 1742, I was full of doubts as to my Interest in Christ, & so did not come forward to that Ordinance at that time; on Sabbath morning that word came into my mind, Why dost thou doubt, which composd me a little. A Minister (12)[9] seing some confusion in the passes, in time of serving [553/−] Tables, said, If ye will not enter into the kingdom of heaven your selves, why would ye hinder others, your brethren & sisters that are entring in: at hearing of which I would gladly have come to the Table, but could not for want of a Token. In hearing the Evening sermon (12) that day, on that text, Thy maker is thy husband,[10] my doubts were removed, and I found much love comfort and composure in my heart: but still I found my heart hard as rock.

---

5   William McCulloch (1691–1771) – minister, Cambuslang.
6   Jn 3:36.
7   Rev 3:1.
8   Ps 149:2, Scottish Psalter (metrical).
9   George Whitefield (1714–70) – evangelist.
10   Isa 54:5.

One night at prayer in Harvest 1742, when I was much afraid that all I had met with, would have vanished & that my heart would turn as bad as ever it was, that word came into my heart with much life & power, My grace is sufficient for thee, my strength is made perfect in thy weakness,[11] which quickened me & warmd my heart with love to Christ.

At the ~~1st~~ 2d Sacrament at Camb. in ~~1742~~ [ ][12] & the ~~first~~ 2d Sacrament that same year, I found my heart warm'd with love to Christ, & some heart melting for sin, tho' not so much as I would have had; and felt it to be sweet time to my Soul.

[554/–] In talking to a Minister (16)[13] and telling him of my hardness of heart & other plagues, as he repeated over some sweet passages of Scripture, exhorting me with the Spouse to go yet a little further, & to say with the Psalmist, O Why art thou cast down O my soul & so disquieted within me &c:[14] I felt what he said attended with such power as took as it were a great load off my Spirit. My doubts as to my Interest in Christ were scattered, & my heart enlarged.

Several promises have at times been brought into my heart with much life & sweetness, & particularly at the 2d Sacrament at Cambuslang in 1743, as Ye have not chosen me but I have chosen you, and ordained you that ye should go forth & bear much fruit & that your fruit should remain.[15] O my Soul thou hast said unto the Lord, thou art my portion,[16] Thou hast got a sight of the promised land but it is yet afar off &c: [ ][17]

The chief thing I for ordinary most breathe after is Sanctification & holiness: the chief grievance I have, is that I have so little love to God, & that my heart is so hard, that I can mourn so little for dishonouring him, & that I should be so careless & secure. My chief delight is in Communion with God, and when he is pleased to give me something of it, I then long for death & heaven. To his name be praises.

[555/– and 556/– blank]

---

[11]   2 Co 12:9.
[12]   '1743' superimposed over '1742'.
[13]   Alexander Webster (1707–84) – minister, Tolbooth/Edinburgh.
[14]   Ps 42:5, Ps 42:11, Ps 43:5.
[15]   Jn 15:16.
[16]   Ps 119:57.
[17]   Insertion ['and at sometimes, I have been made to ~~close~~ give up my self to Christ to be saved by him in his own way.']: McCulloch.

[557/1] A. C. A Married Woman, aged 32 years.[1]

I was only taught to read the Catechism[2] when I was a Child: and I was careless about [ ][3] till last year (1742) when it pleased the Lord to take some dealing with my heart: And then I was much grieved that I had so long neglected to learn to read, & would have given never so much that I had learned to read the Bible: And by applying carefully to learn ~~to read~~, I bless the Lord, tho I cannot pretend to read it perfectly, yet I can read much of it: when I take it up in my hand to read, I know not how to part with it or lay it aside again. And by reading much & oft in it, when I hear passages of it cited, as I am hearing Sermons, I can now turn to them in my Bible, & find many of them there, tho' the particular Book Chapter and verse be not mentioned by the Minr. And O how wonderful is the change now with me from what was the Case before, in this & almost every other respect! For tho' I was never given to things outwardly gross before the World; yet I liv'd all along till last year without the fear of God in my heart. Formerly I did not use to pray, but sometimes when I was dragged to it by natural Conscience & fears of Hell: and tho' I usd to go to the Kirk on Sabbath days for ordinary, [558/2] because others went & it was the Custom of the Place where I livd, yet when I came there, tho I took heed to what was said, yet the Word just died away as I was hearing ~~of~~ it: And when the Minr would have been speaking of particular Cases, I would have said in my heart, Let them take that to them to whom it belongs: I have nothing to do with it; and it would have been just my case for all that: but I had no delight to pray or hear the word preached, or in any thing that was like good: only because I could not read my self, I would sometimes have drawn near when I heard a person read the Bible, or a Preaching—Book, & listened with some kind of pleasure.

    About 9 years ago, a Minr (26)[4] coming thro the Parish visiting, took me aside by my self, & among other things told me Except you be born again, you can never see the kingdom of heaven: that word for a long time after haunted me often, & came frequently into my mind, but I knew not what to make of it. On the last Sabbath of Decr. 1741, hearing a Minr (26) preach, I felt ~~a great sweetness~~ [ ][5] in that Sermon than ever I had found in any Sermon

---

[1] Janat Struthers – the shorthand text in McCulloch's 'Index of persons' names who gave the foregoing accounts to Mr. McC' states: possibly from Shawfield, lived with spouse George Darling in Cambuslang.

[2] *Shorter Catechism of the Westminster Assembly* (1647).

[3] Insertion ['learning to read more']: McCulloch.

[4] William McCulloch (1691–1771) – minister, Cambuslang.

[5] Initial insertion: [~~'more desireableness'~~]; subsequently replaced with: ['more sweetness and delight'].

before and resolv'd I would never stay away from the Kirk again when I could get to it. And all that Winter over after that, I was often under fears about my Souls Salvation, & had more than Ordinary Concern upon my Spirit about things of that kind. After the awakening brake out in Febry 1742, my concern still increased from time to time but [559/3] I endeavoured to keep all the concern I was under as close as I could, that no body might know of it: for I heard many were calling the Work all a delusion; & tho' I did not think it was so; yet I thought they would be the more ready to call it so, if such a poor worthless ignorant Creature as I had any Concern in it. But the Effectual Awakening did not come till about five weeks after that Work broke out publickly in Camb: when I was hearing a Minr (26) preach [ ]⁶ on that Text, I know you that ye have not the love of God in you:⁷ What was then said, came with such power, That I saw I had nothing of the Love of God at all in me then & never had it before: & that all the Curses pronounced in the Word against these that have nothing of the Love of God or Christ in them belong'd to me, and I thought I saw (not with the eyes of my body but of my mind) my sins as a Cloud separating between God & me; & the black Cloud of God's wrath ready to break upon me: and when he said, I have [ ]⁸ that you that have nothing of the Love of God in you should be afraid that the very Stones of the fields or streets should fly in your face: I found this was indeed my Case at the time: But tho' my distress was great yet I did not cry out among the people nor till I got home to a place by my self, & went to Secret Prayer, & then when I thought none but God saw & heard me, I gave vent to the Sorrows & anguish of my heart in earnest cries to God for mercy.

[560/4] For five weeks before this, I had slept and ate & wrought but little, & sometimes awaked out of my sleep crying & weeping, some days I ate none & wrought as little, because I could not: But now my distress came to a greater height than ever: and could now do scarce any thing but bemoan my own condition, & run to my knees every now & then, & hear Sermon when the time of hearing came about [ ].⁹ Sometimes when I essay'd to pray, I could do nothing almost but sigh & groan before the Lord. I did not want to be free of the distress I was under, but thought it was not so great as I would have had it, and as I saw some other under, & begg'd of the Lord that he might send me more powerful awakenings & a deeper Sense of Sin, & was willing to bear whatever he might be pleased to send, that was needful to humble me & bring me to Christ: & was afraid of nothing more than that my Convictions should wear off before a gracious change was wrought. But amidst all my distress the Lord still kept me from sinking in despair, & gave me to hope, That he would

---

⁶   Insertion ['on a Thursday']: McCulloch.
⁷   Jn 5:42.
⁸   Insertion ['Methinks']: McCulloch.
⁹   Insertion ['which had also been much my way before this for some weeks']: McCulloch.

some time or other show me mercy. Before this Thursday, I had been much under fears of hell, and any sorrow I had for sin as dishonouring to God, was never so kindly till I heard this Sermon, and then the chief ground of my fears & griefs & of all my distress, was That I thought I had not the Love of God in me: And this sort of distress continued with me from this Thursday to Saturday night thereafter, when I was at Secret Prayer, in the Twinkling of an Eye, when I was not [561/5] expecting any such thing, that word came into my heart with great Power, darted as it were into my Soul, so as I felt it in the most sensible & surprizing manner, I will blot out thy sins out of the Book of my Remembrance: immediately after that, as in a moment, came that other word in the same manner, He will not chide continually, nor keep his anger still; with us he dealt not as we sinn'd, nor did requite our ill: after this I said [ ][10] Lord may I believe, & it was instantly added, I will sprinkle clean water upon you ~~and ye shall be clean~~ I will take away the stony heart, & give you a heart of flesh. I then got a view [ ][11] of the Golden Sceptre of free grace stretched out toward me, & was made Spiritually to behold the clear Streams of the Water of life before me: & had the most earnest & panting thirst after them. I had also some measure of love to Christ & joy in him, tho but little compar'd with what I have had since. And at that moment, I had a longing desire put into my heart after Communion with Christ at his Holy Table, & feeding by faith on his broken body & shed blood in the Sacrament of the Supper. Immediatly after these words had been sent into my heart, I got the most affecting & humbling sight of my own loathsomeness by sin, as a rotten putrified dead Carcase, by nature & by my actual Sin: which made me to loath & abhor my self in the sight of a Holy God: but this sight continued but a very little, as for a minute or two or so. And after this, I immediatly fell into doubts & fears again: especially when [562/6] I could not for some time find out the Psalm where the second word was: as for the other two I knew certainly they were Bible-words: but for that other word, I thought it was some where in the Psalms, but when I could not find it there, on that or the next day, I was much troubled thinking that it might perhaps not be from the Lord. At length I was shew'd it by a Woman whom I had desir'd to help me to find it: & rejoiced when I got it. I continued with longing desires after Christ, & in that frame the Psalmist describes Ps. 123. O thou that dwellest in the heavens, I lift mine eyes to thee, Behold as servants eyes do look their masters hand to see, As handmaids eyes her mistress hand &c:[12]

On ~~Friday next~~ Sabbath about the middle of April 1742, I was much refreshed and comforted in singing the first Psalms: & ~~when~~ the first words spoken

---

[10] Insertion ['in my heart']: McCulloch.
[11] Insertion ['by faith']: McCulloch.
[12] Ps 123:1–2, Scottish Psalter (metrical).

by a Minr (13)[13] going to preach, Lord what is man that thou art mindful of him, or the Son of Man that thou shouldst visit him,[14] I found coming with great power & sweetness to my heart. And so also all along the time of his Sermon. In the Evening of that day, coming into the Manse, & speaking with that Minr, I could not forbear crying out in the midst of all the Company then about him, That Christ was king in my heart. On Tuesday next I fell under doubts, and having fallen asleep, I awaked in a great fright, finding nothing like the signs of a Change of heart I usd to have; but a Woman (70)[15] coming & reading a Chapter to me (Is. 54) I got some comfort from hearing it read. I was however displeased with my self, for crying out so publickly in the Manse Sabbath before, That Christ was King in my heart, fearing some present might think I had been saying what was not true. On Friday next hearing a Sermon (26) on that Text, awake thou that sleepest, [563/7] arise from the dead & Christ shall give thee light.[16] I found it made sweet to my Soul: & all the promises in it applied to me as particularly as if there had not been another but my self to hear.

I continued in this sweet frame: and had so much delight in hearing of Sermons from day to day, and was allowed so much sweet Communion with God in them, That I could gladly have said with Joshua, if it had been warrantable, Sun stand thou still:[17] Let me have yet more & more of this time of Communion with God in his Ordinances, & get more & more power over my heart Corruptions.

One week day fearing I would not get access to attend the Sermons, as I greatly desired, because I had some Family affairs to look after, & I knew I must work some, else how would I and mine be provided for? When I was going to the Well with such thoughts, these words, For thou art gracious, O Lord, & ready to forgive, & rich in mercy all that call upon thee to relieve;[18] came to my heart, & banished my fears of being reduc'd to ~~Sermons~~ straits by attending Sermons, and made me cast all my care upon God [][19] & to trust in the riches of his mercy for relieving me in all my wants, & I car'd for no more of the World than what might answer present necessities from day to day. And from that time to this, I have it to remark, That I have been so mercifully provided for, with any that depend upon me, that I have never been in want, or oblig'd to stay away from Gospel Ordinances, thro' worldly Incumbrances.

[13] John Willison (1680–1750) – minister, South Church, Dundee.
[14] Ps 8:4.
[15] According to McCulloch's index, '(70)' is identified as Mr Sinclair. The woman here may be 'Janat White' (originally coded as '(69)', but then replaced with 'George Wishart').
[16] Eph 5:14.
[17] Jos 10:12.
[18] Ps 86:5, Scottish Psalter (metrical).
[19] Insertion ['and go to Sermon']: McCulloch.

One day hearing a Minr (12) on these words, Mark 16. And he said unto them, Be not affrighted, Ye seek Jesus of [564/8] of Nazareth which was crucified:[20] I found so great satisfaction & so great joy & peace in believing, that I could not forbear saying to some that sate beside me, Saw ye ever such a Morning as this! But received no Answer.

I long'd much for a Sacrament-Occasion; and attended at the first of that kind that offered, which was at Kilbride. On the Fast-day I had great comfort in hearing the Sermons there, and found all the Promises mentioned to believers, applied to me in particular. I came to a Minr (26) to get a Token in order to communicate, who ~~after~~ bade me look to it, that it was not to to be seen of men & to get a name for Religion or for any other base selfish end: This gave a great knell to my heart, so that I had almost cried out, because this was so far from ~~my heart~~ me that I could appeal to the Lord that knew my heart, that it was not for any such base Ends: I heard the Sermons on Saturday with much pleasure, but was still longing to get to that holy Ordinance, yet afraid of a rash approach, & I turn'd the more afraid, that the people about me seem'd to be so dead: but that word, when the sweat was breaking upon me, my fears were so great, came into my heart, tho not uttered by Minr speaking, But yet with thee forgiveness is that fear'd thou mayest be,[21] which gave me more Encouragement to look forward to that Ordinance. On the Sabbath at the Close of the Action Sermon, that word (tho not mentioned by the Speaker) came into my mind, while I was sweating thro' fear, Daughter be of good cheer thy sins are forgiven thee,[22] which have me much freedom to go forward to the second Table, which, after retiring by my self for prayer, I accordingly did.

[565/9] At the Table, I can say I sate under Christs shadow with great delight & found his fruit sweet to my Taste: & after communicating retir'd by my self for prayer: and had a very desirable time of it afterwards that Evening. On the Munday hearing a Minr (26) on that text, Sing unto the Lord a new song, for his right hand & his holy arm has won him the Victory,[23] I found much sweetness & comfort at the thoughts that the Lord had won himself the Victory in my heart, and I hopd also in the hearts of many others. After that, I found much peace in my heart, and much love to Christ & to all that mentioned the name of Christ in a right way.

In hearing Sermon at Camb. on Sabbath before the first Sacrament there (July 1742) I fell under great fears while a Minr (26) discoursd of Self-Examination from that Text, But let a man examine himself &c:[24] but these fears were scattered by that word, (tho not utter'd by the Speaker)

---

[20]   Mk 16:6.
[21]   Ps 130:4, Scottish Psalter (metrical).
[22]   Mt 9:2.
[23]   Ps 98:1.
[24]   1 Co 11:28.

O Woman great is thy faith, be it unto thee even as thou wilt:[25] After that I heard with much composure, & easiness of mind. And so also in hearing the Sermons on the Fast day, & Saturday. In hearing the Action Sermon on that Text, Yea he is altogether lovely: this is my beloved, and this my friend,[26] I was filled with great joy at the thoughts of Christs love & loveliness, and that I was going to meet with such a Friend at his Table, hoping he would not disappoint me of the [566/10] blessings I needed from him. I had no doubts in time of that Sermon, but after it was done some doubts returnd, but going by my self to prayer, I got some soul refreshing and coming to the Second Table, had great joy in the belief that I was of that number for whom Christ died & suffered; & that, as the Minr (12)[27] then Exhorting, said to believers there, That as sure as I was sitting at his Table below, I should sit down at his Table above. I got also much brokenness of heart for sin both at the Table and after it thro' much of that week. In hearing the Evening Sermon that day (12) on that Text [ ],[28] I was made to rejoice in Christ as my Souls Husband, & to adore the free grace of God that he had enabled me to choose Christ as my Husband, & to close with him in all his offices, especially in his Kingly Office, to conquer my heart, & to subdue my strong Corruptions, that are still so frightful to me to think of. I had also much joy & sweetness of heart in hearing the Mundays Sermons, especially one on that text, (12) On the last day, that great day of the Feast &c:[29]

Hearing a Minr (26) Lecture on Isai.12.ch. Thou hast been angry with me but thou hast comforted me &c:[30] I felt it to be a joyful Lecture to me. Hearing another (44)[31] on Joh.1.12. To as many as received him &c: when he said the Believer had supplies from God that the world knew not of, I found it indeed to be so with me. Hearing another (23)[32] discourse from Isai. 53.10. The pleasure of the Lord shall prosper in his hand, while he said [567/11] The Believers Stock of grace is not in his own hand, but in Christs, I was made to see that my Stock was in sure keeping while it was in his hand, & to rejoice that it was so.

---

[25] Mt 15:28.
[26] SS 5:16.
[27] George Whitefield (1714–70) – evangelist.
[28] Insertion ['Is. 54.5']: McCulloch.
[29] Jn 7:37.
[30] Isa 12:1.
[31] Identified in McCulloch's index as '44 Carlile'. This may be a reference to John Carlyle, former minister at Dalton who demitted his ordination in 1710 and seems to have resided in/around Glasgow (Scott, *Fasti*). It may also be a reference to William Carlyle (1689–1765), minister at Prestonpans (and father of Alexander 'Jupiter' Carlyle); Carlyle was a personal friend of Lord Grange (James Erskine), who was a correspondent of William McCulloch (Macfarlan, *Revivals*, 106) and an 'enthusiast' (Carlyle, *Anecdotes*, 8).
[32] William Gusthart (d. 1764) – minister, Edinburgh/Tolbooth (Collegiate or Second Charge).

Hearing there was to be a 2d Sacrament at Camb. shortly, I rejoiced much at the news of it, the first had been so sweet to me. On the Fast before it, hearing a Sermon on that text, He that hath the Bride is the Bridegroom:[33] I had great joy at the thoughts of Christ ~~being~~ the Bridegroom of Souls being the Bridegroom of my Soul, and this, I think, I was then assur'd of by the testimony of the Holy Spirit bearing witness with mine. I heard the Action Sermon with great delight: and at singing of the first Psalms after it, at these words, And let all those that are thy saints shout loud for joyfulness,[34] I was indeed made to sing aloud for joy, humbly believing I was one of these that were called & allowed to rejoice. When I came to the Lords Table, I had sweet and comfortable Communion with him there. On Munday hearing a Minr (12) preach on that, Compel them to come in:[35] when he desir'd the Prayers of the People of God, to help him to compel sinners to come in, I was aiming to do so, & rejoiced in hopes that some would be brought in to Christ, especially seing such a promising like stir among the Hearers.

In harvest 1742 hearing these lines given out to be sung at the Entry of publick Worship, and in singing of them, My heart burst out into tears, When thou didst say, seek ye my face, then unto thee reply, [568/12], Thus did my heart above all things, thy face Lord seek will I:[36] ~~my~~ I found my heart indeed earnestly seeking Gods face & favour. The Minr (3)[37] lecturd on the Psalm: and that part of it that speaks of Gods putting his peoples tears in his bottle, was made particularly refreshing to my Soul. I had also much Comfort in hearing the Sermon (5)[38] that day. In time of the Lecture that word, My soul shall magnify the Lord[39] (tho not uttered by the Minr) came in to my heart, & made me to adore & praise him for his goodness to me at that Occasion & formerly.

Hearing of the 2d Sacrament at Kilsyth in 1742, I resolved that I would go there relying on Christs' strength & would go on in his name: & hearing a Minr (24)[40] preach on these words, Blessed is he that cometh in the name of the Lord[41] to save us: I was thereby much comforted at the believing views of Christs coming to save me. On Sabbath morning intreating Christs presense to be with me at his Table, that word came into my heart with

---

[33]   Jn 3:29.

[34]   Ps 132:9, Scottish Psalter (metrical).

[35]   Lk 14:23.

[36]   Ps 27:8, Scottish Psalter (metrical).

[37]   Matthew Connell (d. 1743) – minister, E. Kilbride. Father to his ministerial successor David Connell (1706–90), E. Kilbride.

[38]   Identified in McCulloch's index as '5 Baillie'. Possibly James Baillie (c. 1723–78); ordained to Shotts in 1754 (Bell, Ministers of Church of Scotland, 21; Scott, Fasti).

[39]   Lk 1:46.

[40]   John Warden (d.1764) – minister, Campsie; son of John Warden (1671–1751), minister, Gargunnock (Macfarlan, Revivals, 242; Scott, Fasti).

[41]   Ps 118:26, Scottish Psalter (metrical).

great power, Come ye blessed of my Father, inherit the kingdom prepared for you[42]—and gave me great freedom to go forward to his Holy Table. When there I thought Christ was standing with outstretched arms ready to receive me & welcoming me there. I got my heart broken & melted down under a Sense of Sin. Coming from it, I went to a retir'd place by my self & pour'd out my soul before the Lord. Hearing a Sermon (32)[43] on that, I have said, That I will keep thy statutes, O forsake me not utterly,[44] I found my heart inclind & resolvd by grace to keep his Statues, and [569/13] pleading that he might not utterly forsake me. Falling under some damps before I came away, that word cheer'd me up again, Blessd are they that mourn for they shall be comforted.

In Novr 1742 hearing a Minr (26) lecture on Lam. 3. I was much comforted, especially when he came to these words vs. 21, 22 [ ][45] They are new every morning &c:[46] where I was made to wonder at the sparing mercy of God toward me, that when I deservd to have been sent to hell long ere now, he had, in stead of that, been renewing his mercies to me every morning.

At a Weekly Lecture in Camb. in Janry 1743, as I came into the Kirk these words were a giving out to be sung, Give thanks & praise unto the Lord, for bountiful is he, &c:[47] at hearing of which, I was instantly filled with great joy in God, & my heart was made to praise him for his goodness to me. And was again much comforted in hearing a Sermon (26) on that Text, so fitted to what had been my former Case, & what was my present condition, As ye have been partakers of the Suffering, so shall ye be also of the Consolation.[48] I found also a great suitableness in another Weekly Lecture to what had been my Exercise just before & that very time, on that text, (26) We had the sentence of death within our selves that &c:[49] Where I was led from Self-judging, and from condemning my self as worthy of Eternal Death, to trust in God thro' the merits of Jesus Christ.

[570/14] In hearing some Sermons (26) in May & June 1743 at Camb. on Eph. 2.4,5 concerning God's great love & the riches of his mercy, my Soul was filld with wonder at the mercy & love of God in Christ toward his people, & to poor unworthy me in particular.

At the Sacrament-Occasion, in Camb. in May 1743, in hearing the Action Sermon (26) on those words, Who loved me & gave himself for me:[50] I

---

[42] Mt 25:34.
[43] McCulloch's records make identification difficult, but (32) is likely John Mackay – minister, Dunoon.
[44] Ps 119:8.
[45] Insertion ['It is of the Lords mercy &c:']: McCulloch.
[46] La 3:23.
[47] Ps 106:1, Scottish Psalter (metrical).
[48] 2 Co 1:7.
[49] 2 Co 1:9.
[50] Gal 2:20.

found love to Christ in my heart, & was made to wonder at his Love to me, especially when the Minr said, Believers tho ye may be vile & low in your own eyes & despisd in the eyes of others about you, yet Christ loves you for all that [ ].[51] Before the Tables came to be served, I found unbelief prevail much, & was afraid to go to the Table, till that word came into my mind, & set me forward, he that having put his hand to the plow and looketh back is not fit for the kingdom of God. Sitting still however, & delaying till I would get better Opportunity toward the last Tables, at the close of the service of the Second Table, these words were pressd upon my heart with great Power, [ ][52] Behold the Bridegroom cometh Go ye forth to meet him:[53] at which my heart was filld with joy at the thoughts of Christs coming to me as the Bridegroom of my Soul: & immediatly upon that I got to the Table; and when there felt my heart burning with love to Christ, and was helped to apply to his precious blood by faith for cleansing from all my sins: & after coming from the Table got my heart enlargd in secret to bless him for his goodness to my Soul; & in pleading for the like blessings to others.

[571/15] And now after all this Variety of frames at particular Occasions, that I may speak a word of the habitual bent of my heart, & course of my life, since the Lord took a dealing with my Soul of late; I find an earnest longing, for ordinary, in my Soul for the coming of Christ, his coming at death & judgment, when I hope all his Enemies in my Soul shall be destroyed, & I shall be for ever with him and made like him at his appearance. And my great concern is, to get ready for my appearance before him. Tho I be very low in the world; yet I am not much troubled with thoughts about my being reduc'd to poverty or want, because I trust in God & his promises to provide for me: but what gives me most trouble of any thing in the World, is to find so many Evils & plagues in my heart, and fears that my heart be not upright & right enough with God. I have oftimes had Assurance of Salvation by the Spirit of the Lord applying his Word to me: but at the other times doubts & fears much prevail. I have now great delight & pleasure in reading & hearing the word in praying & Spiritual Converse, I bear no grudge or ill will at any in the world. I pray for all, even for Enemies: & earnestly long for the advancement of the kingdom of Christ: to him be glory for ever.

[572/– blank]

---

[51] Insertion ['and could say Christ loved me & gave himself for me']: McCulloch.
[52] Insertion ['at midnight there was a cry']: McCulloch.
[53] Mt 25:6.

[573/−] b.i. A Woman of 44 years.[1]

In the former part of my Life before the last year I had along been kept outwardly blameless before the World: and by my Acquaintance was reckoned a very good naturd sort of Woman. And beside outward Civility, I had all along from my Childhood a form of Religion. I had a way of praying in Secret for ordinary once a day, and that was before I went to bed at night and when I happened to go to bed without minding it, I would have been very uneasy and sometimes in that case I would have risen again out of my bed & gone about it, fearing I might perhaps die before tomorrow, and thinking I was very unfit for it! And sometimes when I fell into straits or troubles I would have prayed after than once a day. I usd also for ordinary to go to the Kirk on Sabbaths; seeking food to my Soul, & sometimes I thought I got something & sometimes nothing. One Sermon particularly I heard ( ) on these words To them that believe Christ is precious,[2] affected me much: & tho I thought all along that I had not an Interest in [574/−] Christ, yet I had a great desire to have an Interest in him, & I thought I would not rest till I got it. When I read or heard the word preachd formerly, & continually all was dark to me, I knew nothing of God or Christ to any purpose, I felt nothing of the life and power of godliness as, blessed be God, I now do. And I really think and feel in daylie Experience now, when I compare my present with my former state, that there is as great a difference betwixt what I am now by grace, & what I was formerly, as betwixt the darkest night & the clearest day.

When the Awakening at Cambuslang in Spring 1742, was much talkd of, and some brought me good accounts of it, and some bad; yet I did not at all believe the unfavourable Accounts, but still thought well of that Work, and what I thought others were getting there, I came and thro' ~~mercy~~ preventing mercy, got the same my Self. On the first Thursday of April I came to that Place, & heard a Minister (26)[3] preach on that Text, I know you that ye have not the Love of God in you,[4] where he gave many Marks and [575/−] Evidences of these that had & had not the Love of God, & found what was said, brought home to my heart, & was made clearly Sensible that I was one of these that did not love God: and particularly when he said, Those that loved God servd him out of free choice & inclination, & would do so tho there were no rewards or punishments hereafter: but they that did not so love God could not serve him;

---

[1]   Marien Calendar – the shorthand text in McCulloch's 'Index of persons' names who gave the foregoing accounts to Mr. McC' states: spouse of [. . .] Ballie. Taught to read the Bible when a child, got the Catechism to heart, and retained it.

[2]   1 Pe 2:7.

[3]   William McCulloch (1691–1771) – minister, Cambuslang.

[4]   Jn 5:42.

or words to that purpose: I then saw that all my pretences to serve God were just nothing, and that I had never serv'd God, or could not serve him, because the love of God was not in me. Upon which I found a thirsting in my Soul after the Love of God, & a restlessness of Spirit to get the Love of God put within me, without which I saw I could never serve him: & how I might be found in Christ having on his righteousness. After I went home this Restlessness of Spirit continued with me, till I came back, which was about a month after, & then I heard a Minister (26) on that Text, He that believeth not on the Son shall not see life, but the wrath of God abideth on him. Joh. 3. last verse[5] & there I was made Sensible of my being an unbeliever, & that the wrath of God was abiding upon me: & thereupon I fell into great distress of Soul, for want of the Love of God and [576/–] that I had never serv'd God out of Love that I had done nothing right but all was wrong, that I did nothing but sinn'd thro my Life, that I wanted an Interest in Christ, that yet I had come so oft to the Lord's Table, and had there communicated unworthily, and ate & drank judgment to my Self. And after I went home, tho' I essayd to work, yet I could eat drink or sleep little or none for several days. About ten days after this I came back to Cambuslang, & while I was at Secret Prayer, after I had gone to bed & could not sleep, & rose again, & was for a good while very dead & lifeless in that duty, at length in the morning, it pleasd the Lord to loose my bands, by pouring out a Spirit of Supplication on me, & enabling me to pour out my heart before him, in another manner than ever I had done before. I cannot now remember one word by another that was then set home on my heart: but my heart was eas'd of all my griefs & sorrows; and fill'd with comfort. That day hearing a Minister ( ) preach, I immediately fell into a Swoon thro' joy & could hear no more of that Sermon. At night when I went to Secret Prayer I found my self much straitned, & nothing of the mornings frame remaind. [577/–] I came in to the Hall of the Manse at first very dead, but was there filled with joy before I went out. ~~I continued~~

For some time after this, I continued restless in my Spirit, suspecting I might be in a delusion, & that matters were not right with me, till one day at Secret Prayer, that word came into my heart I will keep him in perfect peace whose mind is stayed on me:[6] which was so particularly applied to me, as if the Lord had said, I will give thee perfect peace. Formerly, I had many cares how to gain & gather more & more of the things of the world, & these carking cares were a burden to my Spirit; but after this, Glory to God, he easd & freed my heart of all worldly cares, & I car'd not what might befall me in the world, provided I might have the love & favour of God in Christ toward me, & might have grace to love & serve him. And from that time forth my mind was kept stayd on him; & the Concerns of his glory and Interest

[5]   Jn 3:36.
[6]   Isa 26:3.

lay nearer my heart than any Concerns of my own; I became concern'd for the Salvation of others as much as my own, and prayd as heartily for them as for my self, & every thing I see or hear of that dishonours him is grieving & wounding to my Soul.

[578/–] And from that time to this (Novr. 14. 1743) I have been kept trusting in him: tho I sometimes now & then when I fall under clouds & darkness, when I find corruption prevail, so as to be much troubled for sin as dishonouring to God, yet so far as I remember, I have not had any one doubt or fear of my Interest in Christ. And the Lord has in mercy so sanctify'd & sweetned every Lot I fall into, that nothing now falls amiss to me, because it is the holy Will of God & because he has given me himself for my portion. I am now helped to bear with ease & cheerfulness, many tryals that were formerly most afflicting & distressing to me, under which I was often ready to sink. I have now no Cross in the world but a body of sin & death. So gracious has the Lord been to me ever since, that he never one day leaves me comfortless. Christ is now become all in all to me; I know not how to live without him: & the evidences of his love to me, & often feel a most fervent love in my heart to him: I lov'd him for a while, mainly because he has done and suffered so much for me, but now I love him for himself, and because of his own Excellency & loveliness, which he hath discovered to me: & every day I see always new cause to praise him, for new discoveries of his Love [579/–] and loveliness: and the thoughts of Eternity are sweet to me, because then I'll then get time enough to praise him, & be put in a capacity to do it, without any Sinful imperfection. He has often manifested forth his Glory & his love to me in Private duties & Publick Ordinances, particularly at several Sacrament-Occasions at Cambuslng last year & this, & my joys have then & at other times so overflow'd, that my Body has been made to shake & tremble. I am now afraid of nothing but offending & dishonouring him by sin. Death that was a terror to me to think of, is now become a pleasure to me: he has been pleasd (in condescending grace) to make it known to me, that he has taken me (poor deform'd hell-deserving me) for his Spouse, that he hath betrothed me to himself: and I now consider Death as a messenger to come & call me home to my Lord & Husband, to be where he is: and, tho' I do not know how matters may alter with me, yet for the present, & for a long time past, the thoughts of Death are as pleasant & delightful to me; as a message would be to a Loving Wife ~~would be~~ to come away home to her Husband. Until the day break and the shadows fly away: make haste my Beloved & be thou as a roe or a young hart upon the mountains of Bether,[7] Even so come Lord Jesus. Amen

[580/– blank]

---

[7]   SS 2:17.

[581/–] b.r. A Girl of 13 years of age.[1]

In reviewing my life before 1742, I see reason of thankfulness to God for keeping me outwardly civil & moral in my behaviour, before the World; but at the same time I see much reason to be humbled, that all that time I was quite a Stranger to all Serious Religion. I was indeed train'd up to a custom of praying by my Self twice a day, & for a while to the Seceders meetings; but it was only because I saw many others, & especially my friends and neighbours going, & to comply with my Parents desire: for my heart did not ly to these things, I could make no distinction between one Preaching & another, but only as they were long or short: to me a Short Preaching was a good Preaching, because I got soon away; but a long one was always a bad one; I could not away with it, & I was ~~extremely~~ exceeding weary till it was over.

When the Awakening brake out at Camb. In Febry. 1742, I heard a Woman tell a friend of it, & call it Delusion: to which my [582/–] friend answered, That if it was Delusion, she was sorry that it had fallen out where such a one who was Minister there, was concern'd. I heard these Persons & others at home also talk much about that time of Conversion, and these they call'd Converts at Cambuslang. I went to that Place soon after that & heard Sermon there about the latter end of Febry 1742, but was not at all affected with what I heard [ ][2] as I look'd about me, I saw a Woman weeping much, & said, pointing at her, to a Friend that was by me, It may be that Woman is one of them they call Converts. I went home that night little or nothing at all touch'd with what I saw or heard. I came back next Tuesday, & heard Sermon, & saw several weeping for their Sin. Next time I came there shortly after this, I heard a Minister (26)[3] preach on that Text, He that believeth not is condemn'd already:[4] As these words were repeated in the Sermon, I found them come close home with power to my heart, & made to awaken my Conscience, and to bring me to a Sight & Sense of my Sins: and the first Sin of all I was convincd of was my Unbelief, and [583/–] I saw ~~when~~ I was condemn'd already & lost for ever without Christ. Convictions of this & many other Sins after this, were set so close home upon me by my Conscience, as clearly and distinctly, as if they had been all set down printed on a Paper before my eyes, & as if there had there had been never so many witnesses, telling me of them, & so

---

1   Catherine Anderson – the shorthand text in McCulloch's 'Index of persons' names who gave the foregoing accounts to Mr. McC' states: daughter of William Anderson, portioner in Little Givan. Taught to read the Bible, got the Catechism to heart, and retained it.

2   Insertion ['I wondred much what sort of Creatures these were they called Converts &']: McCulloch.

3   William McCulloch (1691–1771) – minister, Cambuslang.

4   Jn 3:18.

many persons, all confirming the truth of what I was chargd with, one after another. Upon this I fell into great distress of Spirit, partly at the thoughts of my being a poor condemn'd Sinner, & I was verily persuaded that if I had died then or before I got out of that State I was then in, that I would gave gone to hell, & that it would have been perfectly just with God to have sent me there for ever: but my Grief & Soul-distress was chiefly & above all things because I had so dishonoured God by all my Sins, & especially that I had so dishonoured Christ by my Unbelief, and this was a thought I could now bear up under, because I knew & was now persuaded, that as he was the [584/–] worst & most dreadful of all Enemies that ever I could meet with; so he was the best of all Friends; and the Lord gave me at that time a heart to melt into Sorrow on this account; to look to him whom I had pierced by my Sins & to mourn as one mourns for the loss of the dearest friend, for the death of an only Son or a first-born. I did not however cry out, either at this time or any other, nor did I ever Swarf nor had I any visions. I was made however at this time & afterward sometimes to weep abundantly. And sometimes after this, when I have been hearing Sermon on Cambuslang Brae, & siting ~~hearing Sermon~~ before the warm Summer-Sun I have been ~~like to~~ made to tremble with grief for Sin, as if I would have been all shaken to pieces.

From this time I continued till August next in darkness & distress of Spirit, before I got any Relief or Outgate, and got nothing [ ]⁵ all that time Sensibly applied to me, and could my Self apply nothing that I read or heard for my comfort. [585/–] Yet the Lord was pleased in mercy to keep me all that time diligent in the use of the means of grace: I came for a long time almost every day to Camb. & heard Sermon there: I often read my Bible by my Self; and was much taken up in Secret Prayer & mourning for Sin: & tho I was often at the point of despair, sometimes for a little while, seem'd to sink in despair, yet the Lord kept me from sinking quite in that horrible pit of despair & gave me some little glimmering of hope again, so much at least as to keep me close to the use of the means of Salvation.

At length, while I was sitting on the Brae at Camb. On a Thursday about the beginning of August 1742, before Sermon began, that word came into my heart with power, Who is there among you that fears the Lord that obeys the voice of his Servant, that walks in darkness & hath no light, let him trust in the name of the Lord and stay himself on his God. These [586/–] words were apply'd to me with that Light and Power that made see that the Lord had wrought in me these Qualifications there mentioned, & was made to trust & stay my Self on God in Christ, with some hope of his being my God: and in being helped to do so, much of the Burden that was upon my Spirit was taken off, & I was much eased and comforted. Next Lords day, which was the Preparation Sabbath before the 2ⁿᵈ Sacrament there in 1742, I was under

⁵   Insertion ['comfortable']: McCulloch.

some damps at the thought that I had been taking that Comfort that did not belong to me; but was again encouraged to hope that that gracious promise, I had met with a few days before, was from the Lord, & that he had allowed & enabled me to trust & stay my self on him, & was enabled again to do so. Fast day & [ ][6] all that week, I found a sinking on my Spirits, & was in great difficulties whether I should seek to be admitted to the Lords Table or not: but tho I saw great danger in a rash unprepared approach, I durst not however venture to stay away. A Sermon I heard preach'd by a Minister (20)[7] on the Text, He hath put him to grief,[8] was made very useful to me for this purpose, and I was somewhat comforted by it. On Sabbath, when I came to the Lords Table, he was pleased to give me much of his gracious presence; & I may say, He took me into his banqueting-house, and his banner over me was love.

[587/–] At Cathcart Sacrament in May 1743 when I was at the Lords Table, and was coming away, that word came to my mind with much power, I am he that blots out thy transgressions as a Cloud, and as a thick cloud thy Sins.[9] I was made to believe that the Lord had ~~done~~ accordingly pardoned all my Sins for Christs Sake, & this was matter of great comfort to my Soul.

At the Second Sacrament at Cambuslang in 1743, when I was at the Lords Table, I could say with the Spouse that I was sick of Love to Christ: and I was made greatly to rejoice that he had taken the Throne of my heart, & shed abroad his Love there; & I was so filled with joy on this account, that it was with great difficulty that I could refrain from crying out for joy among the people.

But that I may not be tedious, I shall only further notice some few things in general. It is now (March 8, 1744) about two years since I was awakned from my Sleep in Sin, & I would also hope raised from a Death in Sin: For when I look back upon these two last years, & my temper of Spirit & way of life in them, I cannot but notice a very great difference and opposition. Formerly, I was indifferent whether I went to Publick Ordinances or no, & whether I heard or no: now, I could [588/–] not think of staying away, except necessity oblig'd me: & when I come, I take great delight in hearing the Gospel preach'd, & in joining in the other parts of publick worship. I come to hear the word, believing that Christ is to speak in a preached Gospel to his people, & hoping that he will speak something home to me in particular, for seasonable instruction in duty, conviction of Sin, or comfort & establishment in his way, as I may stand in need: and I find ~~it to be so~~ him graciously doing so accordingly from time to time. Formerly my heart did not ly to Secret Prayer at all; now I find the quite contrary with me: I know not how I could

6   Insertion ['almost']: McCulloch.
7   James Robe (1688–1753) – minister, Kilsyth.
8   Isa 53:10.
9   Isa 44:22.

live without it one day: I take great delight in it as a Service to God in Christ; and because I find much benefit to my Soul by it; and the Lord has been pleased for Jesus Christs sake to give me many answers of Prayer, to bestow upon me many Spiritual blessings I have been asking of him. Formerly I did not know what heart-Corruptions were, or what it was to be troubled for them or even to notice them: now I feel them very Sensibly, & bewail them in Secret before God & have many Errands to Christ that he may conquer them all and take my heart wholly to himself. Formerly I knew not what it was to have recourse to Christ at all: of late, I think I have often closd with him in all his offices with all my heart & Soul. I pretend not to be assured of Heaven, but I desire humbly to wait & hope for the mercy of the Lord Jesus Christ unto Eternal Life. To him be all Glory and honour now & forever. Amen.

[589/–] c.d. A Young Woman of 20 Years[1]

In my younger years, I was traind up to pray in Secret: when I came to years I sometimes minded it, & sometimes laid it aside: I usd all along to go to Church on Lords days for ordinary, reckoning it my duty to attend Publick worship: and likd to sit and hear, tho it was but to little good purpose. [ ][2] I did not think I was in a right state, but little minded what would become of me after death, except that at some times, I would have been more serious & thoughtful.

About a year 1741, I fell under Reproach, which, knowing I had given no ground for, was very affecting to me, & like to break my heart. I was then led to be much more serious & concern'd about my Soul than formerly & made to bless the Lord for ordinary [590/–] that Tryal for me. I went oft to Cambuslang in the year 1742, and tho' I was never under any great terror or sudden awakenings, I came gradually to feel more & more of concern about Salvation upon my Spirit, & found my heart turn more & more tender, and was made to see more & more of my own sinfulness & unworthiness and was sometimes made to loathe my self on the account of my vileness by sin. Sometimes that Summer, particularly, one Sabbath day I went to hear Sermon at Dalyell; and for a day or two before & after that, I felt my heart within me, as it had been all in a flame burning in love to Christ: and was much delighted in hearing Sermon ( ) there.

One night I fell under a strong apprehension that I was going to die: & the Lord was [591/–] pleased to give me such a sense & persuasion of my Interest in Christ, that I could not doubt of it: I was not then at all afraid to die, but was even longing for death that I might be freed from Sin & might be with Christ in heaven. And that word was then cast into my mind, This day thou shalt be with me in paradise,[3] which made strongly to apprehend that I was to die that very night, & to go to heaven. But not finding things fall out as I expected, I fell under a very damp next day, apprehending that all I had met with was but delusion. But I have since been made to conclude, that that last mentiond text of Scripture, had been thrown into my mind by Satan that subtile adversary, when he saw the frame I was in, thinking I was ~~shortl~~ to die 'ere long, & longing for it, with a design, to drive me to despair,

---

[1]   Agnes Hamilton – the shorthand text in McCulloch's 'Index of persons' names who gave the foregoing accounts to Mr. McC' states: daughter of 'widow Hamilton' of Evamiln in the parish of Hamilton. Taught to read the Bible and write, got the Catechism by heart, and retained it.

[2]   Insertion ['I cannot charge my self with any things outwardly vicious before the World']: McCulloch.

[3]   Lk 23:43.

or [592/–] to make me look upon all I had met with, as delusions, when the Event did not fall out as I expected in this Instance. But after some days, I gradually recovered my former composure of mind.

Several Promises of Scripture have at times been brought into my heart with great sweetness; on a Fast day before the Sacrament, as I was going to the Church in Summer 1743, that word came into my heart, I am come into my garden, my Sister, my Spouse,[4] at which I felt my heart set all as in a flame with love to Christ: and that day hearing a Minister ( ) preach on a Text in the Song of Solomon, I had difficulty in time of that Sermon, to refrain crying out for love & joy. [ ][5]

For ordinary my chief Concern is about Securing an Interest in Christ; The motions of Sin are my grief & burden; & sometimes I could be glad to die to get free of Sin. I find much deadness on my Spirit for some time past; but I am living in hopes that God will yet be pleasd to quicken me. To his name be glory.

---

4   SS 5:1.
5   Insertion ['I think I can say in the sight of the heart searcher, that my heart has some times been drawn out to a closure with Christ in all his offices.']: McCulloch.

[593/–] A Married woman of 36 years.[1]

In my Childhood I some-minded Prayer in Secret & sometimes neglected it. When I came to Womans years, I durst not ~~altogether~~ neglect Secret Prayer, ~~but~~ reading & hearing of the Word at stated times, and sometimes I felt some desires after Christ, ~~at~~ but I think I have reason to conclude that all that time I was a Stranger to Communion with God. I had also at certain times, a great Fear & Concern upon my Spirit, apprehending that I would die soon; ~~but~~ and under ~~these~~ fears of perishing for ever, if I dy'd in the Condition I was in, I would have sometimes have been made to cry out in the night time on my bed: but when these apprehensions of approaching Death wore off, these fears wore off also & I ~~was~~ returned to what I was before. And very often ommitted Secret Prayer.

When the Awakening brake out at Cambuslang, I came there, & was mighty desirous to hear & see these that were under great concern, & to hear & know what they said as to their Convictions of Sin & workings of Grace, & earnestly desir'd that I might be the next, that might fall under Awakenings. I then found my heart [594/–] drawn out to a choice of the ways of God. At Blantyre Sacrament in 1743, hearing a Minister on that Text on the Saturday, The Lord is my portion saith my soul therefore will I hope in him,[2] I was much concernd to be able to saith so. On Munday hearing a Sermon in these words, Christ in you the hope of glory[3] I found what was said brought home with much delight to my soul. On the Munday Morning immediately after the Sacrament at Cambuslang that year, I was awak'd with many Convictions & Challenges for Sin, & made to see that all I had ever done ~~had~~ was sin. While in this case One in the form of a beautiful Man appeared to me ~~for~~ as in a Vision, and then vanishd away as it had been out of sight.

---

[1]   Partial account with no record of respondent's name.
[2]   Lk 3:24.
[3]   Col 1:27.

[595/–] b.u. A woman about 26 years.[1]

Before I was awakned in the year 1742, tho' I was kept outwardly moral & civil in a good measure, & free of the more gross sort of Outbreakings, & had some kind of form of Religion; yet I knew no more of the power of godliness, than things that have no life. I would have sometimes gone about Secret Prayer, tho but very seldom, if it had not been for a week or two before a Sacrament-Occasion or so, & a little after it was over, and then would have in a great measure laid it aside again, or when at any time I would have set about it, I perform'd it but in a very cold rife and careless manner. I usd however to go to Church on Sabbath-days, but I know not for what end, if it was not to see and be seen & to comply with the Custom of the Place. I also sometimes communicated but in a very formal manner.

Hearing of the Awakning at Camb. in February 1742, I came out of curiosity to that Place in March 1742, but nothing touchd me the first Sabbath I came: next Sabbath, while I was hearing a Preacher (35)[2] there, the Lord was pleased to give me a Sight & Sense [596/–] of my Sins, tho, for any thing that ever I could remember, it was not by means of any thing uttered but the Speaker: I then particularly got an affecting sense of my Sin and Unworthy Communicating, neglect & careless performance of the duty of Prayer, slighting Gospel Ordinances, & many heart sins; I saw I had a heart as black as Hell, & was made to cry out that it was so after I was gone home. I was also made to cry out when among the People when first struck with a Sense of Sin, & was then made to tremble to a great degree, so that my flesh seem'd all to be loose, as if it had been all coming off from the Bones. I continued in distress under Convictions for about five weeks after this, before I got any Comfort or relief; only one day when I was at Cambuslang, as I opened my Bible & read that word, The law of the Spirit of life in Christ Jesus hath made me free from the law of sin and death,[3] I felt a Sweet and Secret Power applying these words to me. I was all that time when I was awake, almost constantly Praying in my heart: I essayd also to follow my [597/–] Work on week days, tho' I could do little at it: & long'd much for thro' the day, for night, that I might get my heart pour'd out before God, after the rest were gone to bed, & was often helped to do so.

---

[1] Agnes Young – the shorthand text in McCulloch's 'Index of persons' names who gave the foregoing accounts to Mr. McC' states: daughter of John Young, a smith in Campsy. Taught to read the Bible when a child, got the Catechism to heart, and retained it.

[2] James Young – probationer minister, Gorbals and Falkirk (Robe, *Short Narrative*, 8, 142, 163–8).

[3] Ro 8:2.

About five weeks after my first awakning, after I had been at Cambuslang & was very dead & stupid while there, & was coming home, without any Company, after I had been praying in my heart, that I might not be left alone, but that the Spirit of the Lord might be with me, as I walk'd on my way, that word came into my heart, Fear not for I have redeem'd thee:[4] & such a power came along with it as filled me with the love of Christ, & with such a joy that I did not know whether I was on the Earth or not; & I was then so assur'd of the love of God to me & my Interest in Christ as my Redeemer, that I thought I would never doubt of it again. And this frame of love and joy & assurance lasted with me in a good measure for about half a year after this; during which time I was much in the joyful praises of God, and would have often sought & wishd for opportunities to get alone to places [598/–] distant from all houses that I might there sing Psalms & praise God all alone, and oftimes did so with much joy.

After this I fell into great deadness: but the Lord was pleased now & then to send me Revivings again. And in such Ups & Downs, I have continued from that time to this (June 18. 1744). I have often found great Sweetness in hearing the Word, & partaking of the Lords Supper, and particularly at the 2d Sacrament at Cambuslang in 1742: & for about two weeks after the first Sacrament there in 1744. At Secret Prayer, I often find my heart very dead, at other times the Lord gives me much freedom & enlargement in pouring out my heart before him. When he hides his face I am troubled, not indeed so much as I ought to be, but I am troubled that I cannot be troubled & affected enough, & I remain unsatisfied, till he hive me the light of his Countenance again. The Sin of Unbelief has often been my grief & burden: and I have several times, particularly at Camb. felt a Secret power drawing my heart to close with Christ in all his offices as my Prophet, Priest & King; and I truly think he has made me as willing [ ][5] to be ruled by his Laws, as to be saved by his Love & the merit of his Death. To his name be Glory. Amen.

---

4   Isa 43:1.
5   Insertion ['& desirous']: McCulloch.

[599/–] Issobel Matthie John Yools Wife and [. . .] wife Widow in the Town of Kilbride, age 26.[1]

I was put to School & taught to read the Bible when I was a Child, & got the Shorter Cat. mostly & retain it in a good measure still. I had an outward Civil walk before the world all along: I had a religious Education & usd sometimes to pray by my Self in Secret & sometimes neglected it: but it was only a Custom I got that made me mind it at any time. I always usd to go the Kirk on Sabbath days, but it was only to see and be seen & out of fashion. I sometimes had some desires to be where there was any thing of good, tho I had none in my self. I usd to read the Bible sometimes, & when I read, I thought that they were happy that were truly religious. I sometimes thought of heaven & hell, but any worldly fancy would have out it out of my head again, I never had any Convictions of Sin, till last year, tho' I had some resolutions to mend my life ~~till~~. I came to Camb. about the first ~~Sabbath~~ Munday of March 1742, & saw several people in distress, & wishd I were like them, & thought Surely if I got a Sight of my Sins it would be a very dreadful sight, & could not endure to hear any speak evil of them: I would gladly have come again to Camb. but could not have opportunity to come till about the last Sabbath of March, & in time of the first Psalms Singing, I felt a great heaviness come upon me & my heart like to faint, & said within my self, Lord whatsoever is for thy Glory and my good, I am willing to Suffer it. And hearing the Minr Mr McC on that text, He that believeth not on the Son shall not see life, but the wrath of God abideth on him;[2] & that word in the Sermon He that believeth not the Gospel to be God's word is condemnd already,[3] struck my heart with power, and I was put to examine Self, & all the way going home, I was kept thinking upon it, & made to think [. . .] [. . .] [. . .] [. . .] [. . .] [. . .][4] I been doing all this time that I have [600/–] never yet believd the Gospel, & had never received it as God's Word, but livd in a secure carnal state. That night I slept some: and my mother in the morning telling me of one that had slept well, I said Oh mother, we have got too many of these sound sleeps. Next night I was so frighted, when I came in from Prayer, when I went to bed, with the terror of Satan that fell upon me [when I though I saw at the side of the bed as a rough tautie dog] and came out of the bed again: and a Neighbour man (John Allan) ~~coming on~~ being calld by my sister, when she saw I was so frighted, & he saw The night was ordaind for sleep, & bade me

---

1   This partial duplicate account is an earlier version of that found in Volume I:312–21.
2   Jn 3:36.
3   Jn 3:18.
4   The duplicate account in Volume I (p. 312) reads: 'Alas! What have . . .'.

go to my bed, & see if I might get some rest. I answered ~~that~~ How can I take rest; when God has sent his own Son, to save Sinners, & I ~~will not be~~ am not willing to be saved by him: and before I went to bed, I was so strengthned in that duty, that I thought tho Satan should come and appear never so near me he could do me no harm, being made to hope & trust in God that he would save me from that Evil one. I went to ~~my~~ bed & got some rest: my convictions continued with me & I was made to grieve much that I had so long despised and contemnd the Son of God. I came down to Camb.: on Thursday but going sensibly, but still that conviction continued That I had despisd the Son of God: & I was much distressd under it [†]:[5]& remained in this distress for some days after. On Sabbath night I hard a Minr (Mr McC) preach again concerning Unbelief, & fell under such distress at the thoughts that I had by Sin wounded a dear Saviour, that I fainted three times on the Brae where I was hearing Sermon, I fell into a Swarf three times being all the times of these Swarfs, still well enough in the exercise of my Reason, & my bodily eyes being shut, I saw as it were great darkness: but could [601/–] not hear what was said distinctly. But only as it were a confused sound: and all the three times just as I was coming out of these three Swarfs these words came to my heart with power Fear not Daughter for thy Sins are forgiven thee I took up my bible not minding one passage of it more than another and my eye lighted upon that passage which I did not remember was in the bible Isa Let the wicked forsake his ways and the Unrighteous Man his thoughts & let him return unto y Lord & to our God for he will abundantly pardon[6] this word was of great use to relieve me from my distress at that time & I had a greater inclination to duty than before and I then thought God was calling me to return from my sins & to come unto him & promising pardon. I came up to the Manse after Sermons: & I heard a preacher (Mr Davidson)[7] Lecture abt Zacheus and who observed that our Lord did not quarrel Zacheus for his Sins but as soon as the Spirit of God entered into him he quarreld himself that preacher also observed the Redeemer had to go thro' Samaria to bring home ane adulterous Woman and Who Knows but he will go thro' this room to bring home some of the Chief of Sinners among us. I thought I was the very Chief of Sinners present and I had hopes the Redeemer would come to save me After that immediatly I lost hope and Cryed out O ~~was The~~ is my Redeemer gone. The Minr of the Place said will ye wait I answered but I cannot wait ~~after which~~ That Minr urged me again to wait with patience I said that neither He nor any other ~~person~~ man was able to relieve me for none

---

[5]   Insertion ['† And after Sermon coming into the Hall <....> in the Manse & crying out, there, some calld to me to hold my peace, I answered in great bitterness, How can I hold my peace, when I have trampled the Son of God under my feet.']: McCulloch.

[6]   Isa 55:7.

[7]   Henry Davidson (1687–1756) – minister, Galashiels (Fawcett, *The Cambuslang Revival*; Scott, *Fasti*).

could do it but Christ. After this I returned home and continued in great distress till Wednsday and them I thought that Satan was not only about me but drawing me by the feet down to Hell A preacher [†][8] came to see me when I was under this apprehension but I would not allow him to speak any words of comfort to me I said none could relieve me but He that had trode the wine press of the Fathers wrath alone when of the people there was none to help him But I desired that Preacher to pray for me when He desired me to lay hold of a promise of the Bible he had before been speaking of ~~But~~ I said I cannot not lay hold of any one promise in all the Bible. I found I had no strength in my self ~~but I saw all to relieve me~~ But I saw that all my strength must come from the Redeemer to relieve & save me yt Preacher desired me to shew my bible to him [ ][9] but I would not let it go saying it was Gods Holy Word I would not part with. After this He desired me to take some refreshment to my body by meat & sleep, but I said I could rest none till I got a Saving interest in Christ immediatly after this These words came into my mind with power fear not for I will work a thorough work and a [602/–] saving change and thou shalt taste of the Cup of My Wrath but not forever and in a little after that word came also wt such poverty y I was forced to cry out with Joy fear not for I am with thee[10] I will lead the by the Hand whethersoever thou goest After this I said O this has been a sore fore noon but this is the sweetest ~~fore~~ afternoon yt Ever I had. Towards the end of that same week it came into my mind that all I had met wt was but a delusion On Sabbath a Minr (Mr Mat Connell) preached from Rom 8.15 Ye have not received yt Spirit again unto fear but ye have received the Spirit of Adoption whereby we cry Abba Father where he opened up the way how the Spirit of God wrought upon the Hearts of his people I then found that what I had met with exactly agreed to what yt Minr said about the Operations of the Spirit of God and this was the means that relieved me from distress at that time. Next day I came down to Camb: and heard y Minr there describe the nature of unbelief and I was greatly affraid that I was still under its power & I thought there no sinner among all ~~that~~ the people I saw like my self I saw myself so vile in my own eyes because of my sins that I was forced to Cry out O what have I been doing all my life against God and I thought I was more vile than any creature & loathsome upon the account of my sins I saw I brought a polluted nature into y world with me & that I had gone astray as soon as I was born I thought I saw I justly deserved Gods wrath yea that a 1000 hells were little enough for me considering what I had done agt God. I was then affraid of nothing but of God whom I had grievously offended

8   Insertion ['† Mr David Connelll']: McCulloch; David Connell (1706–90) – minister, E. Kilbride.
9   Insertion ['to point out a passage to me to meditate upon']: McCulloch.
10   Gen 26:24, Isa 41:10, Isa 43:5.

when I was in my way home these words came into My mind w' power thou
shalt be pure as gold and fine as Ophir & they made such ane impression upon
me that they greatly raised up my Spirits I did not know where to find that
passage but resolved to make search for it till I got it And the first time I took
the bible into my hand after this I happened to lookd upon Isa:13.12 [†][11]
where thus it is written I will make a man more precious than fine gold Even
a man [ ][12] the golden wedge of Ophir. I was glad that I had met with that
passage as being the same in Scriptures with having some relation to what
was spoken to my heart in my way home Which gave me great ease and
Comfort for I thought those whom God had purged from their Iniquities
were made more precious than pure Gold pure as gold & precious as the
Wedge of Ophir but after this I doubted if I had any interest in these words
spoken inwardly to my soul and then it came these words came also into my
mind I will cover thee under my wings till the Day of adversity be [603/–]
over. I was then in such a condition and Christ was precious to my soul that
I thought I could have parted will all I had for out of love to him. I continued
for some days after this in such a frame that nothing could divert my thoughts
from Christ and Inclined then resolved to lay my self down for ever at his
feet for mercy and his free grace to Save me I was filled with high Esteem of
His blood which alone could Save me and I saw if I had once got one interest
in Christ Indeed no oyr Saviour

   After this Satan began to tempt me to Deny Christ but I was helped to
resist him Replying again No no I was willing to be denyed to all and to part
with all but that him I would not deny him. I cannot want This temptation
wrought within me for about a 14 days before that temptation left me I was
coming to Camb. to hear a Stranger Minr (Mr Wh——d) and two or three
days before I heard him it was constantly urgd upon my mind that if I went
& heard that Minr I would go mad when I The day that I came to hear him I
got great liberty to pray for that Minr and for all that should hear him After
I heard his first sermon I was some what revived but got no particular word
to my Soul. The Tempter began again to urge me wt his former temptation
next day I could not win back that day to hear him but I could not stay at
home [ ][13] I went therefore to the fields with my Child and waited upon God
When I was a mile from home I heard a great Crack of thunder which used
to affright me much and I Knew not whither to return to my own house or
go forward to a friends House whom I was intending to see that Day Then I
resolved in the Strength of the Lord to go forward When I had gone a about
half a mile further I was made to believe that [ ][14] I dyed that day it should

---

[11]   Insertion ['with the first glance of my Eye']: McCulloch.
[12]   Insertion ['than']: McCulloch.
[13]   Insertion ['at my own house']: McCulloch.
[14]   Insertion ['if']: McCulloch.

be well wt my soul and if I lived it would be well also ~~and~~ My faith in y'
Lord Jesus was made so strong that nothing could trouble me & My heart and
my mouth were filled with his praises so that I could not intertain any other
Subject in my mind & I was made to believe His eye was upon me And He
was altogether precious to my Soul. this good frame continued with me all
that day and night thereafter and next day also I returned home with a heart
full of love to God and was inabled to say My Beloved is mine & I am his[15]
this frame continued with some abatement for a considerable time after this

And after this pleasant time I found my heart hard and that I had no liberty
to pour out my soul to God for about a fourthnight But that word in Mal:
was of great use to soften my heart [604/–] and to make Christ precious to
my Soul But unto you that fear My Name will the Sun of Righteousness arise
with healing under his name[16] After this I continued in a heavenly frame
still meditating upon and praiseing God till the first Communion in Camb.

I heard on Saturdays Night before that Communion that Stranger Minr
formerly mentioned speaking of the Blessed Redeemers Sufferings and that
he bare all the sins of ane Elect World till he fell to the Ground and perhaps
his blessed lips licked the dust I thought this my ~~wounds~~ sins had made the
wounds in his Side and put the Crown of thorns upon his head the Very
thought of this deeply pierced My heart. In my way home I then began to
Reflect upon the many wants I had and my great necessitys I had ~~not~~ no
doubt of Gods willingness to relieve them but I doubted of my willingness
to receive from him then that word came into my mind with great power I
will supply all thy need I was then oblidged to tell my Neighbours on the
Way what God had said to my Soul

I heard a Minr [ ][17] Preach on Song before the Action Yea he is altogether
Lovely this is my beloved & this is my friend O Ye dauters of Jerusalem[18] in
time of that Sermon I found my heart greatly and sweetly drawn out after
Christ and He rang King in my heart He was above all things to me and above
all my troubles At the Communion table he was altogether lovely & precious
to me and it was then said to my Soul He was become My salvation I heard
a Minr in the evening preach on Isa: Thy Maker is thy Husband[19] who said
Come and ~~marry~~ be married to Christ and you'll have a dear Husband. I was
so filled wt love to Christ and Esteem of him that I wondered if there were
any amongst that great multitude that were unwilling to Close with him. but
still I wanted more & more of Christ for my self and I had great hope that
I would get more of Christ before that occasion was over Next day I heart

---

[15] SS 2:16.
[16] Mal 4:2.
[17] Insertion ['Mr Mc Culloch']: McCulloch.
[18] SS 5:16.
[19] Isa 54:5.

the same Minr from Ph: 2. let the same mind be in you &c:[20] in time of that Sermon I was made so full of the Love of God in Christ that I fell back from the seat I was sitting on and made to cry out O all you that's There O praise The Lord for what he has Done for my soul I was made to Swoon a way and when I was in the Swoon I thought I saw [...] [...] [...] [605/–] The Redeemer then said unto me There is the Seal of Your salvation and I saw Clearly The R as it were ane Z of blood for along time after this occasion was over my heart continued full of Love and joy and praise.[21]

[20] Php 2:5.
[21] The remainder of this narrative is found on pp. 282–5.

Janet Jackson Daughter to James Jackson Elder in Camb aged about 24 years[1]

I was taught to read my question Psalm book at the publick School and learned to read my bible by my Parents at home I was set to read my bible and pray unto God by my parents when I was young but I was very indifferent about it. After I came to some years I had some concern to mind my duty and I went about it chiefly because I saw others minding it I keept the Kirk but minded Little what the Minr said nor did I under stand what I heard and I was easy whither I heard or not. I was not vicious or immoral in My Life and when I heard others banning and swearing I turned fear'd and Sometimes I have reproved them and asked why they Bann'd for I thought it was a sin in them to bann But tho' I was soberer than some others before the World I was as ill as they for all that for my heart was as ill as theirs and I had no love to God and Christ and I did nothing to please God I was always provoking him tho I was insensible of it. All this time my Conscience was asleep and did not rise up against me for Sin

Some years before the Awakening I was in service in a Minrs family [ ][2] who took great pains upon me and I attained to some more Knowledge and had some concern about My Soul I minded My duty more closely both to God & Man but I had no discoveries of my lost state & Condition by nature Only I had somewhat more concern about the external part of Religion I had some pleasure in duty sometimes when I thought I had any liberty in it but my heart was never truly affected with what I was about. About five years ago at a communion occasion when I saw some young folks coming to My Mr about their soul-Concerns and seem'd to be affected I wondered what it was they were affected about & that I was not affected about my Souls State as well as they I was in some little concern at that Occasion but it went intirely off after the Communion was over ~~Before the Communion tho' I had been at the Lords Table~~ The next year after when the Communion came to be dispensed again in the Parish [ ][3] My Concern Revived and I saw some of my Heart plagues such as wandering in time of Religious duties I was about that time in Company speaking with some of my Acquaint [...] [...] [...] [...] [...][4] and about the

---

[1]   Janet Jackson – spinner in Cambuslang; former servant of McCulloch. Daughter of James Jackson, elder at Cambuslang. Sister of narrative respondents Elizabeth Jackson (I:67) and Catherine Jackson (II:122). This partial duplicate account is an earlier version of the version found in Volume I: 15–25. This account begins on p. 605 of Volume II in McCulloch's manuscripts, directly following the conclusion of the previous account.

[2]   Insertion ['Mr McCulloch']: McCulloch.

[3]   Insertion ['being 1739']: McCulloch.

[4]   Illegible text due to worn tail-edge. The duplicate account in Volume I (p. 16) reads: '. . . ances about religion'.

disposition of my heart & [606/–] one in the Company said nothing ailed their heart I wondered what had made my heart worse than My N̶e̶i̶g̶h̶b̶o̶u̶r̶s̶ I then prayed to God that he would stay my wandering heart I w̶o̶u̶l̶d̶ fell under great concern whither I should got to the Lords table or not and when I was in this Concern one morning that word came to my mind in Isa: I will strengthen y' Yea I will up hold thee with the Right hand of my righteousness[5] but it did not come into my mind with any power My desire continued to go to the Lords Table I went accordingly into it at that occasion but cannot say I had faith to discern the Lords body in that ordinance or Love or repentance Only I resolved I would never be as I had been before. for a considerable time some concern to do better after that Communion remained with me and I reformed in some things I saw I had d̶o̶n̶e̶ been wrong in before but my righteousness was as the Early due & morning Cloaud it vanished away. The next year after this when I was hearing a̶ ̶S̶e̶r̶m̶o̶n̶ ̶a̶t̶ ̶a̶ ̶c̶o̶m̶m̶u̶n̶i̶o̶n̶ a Minr exhort a̶t̶ ̶t̶h̶e̶ ̶L̶o̶r̶d̶s̶ T̶a̶b̶l̶e̶ Communicate at the Lords Table in a Neighbouring Congregation (Carmunnock) I was greatly affected at the time with these words Spoken to by him viz: Only Those that had Clean hands and a pure heart[6] had right to sit down at that table they came into my mind wt Power and made me shed abundance of tears I then clearly saw I had no right to that ordinance and I had some general concern about my state but I had not particular Convictions of my Sins Yea I did not reflect that I sinned last year in going to the Communion table and eating and drinking there while I was not prepared in heart for that duty All that Summer after some concern remained upon me but after that it wore off intirely Only I thought it would be well enough with me if carried as I saw other Devise people carry B̶u̶t̶ and so I keept up a form of Religion and rested there.

In Septr 1741 I heard a Stranger Minr [ ][7] at Glasglow preach two sermons in the High Church yeard one in the morning and thoyr at night Who in one of these sermons frequently spoke of Those people to whom God spake no peace and [ ][8] I was in some concern to know who these people were and in what condition t̶h̶e̶y̶ yt people were in & how they carried in the world. And after I heard of Severals that had been awakned in hearing that Minister I fell into new concern about my self. And I h̶a̶d̶ saw one of my sisters[9] greatly altered in her way that had been hearing him yt she spent much time in prayer by what she used to do and read that Minrs sermons often and made much use of her Bible. I thought certainly I was not like my sister now [. . .] [. . .]

---

5   Isa 41:10.
6   Ps 24:4.
7   Insertion ['Mr Wh—d']: McCulloch.
8   Insertion ['in time of hearing']: McCulloch.
9   Duplicate account in Volume I (pp. 15–25) identifies this person as Elizabeth Jackson (81) – lay person, Cambuslang.

[. . .] [. . .] [. . .] [. . .][10] But I was [607/–] not much concerned about my self
as yet only I prayed more frequently ~~on my bible~~ and read my bible oftener
and took pleasure ~~and~~ in reading yt Minrs Sermons and the Weekly History
after it was published And I thought my own Minr preached much better
then he usd to do. In the month of December 1741 my own Minr[11] had his
text in ~~Now is the accepted time and~~ We beseech you that y[e] received not y'
Grace of God in vain &c:[12] Who said people heard the gospel as if they heard
not and heard it slightly I thought the minister was preaching to me when
he had that note and pointing at me as distinctly as if he had named me out
all the time of that sermon and I found I was one of these Sinners who had
received the Grace of God in vain which affected me so greatly that I was like
to cry out before the Congregation under a deep Sense of this and My other
Sins and how my unworthy communicating stared me in the face and Pierced
deep into my Conscience and my often allowed heart wandering in time of
Dutys of prayer and Praise and that I thought so little of Publick ordinances
dispensed by the Minrs after I had heard some of the North country Minrs
of whom I had a great opinion I saw it was wrong in me to despise and under
value the Ministers of this Church These and many other Sins which I do
not now distinctly remember were very grievous to me After Sermons I went
home in great grief for the evils I had done and I never had any such sight
Sights of Sin all my by past life as now I got of it I saw it as dishonouring &
provoking to a Holy God and I do not remember I was in any fear of hell at
all tho I had got a great sight of my sins After I went home I prayed to God
with more earnestness than ever I had done and I did not know that convictions
were dealing with me but I thought no body was so sinful as I in the Sight
of God I did not discover my Case to any mortal [ ][13] &c For several Sabbath
Days after this I thought the Minister was preaching preaching against my
sins and no other bodies but my own and I got more discoveries of y' Evil of
my ways from time to time. And I thought sin was anoyr thing than ever I
had discovered it to be & I saw the corruption of my nature & my Evil heart
of Unbelief and that I could not be saved while I continued in that State of
Sin and under the power of Unbelief and I began to be afraid that God would
not have mercy upon me because I saw my sins so great & provoking to God
About this time one of my Sisters[14] went and stayed with my Married Sister

---

[10] Illegible text due to worn tail-edge. The duplicate account in Volume I (p. 17) reads: 'About
     this time also, I was frequently hearing one of my Neighbors (61) speak of some people that
     had been awakned at Glasgow, on whose lives there was a great change to the better.'
[11] Duplicate account in Volume I (pp. 15–25) identifies this person as William McCulloch
     (26) – minister, Cambuslang.
[12] 2 Co 6:1.
[13] Insertion ['that had been awakened about that time on whose lives there was a great Change']:
     McCulloch.
[14] Duplicate account in Volume I (pp. 15–25) identifies this person as Elizabeth Jackson (81) – lay
     person, Cambuslang.

for some time and I having a good opinion of her I thought I was not worthy of her company and yrfore she was taken away from me Still my Convictions turnd more cutting and deep but at this time it was not known that I was under any [. . .] [. . .] [. . .] [. . .] [. . .] [. . .][15] do I keept all within my self I [608/–] wrought my work and forced my self to take my meat that I might not be discovered to be in distress. But sometimes I did not sleep for the concern upon my Spirit and when I was keept awake some passages would have came into my mind with sweetness and I was made frequently To bless the Lord that such comforting words to distressed souls were in the bible But the particulars I do not now remember. My Convictions still continued only I got more hope that God would shew Mercy to my Soul. I heard one of my acquaintances[16] in my Fathers[17] house about the 12th of Feb. telling him of Severals in y' Congregation who had fallen under convictions A thought came into my mind that ~~nothing~~ was ailing me ~~and~~ that others would get mercy but I would be left of God in my Sins. that night I heard My Father reading from Mr Guthries Tryal[18] and by what I heard from that book my convictions and distress increased so greatly upon my spirit y I was very near bursting out before all in the House but I went out to the door to get my distress concealed & to prevent my outcrying in their hearing When I had gone to the door that word in Psal: 51 came to my mind with great power a broken and a Contrite heart Lord thou wilt not despise[19] which took off much of the weight on my Spirit I was then made to see my heart was truly broken & contrite under a Sense of my Sins and to hope ye Lord would not despise me altogether and I was inabled to bless and thank God for what encourgemt I had got at that time after which I went to one of my acquaintances [ ][20] who knew of my youngest Sisters distress and Outgate and we spoke of her ~~together~~ But my own distress for sin as dishonouring to God was so great that I was forced to burst out in tears before her tho I did not tell her ye reason that made me do so My Soul trouble continued upon me very heavy Next day I went in to see another Neighbour [ ][21] experienced in religion who had observed me under concern by my face and actions and Strictly charged me to tell what was dealing with me and no more to conceal my case for that she was sure something ailed me by ordinary but I could not speak out one word to her of my Case and went immediatly out from her and returned to my

---

15   Illegible text due to worn tail-edge. The duplicate account in Volume I (p. 18) reads: 'my distress was not known to my Friends'.

16   Duplicate account in Volume I (pp. 15–25) identifies this person as Jean Galbreith (61) – lay person, Cambuslang.

17   Duplicate account in Volume I (pp. 15–25) identifies this person as James Jackson (67) – elder, Cambuslang.

18   William Guthrie, *The Christians Great Interest*.

19   Ps 51:17.

20   Insertion ['Jean Robertson']: McCulloch.

21   Insertion ['Jean Galbreath']: McCulloch.

work in my Fathers House As I spun at my wheel I read on my bible upon
my knee and shed many tears & my distress continued some time of that day
being Saturday Feb: 13. 1742. That word came to my mind with power &
supported me much as in Ps. 72. The prayer of y Destitute he surely will
regard[22] I thought I was [. . .] [. . .] [. . .] [. . .] [. . .][23] [609/-] destitute and
made to hope from that God would regard Me in great concern at that time.
I spent a good part of that day with anoyr of my Sisters[24] & and a comerad
and none of us could speak to anoyr because our grief was so great & sorrow
had filled our hearts On Sabbath as I was in the Church a good number of
people being there and many of them standing for want of seats My sister[25]
first mentioned having for a seat to sit down upon from a Neighbour and I
being left to stand I thought that I was not worthy of a seat and therefore got
not a seat and I thought every body knew I was a great Sinner and not worthy
of the Regard of others I stood with great difficulty and was often at the
point of crying out all that day & I thought all I heard in Sermon was levelled
against Me in the afternoon I remember the Minr[26] said [ ][27] Some would be
greived because y^t God was pleased to bring home to himself others by
converting grace and murmuring t God that he was not pleased to call
themselves. I thought this was exactly my case for I was quarreling and
murmuring in my own mind ag^e God y^t he seem'd to take my Sisters friends
and leave my self as I then apprehended I saw the evil of this and was convinced
God might in justice pass me by and suffer me to perish in my sins and yt it
was ane Act of Grace in God to Save any of the Sinfull Children of Men and
I thot my heart was humbled under a sense of Sense of my rebellion against
God. In time of that Sermon The Minr shewed what way a concern upon a
persons spirit about Salvation differed from Convictions of Sin and how the
one was distinquished from y' oyr. And this was the first time that I knew I
was under convictions for I Knew not before this what convictions mean'd
at hearing of this I was somewhat glad when I knew what was dealing with
me and also at the same time almost like to cry out of sorrow for my sins yea
the most part of that afternoon day after Sermons in whatever places I was I
was at the point of Crying out This being the Sabbath when my Sister (Kat.)
was under very deep Convictions and bro't to the Minrs Closet The person[28]

---

[22] Ps 102:17, Scottish Psalter (metrical).
[23] Illegible text due to worn tail-edge. The duplicate account in Volume I reads: 'a person truely'.
[24] Duplicate account in Volume I (pp. 15–25) identifies this person as Catherine Jackson (83)
      – lay person, Cambuslang.
[25] Duplicate account in Volume I (pp. 15–25) identifies this person as Elizabeth Jackson (81) – lay
      person, Cambuslang.
[26] Duplicate account in Volume I (pp. 15–25) identifies this person as William McCulloch
      (26) – minister, Cambuslang.
[27] Insertion ['words to this purpose']: McCulloch.
[28] Duplicate account in Volume I (pp. 15–25) identifies this person as Ingram More (59) – elder,
      Cambuslang.

who came about her to carry her to the Minr not knowing as I suppose my Distress & not desiring me to go along with her I was greatly affected with this and thought that I was neglected by every body I then Cryed out in the House where we were that tho' I was yet despised by Every body I would trust in God. I ~~was~~ then went along wt my Sister & that oyr Person to the Minrs Closet and all the times she was in her bitter Soul agonie for her Sins. I found my heart stupid & hard After she got her outgate and was commending the Riches of free grace to oyrs and came to speak to me I then thought there was no mercy for me that had been so great a Sinner and when I was in this Case immediatly these words came to my heart with great power & sweetness as in I will draw thee wt y' cords of love and y' bands of [610/–] a man[29] and that moment I found my heart drawn out in love towards God Immediatly after this that Scrip: Mat: 11.28 came into my mind both with power Come unto Me all ye that labour and are heavy laden & I will give you rest and As in I will make Crooked places Straight & rough places plain.[30] Immediatly I found the gracious presence of God wt drawn from me which made me cry out and before the Company when I found ~~God~~ him Hiding his face from me But I said I would trust in God. I continued under Damps and in doubt of my interest in Christ all the after part of that Night & Next day because I was like my Sister[31] who had got ane Outgate on Sabbath night & could do nothing but bless & praise God for a long time after. I remember also on that Munday a Young Man (Ja: Millar Weaver)[32] asked me if I was in fear of hell he wanted to know this because he had a Broyr under great fears of Hell at that time I answered him I was not in fear of hell. He asked me again what made me so concerned then I answered because by My Sins I had so greatly dishonoured God That Young Man desired me to take some courage and hope in the Salvation of God. That Evening I went to That Experienced Christians[33] house formerly mentioned where there was about Eight or Nine Young people that had lately falln under distress and a Preacher[34] & Elder[35] and anoyr Man[36] who had been lately awakned by means of Mr. Wh——d came down to Converse wt the Wounded That preacher exhorted not to read so

[29] Hos 11:4.
[30] Isa 40:4.
[31] Duplicate account in Volume I (pp. 15–25) identifies this person as Catherine Jackson (83) – lay person, Cambuslang.
[32] James Miller – weaver.
[33] Duplicate account in Volume I (pp. 15–25) identifies this person as Jean Galbreith (61) – lay person, Cambuslang.
[34] Duplicate account in Volume I (pp. 15–25) identifies this person as Alexander Duncan, licensed probationer preacher, Cambuslang; later an elder at Cambuslang (Robe, *Short Narrative*, 8, 28–30, 290; Fawcett, *The Cambuslang Revival* 83).
[35] Duplicate account in Volume I (pp. 15–25) identifies this person as John Bar (58) – elder, Cambuslang.
[36] Duplicate account in Volume I (pp. 15–25) identifies this person as Ingram More (59) – elder, Cambuslang.

much on other prackical books as the bible for that was the ~~most safe~~ fittest book for persons in their Condition I thought what was then said was ane proof to me who had read more on Sermons and other practical books than my bible. I then betook my self more to my bible and had more pleasure & profit in reading it than I had met wt before, Next morning shortly after I arose from my bed these words Act: struck my heart wt great power Believe on y' Lord Jesus Christ and thou shalt be saved[37] I thought I was in some measure inabled to believe and I attained to some more peace than before but I did not attain at that time to Joy and I began to suspect myself that I was not in a right way because I was not so full of Love and Joy and Praises to God as My Sister[38] That Night my other Sister (Eliz:) got her heart opened and her Country tongue Loosed to sing the praises of God and Desired all in that little town where she was to be brought unto her that she might tell them how good and Gracious God was I was much sunk that I took & thought my heart was not so much filled wt the Love of God as My Sisters were and my doubt about Conversion was the more increased on the 18th of That Month I heard that sermon where in so many fell under [. . .] [. . .] [. . .] [. . .] [. . .] [. . .] [. . .][39] [611/–] Minrs Text was in Jer.23.6 And this is the Name where wt he shall be called the Lord our Righteousness I thought That Sermon was as it were a New Gospel to me I had great pleasure ~~in hearing~~ & satisfaction in hearing it But I do not remember I could say assuredly the Lord is My Righteousness. I came into The Minrs Dining room and was greatly rejoiced to see so much under Convictions of Sin and Getting Sensible reliefs and commending Christ to one anoyr And My Broyr in law being under great Distress for his sins I thought I was in some measure helped to speak to him of the riches of free grace in the Redeemer to Heart broken Sinners. I got ~~nothing of Sensible~~ more of that Sensible presence of God on that day. But my doubt still increased about my being converted when I saw others so much inlarged in singing the praises of God and Especially when I heard a Young Man[40] the following day speaking ~~several~~ a long time so greatly in commendation of Christ ~~to others~~ and telling ~~the many~~ what promises ~~that~~ had been spoken to his heart & yt particular that God had said to his Soul I will never leave thee nor forsake thee[41] and many oyrs ~~great & precious Promises~~ like promises I then thought t myself was no thing at all and began to be greatly discouraged and I continued in this doubt about my Conversion without any Sensible

37   Ac 16:31.
38   Duplicate account in Volume I (pp. 15–25) identifies this person as Catherine Jackson (83) – lay person, Cambuslang.
39   Illegible text due to worn tail-edge. The duplicate version in Volume I (p. 21) reads: '. . . Convictions, The . . .'.
40   Duplicate account in Volume I (pp. 15–25) identifies this person as James Millar (62) – weaver, Cambuslang.
41   Heb 13:5.

Releif for a Considerable time. When I saw the persons that had been in distress getting such great manifestations of the Love of God I was heartily willing to go ~~throw their soul trouble as for sins~~ thro any trouble rather on Soul or body that I might get their Strong Consolations. One morning I was longing ~~for such a distressing Sight and sense of Sin as I had seen others in before they were comforted~~ [ ]⁴² That word in Ps. came to my Mind wt Sharp rebuke Why Dost thou boast O Mighty Man of Mischief and of ill⁴³ I thought then it was a sin to Wish for such troubles upon my Soul after which I durst not long for such ~~a distressing Sense of God and Sight of My Sins trouble~~ tho' I should want the Comforts of ~~y' Distressed~~ others But still it was grievous to Me that I thought I had not such Strong Comforts as others till one morning I was awaked out of sleep with these words struck into my heart wt great power as in Ps Cast thy burden upon y' Lord & he shall sustain thee⁴⁴ About the 11ᵗʰ of Ap: I heard a Minr (Mr McCulloch) preach on Psal: Today if Ye will hear his voice harden not Your Hearts⁴⁵ I thought I heard indeed the Voice of Christ to my soul in time of that Sermon and I was inabled to believe upon him wt my heart and to Receive him as offered in y' Gospel and for along time after that I thought I had faith in and Love to God in a lively exercise and that I was inabled to walk by faith & to live in the flesh by faith [612/–] on the Son of God and I took great delight in that life and indeavoured to have my conversation becomeing the Gospel & to walk Worthy of the Lord to all well pleasing. but I lost sight of my interest in Christ by accidentally happening upon some loose leaves of a printed book and there finding the [ ]⁴⁶ great Lengths Hypocrites might come in Religion I then lost all hope of My interest and concluded My self a Hypocrite and thought I had been but deceiving My self and the World with a profession of Religion all this time I then betook my self to Prayer to God begging that He in mercy might Search & prove Me and might not Suffer me to put a Cheat on my self or others And sometime after this that word came in [ ]⁴⁷ Rom: to be carnally minded is death but to be Spiritually minded is life & peace⁴⁸ and after this anoyt ~~passage~~ sentence once came in with great power Nevertheless ~~not~~ the Spirit Liveth in Me I came and asked My Experienced acquaintance⁴⁹ where to find any Scripture Word Like that sentence ~~I have not spoken~~ and she told me it would be that in Gal. 2.20 Nevertheless ~~not I but Christ liveth in me I~~

---

42 Insertion ['much for these comforts and willing to suffer any trouble to get them']: McCulloch.
43 Ps 52:1, Scottish Psalter (metrical).
44 Ps 55:22.
45 Ps 95:7–8.
46 Insertion ['seeming']: McCulloch.
47 Insertion ['but not with great power']: McCulloch.
48 Ro 8:6.
49 Duplicate account in Volume I (pp. 15–25) identifies this person as Jean Galbreith (61) – lay person, Cambuslang.

live yet not I but Christ liveth in Me[50] where the first passage when it Came to my Mind I thought That I was indeed carnally mind that I had all along been carnally mind and that had never hitherto been Spiritually mind and I was perplexed to think that I had been so And I could not say that the Spirit liveth in Me and I fell into greater darkness than ever till one day when my distress and darkness was exceeding great and I was spining on My Wheel These words came into My Mind wt great sweetness & power Thou art a New Creature[51] and then I was made to believe I was no Hypocrite but a new creature for a light shone into my mind along with these words convincing & showing me that old things were passed away and all things were become New And then the thoughts of my Hypocrisy evanished for a Considerable time but after that I fell into strong convictions of the Evil of Sin one night in a meeting for prayer and conference in time of the when the 13 Psal and these words in Ps 41: Gainst thee the only have I sinned[52] were sung and I was at the Point of Crying out but got my Case pretty much concealed from those in the meeting only my old Experienced acquaintance observed me in disorder and afterwards asked My Case I told I was under deep convictions of the Evil of Sin but I durst not altogether doubt of my Interest in Christ These Convictions continued with me for a Considerable Time and one day [. . .] [. . .] [. . .] [. . .] [. . .] [. . .][53] [613/–] wanting some sensible comfort amidst my distress and casting about in my own mind what way I would get it These words came into my mind wt great Power as in Ps: Thou Hast arm y' full of power[54] I was then made to look to the Power of God for support & Comfort and shortly after this when when I was in disorder upon the account of my Sins these words came into my mind with great power Thy Warefare is accomplished[55] and immediatly I was releived from the Burdensome Sense of My Sins and made to bless & praise God for this seasonable Relief to my soul[56]

---

[50] Gal 2:20.
[51] 2 Co 5:17.
[52] Ps 51:4.
[53] Illegible text due to worn tail-edge. The duplicate account in Volume I (p. 23) reads: '. . . when I was . . .'.
[54] Ps 89:13, Scottish Psalter (metrical).
[55] Isa 40:2.
[56] The duplicate narrative text continues in the account in Volume I (p. 24).

Isobel Mathies Account Continued.

After which I was greatly troubled with hardness of heart and could get no rest and I was still seeking from & praying to God for deliverance from the body of sin and many a time when I essayed duty I could do nothing but groan I was some what relieved from that in hearing a Minr [†][1] (Mr. Robe)[2] preach on Isa 53. He hath put him to grief when thou shalt make his Soul an offering for Sin[3] the words of the text were very reviving to Me. I heard also anoyr Minr on yt same day (Mr Henderson)[4] on Rom 8. Who shall lay anything to y' Charge of Gods Elect[5] & That Minr gave some of the Marks of the persons who ~~could~~ might say with the ap there and I thought I could apply them which was a means of comforting Me. On Saturday I heard anoyr Minr (Mr Webster)[6] from P: Unto you there for y Believe he is precious[7] My faith was then in lively exercise and I thought tho C should stay me yet I would lay me down at his feet for Mercy and The Redeemer was precious to my Soul. The Minr of yt Place had his Action Sermon text from 1 Jo: ~~Here is Ch~~ herein is love &c: in time of that Sermon I found my heart greatly drawn out in love towards Christ and I continued in this frame at the Lords table as I was going forward to the table that promise in Zech: was very refreshing to me which came in with great power & sweetness I will pour out the Spirit of Grace & Supplication[8] [614/–] and I found the desires of My heart greatly inlarged for greater measures of grace and The Redeemer in his person and benefits was altogether lovely to my Soul In my way home that night temptations came into My Mind but I got strength to resist them.

On the Munday I heard a Minr (Mr Hamilton[9] on Eph: pray without ceasing[10] And he was shewing by what marks a person might Know that they got returns of prayer from God amongst others he named this that it was a good evidence God answered our prayers when in time of temptation we got Strength to resist them I could not but say God had upholden me in time of my troubles frequently and strengthened Me to resist temptations and ~~my reflecting on this~~ when I reflected on this it was very sweet to me & I was inabled to bless & praise the name of God for helping me in the time of my need and supporting Me in the dark hours of temptation after this occasion was over I continued in a humble & thankfull frame for what God

---

1   Insertion ['† on the fast day before ye 2d Communion']: McCulloch.
2   James Robe (1688–1753) – minister, Kilsyth.
3   Isa 53:10.
4   Richard Henderson (d. 1769) – minister, Blantyre.
5   Ro 8:33.
6   Alexander Webster (1707–84) – minister, Tolbooth/Edinburgh.
7   1 Pe 2:7.
8   Zec 12:10.
9   William Hamilton (1689–1769) (11) – minister, Douglas.
10   1 Th 5:17.

had done for Me for some time ~~till~~ One day these words ~~in Jer.~~ came into My
Mind he that breaketh one Commandment is guilty of all[11] and I was filled
wt great horror and fear I got liberty to power out my soul to God in prayer
for strength to obey & serve him and I plead much that I had no strength in
my self and yt his grace was only Sufficient for me. I said I would only lean
upon his strength and upon the back of this petition these words Came in
with power & Sweetness My Grace ~~is~~ shall be sufficient for thee[12] ~~After this~~
immediatly after this I was so filled with a sense of his goodness to my Soul
that I was filled with thankfulness and praise and that of redeeming love was
above all his mercies I was in the Lively exercise of faith & love after this day
till Kilsyth Communion and ~~a sense~~ of The Redeemers Love constrained
Me to go there and Commemorate his Death. On Saturday I heard a Minr
~~preach~~ (Mr Warden in Camp:)[13] on Ps 118 Blessed is he that Cometh in the
Name of the Lord to save us[14] I then had a full assurance of faith that C was
Come to Save Me and I blessed the Lord for his Coming to save My Soul. I
heard anoyr Minr on Isa 62.7 Give him no rest till Zion be made a praise of
the [615/−] whole earth after this I think I was helped much to wrestle with
God that he might make Jerusalem a praise of y Whole Earth and I prayed
much for this & ~~expected~~ continue in expecting ane answer from him On
Sabbath Morning I heard anoyr Minr (Mr Gillespie)[15] on Isa I even I am he
yt blotteth out thine iniquities and will not remember thy Sins[16] I was made
here also to believe God would fulfill that promise to My Soul and I had great
peace. I intended to have gone to the Communion table but it so fell out that
I was dissappointed of a token ~~My Parish Minr~~ which was a great trouble to
Me for I had a great desire to go to the table and the dissappointment was the
heavier upon Me. I heard anoyr Minr whose name I did not know preach on
if I by the finger of God Cast out Devils then is the Kingdom of God Come
unto you[17] where he shewed what these devils were that the Spirit of God did
cast out of the hearts of men he named Several Sins such as pride & Unbelief
and gave the marks by which a person might know y' Kdom of God was
come unto him I was enabled to apply the marks and I was releived from the
disorder that had been upon my Spirit by reason of my disappointment of a
token After this thro' the whole day I was filled with joy & peace in believing.
On Munday morning I heard the Minr of the place explain a part of the 118
Psalm before it was sung ~~and when he was~~ & when he was explaining these

[11]   Jas 2:10.
[12]   2 Co 12:9.
[13]   John Warden (d.1764) – minister, Campsie; son of John Warden (1671–1751), minister,
       Gargunnock (Macfarlan, *Revivals*, 242; Scott, *Fasti*).
[14]   Ps 118:26, Scottish Psalter (metrical).
[15]   Thomas Gillespie (1708–74) – minister, Carnock; founder of Relief Church in 1761.
[16]   Isa 43:25.
[17]   Lk 11:20.

words Bind ye unto y' horns wt cords y'sacrifice[18] I fell into such a frame as I knew not whether I was in heaven or Earth and I got a clear faiths view of y'ocean of the Redeemers blood shed for the remission of Sins I was filled with unspeakable love & joy and sank down upon my seat and my heart was full of praise & thanksgiving I continued in this frame for a little while. And while I was continuing in this heavenly frame after I came home I suppose more than a fourthnight a ~~Temptatio~~ fiery dart came into my mind ~~calling~~ to me [616/–] tempting me to doubt if there was God and it was urged if there was a God how has he a begining. I was put all in to confusion And greatly affrighted with such thoughts but I resolved to seek the Lord and his face and to trust to his power to ridd me of it and I was keept a wrestling agt it & beging for deliverance. I got no rest for the space of six [ ][19] days nor night for it hanuting me when it was Evening I wished for the Morning [ ][20] & when it was morning I wished for y' Evening expecting the relief then. I bless y' Lord I was helped to wrestle &trust he would come and deliver me and one day yt word was brought into my Mind I will wait upon y[e] Lord and I got some more strength and ~~sometime after this I felt Relief came by means of these words Behold he Even~~ when I was meditating on y' ~~Redeemer by means of these words Behold he and~~ He only is Y[e] Almighty God. ~~And this was on a Munday~~ on the Sabbath before [ ][21] I heard My Parish Minr on y[e] words in Ecl: it shall be well with the Righteous but it shall be ill with the wicked[22] and He gave the Marks of the Righteous and I got liberty to apply them to my self which was very comforting to Me. After Sermons Satan came upon me strongly tempting Me to destroy my Child I was helped to say in faith My God will never leave Me to do that that night I had strong hopes I would get relief from this & my former temptations that night ~~but it came not that very night~~ My body was refreshed wt sleep but when I awoke I was not refreshed in Spirit I fell asleep again in the morning and had sweet meditations in my sleep upon the precious blood of Christ and when I awaked out of this sleep these words came with power Behold he and he only is the Mighty God the Lord[23] and at this time all y[e] Promises Ever I had got came fresh into My Mind and I was strengthned to rely by faith on the merits of Christ and my heart was filled wt love And I was not [617/–] haunted wt that temptation. Sometime after this as I was one day going to my secret duty a great fear came upon me that I ~~had~~ might be grieving the Spirit of the Lord ~~and that~~ but I was sure I thought if I was doing so it was not wittingly in Me and then These words came in with great sweetness and gave Me great

---

[18] Ps 118:27, Scottish Psalter (metrical).
[19] Insertion ['weeks']: McCulloch.
[20] Insertion ['expecting relief']: McCulloch.
[21] Insertion ['my releif came']: McCulloch.
[22] Isa 3:10–11.
[23] Ps 105:7, Scottish Psalter (metrical).

liberty & peace in believing I will be your God & Ye shall be my people[24] I got near access to God in that duty

Some time Lately I was cast down & discouraged when I thought upon my own weakness & insufficiency and greatly afraid that I would draw back from God & My Duty and but one Day ~~My Parish~~ The Minr was lecturing one yᵉ Ps. in his ordinary place from upon yᵉ words O God thou wilt strengthen that which thou hast wrought for us[25] And as he was explained these words he had that Espression which came with power upon my heart & strengthened my faith God will perfect that which he had begun

And now since my first effectuall awakening to see my danger by sin and I hope Saving inlightning to see the remedy it is my constant business to travel betwixt the Redeemers fulness and my own Emptiness I am still desiring more of him and habitually Meditating upon him and I endeavour to make the Glory of God My Chief End My sins are the greatest grief in this world I long to get rid of all Sin and to Enjoy God forever & ever

I heartyly pity them that oppose what I find to be a Work of Gods Spirit I have suffered the persecution of their tongues I am helped patiently to bear it and I have no rest upon my mind till I get them heartily forgiven & my Soul pourd out before God in their behalf that he may forgive and inlighten them and let them see that it is Jesus Whom they persecute I am in good hope the Lord will hear in his own good time

[618/– blank]

---

24 Jer 7:23.
25 Ps 68:28.

[631/1][1, 2] Octtober 1741. I ~~rember~~ remember on Sabboth I was going to the church I ~~had~~ communed with my self now many a time have I been in that place with a grave countenenc whil my heart was with the foolyees and littel harkening to what was sead and more espeshaly in the time of the communion and likeness had some heart melting under a senc [. . .] abut this time one night whils I was at my work I was verry much troubled with worldly thoughs I though I would reed on my bible ~~when~~ whear I hepened upon that place whear it says ~~God forbid that I should glory~~ [. . .] [. . .] [. . .] [. . .] [. . .] ~~cros of Jesus Christ which then~~ but God forbid that I should glory save in the cross of our Lord Jesus Christ by whom the world is crucified onto me and I onto the World[3] and this was my hearts prayer unto God that he would crucifie the world to me and I onto it thoron the cross of Jesus Christ

September 1745 one night while I was at my work I was troubled with such thoughs as thes that God could did not know my thoughs after I left work I went to prayer and endevoured to confess and bewaile the unbelife of my heart unto God but found no Outgeat the seame night I read a sermon [632/–] preached upon thes words but of him are ye in Christ Jesus who of God is made unto us wisdom and righteousness and sanctification and redemption[4] but when I read that sermon I thought I had no experrinencess there of which damped me very much so I retured to prayer and be moned my keus unto God whear I got som utterence so I went and read the sermon over agine whear I thought I had some experriences thereof and also comfort there from but especaly from the letter peart of it and this was all the experriences I had of my unbelife when I once heard you upon thes words John 4.10 he that believeth not God hath made him a liar because he believeth not the record that God[5] of his Son and if I remember you sade that Those that had not been sencabel of there unbelife had nothing of a right wasting of a Work yet ~~in there after~~ in the summer Thereafter on a morning I had upertunnity to read where I chuse durran[6] upon death expacting to heve receved som comfort from death but when I opened the bood (it was the letter peart of it) it was titeled selfe denyall so I thought I would read that peart of it wheare I met with great

---

[1]   Primary pagination number [619]–[630] omitted by McCulloch.
[2]   A partial account with no record of respondent's name begins here.
[3]   Gal 6:14.
[4]   1 Co 1:30.
[5]   1 Jn 5:10.
[6]   James Durham, *The Great Corruption of Subtile Self, discovered, and driven from it's lurking-places and starting-holes And the contrary grace, self-denyal commended, as an indispensably necessary requisite to the acceptable and successfull performance of all commanded-duties, and as notably fitting for taking up of the cross, and following Christ. In seven sermons. By master James Durham, late minister of the gospel in Glasgow* (Edinburgh: printed by the heir of Andrew Anderson, printer to the King's most excellent Majesty, 1686).

convictions of selfe whear I was even pricked to the heart especialy when I
read that [633/–] place wheare he gave som marks and evidences when selfe
bear the way in duty so he sade when selfe bear or had dominion the heart
was nothng the betterd there by and was as light and frothy when it had dun
as when it began it was a sein that selfe had the dominion and sway This and
the like was very weighty upon my spirits so tha I could not wheave eas my
smart it was my earnest prayer to God that he would mortifi it in all it motions
and actings for I thought that I could do nothing but it was allways present
with me and that dally and is to this day in a great misour venting it self in
me and in al my dutys and performences I was ignorent of My great idol selfe
untill this time in a great misour I found also some comfort in the seam book
but I do not mind distinkly now what this markes ~~ware~~ was

When this work began with me or a litel after I found my heart willing
to peart with the World and all things therin I thought sometimes can I had
happened to heve been awe longer [634/–] a knowing religon for now I
thought I would los all my worldly plesours and delights Sometimes I had a
very delutious sence of them upon my heart so that I thought that there was
avere great on willingness in me to peart with them other times. I thought
that I could a pearted with all things what sover Yea I could say that God was
mor pretious to me then ~~gold~~ thousands of gold and silver more desierabel
then mountens of pry On day I was vere much trobled there with I thought
with my selfe if I weres once in a good fream agien I will then try what
inflewence the world will heve upon my heart which acordingly as I belive
God did shein in upon my soul with the Light of his countenence the seam day
then I thought with my selfe—now world do thy worst but I then counted
the world nothing Yea bes then nothing and venity I was for three quarters
at the first of a year verry ignorent of my heart corruptions only I was verry
much trobled with a wandering heart [635/–] it was verry trobelsome to me
for a long time I knew not what to do meneatime upon the a count there of
I indeed was vere senceabel that I was urigenale corrupe liket I had not such
a heart burding of it as I heve found sume times since.

Aprile 1743 I whent unto the Sacrament of Glasgow where I whent into
the ramshorn church where you preached but heard verry littel seve only
when you gave out the psalm where I got the excersies of desier and longing
for the new heart and right spirit and also helped to plead ~~that God would
give me the same~~ by preases That God would geve me the seame after I went
from the church to my quarters I was lead awy with some world company
and spent a good peart of that eving there in which was a vere sore cheke
knowing that I should heve been about another work but when I releeved
to my duty I found my heart ~~all the alltogeder all to this alto gether~~ out of
fream for the senn [636/–] and continowed all that night in the next morning
I went out into the green where I lamented over my one belife and over the
weakness of my faith and the want of excerseas of what I thought I had by

prayer and medetation: and also pleading for faith and the excerseas there of: by the seam where I got some heart melting there by under a sence of want and of the preciousnes thereof Yet when I went to the church I was much under the power of a body of sin and death Yea every way of onfit for the duty of the day and in much pain and uneasenes of heart and when the time drow one of aproach onto the Lords table in this condition which in creased my oneasenes and desier to be there I went out of the church and went to prayer where I got my heart poured out in some misour yet I was not setisfied yet I thought I would ventour to go to the Lords table as I was for I thought to stay away til I was in a good fream was upon the matter that I would not go til I had a price in my hand so I [637/7] went professing to depend upon his own strenth but met with nothing remarkeble Next morning I went out into the green where I opened my bible and hepened upon the 18 ch-p of John but when I looked upon the ch-p these words came into my mind Judas betrayest thou the Son of Man with a kiss[7] I then thought with my selfe that I had betrayed him with a kiss I closed the book and went to prayer where I got my heart poured out in a great misour with meny tears I went unto the church hoping that the last day of the feast might be a great day o the feast to me as it had been my prayer before but I then found that my toroble was more in crased then before and in stead of geven thanks onto the Lord (as both the day requered unto being preached from the 106 psalm praise ye the Lord O give thanks unto the Lord for he is good for his mercy endureth for eve[8]) I found that in my heart that would not give thanks unto [638/8] Lord I though it was Satan that trobled me for I was under amighty lod of troble and a mighty pain and oneasenes was in my heart and next Mr warden in came preached hebrews 10 v 38 now the just shalt live by faith I then thought with my selfe I shall now be cut of for I heve no faith which in crased my troble and oneasenes but when he came to the letter peart of the sermon if I remember he sade that some profesed to heve faith who know nothing of the trobles and deficultys that ~~they~~[9] were in some times this thought that they should on day fall by the hand of Saul other times this thought they had not the spots God children and severl others trobles he mentioned and when he be gane to mention thes trobles my heart did apeal unto God that this was my Real and present condition I then found the imprestions of his holy spirit so warm upon my soul that the sweet did brak [639/9] upon my body he spoke not to a keas but I could apeal unto God with abroken heart [ ][10] and a contrite Spirit he sent from above he took me he drew me out of meny waters he delivered me from my strong enemy and from them which hated

---

[7]   Lk 22:48.
[8]   Ps 106:1.
[9]   Insertion ['the people of God']: McCulloch.
[10] Insertion ['that I had exparenced it']: McCulloch.

me for they were too strong for me as it is in the Psalms 18 v16.17 About July
1743 I heard Mr Gilles[11] upon Psalms 145 v 9 the Lord is good to all and his
tender mercies in over all his works I then thought to heve receved it in the
truth and Love of it and in thankfulnes for his great mercies meny fold but
I then began to find nothing but a unbeliving heart which in creased mightely
so I thought that I was nothing but a meer hypocrite when I went home I
had mind of a passeg of Mr Willesons upon the Sacarmental cattishisem[12]
he sead the best way was when on was under tentations of Satan to come and
act faith on Jesus Christ as this had never dune it before so I went to God by
prayer and profsed my willingnes to receve the Lord Jesus Christ upon his
oun terms and pleading upon that promes in 50 v i of Isaiah where I wan to
much brokennes of heart and I thought was helped so to do yet my heart was
[640/10] not halted but by degrees in reedings that night I cannot geve you
any more of my expareances in plean words but thesse and the like when I
cam from you last I was very much trobled with what you sead concearning
unbelif and origenal sin and I belive not without Just rason As I went home
I found in my heart to geve thanks to God that I had hepned to come unto
you for I ought that I had not yet mourned for my origenal sin acording as
I had sined in Adam I indeed at the first was mad Sencabel that I was with
out God and with out Christ and so cosequantly with out all hop in the world
I also had sevarl times my heart melted with soul refresshing under a sence
of that inward ~~sence~~ conterriaty that was in me to God and Godlynes but
never as I had sined in Adam so far as I remember and can Judg there for I
thought that I could not heve nothing of a seaving work be gune with me
yet but was yet a rebel and the chife of hypocrites I then purposed to pray
that God wold a waken me out of this sleep of ~~and~~ security and that he wold
convince me of all my sins and espashaly my orignal sin and actwul onbelife
but I [641/11] found nothing but deedness only I was Sencabol that I was
onsencable ~~thess was~~ There was some scriptours now much in my mind such
as because that when they knew God they glorified him not as God neither
were thankful but became vain in their imaginations and their foolish heart
was darkned professing themselves to be wise they became fools[13] he is proud
knowing nothing[14] heady high-minded lovers of pleasures more than lovers
of God.[15] I endevoured to aplay thess to my oun heart but I could not win

[11]   John Gillies (1712–96) – minister, Glasgow/College-kirk; historian of revival movements,
       and son-in-law of John McLaurin (1693–1754), minister, Glasgow/Ramshorn (Macfarlan,
       Revivals, 223; Scott, *Fasti*).
[12]   John Willison, *A Sacramental Directory: Or A treatise concerning the sanctification of a communion
       sabbath, The Whole Works of the Reverend and Learned Mr John Willison, Late Minister of the Gospel
       at Dundee, In four volumes* (Edinburgh:1716); J. Moir, 1797.
[13]   Ro 1:21–2.
[14]   1 Ti 6:4.
[15]   2 Ti 3:4.

to such a heart seance of my sin as I would a been at upon thursday when I
was had littel of a broken heart But it was but like a moment of time upon
friday I had some heart meltings wile I was in the felloshep milting but stile
I remenide acusing my selfe with origenal sin I could not wine to such
brokennes of heart and contrition of spirit as I under this for this sin so that
I porposed with my selfe to come down doun to you the feirst Saboth after
I came from you and just to tel you that I was nothing but a meer hypocrite
and to seek your advice what to do upon satter day before this I went up to
egalsom where the sacarment of the Lords Super was to be dispenced if hapely
I might get some soul good [642/12] but durst not presoum to joine with
them I found nothing while the letter ende of Mr edom[16] sermon where he
sead that none had a right to come their but such as had love to God love to
Christ love to his people love to the whol world and eve love to their ennemeies
these and the like qualeficatiens he mentioned and then he aded but let no
pretend to stay away upon the account of the want of these in dutey afected
there by the want of thereof for where shall this get them but at this and the
like a bestion these winos came with some inflewence upon my heart making
me to belive the seam I thought this was a cal to me to jion in this ordenance
so I went and got a token I thought the time was indeed short but porposed
by his grace to inprove it the better so after I went home I endeoured endevored
endevoured to spend the rest of that day in the dutys requiered requiered but
to no porpose for I could not wine to so much as a good form next morning
I indevoured to covenant with God but was deed and lifeles there in I could
not examine my selfe nether could I make any porgras in medetation so I
thought I could not go to the Lords table and I thought when I would hear
the ministers inviting the comunicants to go to the Lords table I thought how
miserabel wold my keas be so I thought there in remenid nothing but a fearful
look- [643/13] ing for of judgment and afirery indignation which shall devour
the adversary[17] for the Wrath of God is reveled revealed from heven aginst
all ongodlines and onrighteousness of men who hold the truth in
onrighteouness[18] so I endevoured to aplay these words to my heart as close
as I cold all the time that I was meking ready to go to the church and while
I was going to the church I was very heve in spirit and when I was about
midway to the church I though I should afallen doud (for I was still condeming
my selfe) and my spirits was like to sink within me at lenth I began to cast in
my mind about the four leprous men in the 7 ch-p of the 2 kings for I thought
if I stay away I will ondoutedly dy and if I come I can but dy so I porposed
to come which was great ease to my spirits wen I came to the tent I heard

---

[16]   This is probably a reference to George Adam (d. 1759), minister at Cathcart, who participated
       in the revival activities and is identified in McCulloch's index as '2 Adam'.
[17]   Heb 10:27.
[18]   Ro 1:18.

M-r Cherles Cotes[19] preched upon Jeremiah 30v21 and their nobels shall be of themselves and their governor shall proceed from the midst of them these were the words and I will cause him to draw near and he shall aproach unto me for who is this that engaged his heart [644/14] to ~~draw~~ aprouch unto me saith the Lord he geve some marks from these words but I can not now disstinkly tell what ~~their~~ this were but I thought in the mean time I could leclame to some of them with out presumtion I heard another ~~miste~~ minister upon exodus 33v18 and he sead I besech thee shew me thy Glory if I remember his doctring was that it was the desire of every beliver to the glory of God in the face of Jesus Christ it was the prayer of my heart and the desire of my soul that the Lord would shew me his glory in the face of Jesus Christ yet I met with nothing remarkabel till that night at Secret prayer were I got my heart poured out and espechally wen I praed for heart estebelen grace the morrow their after I heard M-r Cherles Cotes upon these words thessalonians 4 ch-p 15 ver Wherefore comfort one another with these words and when he came to speak to the charecter of those that be longed to this text [645/15] with the context he confined him self to this epistle ch-p i v3 Remembring without ceasing your work of faith and labour of love and patience of hope in our Lord Jesus christ in the sight of God and our father[20] and when he expleaned the work of faith I thought I could le cleam their onto and also the labour of love but when he expleaned the patience of hope in our Lord Jesus Christ I thought I could not le no cleam their onto so I thought that all the rest was nothing seeing for I thought reather he might come before I was ready

[ ][21] I came away from this place yet in doutting about my Heat and condition I might write more of my exparrinces but they are much to the seam purpose Therefore I think it needles I shall now give you a Jenneral hint of all at the first I had for the spease of tow months or more I had much cominone with God as I thought in almost every duty I was enployed in I found [646/16] for the most peart of this time [ ][22] great ease pleasour and delight in reading praying and inprexsing God not only in femily duty and seakret prayer but also throw the day and ~~in~~ also in murning for my sins so that I ate my meat with pleasor and seinglenes of heart ~~and the way~~ I then began to find that all musecks ~~and dancin~~ of all kinds and dancings and all need-les world discourch and fullesh Jeistings and going to markets and fears and bridals were very hurt full to me and every worldly recrations what some ever for when I reteared from any of these I then found my heart out of fream for wirsheping for God

---

19   This is probably a reference to Charles Coats (d. 1745), minister at Govan, whose name does not appear in McCulloch's index.

20   1 Th 1:3.

21   Insertion ['My heart was very much drawn out after this sermon until he came to explean this patienceof hope in our Lord Jesus Christ and']: McCulloch.

22   Insertion ['I had']: McCulloch.

and I found that God hid his face from me before I thought that their was nowel in any of these and wondred when I heard of good people that wold not hear nor alow yet I could see no eivel their in and I thought that I might duit with out any harm ~~yet I thought their was~~ yet self being greatly if not altogether one mortified I thought that I might go to markets and [647/17] fears and bridals upon some laful reences but I found that it was nothing but the one mortified lus and corruptions of my heart their is one great abomination ~~that I heve no [...]~~ that I had practised some times before and that was running in the night time tow or three ~~mil~~ meils orsles our more as I had opertinity to see young wemen pretending courtasce to them whiles to one and whiles to another I thought their was no eivel in this also and it is to be regreated that it is the practic of the jennural peart of young men at this day and in this pleace and as I sead before their was that in me that wold heve keep both God and the world until shuch times that he mead me to know that I was ether to peart with God in Christ or peart with the World

I had a great concern for some of my relations and for my comrads that I had spent much of my time amoung but being ignorent of the disetfulnes of my heart I be came vein in my imagenations thinkine with my self that I could now say a great deal to the convictions of others and I thought time after time that I wold tel my comrads of the their ~~ve~~ eivel ways but when I had upertunnity after upertunnity ~~that~~ I then found that I had neither spirit nor courage nor could say anything to that purpose I was often venting my self in [648/18] a presumtous carnual selfis way after some time I began to jeolus that it was nothing but saten deverting me from my duty: and from the right path: and it was so violent I found no power to resist it so that some times I thought it was right and some times it was rong and was never throuly convinced of its being ron till I was convinced []²³ by M-r duram²⁴ and then I saw that their was a byas in it and in many other of my actings that I had actted their was for the peas of three quarters of a year at the first a great evedenc of my ignorenc and that was wen I heard others recomending them selves to the prayers of others I did not find that ~~concearn~~ concearn in my heart that I oght to heve had ~~that~~ their was another great mark of my ignorenc of my self be cause I was not so concerned to search out the evels of my heart as I should heve been: untile I was convinced of the desetfulnes of heart ~~you~~ by you preaching upon the desetfulnes of heart by you preaching upon the desetfulness of the heart I then thought with my self their might be much more evels with me that I might yet be on sencabel of and it was but a littel after this tille I was convinced of the idolatry of my heart by M-r duram upon self in deed I cannot say of but I had some knowleg of self but I [649/19] had no power to resist it nether had I such a cleer vew of it nether did I find

²³ Insertion ['upon self']: McCulloch.
²⁴ James Durham, *The Great Corruption of Subtile Self.*

that great evil in it that I then found in it and ~~it was~~ is very streang to think
how it wold heve come in upon me for their was no ~~duty~~ menner of duty
that I had performed but I had found it their in and it was after this menner
ordenarly if I had been in the church I ordenarly had some perplexing thoughts
and ~~akeseeity~~ ancseeity of mind so as to draw away my heart from the duty
in hand if it had been ~~weare wear~~ wearenes in duty then I wold thought with
any if the church weare skieled: their was allways some duty wold heve
presented it self to me eather in reading of my bebile or praying and then the
breve fream that I wold be in what great dlight wold I heve in reading and
what great fervence and heart meltings I wold heve in prayer and ordenarly
these thought wold heve come in upon me with menny tears and in sakret
prayer it wold come in the seame way and in publeck prayer holy like thought
wold heve risen in my heart and good like imprestions in various ways but
their it was conterry to the duty in hand so after this I heve it to remark that
I heve been enabled to resisit when it his come in upon me verry stronglay
and then ordenarly after [650/20] ~~a presumtous carnal selfishning~~ I was enabled
to resist it I heve found the ~~immediat~~ imprestions of God Spirit immedeatly
but then thought that I was no better in Gods sight then a beast because of
my idolatry about this time I began to find grat deficulty in walking with
God as I had don for some time before and could not delight in God not find
that delight in God that I had found before and no wonder for my folly made
it so for the Lord was provocked to hid his face from me and I could not be
but trobled and althogh I thought it was my duty to trust in the Lord yet I
could not do it so constanly as I should heve don and then when I tourned
onwachful then saten wold heve come in by tentations and made me to freat
and repine at Gods holy ways a deling with me and when these tentations
would heve leaft me then I would heve regreated that I had so much yeilded
to saten and would heve porpoused with my self no to yeild ~~agan~~ ageine but
I would not for this were stron and violent so that I would heve been made
to freat and repine and even to curs the day of my birth and to despear of
ever being hapy yet I can not say that ever I dispeared of Gods being [651/21]
eabel to helpy me but I thought that he would not help me one Lords day
whils I was in the church and when I was singing these words by this I know
that certainly I favour-d am by thee because my heteful enemy triumphs not
over me[25] and I think this were aplyed to my soul ~~for it was~~ by the imprestions
of Gods Spirit for I was under some perplexity of mind at the seam time I
thought it was a streang thin to be in such keas for I then was ready to think
that the Lord had cast me of altogether because I could not win to such delight
and such satesfaction in duty as I had found before then I was ready to think
that I had no grace nor did not belong to God I heve been leatly convinced
agine by M-r duram upon self that their is much of thes perplaxcietys of

---

[25]   Ps 41:11, Scottish Psalter (metrical).

mind belongs to on mortifyed corrup self and in deed I mey say that the Lords mercies are over all his other works upon this seam acount as for the lust of the eye the lust of the fleash and the pride of life thes are very frequanly leading me captive to the law of sin and death how frequantly am I found gowing afte my [652/22] detestabel things and looking after others gods some times I think that I heve the mestry over them but wear I be aware I ame just where I was some times I heve eyes ful of adultry so that I can look no where but my corruptions vented them ~~selve~~ selves in some shep or other and altho I get some of victory over them at some times espeshally at sacraments yet they stil over comin me agin their are some things that ar lafull that I heve been obliged to peart with and for sake and as for my onbelife now I think that I heve nothing els for the most peart of my time but a onbeliving onrenewed hard heart void of the trew heat of God heveing no love to God no love to Jesus Christ no consearn for his Glory on consearnt for my self and others and altho I meet with some brokenes of heart and spirit in dutyes and ordenances yet I hink I meke little or no progres in the way heven ward I ame easy lift up and easy cas down some times I think that I heve the in dwalling of the Spirit and some times I think that it can not be so when I can neather find nor see nothing [653/23] but thes corruptions and my great miseryes and grife is tha altho I find something of that miserabel seat and condition that I peceve my self to be in yet I am not win to that Godly sorow of heart frmes unbelife as it is dishonouring to God that I would fean heve I think I get some weeping but no washing I think I heve some sence but no sight I think I heve no knowleg of the Glory of Christ person and when I meet with any thing like good then I ame stil ready to flatter my self on day I heard you upon ~~the peart of~~ epheseancs i v i9 and you was upon the axortation I was afraid that I had never gon farther then what you expleaned and altho I could not denay but I desired and endevoured to act to the Glory of God in all things yet I thought that what you sead was very agreeable to what I had found so I persuaded my self that I was yet in a neattreal steat but my great misery was that I could not get my heart to be afeakted there with I endevoured to aplay a the cares and all the Judgments in the bible bu to no [654/24] porpes end I ~~watch~~ I endevoured to pray for seaven conviction of al my sins but could not obtein and I was so for some days at leanth on night I got [ ]²⁶ heart poured out in an extaroudenar menner as I thought yet I wold not let my self think but I was in neattral ~~steet~~ steat and I continued so for the speace of a week and on evening agin I got my heart poured out in a great misour but never wold let my self think that I had any intrest in christ neather could I get my heart afeacted there with afourtnight after I heard you I was reading upon m-r duram upon self on sabbath night where he says that a natural man comes short as to the discerning of selfiness in the matters

²⁶ Insertion ['my']: McCulloch.

of faith he may possibly discern it when he puts him self in the room of God
or his selfies end when it is more gross but when it comes to resting any on
something in self for salvation or sticking to somewhat in duties and in the
most spiritual duties he doth not disern this and the ~~reson is~~ reason is because
that which ~~men~~ manifests this is spiritual light and it is the spirits work to
convince of not beliving on chirst so I thought that I could say with out
presoumtion that I had rested on nothing I in self for salvation nor stick to
anything in [655/25] duties so as to merit any thing their by (al tho I heve
sined hennously ~~there by~~ in and by my duties) so I found in my heart ~~of the~~
~~exer exerces~~ something of the exercies of prais and thanks to God for this
unspeakable gift Jesus Christ and throu him and this continued with me that
night but oh how ~~short~~ soone did I lose both sight and sence there of 5 when
I heard ~~of this~~ that the sacrement was to be dispenced at glasgow I ~~endevored~~
endevoured to prepar for it and on the fast day I heard you preach upon the
parable of the ten virgins where I thought that I was yet nothing but a foolish
virgin and more espeshaly when ~~youd~~ you sead that hypocrites all ways rested
upon the comon operations of the holy spirit for I had been convinced that
I all ways turned secure and did not pres fore ward tuord the mark for the
prayse of the hevy calling of God in Christ Jesus some days before when I
read in the 7 of Joshua concerning the men of israel fleeing before the men
of ai upon the acount of the acurced thing so I thought that I was ready to
say onto the Lord wherefore hidest thou thy face where fore is it that I do
not partake sencablely of the benefeets of this ordenance I thought that my
concienc told me thut it was be cause of the acurced thing ether because that
I wanted preparation or rested upon it and when you apeled onto ~~christiaene~~
belivers and sead that their worst times are better then their best times were
before I thouth that I could not say that and when I was coming home when
I reflected upon thes things my I thought that I could not presume to come
to the lords tabl [656/26] my heart groned with in me saying what will I do
mat wile I do meaning that I know not what to do for I thought that I got
some ~~weping~~ weeping but no washing I thought I had some senc but no sight
the morow there after I thought that I could not get a paralel place ~~of~~ in all
the scriptures sutable to my case at least I had mind of ~~sene~~ that in the Proverbs
30 v 23 Surely I am more brutish then any man and heve not the understanding
of a man[27] I neither learned wisdom nor heve the knowledge of the holy
and when I was aplying thes words to my self my heart bursted out into tears
and there was also another word cam into my mind as on is out of mind when
dead even so I am for got[28] ~~and~~ and when I was ~~adresing my self to be~~
reflecting upon thes words my soul could not refrein it self from adresing it
yel onto God in thes seam words with hive grons for some short time and

27   Pr 30:2.
28   Ps 31:12.

after a littel space thes wordrs cam into my mind arise O Lord ~~thou~~ into this rest the ark of thy strength[29] and thou where onto my soul aded ~~and com onto wer un onto heart and dewel dwell~~ and came thou into my heart and ~~dw~~ dwell thou their for ever yet I thought that I was nothing the better of all this and so I thought that I could ~~not~~ not go to the Lords table whill I wanted a trou evidenc of a intrest in Christ Jesus yet I resolved to go to heare the preachings then I thought what sheme wold [657/27] think when every body wold be notticing me becaus I did not go to the Lors table yet I went in but found nothing remarkable only when m-r Robe[30] med a offer of Christ onto all hearing him it was my grife because ~~I could not except of him~~ my heart would not axcept of him ~~ane~~ one the morrow morning I went out into the green for to medetate I went to prayer where I got some utterenc but I thought I could not ventour to go to ~~the Lords table~~ whil in this cease I thought if it were to the Glory of God I wold go to the Lords table all tho I should get no thing remarckable at al and thes words came into my mind Who shall ~~acend~~ ascend into the hill of the Lord and who shall stand in his holy place he that hath clean hands and a pure heart who hath not lift up his soul onto vanity nor sworn deceitfully[31] when I had conscidered a whell I thought that I could not allow my self in any knowen sin nor in the neglect of any knowen duty so fare as I know I thought that it had been and was the desire and endevour of my soul to heve every ~~thing~~ corruption rooted out of my heart and to heve a the gracess and virtous of the holy spirit in the room there of I thought that ~~I had~~ could not any more be satesfyed with any be mist God I thought that I had given in my self soul and body to the Lords with out reserv or axception to be his [658/28] so I thought I got some evidenc of my intrest in Christ and so I resoveled to prepare for going to the Lords table and so I went but found nothing remarkable only be fore I went to the Lords table thes words came in to my mind hath no man condemed thee[32] and my soul replyed no man Lord and he sade nether I condeme thee on Munday m-r edem[33] preached upon thes words God for bid that I should glory seve in the cross of our Lord Jesus Christ by whom the World is crucified onto me and I onto the World[34] and when he was preaching I thought that I could not hear one word with satesfation for I thought that ~~I could not be~~ I no suner heard the word spoken but it was wipt away so that I could not heve the sence of on word with another so I was perplexed upon the acount there of and when he had shon the nessecty of heveing the world crucified

29 2 Ch 6:41.
30 James Robe (1688–1753) – minister, Kilsyth.
31 Ps 24:3–4.
32 Jn 8:10.
33 This is probably a reference to George Adam (d. 1769), minister at Cathcart, who participated in the revival activities and is identified in McCulloch's index as '2 Adam'.
34 Gal 6:14.

and had given some derictions ~~he sad what blessed thing~~ in order to the
acomplesment of it he sade what a blesed thing was it that God had ~~not left us~~ promised to help in this and in all other dutys and when I heard thes words
there was vertu came along with them impresing them upon my heart I then
heard clearly and could then receve [659/29] it in the truth and ~~and~~ love of
it to viz the word that was spoken and after this sermon we soung in the 17
salm 13v wher I could sing with the spirit and with the understanding but in
a speashal menner the 15 verce but as for me I Thine own face in righteousness
will see and with thy likeness when I wake I satisfy'd shall be[35] ~~and next mor words I~~ and when I was sining this verce I thought that I should never be
satisfy'd with the likeness of God O how did my soul long for it and next
m-r warden prayed and when he mentioned that word God O how dear how
sweet and how pretious was it to my soul but this did not continou long wit
me but very short I shall not troble you with any more only a few words I
think if I heve any faith at all it is of thee weakest sort and altho I think ~~I heve~~
some times that I heve the in dwelling of the Spirit yet for the most peart of
time I think how can it be for I think that I heve not the fear of God in my
heart I heve no love to God nor Jesus Christ I think I heve no sence of the
evel of sin ~~for~~ upon my [660/30] heart and spirit I think that I heve no heart
afeaction to the people of God I think that I heve no concearn for the Glory
of God nor the good of my own soul and others I think that I heve all the
markes and evedences of black nett our such as an unbeliving heart a hard
onrewed heart an on thankfull stupied dead and lifles heart formal and secur
and my greatest meisry is that I can not get my heart afeacted with thes things
so as to be stirred there by to it duty I think that I make no prograss in the
way of holy ness so that for the most peart of time I do not know what to
dow yet I think that thes are acussations of Satan filling me with them and
contemp for when I ame sitten under sermons and hear markes given I then
for most peart esely percev that I heve non of thes marks that are given and
ordenarly I heve my heart broken under a sence of the want there of or els I
ame ready to con clud that I do not belong to God and heve no intrest in
Christ and it is asearting thing that thes corrutptions are dweling in me yet
I think that I can say ~~that~~ with[36]

---

[35] Ps 17:15, Scottish Psalter (metrical).
[36] Partial account ends abruptly.

[661/-] ~~John Parker Walker & Dyer [. . .] [. . .] [. . .] [. . .] aged 23 years age about 23~~

a.e. A young man aged 23.[1]

My Parents being both religiously disposed persons themselves, took care to give me good Education and Example: and ~~I con~~ train'd me up to Secret prayer and to attendance on publick Ordinances and Family Worship: & I conformed to the Example & Instructions they gave me, as to the outward performance of dutys; not only in my Childhood, but all along my life after I came to years, & was kept always civil and sober in my outward behaviour before the World. I thought when I was young, that it was better to pray more seldom than very frequently, because I had then more sins to confess to God, since the last time I prayd, when I did not pray very often, than when I did: and sometimes I would have confessd and bewaild my sins with many tears. Sometimes when I was hearing the word preachd, I have been under fears, because I did not do what was required; but then I would have thought again, What need I be so afraid, there is nobody I know of does all that the Minister bids, no more than I: & so those fears would have worn off again. When I was young I have found my heart much affected in reading some little Books of Devotion, such as Mr Willisons book on the Sacrament,[2] Eliz. West's account of her life[3] and [ ][4] One Sabbath night also reading my Bible concerning Elijahs being carried up to heaven in a Chariot of fire and Elisha's crying out, O my Father, The Chariots of Israel [662/-] and the horsemen thereof[5] I felt my heart melt wonderfully, & think, that it procedeed from the motions of the Spirit of the Lord: but it ~~was~~ lasted but that night, & cannot say, There was any thing of that kind next day. After I had been recovered one time from a fever when I was dangerously sick, my Father coming to me in the fields, & telling me that he had vow'd when I was sick, That if ~~I recovered~~ the Lord was pleased to spare me, I should be his, and that he had devoted & dedicated me to him: & as he exhorted me to give my self to God in Christ, I found my heart very much affected with what he said. At another time I was very much affected in hearing ~~the Tables served and~~ the Ministers exhort at serving the Tables at a Sacrament at Carmunnock, so that I had almost cried out among the people. But yet after all these things,

---

[1]   John Parker – the shorthand text in McCulloch's 'Index of persons' names who gave the foregoing accounts to Mr. McC' states: walker and dyer in Busby Carmunnock.
[2]   John Willison, *A Communion Sabbath: How it may be profitably spent* (Edinburgh: James Taylor).
[3]   Elizabeth West, *Memoirs; or, Spiritual Exercises of Elizabeth Wast* (Glasgow: 5th edn, 1733).
[4]   Insertion ['one of Isaac Ambrose's books &c:']: McCulloch.
[5]   2 Ki 13:14.

I took so great delight in going to fairs & markets & weedings, where young people drink & make merry with one another, that if my time & money could have allowed me, I would have scarce missd one of them I could have gone to. And tho I went the round of all outward duties, yet I think ~~my~~ this was much owing to religious Education, the Example of others, & the force of natural Conscience. I think, when I reflect upon my former life, tho' I had flashes of sorrow for sin at times, & some flashes of the love [663/–] of God melting my heart; yet I never found my life altered or reformed after them. I was four times in my former life admitted to partake of the Lords Supper: At the first I think there was too much of presumption: at the other three, I was more taken up in preparation, & had much heart exercise in strivings against corruption & temptations, & meltings of heart too under the Sense of Sin. But tho' I had some Sense of my lost condition by nature & by actual sin: yet I was not suitably exercised in seeking to get out of that state. Many of these things look very like Saving Grace; but yet yet I really think I was still all that time in a natural state, & that they were nothing but flashes of a temporary Believer, for within a few days after I had met with them at a Communion Occasion or so, I turn'd as vain & carnal and worldly in my disposition & behaviour as ever. And tho' I could lay claim to some marks of Grace, without any heart condemmings, when I was hearing them given by Ministers in Sermons, when I was in some of these passing better frames, such as ~~That~~ Good desires of heart after Christ, yet these good desires of mine were not habitual, & when I was engag'd in worldly business, there were no such thing with me for ordinary. And tho' I often engagd to God to part with all known sin; [664/–] yet I made my self a liar by my after practice in my seeking after occasions & temptations to sin by resorting to fairs & weddings: and I think I never heartily parted with one sin or mortified one lust, not withstanding all these promises.

At length in Septr 1741 hearing a Minr (12)[6] preach in the High-Church-yeard of Glasgow on a Sabbath Morning, [ ][7] They cry Peace, peace, when there is no peace:[8] After he had describd a false peace in many instances, he said, If ye have no other peace but this, it is but a peace of the Devils making: these words came with a dint on my heart: & put me into such confusion That I minded little more he said after that. I went into the High-Church & at singing the Psalms I found some such flashes as I had often met with before. In the Evening of that day, hearing that Minr (12) preach in that Church-yeard on that Text, The kingdom of God is not meat & drinks &c:[9] at the reading of the Text, I felt some kind of softening on my heart, but it came not to such

---

[6] George Whitefield (1714–70) – evangelist.
[7] Insertion ['on that Text']: McCulloch.
[8] Jer 6:14, Jer 8:11.
[9] Ro 14:17.

a melting as I felt afterwards when he explaind the doctrine of the Text in his Sermon: when he shewd what it was not I felt my heart turn hot & melt & overboil in tears: [665/–] especially when he said, There are many of you will be very good & devout at a Communion Occasion or for a few days after it: but within a little you'll be as vain and carnal as ever: at hearing of this, I was made sensible at the heart that I was just the person he spoke of: and if my heart was hot before, I have many a time thought on reflexion, that it was now like Nebuchadnezzars furnace, heated seven times more than ever: and now my heart was melted down within me under the sense of my wanting the kingdom of God within me, & that I was in a lost & undone condition, & I was crying out in my heart as fast as I could, What shall I do to be saved: I got also at that time a deep sense of my Sin as dishonouring to God: and hearing the Minister speaking of looking to him whom we had pierced, and mourning as for an only sin and a first born, I thought at that very time, that if all my friends and Relations in the World had been newly dead, I could not have mournd & sorrowed so much for them all as I was then mourning for Sin as dishonouring to God. But tho tears flowd out abundantly, I did not then [666/–] or any other time cry out in publick or faint or swarf nor had I any bodily pains: but I had much differently to refrain crying out, and wonder that I did not cry. Nor had I at that time nor any other occasion, any dread of hell upon me. I have sometimes when at Prayer had a slavish fear of the devil, but never any terrors of hell or of the wrath to come. When the Minister said, Some of you will be saying, Who then can be saved, I thought he had said, Some of you will be saying, What shall I do to be saved, I would gladly have asked him that question, for I was then willing to do any thing in order to be saved. When he shewed what the Kingdom of God was, I found his words come as breath upon me; & what was said powerfully applied to my heart. At the Close, while he exhorted such as had got a Sense of their lost Condition without Christ, to come and cast themselves at the feet of his mercy, that if they perished they might perish there where never one had perished yet: I thought I was made heartily willing to do so, and found this to be good news to my Soul. In time of the Prayer after Sermon, I stood up & felt my heart much altered, calmd & softned. [667/–] And ~~with~~ in this condition I went home, & look my dinner very heartily: & went to Secret prayer: & among other things, I said Now Lord, I ~~am~~ renounce all righteousness of my own, and am willing to submit to the righteousness of Jesus Christ: And I was helped to close with Christ that night in all his offices: and under a sense that I had nothing that was good and could do nothing, to look to that all-fullness treasured up in store in the Lord Jesus.

I continued for a long time after this, in a very desirable frame, with much sweetness and calmness of heart, frequently even when following my worldly business, mourning and melting under a sense of my sin, and meditations on spiritual things, & frequently retiring to Secret prayer. About two weeks

after this, on the Lords day morning, before I went to the Kirk, I resolvd I
would read a bit of my Bible, that I might meditate on it by the way (which
I had never usd to do before) & that verse casting up first to my eye, That he
would grant that ye may be strengthened with all might in the inner man, by
his Spirit, I turnd it into a [668/–] prayer for my self, & went on so praying
& meditating, with tears flowing down almost ~~always~~ all the way: and felt
much of that frame in time of publick worship: especially in time of the
prayers and psalms. & could not forbear crying out in my heart: Lord I now
feel thy blessed Spirit at work in my soul. [‡][10]

In these times, I broke off that custom I had before this, of joining my
self to a company of others between Sermons, in the Church-yeard or in the
fields near by; and there spending the time in worldly or carnal discourse:
this I observ'd to be the way of many and had been too much my own way
before this: now I was grieved for such a practice, as tending to wear off
any serious impressions persons had got in time of Sermon, & as being a
prophanation of Gods holy day: & therefore I now usd to retire by my self
at such times, & give my self to prayer reading & meditiating on the Word:
& I continue to do so still.

In these times also, I was made to see what I had never seen before, the evil
of carnal delights of getting songs & ballads by heart & whistling & singing
them over, & hearing them plaid on vials & the like, the matter of these Songs
not being very chaste oftimes, & at best but triffling light & vain things, &
serving to make the Spirit light & airy if not worse: & whatever my frame
was before, such things tended still to make me worse. And [669/–] therefore
I broke off these practices: And in stead of these sorts of carnal delights, I got
some Psalms by heart, or some parts of them, and often sung them when I was
following my Work and found great pleasure in doing so: This I took to be
the will of God & my duty, & I now found my self as much in my Element
in ~~doing so~~ praising God in this manner, as in whistling and singing before,
& much greater: it became as agreeable to me then as to take my meat: but
it was not so much I, as the Spirit and grace of God singing in my heart, or
exciting me to do so. And some passages of Scripture came into my heart

---

[10]   Insertion ['‡After I had been praying much, That the Lord might direct his servant whom
I was to hear on Lords days for ordinary ( ) to what might be useful & needful for me, he
preachd on Joh.3.3 concerning the New birth; & as he went along explaining it & the
marks of it, my heart went along with him, & I was made to see these things wrought in
my own soul. ⊗']. Followed by text in side margin of [669/–]: ['⊗ One night after my
Work, reading a little book calld Vincent on True Love to an Unseen Christ: in reading &
praying over some ~~Prayers~~ things he has there, I felt my heart wonderfully warmed with
the love of God: & as I was going to bed, & after I was in it, several passages of the Song
of Solomon were brought into my heart with great love to Christ & joy in him: such as
I sate down under his Shadow with great delight & his fruit was sweet to my taste. My
beloved is as a bundle of myrrhe unto me; he shall ly all night between my breasts.']:
McCulloch.

with much sweetness soul refreshment, & some measure of joy, that tended to engage me still more & more to this way, particularly these two passages, which came one day one after another,

> When thou didst say Seek ye my face
> Then unto the reply
> Thus did my heart above all things
> Thy face Lord seek will I.[11]

And that,

> I did not stay nor linger long
> As those that slothful are:
> But hastily thy law to keep
> My self I did prepare[12]

I did not at the time know where to seek for these lines in the Psalms, but I met with them there afterwards.

Some time after this, that word was impress'd on my heart, with power & sweetness, To me to live [670/–] is Christ: immediatly after which I thought if some might hear me saying these words, they might say What dost thou pretend to be like the Apostle Paul? but I [ ][13] immediatly to reply with much boldness, Tho I be not like the Apostle Paul in many things, yet I heartily agree with him, in this thing That to me to live is Christ.

Family Worship also now became most delightful to me. I can say to the praise of grace, I have many a time had much heart melting and soul rejoicing in it, & it has been sweeter to me than honey from the honey comb. One day in particular, while the master of the family, read a Chapter in 1 Joh. That speaks much of the love of God, I found great sweetness in hearing it, & found what was read particularly applied to me, ~~particularly~~ especially what word God is love, ~~filled in~~ at which I felt so much of the love of God in my Soul, That I could say in sweet experience, That God in my heart or the Effects of his In-dwelling there, was Love.

One day in Secret Prayer, I found my self much enlarged in praying for the revival of the Work of God thro' the Land, & the spreading of the ~~whole~~ knowledge of Christ thro' the whole world: I was also helped to pray much for my Commorades friends & Acquaintances. One time I was at Secret prayer, I fell into a drousy dead stupid frame, & I noticd my self sometimes uttering things that were just non-sense, or very unsuitable. At another time joining in the duty of Prayer with others my mind took a wandring, & was

---

[11] Ps 27:8, Scottish Psalter (metrical).
[12] Ps 119:60, Scottish Psalter (metrical).
[13] Insertion ['was helped']: McCulloch.

carried quite off [671/–] from joining in the Petitions put up by the Speaker, to think of some excellent Spiritual discourse I had sometime before heard, and found some kind of heart-meltings at thoughts of it; but they were not of the right kind: and I was much displeased with my self afterwards for this: for however good & lawful those things might have been at another time, I saw a great unsuitableness in them to the present duty: & therefore have endeavoured, by grace, to be upon my guard against any thing of that kind, since that time.

Hearing a Minr ( ) speak lately of Gods answering his people sometimes by fire, & exhorting people to seek That God might answer them by the fire of Divine Love in their hearts: I could not but reflect on Gods answering me in that manner sometimes: at some Petitions I have felt, at times, such strong & heavenly impressions came down on my heart, such gleams of Divine Love have sometimes come down on my Soul, that have warm'd my heart to that degree, that I have felt them in some measure also warming my body.

At other times I have had great straitninigs of Spirit in Prayer, and great damps & downcastings, under a sense of sin indwelling corruption; so that I have been made to cry out, O wretched man that I am who shall deliver me from this body of sin & death. And one time after it had been thus with me, that word, The Lord will perfect [672/] that which concerneth me,[14] came into my mind with such sweetness, that I could not but conclude it came from the Lord to me as a promise to me, & I was helped immediatly to turn it into a prayer, That the Lord might graciously do so.

When the Awakening brake out in Camb. in Febry 1742, I was much rejoiced to hear of it, & came & heard Sermon there soon after it began, & [ ][15] at Dinner had my heart so overjoy'd at the thoughts of it, that it was with great difficulty I got my self refrain'd from crying out before these present, and going to Secret Prayer had much freedom allowed me, & was made to say God would be holden & not let go, tell he bless'd us.

In the Spring & Summer 1742; I had not so great Love & joy as sometimes formerly; yet I had constant and abiding desires after what was good & holy, & was led to be often in Secret duty; & helped to much earnestness in it. & got more & more of a sight of the Evil of Sin, and some particular Evils I had too much indulg'd my self in; such as vain & foolish talking & jesting which is not convenient: & enabled to mortify and abstain from these Evils. I was often in great difficulties as to many things that concernd my Soul in that time, & had many Conflicts with corruption: but got many gracious Outgates from them: & these oftimes came by means of some portion of the Word, particularly the Psalms, impressd on my Spirit; by turning to which & singing

---

14   Ps 138:8.
15   Insertion ['when I came home']: McCulloch.

them over, my heart was [673/–] greatly enlarged: such as particularly, that portion of the 30th Psalm from verse 6 & downward,

> In my prosperity I said,
> That nothing shall me move:
> O Lord thou hast my mountain made
> To stand strong by thy love.
> But when that thou O gracious God
> didst hide thy face from me
> Then quickly was my prosperous state
> Turn'd into miserie &c:[16]

One time in meditating on the Redeemers Sufferings, I got my heart melted down under a sense of my sins as the procuring cause of his Sufferings, and of his wonderful Love in coming & Suffering & dying for poor sinners, & for my sins in particular.

    Hearing a Minister (26)[17] preach at Camb. in March 1742, on that Text, a bruised reed will he not break, the smoaking flax shall he not quench &c:[18] I was made to attend with great earnestness: and tho I had not so when I went home, I found the Truths I had been hearing made very supporting to me: and particularly several Citations from the 54th Chapter of Isaiah, which I read over at home with great Sweetness & delight.

    [O][19] Finding my self long time in great bondage of Spirit, that I could not attain to serve God with that freedom & enlargdness of heart, that I would not have done, & that I usd to have, that word [674/–] that word, when Zions bondage God turnd back coming into my mind with some sweetness, I turn'd to that psalm & sung it with great delight of Soul, & founds my bands loos'd and that bondage-frame removed: & joy and [ ][20]

    [O] Going to Camb. & hearing a Minr (26) preach on a Saturdays Evening on that Text, The heart is deceitful & desperately wicked &c:[21] I fell under an affecting Sense of the deceitfulness of my own heart; & was much damp'd: Next Lords day, hearing that Minr (26) preach on that Text, Thou hast ascended up on high &c:[22] one Expression he had concerning the necessity of Restitution struck my heart: for now it was brought to my mind, that I had sometimes in my former life, kept up to my self some little thing of what I got for my Master, as a half-penny or so now & then; tho' not very often neither: And I was now afraid, That I was but a hypocrite still, since I

---

[16] Ps 30:6–7, Scottish Psalter (metrical).
[17] William McCulloch (1691–1771) – minister, Cambuslang.
[18] Isa 42:3, Mt 12:20.
[19] (O) Insert corresponding text from [674/–] and [675/–].
[20] Insertion ['sweetness return']: McCulloch.
[21] Jer 17:9.
[22] Ps 68:18.

had never made Restitution to my Master. I continu'd very uneasy till I after this was made offer to him of what I thought was the full ~~value~~ of what I had taken & more: but he only took it out of my hand, but would not take it from me, telling me, That it was but ordinary to allow such little things to Prentices or more. But I did [675/–] not for sometime after this, recover that Sense of my Interest in Christ I had formerly, till one day that I was reading a printed Sermon (12) concerning the Marks of the New-birth,[23] when God was pleased again to lift up the light of his countenance on my Soul. And then after][24]

At the communion at Cathcart in May 1742, I attended & endeavoured to prepare for it; but in time of the ~~Saturd~~ Sermons on Saturday & Sabbath forenoon, found my heart very hard & dead: & it was little better at the Table, which griev'd me much: but a Minr ( ) who serv'd the Table I was at, having spoke much concerning Christs Sufferings, said, That if any of the hearts of those that were at the Table were not affected with these things [ ][25] they had no business there: I was very grieved to find my heart so little affected, but thought this was too far said. Betwixt Sermons retiring by my self, I got some more freedom in prayer, and particularly in reading & praying over the last Section of the 119th Psalm. In hearing the Evening Sermon ( ) on that Text Hab. 'Revive thy work &c:[26] when he said, These that were never concern'd for the good of the Souls of others were not in a good state, I was thereby encouraged at the thoughts that the Lord had given me a heart to pray for others with great earnestness. On Munday I was refreshd in hearing the Sermons, tho' I had not such joy & delight as I would have had.

[676/–] I also attended at the Sacrament at Kilbride in Summer 1742: but got nothing Sensibly in hearing the Sermons on any of the days: only while a Minr ( ) preachd on the Saturday, I thought he had some Expression or other (tho' I cannot now remember it) that invited me to come to the Lords Table: but was but very dead & hard when there: sitting by my self before the Evening Sermon, that word came into my mind, No man cares for my Soul,[27] which I thought very plainly pointed at my Case: but another word came soon after into my heart with some sweetness, I know how to speak a word in season to the weary Soul.[28] After that Sacrament, I continued but very much discouraged, till Friday next, when I was under much uneasiness

---

23 George Whitefield (1714–70) – evangelist, *The Marks of the New Birth: A sermon preached at the parish-church of St. Mary, White Chapel. To which is added, a prayer, for one desiring to be awakened to an experience of the new-birth and another, for one newly awakened to a sense of the divine life* (London: Hutton, 1739).

24 [Bracketed text for insertion on p. 304 at the corresponding ⓪ symbol].

25 Insertion ['he had said']: McCulloch.

26 Hab 3:2.

27 Ps 142:4.

28 Isa 50:4.

of mind, that things did not go with me as I wishd, & as they had sometimes done before; & was wishing for death; when a gracious God shind in to my heart with these words, To you that fear my name shall the Sun of righteousness arise with healing under his wings:[29] I had before been praying, That the Lord might satisfy me with his goodness; & was looking for a Promise in answer, and that word came into my heart, The mountains shall depart & the hills be removed, but my kindness shall not depart from thee &c:[30] This came with such powerful sweetness & love to my Soul, that I was indeed Satisfied with his goodness & at that time could desire no more: & sang the 116 Psalm all over with great delight.

[677/–] At the first Sacrament at Camb. July 1742, hearing a Minr ( ) preach on that Text, To you a Son is given & a Saviour born,[31] I found the Word spoken come home to my heart with great delight under the Influences of the Spirit. On Munday, hearing a Sermon ( ) on that Text, Let the same mind be in you that was in Christ Jesus,[32] that word came into my mind, Write these sayings in a book, and I found the Sayings of that minister, come with such life & sweetness to my Soul, that I put up my Petition to the Lord, that he would write them on the book my heart.

After this, I fell into great damps & was much dissatisfied with my self at the thoughts that I had never got any thing sensibly at the Holy Ordinances of the Lords Supper; & reckoned that surely it had been owing to my self & my not being duly prepared for it. A book called Vines on the Sacrament, falling into my hands at that time, I found the Author speak much of the Qualifications necessary for that Ordinance:[33] & I then saw how far short I was of these qualifications: I essy'd to meditate & examine my self: but found my thoughts confusd & wandring. I then fell to write my thoughts, the better to prevent wandring. And it occur'd to me first, That the Paschal Lamb was separate & brought in & ty'd to a Post for eight days: agreeable to this, I thought I must meditate on Christs death & sufferings before the 2nd Sacrament ~~Occasion~~ at Camb. that I had in view. I did so, [678/–] and while & I was doing it felt love to Christ warming my heart. Next, the leaven was t be search'd out with lighted Candles & put away; & I beg'd the Lord might discover to me if there was any leaven of hypocrisy, malice, or wickedness lurking in any corner of my heart & help me to put it away; & I essy'd to find it out & have it remov'd. I gave my self Soul body & Spirit to God, in

---

[29] Mal 4:2.

[30] Isa 54:10.

[31] Isa 9:6.

[32] Php 2:5.

[33] Richard Vines. *A treatise of the institution, right administration, and receiving of the sacrament of the Lords-Supper. Delivered in XX. sermons at St Laurence-Jury, London* (London: Printed by A. M. for Thomas Underhill at the Anchor and Bible in Pauls Church-yard, near the little north-door, 1656).

way of Covenant, & accepted of God the Father Son & Holy Ghost as my God, Father Redeemer & Sanctifier, & subscribed with my hand to the Lord. I search'd into my Soul wants & plagues, & laboured to have my heart affected with them: & was much & oft in Secret Prayer.

On the Fast day before the 2nd Sacrament at Cambuslang, I came & heard Sermon, & in the afternoon hearing a Minr ( ) preach on that Text, He that hath the Bride is the Bridegroom &c:[34] I found that Sermon very refreshing to my Soul. On Sabbath after three of the Tables were serv'd I went to Secret prayer, resolving that if I got not something sensibly there, I durst not approach to the holy Table: but getting my heart melted in prayer, I went to the Table, but got nothing remarkable: after coming from it, going to hear Sermon at one of the Tents, and hearing a Minr ( ) on these words He is altogether lovely,[35] I found the Speakers words Sweeter to me than honey, & could say, That Christ was indeed altogether lovely to my Soul.

[679/–] Some while after this I fell under terror of Satan when I essayd to pray: & was much discomposd at the least motion or noise of any thing about me, apprehending it proceeded from the Devil. And one morning, I felt a great oppression upon me, so that tho' I essay'd to rise out of my bed I was not able: & when I essay'd to cry to God to help me, it was with the greatest difficulty I got the words uttered. But being at Prayer, I was relieved by these words, Who shall lay anything to the charge of God's Elect, it is God that justifieth who is he &c:[36] Ø I am persuaded that neither death nor life &c:[37] And that word We wrestle not with flesh and blood but with &c:[38] I knew it was to be troubled with what they call the night-mare before this, & was persuaded that this was nothing of that kind, but proceeded from Satan, & was further confirm'd in it that it was so, by these Scriptures that, by the power that accompanied them, were the mean of my Relief.

As for Fairs & Markets, I had often usd to resort to them still, till about this time, when I was thinking of setting up for my self & getting a house of my own, & thought it needful in that view to look out for one to be a wife to me: & for that end allowed my self to go to Fairs & Markets where I might have occasion to see some young Women, out of which I might choose one: but one time before I would go to one of these occasions, begging counsel and direction from the Lord, to guide me right in that matter, [680/–] these words came into my mind, Let every one wherein he is called therein abide with God,[39] The time is short, it remains that these &c:[40] and this was

---

[34] Jn 3:29.
[35] SS 5:16.
[36] Ro 8:33–4.
[37] Ro 8:38.
[38] Eph 6:12.
[39] 1 Co 7:24.
[40] 1 Co 7:29.

followed by that other word, Let us lay aside every weight & sin that easily besets us.[41] These words came with such power, as determined my will to comply with what appeard to be the Will of God, & in the light in which they were set before me, it seem'd to be the Wil of God, that I should not marry in the present Circumstances, & that I should avoid occasions of falling into such ~~things~~ courses as might entice to sin, & draw away my heart from God & my duty; & that therefore I should not resort to Fairs & Markets; and this accordingly I have observ'd from that time to this.

And now to draw to a Close: Whereas I had met with some kind of heart-meltings & flashes of love to God before Septr 1741, and thought my heart sincere and heavenly while these continued, yet they wore quickly off & I had no more of them nor concern for them when I was about my worldly business: but since that time, the habitual prevailing bent of my heart, is after communion with God in Christ & conformity to him: & tho my heart oftimes wanders & runs off from God in duty, yet himself knows it, That ~~my~~ I am very uneasy when it is so, & that my heart is just like the mariners needle, which tho it may be jogg'd to the one side & the other; yet it is never quiet till it point to the North Pole; so neither does my poor heart ever settle or take rest, till it fix on God in Christ, & find rest in him: To him be Glory Amen.

[41]   Heb 12:1.

Index of persons names who gave the foregoing accounts to
Mr McC.[1]

A. B.   Janat Barry Spouse to John Sheddon Carter in Rutherglen. Vol. 4.
        p. I.

A. C.   Janat Struthers a Married Woman about 32 years old. Spouse to
        George Darling [. . .] now living in Camb.

A. D.   Duncan Alge journeyman Weaver in Glasgow w' his Brother put to
        School by Parents & taught to read & write some got Cat. & retn
        mostly

A. E.   John Parker Walker & Dyer in Busby Carmunok aged 23.

A. F.   Eliz. Finlay daughter to John Finlay Tennant & Walker in
        Carmunnock aged about 20. tat t. rd Bible & got Vin Cat.

A. G.   Isobel Watson Spouse to ~~Robert Duncan Taylor~~ in Gl. tat when a
        Child to read the Bibl nglcyd to get the Cat. b @ hv [. . .] aged abt
        ~~38~~

A. H.   Jean Wark daughter to John Wark Weaver in Provam mill Barony:
        aged about 17. put to School wn a Child. taught to read Bible y got
        ô L Cat. by heart, till about a year ago that J bgn t. get S.

A. I.   Daniel McClartie son to Angus McLartie Weaver in Naptal Parish
        or Kirkmichal in verluss in Argyleshire Serv' in Paisley &c. aged 21.
        my fht @ 2 grndfht rknd [. . .] ws morly yigt, got cat. by heart @
        rtn it, c̄ write s

A. K.   Janat Tennant Daut to David Tennant Weaver in Carm Old
        Monkland aged abt 30. tat t. rd Bibl @ hv a gd pt cat. by hrt

A. L.   Janat Reston Spouse to James Allan in Middle Quarter Barony aged
        20 years tat t. rd Bibl got Cat. @ rtn it mstly stil

A. M.   Isobel Moffat daut t. James Moffat a Shoemaker in Mid Quarter. tat
        t. rd Bibl got Cat. @ hv it mstly stil agd ab 2[.]

A. N.   Bethea Davie Daut to John Davie Weaver in mid-Quarter Barony.
        tat to rd Bible got Cat. @ rtn mostly stil. aged 23

A. O.   Agnes More Daughter to John More Tennant in Carmunnock aged
        about 23. pt t. Schl wn a child. tat t. rd t. L Bible got Cat. t. hrt @
        rtn it mstly stil

A. P.   Ann Montgomery to Mathw Montgomery Shoemaker in Glasgow.
        tat to rd Bibl when young, get Cat. by hrt @ hv it mstly aged abt
        [. . .]

A. Q.   Janat Moffat dat t. Alex' Moffat Shoemaker in Shettleston, tat t. rd

---

[1]   This index was originally bound with Volume I, but belongs to Volume II. The indicies in
      this edition have been rearranged so that they correspond with the volumes to which they
      belong.

Bibl @ got Cat. by hrt @ rtn it mostly stil Married to John Paton Bleecher, aged abt 24

A. R.   Agnes Burnside Spouse to James Rob Tenant in Shettleston tat t. rd Bibl & got much of it by heart @ rtn it stil aged 2[. . .]

[New page begins]

A. S.   Margt Borland daughter to James Borland Tenant to Shawfield in Bothwel about 23.

A. T.   Rebecca Reid daughter to James Reid Tennant Eld in the Barony tat t. rd t. Bibl, @ got @ rtn th. Cat. t hrt ptly stil aged 22

A. W.   Margt Clerk Spouse to John McGlass Day Labourer in Gburghs in Givan parish, ~~tat t.~~ aged 42.

a. u.   Margt Givan Sewstress, in Glasgow dat t. David Givan Workman in Glsgow tat t, rd wn y__ got Cat. t. hrt wn y__ rtn it prtly stil. age abt 20.

a. v.   Mrs Sarah Gilchrist dat to James Gilchrist Schoolmstr in Cardoss. tat wn y__ t. rd @ write, & got Sh. Cat. t. hrt @ rtn it stil abt 2[.]

a. x.   Mary Colquhoun Dautr t. James Colqhoun Tenant in Old Monklnd tat t. rd wn a Child got Cat. t.hrt @ hs a gd pt stil age abt 1[.]

A. Y.   Catharine Tennant daut to David Tennant Maltman in Glasgow tat t. rd Bibl got Cat. mstly t. hrt @ hv so stl age 1[.]

A. Z.   Catharine Jackson dt. t. James Jackson Elder

A. A.   James Lang Weaver in Kilmarnock Son to John Lang Weaver in Kilmarnock tat t. rd th Bibl @ write, got L Cat. by hrt w^t agt prts [. . .] [. . .] it mstly

B. A.   John M' Alay born in Glsgw, a Gardiner there aged abt 27. tat t. rd. th Bible @ write, & got th Cat. t. hrt. @ hv [. . .]

B. B.   Charles Thomson Shoemaker in Glasgow aged 36 tat. t. rd Bibl @ got th Cat. t. hrt @ hv it mostly stil.

B. C.   Robt Hamilton Weaver in Anderston tat t. rd @ wrt @ hv Cat. t. ht aged 29.

B. D.   Isobel Provan dat t. Robt Provan in Calder Tennant there tat. t. rd Bibl wn a child got th Cat. t. hrt @ rtn it stil, age abt 36 years

B. E.   Agnes Buchanan dat t. James Buchanan merch. in Shots tat wn a child t. rd Bibl @ got Cat. t. ht @ rtn it mstly stil age [. . .]

B. F.   Janat McAlpin dat to John McAlpin Wool-mercht in th twn @ Girth tat y__ t. rd @ got th Cat. in my Childhd t. hrt t, aftwrd lst. u rd —@ Cat. Age aged 2[.]

B. G.   Charles Cuninghame Shoemaker in Glasgow born in Carluke tat t. rd Bible & got th. Cat. t hrt @ write s age 21

★B. F.   Jean Walker dat^r t. Arch. Walker Shoemaker in Calder tat t. rd th. Bibl @ got pt of th. Cat. to hrt @ rtn Agd 19

★B. G.   Christine Lamont dat to James Lamont Tennant in Rosneath. tat t. rd a little wn a Child. Aged 44.

[New page begins]

B. H.   Margt Richie [ardson] dat t. James Richardson wright in Gorbels tat wn a child t. rd Bibl, got Sh. Cat. t. hrt. @ rtn it stil age 20

B. I.   Marien Calendar is Mrs Baillie tat t. rd Bibl wn a Child got th. Cat. t. ht @ hv it stil. age 44.

B. K.   Janat Park dat to Gavin Park now living in Carmunnock Town formerly a Packman in England tat t. rd Bible & got the Cat. t. ht @ hv it still age 20.

B. L.   Mary Shaw dat t. Duncan Shaw Ship-carpenter in Greenock tat t. rd Bibl wn a child got Sh. Cat. t. ht @ rtn it stil.

B. M.   Andr. Falls son to Robt Falls in Cambuslang Town tat t. rd t. Bibl wn a child got t. Cat. t. ht. @ rtn it mstly stil age abt 21

B. N.   Jean Anderson dat' t. James Anderson Tennant in Shawfield tat t. rd th. Bibl, got Sh. Cat. t. hrt. @ rtn it mstly stil. age 19

B. O.   Janat Turnbull dat' t. Wm Turnbull Taylor in Ruglen tat t. rd Bibl wn child got Cat. t. hrt. @ hv it t. hrt age 19

B. P.   Margt Barton Dat' t. Wm Barton Tennant in Calder tat t. rd Bbl wn y__ got th. Cat. t. hrt. mstly @ hv it mstly stil Age. 26.

B. Q.   Bessie Lyon dt' t. John Lyon Cooper in Blantyre tat t. rd Bbl got Cat. t. ht @ hv it pretty wl stil [hr fth' agd \ rpld] age 23.

B. R.   Catharine Anderson dat' t. Wm Anderson Portioner in Little Givan tat t. rd Bible @ got Cat. t. hrt @ hv stil age abt 13

B. S.   Margt Carson dat t. John Carson sailor in MacCairn Parish in the Highlands tatt t. rd Bibl @ got Cat. t. hrt. @ hv it mostly still. fth' a litl lk rel. mt' rlgy lk. abt 16.

B. T.   Janat Lennox dat' t. John Lennox Gardiner in Glasgow, tat t. rd Bibl wn y__ & got t. Cat. t. hrt. @ hv it stil. age abt 20.

B. U.   Agnes Young dat t. John Young Smith in Campsy, tat t. rd Bible wn a child got th Cat. t. hrt @ rtn it stil age 26.

B. V.   Janat Bredan mrd t. Jolhn Murdoch Soldier tat t. rd Bibl got Cat. t. hrt @ hv it so stil. aged 39

B. W.   Bailie Wier in Hamilton tat t. rd @ write and lrnd S- Latin got Cat. t. hrt rtns it stil age 50

B. X.   Mrs. Wier, in Hamilton tat t. rd @ write got Cat t. hrt rtns it stil age about 28

B. Y.   Margt Boyle Relut of James Scot Shoemaker tat t. rd got Cat. rtns it mostly still age 34.

B. Z.   Jean Morton, Relut of Wm Edmiston Weaver [. . .] tat t. rd got Cat. hs stil. age 37.

[New page begins]

Daniel Forbes Sergeant of the [. . . . .] [. . .] Ednr tat t. rd @ write S- Latin
     got Cat. it stil aged 29

c.b.   Archb^dSmith Mason in Kilbride tat t. rd Bibl @ write S- got Cat. t.
     hrt @ rtn it stil mostly. Age abt 40

c.c.   Helen Finlay daughter to John Finlay Farmer in Calder tat t. rd the
     Bible, got the Catechism by heart, has it still. aged 26.

c.d.   Agnes Hamilton daughter to Widow Hamilton in Evamiln in the
     Parish of Hamilton, taught t. rd Bible & write, got t. Cat. by heart
     & retains it still. Aged about 20

c.e.   Margt Brownlie dat' t. James Brownlie Smith in Hamilton taught
     to read the Bible when young got Cat. t. ht. rtns it age 25

c.f.   Janat Alston dat t. Gavin Alston in Dalserf: She resides in Milton
     tat t., rd th. Bible wn young got Cat. by hrt rtns it mstly stil

c.g.   Margt Smith Spouse to John Hamilton in Lettrick

c.r.   An old Soldier of 51 years.

c.h.   Thomas Foster in Ridley-wood

Index of the Ministers & Others made useful to Persons Apointed at By Figures

Mess	36	Nasmith	M^r. Sinclair	70
1	—Henderson	37	Wm Brown	Mr J : Bane Junr	71
2	Adam	38	Scot: Stonhouse	Jo Currie O. M.	72
3	Mat: Connel	39	Wm Maxwell	Fair Mr Walker	73
4	D: Connel	40	Davidson	Robt Donald	74
5	Baillie	41	Gillespie	Wm Bogle	75
6	Duncan	42	Dovehill★	Sergeant Forbes	76
7	Buchannan	43	Pinkertoun	Mr Warden Preacher	77
8	Zuil	44	Carlile	Mr Wilson in Carstair	78
9	Currie Munk East:	45	Semple	Mr Hill in Km—k	79
10	Ham: Bothw	46	Lawson	~~Mr Currie O Munk~~	~~80~~
11	Ham: Douglas	47	Wm Steel	M^r McMillan	80
12	Wh———d	48	Lining	Eliz Jackson	81
13	Willison	49	H: Cross	Jean Robertson	82
14	McLaurin	50	Jo: Cross	Cath: Jackson	83
15	Stirling	51	P Potter	Jo: Wark	84
16	Webster	52	Muirhead	Mr Wharry	85
17	McNight	53	Mathieson	Mr Park	86
18	Walker Josiah	54	Fisher	Mr Spence	87
19	Ham: Barony	55	Eb: Erskine	Mr Jo Erskine	88
20	Robe	56	Ro^t Wright		
21	Bonnar	57	Arch: Fife		
22	Currie King:	58	Jo: Bar		
23	Gustard	59	Ing: More		
24	Warden Camp	60	Bartle Somers		
25	Warden Cader	61	Jean Galbreith		
26	McCulloch	62	James Millar		
27	Burnside	63	Ro^t Bowman Junr		
28	Anderson	64	Pat Maxwell		
29	Speirs	65	Col: Campbel		
30	G: Campbell	66	Glaud Somers		
31	Gillies	67	James Jackson		
32	Mackie	68	~~Chappel~~		
33	Arrot		Mr Tho: Walker		
[34]	Glog	~~69~~	~~Janat White~~		
[35]	Young		Geo Wishart		

★   Positive identity cannot be made, owing to illegibility.

APPENDIX 1

LETTER OF DONATION FROM MRS COUTTS

17 Argyle Square
1st May, 1844
My Dear Sir

It has been my wish to send a few of my Books to the Library of the Free Church and I have them now ready—I think in all 43 [ ]^{1} vols.—

Would you have the goodness if not inconvenient to send the Library Porter here, for them, at an hour when they could be taken in. A list shall be sent along with them.

I remain My Dear Sir,
Most respectfully yours
J Coutts

---

^{1} ['34'] Bottom margin note: 'A mistake. 34 books is the number.'

APPENDIX 2

DONATION INVENTORY FROM MRS COUTTS

May 1ˢᵗ 1844

List of books presented by Mʳˢ Coutts to the Free-Church, or New College Library.

1 Sermons by the Revᵈ Wᵐ Macculloch of Cambuslang. 1 Vol. Glasgow, 1793
2 Examinations of persons under Spiritual Concern, at Cambuslang, during the Revival, in 17-41–42 by Revd Wm Macculloch, with Marginal Notes by Dr. Webster and other Ministers. 2 Vols M.S.S.
3 Lectures on Isaiah by Dr. Macculloch of Dairsie. 4 vols. —— London 1791
4 Sermons by Dr. 2 Vols Ednʳ 1803
5 Sermons with Short Memoir, of Revᵈ Robᵗ Coutts of Brechin, 1 Vol.—— Aberdeen, 1806.
[new page begins]
6 The Nonconformists Memorial by Dr. Calamy and Samuel Palmer, 5 Vols. London 1802
7 Acts of General Assembly from 1638 to 1720. 1 Vol. Ednʳ, 1721
8 Romaine on the Song of Solomon. 1 Vol. London, 1759
9 Discourses by the Revᵈ Chaˢ Irvine. 1 Vol. —— Ednr 1772
10 The Parable of the ten Virgins by the Revᵈ Thoˢ Shepard. 1 Vol. —— Falkirk 1797
11 Sermons On The Seasons; by The Revᵈ Dr Thoˢ Gillespie; 1 Vol Ednr 1832.
12 Lives of eminent persons by Samuel Clark, 1 Vol. London 1683
13 Memoir of Dr. Macgil by Dr. Robt Burns, 1 Vol. Ednr 1842.
[new page begins]
14 Sacred Tropology; by Revᵈ John Brown. 1 Vol. Ednʳ 1768
15 Domestic Encylopaidia; by Dr. Willich, 4 Vols. London 1802
16 Flavel's Works. 1 Vol. Ednʳ. 1731
17 Monthly Review or Literary Journal, for 18-40, –41, & 42 being Vols 28 to 35.——
In all 34 Vols——

APPENDIX 3

A BRIEF ACCOUNT OF THE LIFE OF
THE REVEREND WILLIAM MCCULLOCH

The Revd Mr William McCulloch minister of Cambuslang whose dyath we mention in our last, dyed in the 80th year of his age & 45th of his Ministry.—He was a man of uncommon & remarkable abilities————

As a schollar his knowlege was acurate & extensive. The Languages, Mathematics, Algebra, Astronomy & Geography, he had studied with the utmost attention, tho his masterly acquaintance with them, was but little known, except to those who receivd Instruction in them from him in his early days.—

As a Christian he was modest & humble, loving spiritual & resignd; watchful & circumspect in his conversation & conduct.

Perhaps few men ever examplifyed the high Character of a Christian with more sweep yet at the same time with less Shew. But this is what he wish'd to pass []^{1} thro' the vale of life unnoted unnoticed———— As a Minister, He was an earnest affectionate Preacher of the gospel of Jesus Christ, & a laborious Workman in the Church of God: careful, studious & exact in his preparations for the Pulpit—Tho' oft times oblidged to preach in the course of Providence with after short notice, yet he always approved of studyed well digested Scriptural discourses, [new page begins] & what he approved he practised—as his numerous acurate Manuscripts abundantly testify—And he was honourd to preach the Gospel with much—with remarkable success, to the comfortable experience of many. His desires to promote the knowledge of Salvation were ardent & intense, as his last Testament most fully evinces / where failing his wife & son / he left his all for this purpose to the management of a few Executors whom he earnestly intreated, as his last request, to conceal his name.

He was loved by his Parish, esteemd by his friends & respected by all. Words are insufficient to describe his character.

But these few words hints, were intended to suggest to those who knew him not, the heavy loss which his congregation, his Friends & many in the church have sustaind by his death, &—which they are now deeply lamenting.——

M^{r} MCulloch died in 1771 or 1772.

---

^{1} ['unnoticed'].

APPENDIX 4
EXPLANATORY NOTE ATTACHED TO THE MCCULLOCH MANUSCRIPTS

These 2 (4to) Vols of M.S.S. were long in the family of Mr Maculloch of Cambuslang (& are in his own writing) they were afterwards in the possession of his Son the late Rev Dr Maculloch Minister at Dairsie (in Fife) & were after his death presented lately to the Free Church College Edin^r by his surviving daughter – Mrs Coutts

    13 June 1844

INDEX OF BIBLICAL CITATIONS

INDEX OF RESPONDENTS

INDEX OF MINISTERS AND OTHERS CITED

INDEX OF TOWNS AND PARISHES

INDEX OF ORIGINAL SOURCES

GLOSSARY

banning	swearing, cursing		a moral or spiritual
Candlemass	(or 'Canlemas') – 2		problem
	February; a Scottish	overloup	(overlope), archaic,
	quarter-day.		trespass, transgression
carking	'cark' – a certain	prentice	apprentice to trade or
	weight, load, anxiety		craft
Chopine	a Scottish half pint	pry	One of the various
	(an English quart)		species of sedge
cumber	difficult to pass		common in southern
	through, full of		Scotland and used for
	obstacles		sheep-feeding
dint	blow, shock assault,	refect	recover, refresh
	deep impression,	roe, rae	a deer
	impact	sclate	slate
douce	sedate, sober,	seet	or 'suit' – to pursue,
	respectable		aim at, seek to obtain
essay	*obsolete* a tentative	snell	quick, active, severe
	effort, a trial	steek	keep a quick rate or
embruing	staining or dyeing		pace
Haith	*interjection* a mild oath	straitned	*archaic* confined
	or exclaim of surprise		within narrow limits
Lambas	or 'Lambes',	slockned	extinguished,
	'Lambmes', or		quenched, or
	'Lammas' – 1 August,		appeased thirst
	a Scottish quarter-	tautie	matted, tangled
	day	thraldom	servitude
Line	a line of writing;	thole, tholl	to suffer, bear,
	any piece of written		endure with patience,
	authorization;		tolerate, be subjected
	a certificate of church		to
	membership	upbraid	to cast or pull
Martinmass	The feast of	wass	wash
	St Martin, 11	wast	waste
	November; a Scottish	wresting	twisting
	quarter-day	y^e	the
Minr	Minister	y^r	there
minting	attempting, trying	y^s	this
outgate	outlet; a way out of	y^t	that